Antiquarians of Nineteenth-Century Japan

Antiquarians of Nineteenth-Century Japan

The Archaeology of Things in the Late Tokugawa and Early Meiji Periods

Hiroyuki Suzuki

Edited and translated by Maki Fukuoka

Getty Research Institute
Los Angeles

The publication of this book has been aided by a grant from the Ishibashi Foundation.

The Getty Research Institute Publications Program
Mary E. Miller, *Director, Getty Research Institute*
Gail Feigenbaum, *Associate Director*

English translation © 2022 J. Paul Getty Trust

Published by the Getty Research Institute, Los Angeles
Getty Publications
1200 Getty Center Drive, Suite 500
Los Angeles, California 90049-1682
www.getty.edu/publications

Mary Christian, *Editor*
Jim Drobka, *Designer*
Michelle Deemer, *Production*
Karen Ehrmann, *Image and Rights Acquisition*

Distributed in the United States and Canada by the University of Chicago Press

Distributed outside the United States and Canada by Yale University Press, London

Printed in China

Originally published in Japanese as *Kōkoka-tachi no 19-seiki*
Copyright © 2003 by Hiroyuki Suzuki
First published in Japan in 2003 by Yoshikawa Kobunkan Co., Ltd., Tokyo
English translation rights arranged with Yoshikawa Kobunkan Co., Ltd. through Japan Foreign-Rights Centre

Front cover: Case 2, Japan Prehistoric and Early, details. From Edward S. Morse, *Catalogue of the Morse Collection of Japanese Pottery*. See fig. 24.

Back cover: Ichiyōsai Kuniteru (Japanese, 1830–74), *A View of a Collection of Things Past, Present, and Novel*, 1872, detail. Triptych, multicolor woodblock prints. See plate 1.

Library of Congress Cataloging-in-Publication Data

Names: Suzuki, Hiroyuki, 1952- author. | Fukuoka, Maki, 1972- editor, translator. | Getty Research Institute, issuing body.
Title: Antiquarians of nineteenth-century Japan : the archaeology of things in the late Tokugawa and early Meiji periods / Hiroyuki Suzuki ; edited and translated by Maki Fukuoka.
Other titles: Kōkokatachi no 19-seiki. English
Description: Los Angeles : Getty Research Institute, [2022] | Includes bibliographical references and index. | Summary: "This volume explores the changing process of evaluating objects during the period of Japan's rapid modernization"— Provided by publisher.
Identifiers: LCCN 2021013510 (print) | LCCN 2021013511 (ebook) | ISBN 9781606067420 (hardback) | ISBN 9781606067437 (pdf)
Subjects: LCSH: Antiquarians—Japan—History—19th century. | Antiquities—Collectors and collecting—Japan—History--19th century. | Japan—Antiquities—Collectors and collecting—History—19th century.
Classification: LCC DS815 .S98313 2022 (print) | LCC DS815 (ebook) | DDC 952/.025—dc23
LC record available at https://lccn.loc.gov/2021013510
LC ebook record available at https://lccn.loc.gov/2021013511

Contents

vi   **Preface to the English Edition**
1   **Introduction** Maki Fukuoka
9   **Translator's Note** Maki Fukuoka
11   **PLATES**

	16	**Prologue: The Order of Things**
CHAPTER 1	21	**The World of Things Past and *Kokikyūbutsu***
CHAPTER 2	53	**"The Past and the Present" and "The New and the Old"**
CHAPTER 3	71	**The Season of Exhibitions**
CHAPTER 4	116	**Active Antiquarians**
CHAPTER 5	159	**Antiquarians in Nineteenth-Century Japan**
	214	**Epilogue**

APPENDIXES

TABLE 1	217	**Exhibition Practices and Policy Changes from the Late Tokugawa to Early Meiji Periods**
TABLE 2	224	**Significant Meiji Publications with Reproduced Illustrations**
TABLE 3	227	**Glossary**

229   **Works Cited**
236   **Illustration Credits**
237   **Biographical Notes on the Author and Translator**
239   **Index**

Preface to the English Edition

HIROYUKI SUZUKI

Fifteen years have passed since this book, originally written in Japanese, was published in 2003. It may be helpful for readers to make brief reference to a background of the publication and progress, or regress, after its publication. It is hoped this review will help them gain a clear vision on the state of the field of art-historical studies in Japan.

As mentioned in the epilogue of the original, the 1990s was the decade—in particular for historians of Japanese art—that was memorable for shaking the status quo of disciplines to their foundations. Revisionist art historians and critics of the time opened a Pandora's box that, a hundred years before, Basil Hall Chamberlain had sealed under a spell. "To translate the European term 'fine art,' there has recently been invented the compound of *bi-jutsu*," he wrote in *Things Japanese: Being Notes on the Various Subjects Connected with Japan* (1890). Discovering the exact date of the term's origin, in an official document the Meiji government issued in 1872, their quest for the truth located uncertainty, non-universality, and mortality in the concept of *bijutsu*, upon which the study of Japanese art history had long been predicated.

Following the current of critical studies in the 1990s, the original version of this book was published in a series entitled The Direction of Modern Art (Kindai bijutsu no yukue). The initial editorial plan of the series was to publish seven volumes of critical research inspired by revisionist art-historical studies of the 1990s, but for various reasons this challenging plan ground to a halt after three volumes and remains incomplete.[1]

In retrospect, however, the fate of the plan might reflect a limit of revisionist studies of modern art history in the 1990s. It is true that the revisionists awakened historians of Japanese arts to an insight into the historicity of the concept of *bijutsu*. Yet, their studies brought about fluidity in the field of art-historical studies, because the updated recognition of *bijutsu* seemed, for some, to deconstruct the established framework of the discipline. This response would be reasonable if they bitterly remembered the bygone years, when they had taken great effort to establish art history as an independent discipline separated from the field of aesthetics. Oddly enough, art history in Japan started its academic career as a branch of aesthetics in the 1890s, and, for example, a nationwide academic society of art history was not established until the late 1940s, after the Pacific War. Setting aside such a tangled background of the discipline, however, among the negative responses to revisionist studies, the most typical one was the criticism that they simply examined art or *bijutsu* from the perspective that art was first and foremost a part of the institutions organizing various systems of the society—and that, as a result, they deliberately ignored the most important thing for the study of art history, namely, art objects themselves.

Responses both positive and negative to the revisionist studies more or less reflected the state of the field of historical studies of Japanese art in the first decade of the new century. In reviewing the academic scene in Japan during the 1990s, revisionist studies in the field of art history were inspired and influenced by contemporary critical theory developed in the West, particularly in the United States. Gender theory, for instance, was earnestly introduced and applied to Japanese arts; methods of social history also inspired some art historians to try them in the field; and so forth. These trials were often bundled together with the seductive label "new art history."[2] However, their outcomes varied. Some were seen as introducing new insights into the field, while others were understood as the works of parrotlike followers of critical theory imported from the West.

In considering the present situation in which no alternative theory, method, or insight has taken shape, it is still unclear what vision the second decade of the twenty-first century will provide us for the field. However, in my view there is a conspicuous inclination in historical research of Japanese arts that did not change, even in the 1990s: the scholarly estrangement between histories of premodern and modern art. Largely due to a lack of expertise in the other's area, art historians often look with disinterest at the other side. It is obvious that this peculiar rift is rooted in the invention of the term *bijutsu* in the Meiji era, which caused a discrepancy of the research field between premodern and modern art histories.

For the future historical study of Japanese arts, it would be crucial to build a strong bridge with which one could span the brook separating those two fields within the same discipline. If one could manage this, then art history might be able to take steps forward toward more universal issues—for example, how to free art history from the framework of the nation-state, and how to settle the confrontation between globalism and regionalism in art-historical studies.

Acknowledgments for the original book appear in its epilogue, according to the editorial custom of Japanese publications. For this English edition, first of all, I would like to thank Maki Fukuoka, who generously agreed to undertake the laborious work of translating the original Japanese text into English. I also express my special thanks to the Ishibashi Foundation for their financial aid. Without their thoughtful consideration and extensive help, this plan to publish the English edition could not have been realized.

NOTES

1. Later the publishing plan was reorganized to include other volumes in the series, and an additional five volumes were published by the summer of 2018.

2. For reviewing the state of the field in the 1990s, see Namiki Seishi, "Nihon bijutsushi kenkyū no genzai," in Ōta Takao, ed., *Geijutsugaku o manabu hito no tame ni* (Kyoto: Sekai Shisōsha, 1999), 122–25.

Introduction

MAKI FUKUOKA

In "Meditations on the Frame" ("Meditación del marco," originally published in Spanish in 1943), philosopher and social theorist José Ortega y Gasset noted, "We are not used to *seeing* a frame except when it is in the carpenter's shop, bereft of a painting: that is, when the frame is not fulfilling its function, when it is, so to speak, out of a job."[1] At the same time, its Spanish title, "Meditación del marco," calls for another English translation, "Meditation from the frame," since the preposition *del* (and its component *de*) can function as both *of* and *from* in English. Thus, the second translation indicates another way that Ortega y Gasset viewed a frame (*marco*): a way to position himself peripherally.

These observations by Ortega y Gasset—on the strangeness of seeing a frame without the painting and the insinuation of frame as a positioning tool—renders a frame both the object of investigation and the designation of his location. This double meaning invested in the idea of frame resonates strongly with Suzuki Hiroyuki's *Antiquarians of Nineteenth-Century Japan: The Archaeology of Things in the Late Tokugawa and Early Meiji Periods*. If a frame, or a gilded frame to be precise, is an analogue to the epistemological structure of art history—a constructed device that isolates art objects from other "things" to provide space for reflection and contemplation for the viewers—then Suzuki's book invites us to study this frame being assembled in the carpenter's shop.[2]

Suzuki focuses on individuals whose collections and practices of sharing and showing their objects are hardly a common topic in the discipline of art history. Through his analyses of primary sources on these individuals, Suzuki highlights their collective interest in and attitudes toward their things within the context of the changing social environment of mid-nineteenth-century Tokyo. As readers, we witness the intricate and often idiosyncratic dynamics of individuals whose commitment to assemble these frames was both serious and extraordinary. Unlike the arc of the received narrative, where the chronology of Japan's art follows a periodization based on political events, Suzuki's narrative posits that it is strategically significant and reasonable to regard past practices related to objects nurtured during the previous Tokugawa period as inseparable from and contiguous with the birth of the concept of fine art in Meiji Japan.

How was the frame constructed? From where did the measurement of its parts and the decisions on its materials emerge? Who assembled it? Suzuki answers these questions through archival resources, publications, and the diaries of several individuals who occupied a significant space within the figurative carpenter's shop.

To extend this analogy further, Suzuki also attends to the interactions at the shop. A range of individuals—from Takamura Kōun, a famous sculptor of Buddhist icons, and Murata Fumio, who unofficially traveled to England and became a publisher of a satirical magazine, to Edward S. Morse, an American zoologist who befriended many antiquarians during his long stay in Tokyo—come in and out of that shop. Each figure brings in new and old ideas about objects, at the same time the implementation of new cultural policies by the Meiji government is a constantly felt presence in the air. The communications that take place inside and outside the shop, through and about objects and individuals, magnify the process by which the frame came to be framed.

Antiquarians of Nineteenth-Century Japan was published in Japanese in 2003 as the first volume of Yoshikawa Kōbunkan's series The Direction of Modern Art. At the dawn of the twentieth-first century this series provided a venue for art historians in Japan to expand national inquiry into the relationship between modernity and art history. Suzuki, whose career as an art historian began as a researcher of premodern art at the Tokyo National Institute for Cultural Properties, came to write this book in the wake of publications in the 1990s by Kitazawa Noriaki, Satō Dōshin, and Kinoshita Naoyuki that staked out challenging and novel perspectives on the history of art history in Japan.

As Suzuki notes in the epilogue, these new voices of modern art specialists produced distinct traces visible to art historians across the field. In addition to deconstructing the normalized and foundational term *bijutsu* (fine art), these new studies also gave rise to the proposition that contemporary art history could—and should—include objects that had not been considered proper items for analysis under the borrowed scheme of art history originating in the Euro-American context. Since then, many historiographical and historical inquiries into the status and understanding of "nude," "architecture," and "craft," for example, have resulted in amplifying the sense that since its inception in the nineteenth century, art history in Japan had been skewed by the desire to mimic its Western counterpart.[3] Suzuki's book is one example from a group of self-reflective, perhaps even subversive, efforts to challenge this propensity of the field. Its ambition to undo the particular Eurocentric structure of the discipline is thus insistently postcolonial.[4]

Antiquarians of Nineteenth-Century Japan also examines the period just before governmental interest in fine art and art history took concrete shape. Satō Dōshin's *Modern Japanese Art and the Meiji State: The Politics of Beauty* (originally published in Japanese in 1999, English translation 2011) detailed the processes of institutionalizing art, creating museums, and developing official policies by the Meiji government. Suzuki's book strips the layers of historical soil in Satō's work farther afield and deeper in time. *Antiquarians of Nineteenth-Century Japan* focuses on the roles and interests of particularly active antiquarians, their personal relationships, and collaborative projects to expose the nitty-gritty details of the antiquarians who tried to cope with the changing status of objects—*their* objects.

Among the recent calls to reconsider the state of the discipline in light of globalization, particularly noticeable is the fact that anglophone scholars began to investigate the key terms—*global* and *world*—beyond the frame of contemporary art. An edited volume from the Clark Studies in the Visual Arts, *Art History in the Wake of the Global Turn* (2014), Whitney Davis's review of Kitty Zijlmans and Wilfried van Damme, eds., *World Art Studies: Exploring Concepts and Approaches* (2009), and John Clark's "The Worlding of the Asian Modern" (2014) are relevant examples here.[5] In providing commentaries on the publication of *World Art Studies,* Davis notes: "*World Art Studies* contributes to the worlding of art, rather than to globalizing art history. Or more exactly, it tries to ensure that the globalization of art history (long one of the very criteria of art history) effects the worlding of art. Such worlding cannot and should not be taken for granted in any mere globalization—today more than ever. This is the fundamental theoretical advance."[6] John Clark also deploys the term *worlding,* but uses it as a particular historical phenomenon. For him, *worlding* denotes opposition to the hierarchy of historical events determined by colonialism or imperialism. "Worlding," he notes, "from the outset, meant making local interpretive frames visible in a global perspective across cultural and temporal zones because, from the early nineteenth century, there was the potential for local discourses to penetrate the non-local."[7]

These renewed attempts to investigate the terms of the discipline whose uses have become endemic can be read as a symptomatic gesture emerging from the work of anglophone scholars, a collective will and desire to act on the question of boundaries. Does it signal a shift in aspiration, at once aesthetic and epistemic, that is distinctly different from previous critiques of art history in its content and approaches? Notwithstanding the elasticity and elusiveness of the "world" and the "globe," the stakes of these nouns remain unclear. To what extent is this gesture an endorsement of the art market that is inextricably entangled with the neoliberal economy? Whose interest does this represent? What is clear across these recent attempts, moreover, is what they want to move away from: Eurocentrism. In this context, the prefix *de-,* whose Latin etymology carries a sense of undoing and reversing an action, has gained prominence in the appearance of terms such as *decentering* and *decolonizing.*

It is in relation to this contemporary context that I want to situate *Antiquarians of Nineteenth-Century Japan*. Although the political, economic, and cultural conditions differ greatly, the art historians of the early twenty-first century and the antiquarians of the mid-nineteenth century are each faced with a similar challenge: how to navigate different ways of apprehending their world and their worldviews through the objects of art-historical scrutiny. The question of framing has reappeared a century and a half later.

This return strikes me as significant. Faced with a huge and abstract push toward internationalization and modernization, figures such as Ninagawa Noritane and Morse did not completely align themselves with such forces per se. Rather, they carved out their own niches through gathering publications and engaging in deliberate collaborations with the government. In response, antiquarians focused on the modes and techniques of representation, shared systems of evaluation, and the rhetoric of analysis. However small and temporary their niche was, the grandiose political tidal wave of the government did not completely drown their interests. Quite usefully, Suzuki provides succinct analyses of the why and the how of various stakeholders situated in the midst of a worlding that unfolded a century and a half ago.

For Ninagawa and his fellow antiquarians in nineteenth-century Japan, the stakes were high and personal: their cultivated and informed worldview based on their collecting was challenged and deemed old. As Suzuki argues, in their familiarized method of sustaining this worldview, the objects and their knowledge of them had been arranged without reference to the hierarchical structure of art-historical taxonomy. Rather, their world was characterized by its circularity, like a mandala. What did the antiquarians do when this worldview was called into question? This book provides the details of this process and their activities.

In its subtitle and the prologue, Suzuki makes clear the significant debt this project owes to Michel Foucault's *The Order of Things: An Archaeology of the Human Sciences* (1966, English translation 1970). In the chapters that follow, Suzuki steadfastly incorporates what Foucault terms as "archaeological" methodology, one that is invested in "configurations within the *space* of knowledge which have given rise to the diverse forms of empirical science."[8] Chapters 1, "The World of Things Past and *Kokikyūbutsu*," and 3, "The Season of Exhibitions," are devoted to the physical and tangible space in which activities of constructing knowledge about and through objects took place. Chapter 1 is organized around the governmental edict of 1871 to protect *kokikyūbutsu* (old and ancient objects), and then it delves into the question of access. It addresses who had access to things of value and why, where the things were kept, and how the new Meiji government intersected with the existing space of knowledge production. It ends by foregrounding the emergent stakes, both epistemic and historical, that altered the shape of knowledge production of *kokikyūbutsu*. Chapter 3 begins by providing selected Japanese synthesizing experiences of museums and exhhibitions in Europe and America around the time of the Meiji Restoration. It then looks backward in time to analyze *kaichō,* the historical practice of a public display of objects popularized during the Tokugawa period. Treating expositions, museums, and *kaichō* as physical space of knowledge production, Suzuki makes comparisons among them to identify the differences and similarities on the levels of discourse, audience expectation, and infrastructure. The Meiji government's reliance on the idea of "necessary things" emerges here as the pivotal device that encouraged such comparison, through which the viewers judge "the relative merits, superiority, and inferiority" of things. The decisive shift in evaluative standard—and, therefore, the types of knowledge generated—illuminate the historical a priori of the epistemology. Chapters 2, "'The Past and the Present' and 'The New and the Old,'" and 4, "Active Antiquarians," intersect with chapters 1 and 3 by focusing on a more intangible aspect of spaces of knowledge production, such as language, rhetoric, and concepts, through which "the mode of being of things," to borrow Foucault's phrase, were altered.[9] Specifically, chapter 2 interprets the significance of the binary oppositions of the past and the present on the one hand, and the new and the old on the other, in the preface of Ninagawa's *Illustrated Book of Past Things: Ceramics Section* (*Kankozusetsu tōkinobu,* 1877), a seminal publication by an exemplary antiquarian of the period. Suzuki returns to analyze the illustrations of this publication extensively in chapter 5, "Antiquarians in Nineteenth-Century Japan." Chapter 4 expands the discussion of exhibition space detailed in chapter 3 by considerations of the field of *meibutsugaku* (the study of names and things), a study of exegetics of *xungxue* developed first in the fifth to the third century BCE China. Suzuki's approach is to situate this field both historically and historiographically to delineate the changes in *tabula* and grammar, in Foucault's terms. In the concluding chapter 5, the analyses of actual space and abstract concepts merge together. Here, what Foucault termed as "the experiences of propinquity of things" become concretized by the examination of the forms of social assembly that the antiquarians harnessed, unpacking their logic to incorporate new technology such as photography and lithography to address epistemological hurdles of antiquarianism, and the establishment of archaeology as an academic subject. While "things" kept their material forms intact, the historical a priori—specifically, the professionalization of knowledge production—hierarchized and sidelined "the space of knowledge" nurtured by the antiquarians, burying deep their historical roles and works.

At the same time, it is also significant that Suzuki's interpretations emerge out of detail-oriented analyses, supported by his keen investment in discerning subtle differences in language and pictorial representations. Here his interpretive mode mirrors the object of his analyses—the antiquarian and connoisseurial attention to detail. He asks the reader to focus on microscopic details, for example, the historical differences among the concepts of the new, the present, and the novel, explored in chapter 2. The depth and intensity of the sustained attention given to these minuscules construe the microcosm that the protagonists of the book inhabited.

The close-knit community of antiquarian assembly and its eclecticism, coupled with the laser-sharp focus in individual collections analyzed in chapters 4 and 5, further contribute to render the world of nineteenth-century antiquarians through Suzuki's mode of interpretation. As readers, thus, we also witness the extent to which Suzuki's analyses are indebted to the antiquarianism he is describing and analyzing.

Let us return to Ortega y Gasset's essay "Meditations on the Frame." He ended the essay with a section titled "Failure." Here Ortega y Gasset evaluates his own writing, asserting metacritically that his effort to write innovative thoughts on frames had failed, as he had foreseen.[10] He continues: "It would have been worthwhile to pose the suggestive question of why paintings in China and Japan are usually unframed. But how can one approach that subject, which implies as it does the radical differentiation between Far Eastern and Western art, between the Asian heart and the European one?" This prescribed difference is such that he asserts, "in order to understand [the radical differentiation], it would first be necessary to suggest why the Chinese orient toward the south, not the north, as we do: and finally, why, when they want to say 'no,' they nod their heads up and down, as we do when we say 'yes.'"[11] Ortega y Gasset points to the significant challenge that one must commit to when faced with the difference while also hinting at the improbability of overcoming such gap. In this text, too, we come face to face with the sense of uncertainty prompted by the question of worlding.

Suzuki's argument offers an alternative response to Ortega y Gasset's frustrated and frustrating ending. Rather than seeking continuity and translatability among differences, as Ortega y Gasset does, Suzuki treats these differences as potentialities. As he notes, the activities and works of the protagonists in his book are discontinuous with the accepted teleological narrative of Japanese art history. Indeed, they are often overlooked or understood as setbacks. But by taking these failed attempts seriously, Suzuki offers a reading that signals how these activities allow us to come to terms with such differences without the imposition of one stratum of value over the other. In this way, his book undoes and reassesses our own frames of reference.

NOTES

1. José Ortega y Gasset, "Meditations on the Frame," trans. Andrea L. Bell, in *Percepta* 26 (1990): 188. Italics in translation original. I thank John Mowitt for calling my attention to these grammatical and conceptual nuances.

2. "Parergonically" is another way to articulate this. Here, I am evoking "Parergon," the first chapter of Jacques Derrida's *The Truth in Painting*. Derrida posits the question of aesthetics, particularly Kantian aesthetics, as one about "*discourse on the frame*," and argues that this discourse is "against, beside, and above and beyond the *ergon*, the work accomplished." Jacques Derrida, *The Truth in Painting*, trans. Geoff Bennington and Ian McLeod (Chicago: University of Chicago Press, 1987), 54.

3. Indeed, Satō Dōshin noted in his 2006 *Bijutsu no aidentitī*, also published in the same series as Suzuki's, that the gap between the understanding of "Japanese art history" in a Euro-American context and Japan stems from the historical fact that in modern Japan, art history as a discipline demonstrably modeled itself after that of the West. Satō Dōshin, *Bijutsu no aidentitī* (Identity of Art) (Tokyo: Yoshikawa Kōbunkan, 2007), 77. A recent surge in exhibitions of *shunga* prints (mostly pre-1868 images of sexually explicit materials in woodblock prints and hand scrolls) can also be situated in relation to this mode of reconfiguring the elements and limits of the objects considered in the discipline.

4. Here I use the concept of the postcolonial to designate a series of epistemic impingements through ideological systems of Eurocentric origins. That is, my use of "postcolonial" is not determined by and limited to the historical colonialisms, in which Japan, as a sovereign nation, colonized regions of East and South East Asia.

5. As Parul Dave-Mukherji chronicles, James Elkins's *Stories of Art* (2000) indicated an inaugural effort by Euro-American art historians to bring in "non-Western" visual practices to the platform of art-historical survey. The title refers back to Ernst Gombrich's *The Story of Art* (1950), a popular and influential text to this day. Her criticism of Elkins's effort and her timely assertion that a critique of cultural nationalism must be included in any such globalization of the field remain unfulfilled. Parul Dave-Mukherji, "Art History and Its Discontents in Global Times," in Jill H. Casid and Aruna D'Souza, eds., *Art History in the Wake of the Global Turn* (Williamstown, MA: Sterling and Francine Clark Art Institute, 2014), 91–95. Also see Parul Dave-Mukherji, "Whither Art History in the Globalizing World," *Art Bulletin* 96, no. 2 (2014):151–55.

6. Whitney Davis, "Comment: World without Art," *Art History* 33, no. 4 (2010): 712.

7. John Clark, "The Worlding of the Asian Modern," in Michelle Antoinette and Caroline Turner, eds., *Contemporary Asian Art and Exhibitions* (Canberra: ANU Press, 2014), 67–88. In light of Davis and Clark's broad ambition, W. J. T. Mitchell's cautionary skepticism is noteworthy. Mitchell noted how such a notion itself is overwhelming as it hints at totality and universality. W. J. T. Mitchell, *Image Science: Iconology, Visual Culture, and Media Aesthetics* (Chicago: University of Chicago Press, 2015), 93.

8   Michel Foucault, *The Order of Things: An Archaeology of the Human Sciences* (New York: Vintage, 1994), xxii. Italics in original.

9   Foucault, *The Order of Things*, xxii.

10 As he reflects here, Ortega y Gasset's aim was to find "a humble theme," a topic for which he will be able to write no more or less than one folio.

11 Ortega y Gasset, "Meditations on the Frame," 190.

Translator's Note

In this translation, I have minimized the number of romanized Japanese words in the main text, moving information and descriptions of events, places, and names in Suzuki's original to endnotes when appropriate. Similarly, since the text itself mentions and discusses many Japanese books, rather than providing the conventional sequence of a Japanese title followed by its English translation, in the text the publication titles are styled as English titles followed by romanized Japanese, with the English translations alone used in a chapter text's repeat references. This is intended to aid interested anglophone readers from many disciplines to follow the narrative more easily. The notes provide references in romanized Japanese for researchers. In addition, further information on key publications and terms is provided in the appendixes.

There are a few terms for which I have retained romanized Japanese in the text. One key term is *kokikyūbutsu*, "old and ancient objects." The interpretive differences between the concepts of old and ancient are at the center of Suzuki's analyses, and as he argues, the term *kokikyūbutsu* itself was a novel invention by the Meiji government. Likewise, the Japanese noun *shūkokan* is used: as Suzuki notes, *shūkokan* refers to individuals' experiences in the West, at museums such as the British Museum; as his analysis of the primary sources also indicates, the idea of *shūkokan* also encompassed the role of recordkeeping, an archival facility in a contemporary sense. Rather than translating this term as either "museum" or "archive," the aim in keeping *shūkokan* is to suggest its distinct sense—modeled after European precedents but also conceived as a particular structure fit for the historically shifting environment of its day.

The historical and cultural nuances of the difference between the terms *exhibition* and *exposition* in English on one hand, and *hakurankai* and *tenrankai* in Japanese on the other, are opaque and confused. The lack of articulated difference, or the hesitation to gesture toward them, is palpable in surveying the English–Japanese dictionaries published around this period. For instance, in editions of Hepburn Japanese–English and English–Japanese dictionaries, the term *exhibition* is defined as both *misemono* and *hakurankai,* while the term *exposition* is rendered only as a noun meaning the "act of pondering." The Japanese term *hakurankai* is defined as "an exhibition of rare and curious things" and "an exposition," and *tenrankai* as "an exhibition or collection of rare and curious things for show."[1]

While definitions from historical dictionaries serve as one among many sources, I took these examples to guide my translation. For the national exhibitions modeled after the international expositions in the mid-nineteenth century, I have opted to use the word *exposition* to register its resonance of their Western counterparts. Otherwise, I translated the term *hakurankai* in both primary sources and Suzuki's writings as *exhibition.* In chapter 3, historically entangled back and forth between the display formats known as *misemono* and *kaichō,* exhibitions and international expositions play a critical role. Here, to uphold the logic of the argument over semantics and nominal confusion, I also rendered Suzuki's term *hakurankai* as "exhibition practices" or "display techniques" to signal that their meaning in contemporary English includes both "exhibitions" and "expositions."

Japanese names in this translation follow the Japanese order, with family name followed by given or literary name. It is standard practice in the study of Meiji Japan to refer to historical figures by their surname rather than given or literary name; I have adopted this convention in this translation. For the sake of consistency, I also use the surname to refer to historical figures in Tokugawa Japan, though the use of given or literary name would otherwise be the convention.

To produce this English translation, the cooperation of its original author, Suzuki Hiroyuki, has been both instrumental and exceptional. I thank him for providing copies of primary materials and for his willingness to articulate the nuances of his argument. In editing the English translation, Daniel Abbe, a PhD candidate at UCLA, assisted with remarkably concise and constructive suggestions. I am grateful for his assistance and patience. The thorough and reassuring editorial touch of Mary Christian was also significant. I thank Mr. Hot Sauce, who provided unparalleled comfort and joy. Finally, I am grateful for the support of the Getty Research Institute—Michele Ciaccio, managing editor, and Laurie Bolewitz, project management coordinator—for their understanding and patience in completing a manuscript during the ongoing global pandemic.

NOTES

1   Curiously and tellingly, Japanese terms for gathering, such as *honzōkai, shogakai, bussankai,* and *yakuhine,* do not appear in the editions of English–Japanese dictionaries I consulted. Digital Waeigorinshūsei, http://www.meijigakuin.ac.jp/mgda/waei/search/.

Plates

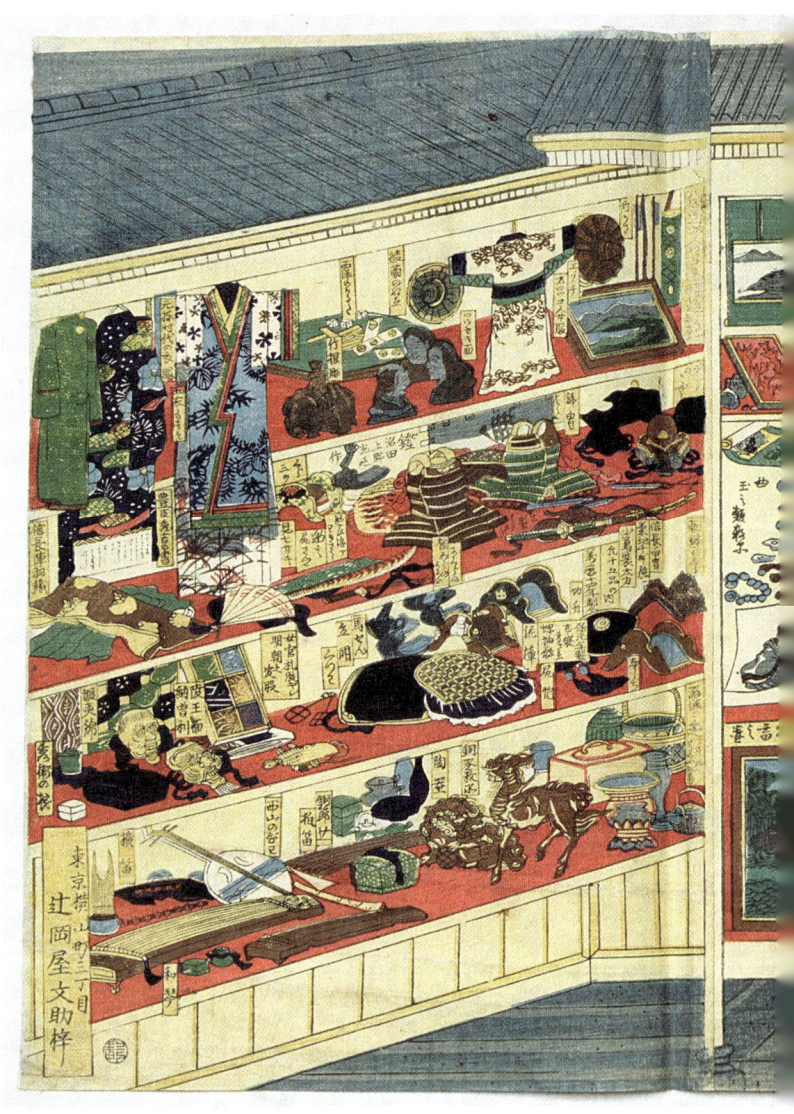

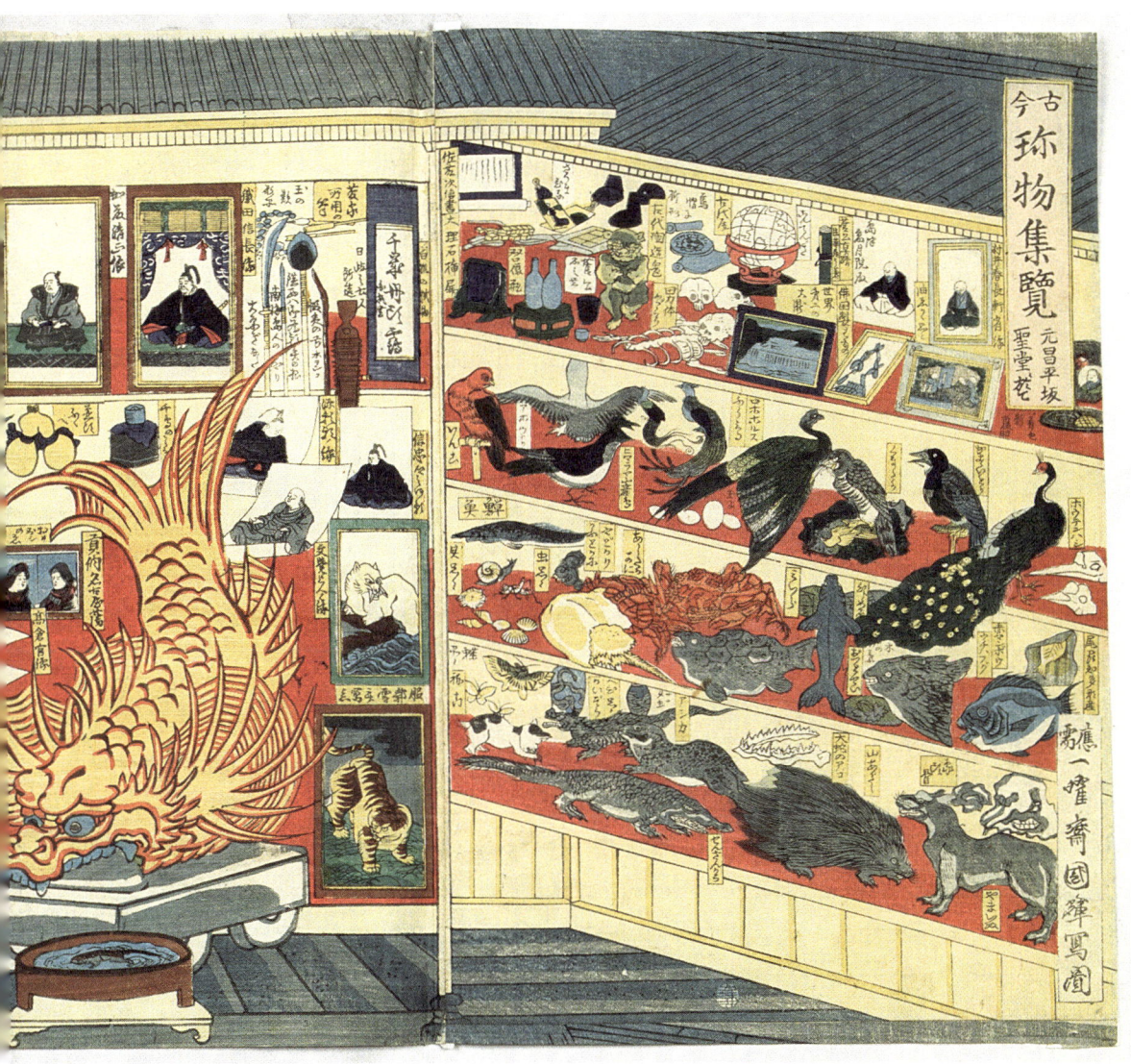

PLATE 1.

Ichiyōsai Kuniteru (Japanese, 1830–74). A View of a Collection of Things Past, Present, and Novel (*Kokinchinbutsu shūran*), 1872. Triptych, multicolor woodblock prints, 36.5 × 73.8 cm. Tokyo Kokuritsu Hakubutsukan, C0057548.

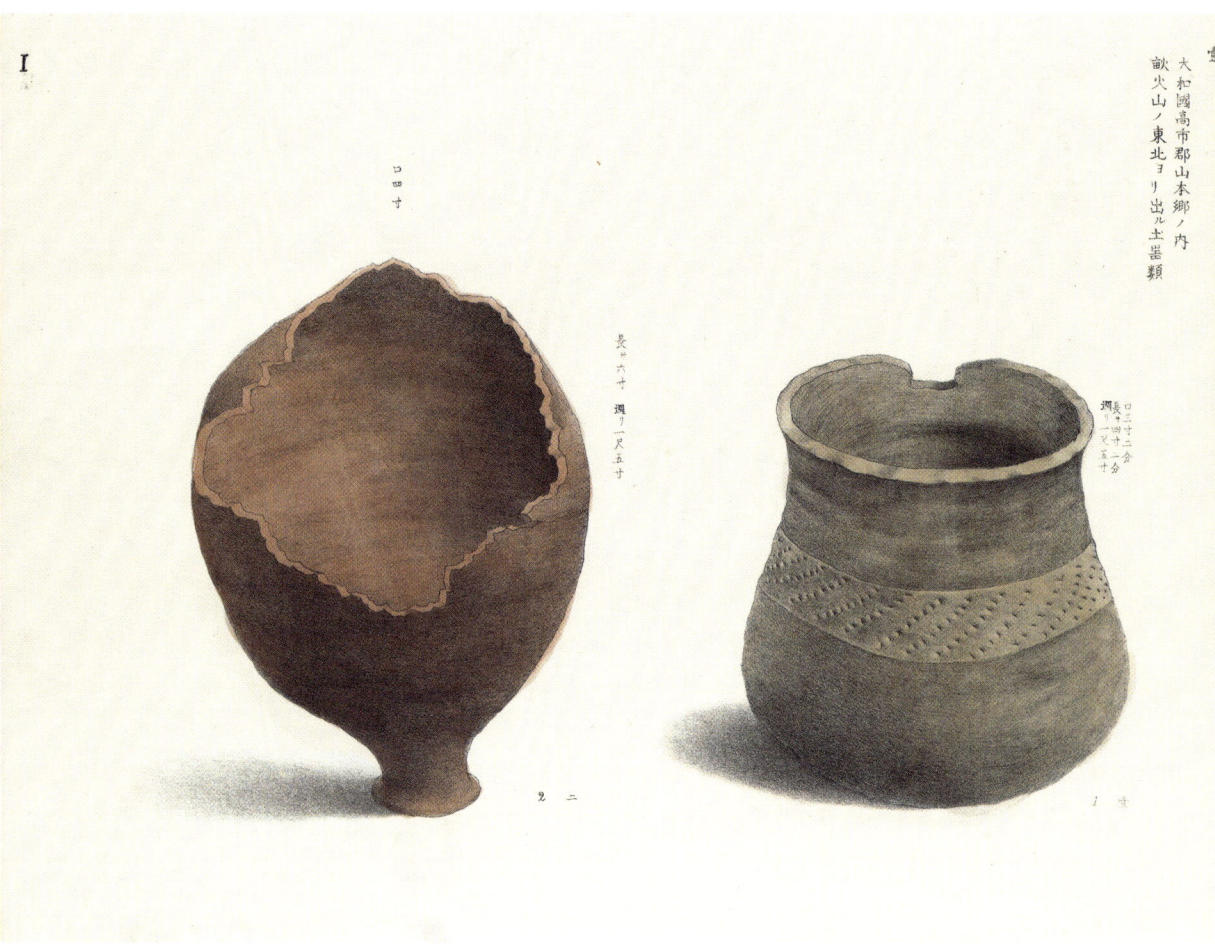

PLATE 2.

Ninagawa Noritane (Japanese, 1835–82). From *Kwan ko dzu setsu: Notice historique et descriptive sur les arts et industries japonais,* vol. 1, fig. 1, 1876. Hand-colored lithographic print, 28 × 40 cm. Los Angeles, Getty Research Institute, 2606-493.

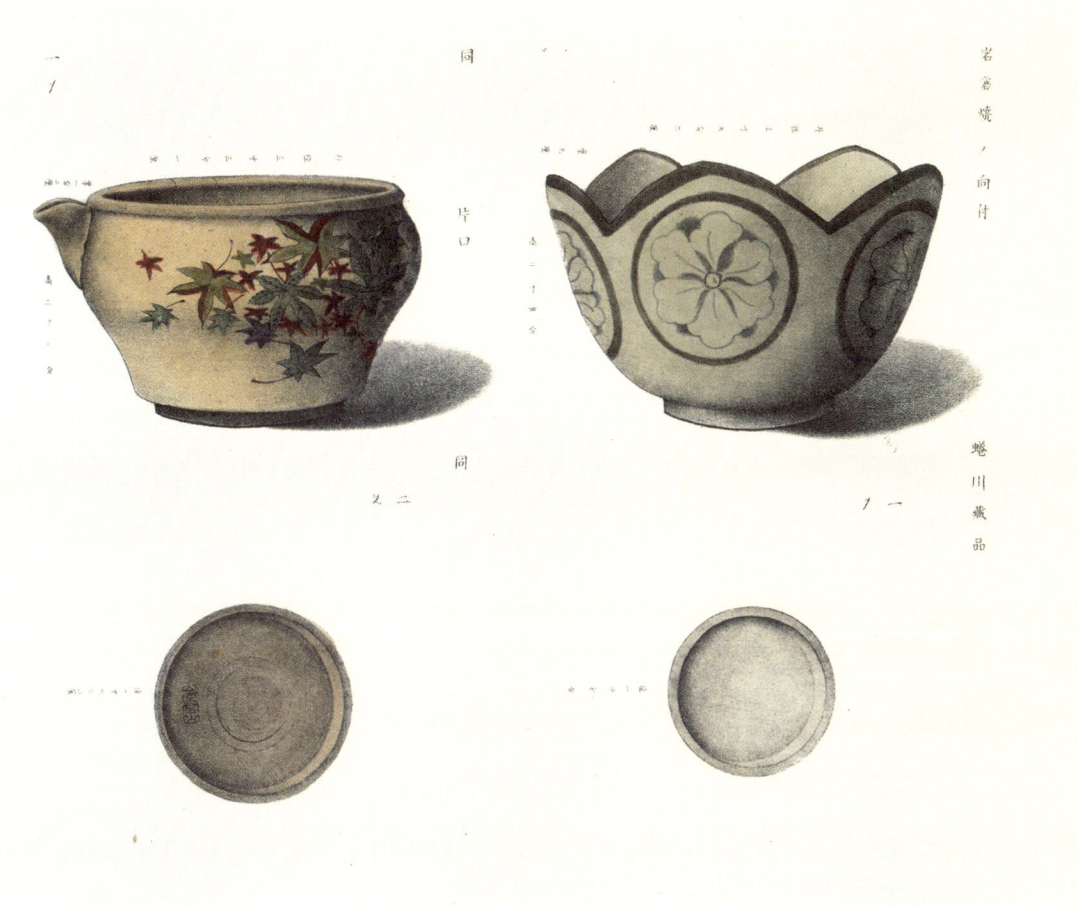

PLATE 3.

Ninagawa Noritane (Japanese, 1835–82). From *Kwan ko dzu setsu: Notice historique et descriptive sur les arts et industries japonais,* vol. 5, fig. 1, 1877. Hand-colored lithographic print, 28 × 40 cm. Los Angeles, Getty Research Institute, 2606-493.

Prologue: The Order of Things

CHANGES IN THE WORLD OF THINGS

This book deals with the world of things past. It covers the time from the Bakumatsu period (1852–68) to the middle of the Meiji period (1868–1912).[1] I propose to analyze how "the world of things past" changed within this time frame. During the thirty-year period from the late 1850s to the first half of the 1880s, the world surrounding "things past" transformed dramatically. Of course, these changes were inseparable from broader societal changes in Japan, beginning with the opening of select ports to expand foreign contacts during the Bakumatsu period. As the conditions around things past changed, the processes of interpreting their meanings and their values also shifted. Quite literally, ways of perceiving things changed.

The term *things past* might seem vague, but these objects undoubtedly constituted a particular type of a world, a cosmos, before they were understood as "art objects," "archaeological remains," "cultural properties," or "antiques." The order of this cosmos, structured by the intimate connections among objects, has long been forgotten. For this reason, I feel compelled to use the term *things past*. What did the order of this cosmos—"the world of things past"—look like? How did this order change? We can hope for more from this line of questioning. Wouldn't tracing changes in the world of things past also allow us to glimpse changes in the world of human beings?

Before we begin the main discussion, let me take a moment to follow the argument that Michel Foucault (1926–84) presents in his introduction to *The Order of Things* (*Les mots et les choses,* 1966). In doing so, I intend to make clear the broader issues my line of questioning contains.

FOUCAULT'S WORDS AND THINGS

The beginning of the introduction to *The Order of Things* discusses a strange classification adopted in "a certain Chinese encyclopedia." It relates to the ways of classifying animals, drawn from a story by the Argentinian writer Jorge Louis Borges (1899–1986). According to this, this Chinese "encyclopedia" classifies animals into: "(a) belonging to the Emperor, (b) embalmed, (c) tame, (d) sucking pigs, (e) sirens, (f) fabulous, (g) stray dogs, (h) included in the present classification, (i) frenzied, (j) innumerable, (k) drawn with a very fine camelhair brush, (l) *et cetera,* (m) having just broken the water pitcher, (n) that from a long way off look like flies."[2] One can easily imagine how fundamentally different this taxonomic system is from one used in zoological studies today. For instance, where would a local stray cat belong in this system? One can also imagine an example that would be classified into multiple categories, especially among the fictional creatures. There is neither clarity nor consistency in the system. According to philosopher and translator Nakayama Gen, if one follows the logic that classification is a method to understand things, "it requires at least three principles: (1) the principle of comprehensiveness, that all existing things are completely absorbed in the order and there is nothing left outside of this order, (2) the principle of exclusion, which eliminates the possibility of overlap within the order, and lastly (3) the principle of non-transcendence, which holds that the classification takes place across a standardized 'level,' and that there is no meta-classificatory standard beyond this level."[3] None of the three principles apply in the taxonomic system of the "strange Chinese encyclopedia."

To be sure, Foucault's intention was not to mock an inefficient or illogical system from "the East." He argues:

> The Chinese encyclopedia quoted by Borges and the taxonomy it proposes lead to a kind of thought without space, to words and categories that lack all life and place, but are rooted in a ceremonial space, overburdened with complex figures, with tangled paths, strange places, secret passages, and unexpected communications. There would appear to be, then, at the other extremity of the earth we inhabit, a culture entirely devoted to the ordering of space, but one that does not distribute the multiplicity of existing things into any of the categories that make it possible for us to name, speak, and think.[4]

In other words, "in our dreamworld, is not China precisely this privileged *site* of *space*? In our [European] traditional imagery, the Chinese culture is the most meticulous, the most rigidly ordered, the one most deaf to temporal events, most attached to the pure delineation of space."[5] Foucault further clarifies: "We [Europeans] think of it as a civilization of dikes and dams beneath the eternal face of the sky."[6] It is easy to say that Foucault's characterization of China evinces nothing but the worldview of the Orientalist who contends that stagnant China, a civilization on the opposite side of the earth, shows its "eternal face" in contrast to the progressive world of Europe. Foucault's point, though, is that this fiction exists "in our dreamworld." Indeed, it is precisely because it's a fiction that it also serves as a compelling site for various other issues.

According to Foucault, "in order for a thing to be apprehended as a thing within an order, there must be a singular perspective, one that has been constructed culturally and historically," and "in order to apprehend the order of existent things, there needs to be a framework before the thing can be apprehended."[7] Foucault refers to this necessary framework as an "episteme." Following this, the seemingly ordered and tidy foundations of the European classification system supported by the three basic principles also appear as nothing but a product of a certain episteme. This allows Foucault to situate the strange taxonomic system found in the Chinese encyclopedia in a relative perspective.

The framework of knowledge required to apprehend the order of things is not a fixed entity. Foucault notes that "there is nothing more tentative, nothing more empirical (superficially, at least) than the process of establishing an order among things."[8] In fact, he assumes that the creation of an episteme is a dynamic process. The classification system of the Chinese encyclopedia, which "establish[es] an order among things," is surely also a process that could not be "more empirical." Foucault claims that "in every culture, between the use of what one might call the ordering codes and reflections upon order itself, there is the pure experience of order and of its modes of being."[9]

This area of "pure experience" is situated between two areas, "the use of what one might call the ordering codes" and "reflections upon order itself." As this might be a bit too abstract, let me pick up more concrete examples from Foucault. On the one hand, "the fundamental codes of a culture—those governing its language, its schemas of perception, its exchanges, its techniques, its values, the hierarchy of its practices—establish for every man, from the very first, the empirical orders with which he will be dealing and within which he will be at home."[10] Opposite this area exist "the scientific theories or the philosophical interpretations which explain why order exists in general, what universal law it obeys, what principle can account for it, and why this particular order has been established and not some other."[11]

Between these two Foucault locates the domain for "pure experience," which he sees as playing the "fundamental" role of "intermediary."[12] He then characterizes this middle domain as "more confused, more obscure, and probably less easy to analyze." But it is through examining this space that a culture, imperceptibly deviating from the empirical orders prescribed for it by its primary codes, instituting an initial separation from them, causes them to lose their original transparency, relinquishes its immediate and invisible powers, frees itself sufficiently to discover that these orders are perhaps not the only possible ones or the best ones; this culture then finds itself faced with the stark face that there exists, below the level of its spontaneous orders, things that are in themselves capable of being ordered, that belong to a certain unspoken order; the fact, in short, that order *exists*. As though by emancipating itself to some extent from its linguistic, perceptual, and practical grids, the culture superimposed on them another kind of grid that neutralized them, which by this superimposition both revealed and excluded them at the same time, so that the culture, by this very process, came face to face with order in its primary state.[13]

Within this in-between space, "order itself" is "liberated" and generates a framework for knowledge that would encourage the construction of the order of things. For Foucault, order emerges from this in-between space "according to the culture and the age in question, continuous and graduated or discontinuous and piecemeal."

Between following the code that reflects the existing order of things, and explaining or interpreting that order, exists the expanding domain of "pure experience" that comes face-to-face with the various modes in which orders of things exist. It is here, in this intermediary domain, that various epistemes change and emerge. To further articulate "pure experience," Foucault explores it "in grammar and philology, in natural history and biology, in the study of wealth and political economy," analyzing the changes in epistemic frames in Europe since the sixteenth century.[14] His approach, therefore, is entirely opposite from an approach that assumes that disciplines today have resulted from a progression directed toward objectivity and logic. As he notes, this is "an inquiry whose aim is to rediscover on what basis knowledge and theory became possible; within what space of order knowledge was constituted; on the basis of what historical *a priori,* and in the element of what positivity, ideas could appear, sciences be established, experience be reflected in philosophies, rationalities be formed, only, perhaps, to dissolve and vanish soon afterwards."[15]

His project reveals "the epistemological field" that is an episteme.[16] Within this space, knowledge is seen "apart from all criteria having reference to its rational value or to its objective forms." This inquiry, then, "grounds its positivity and thereby manifests a history which is not that of its growing perfection."[17] This kind of history does not aspire to the perfection of knowledge. Instead, it is a history full of the potentiality of the various conditions of knowledge. Foucault's account brings forth various arrays within the space of knowledge that has produced various forms of empirical sciences. It is in this sense that Foucault characterizes his inquiry as an "archaeology" rather than as history in the traditional sense.[18]

In this manner, Foucault ends his introduction to *The Order of Things* and moves on to particular case studies—just as we, too, will now move on to explore changes in "the world of things past." In dealing with this material, though, Foucault's archaeological method is an efficacious model.

NOTES

1. Bakumatsu generally designates the last years of the shogunate rule, encompassing the period from 1852, when Russian and American fleets successively came to demand that the Tokugawa shogunate open the country, to 1868, the year of the fall of the shogunate and the Meiji Restoration.

2. Michel Foucault, *The Order of Things: An Archaeology of the Human Sciences* (New York: Vintage, 1994), xv.

3. Nakayama Gen, *Fūkō nyūmon* (Tokyo: Chikuma Shobō, 1996), 76.

4. Foucault, *The Order of Things*, xix.

5. Foucault, *The Order of Things*, xix.

6. Foucault, *The Order of Things*, xix.

7. Nakayama, *Fūkō nyūmon*, 77.

8. Foucault, *The Order of Things*, xix.

9. Foucault, *The Order of Things*, xxi.

10. Foucault, *The Order of Things*, xx.

11. Foucault, *The Order of Things*, xx.

12. Foucault, *The Order of Things*, xx.

13. Foucault, *The Order of Things*, xx–xxi.

14. Foucault, *The Order of Things*, xxi.

15. Foucault, *The Order of Things*, xxi–xxii.

16. Foucault, *The Order of Things*, xxii.

17. Foucault, *The Order of Things*, xxii.

18. Foucault, *The Order of Things*, xxii.

CHAPTER 1

The World of Things Past and *Kokikyūbutsu*

SECTION 1: COMING INTO CONTACT WITH THINGS

THE EDICT ISSUED IN THE FIFTH MONTH OF 1871 (MEIJI 4)

At the end of 1872, the Meiji government adopted the Gregorian calendar. This change rendered the third day of the twelfth lunar month of Meiji 5 as 1 January 1873 (Meiji 6), thus marking one of the enormous shifts that took place in the order of temporality. My account begins in the previous year, 1871 (Meiji 4). In the fifth month of this year, the Grand Council of State (*Dajōkan*) issued an edict regarding the preservation of old and ancient objects (*kokikyūbutsu*).[1] A portion of a document attached to this edict is fascinating, as it includes objects categorized as *kokikyūbutsu* among those deemed worth preserving. There were thirty-one categories in total. In addition, a short description followed each category, and in certain cases an explanation of the categories was also included. For example, the "musical instrument" section included the following description: "Musical instrument section: transverse flutes, pan pipes, recorders, bass drums, gongs, hand drums tapped with sticks, transverse harps, ancient Japanese transverse harps, lutes, ancient Chinese transverse harps, masks, and other objects such as *noh* play costumes and instruments belonging to various dance and music practices."[2]

While masks were surely not musical instruments, the category included objects pertaining to musical performances. It makes sense, then, that *noh* costumes were also included. This demonstrates in concrete detail what the new government thought worthy of preservation in the early days of the Meiji period. While I acknowledge that skimming through the details of all thirty-one categories contained in the attached paper demands the reader's patience, I will list them here because they serve as the starting point for my argument.

Note that I added the numbers given to each category in the list, in order to facilitate the forthcoming discussion. That is, these numbers are not found in the original document. I want to call attention to the notable sentence at the end of the document: "The above objects are presented regardless of their origin in or outside Japan, from the age of the gods [*jindai*] to the recent past."[3] Since these things were brought together under the broad umbrella of *kokikyūbutsu,* the list-makers imagined that the oldest items were produced in the age of the gods, long before the time of Emperor Jinmu's reign (putatively said to be 600 BCE), and did not include objects produced in contemporary times. I also want to call attention to this clause because it did away with the distinction between items produced locally within Japan and those imported from abroad.

1. Ritual implement section: shields, arms, and other items used in Shinto rituals, etc.

2. Old jade and jewelry section: comma-shaped beads, cylindrical beads, glass, crystal, and the like

3. Stone arrowhead [*sekido*] and stone ax [*raifu*, literally, thunder god's ax] section: stone arrowheads, stone axes, stone rods [*hekirekichin*, literally, thunder god's drum rods], stone daggers, spoon-shaped scraper stones [*tengunomeshigai*, literally, rice-spoon of the long-nosed goblin Tengu], etc.

4. Old mirror and old bell section: old mirrors, old bells, etc.

5. Copper vessel section: *tei* [Ch. *ding*]*, shaku* [Ch. *jue*], and various other copper [and bronze] vessels

6. Old roofing tile section: famous things [*meibutsu*] and old tiles in general regardless of fame

7. Weaponry section: swords, bows and arrows, banners used on the battlefield, helmets and armors, harnesses, ancient weapons made of bronze [*ka*, Ch. *ge*, and *geki*, Ch. *ji*], a pair of large and small swords [*daishō*], guns, bullets, drums used on the battlefield [*senko*], horns used on the battlefield, etc.

8. Old calligraphy and painting section: things of fame, portraiture, hanging scrolls, handscrolls, albums of exemplary calligraphy [*tekagami*], etc.

9. Old book and old sutra section: books and pictures to consider the past, old woodblock prints and old manuscripts, and other items, including popular novels [*gesaku*], predating the middle past [*chūko*] and therefore belonging to the ancients

10. Tablet section: *hengaku* tablets in shrines and Buddhist temples, as well as tablets of calligraphy and paintings by notable persons

11. Musical instrument section: transverse flutes, pan pipes [*shō*], recorders [*hichiriki*], bass drums, gongs [*shōko*], hand drums tapped with sticks [*kakko*], transverse harps [*sō*], ancient Japanese transverse harps [*wagon*], lutes [*biwa*], transverse harps [*shitsunokoto*], masks, and other objects such as *noh* costumes [*sarugaku*] and instruments belonging to various dance and music practices

12. Bell inscription epitaph section, and ink rubbings of exemplary calligraphy of the past [*hōjō,* Ch. *fatie*]: old things, both famous and not

13. Seal section: ancient seals, etc.

14. Stationery section: writing desks, ink slabs, carbon ink, brush racks, ink slab screens, etc.

15. Agricultural implement section: ancient items

16. Carpentry tool section: same as above

17. Carriage and palanquin section: carriages, palanquins, bamboo palanquins, etc.

18. Furniture section: bedding furniture, screens, lanterns and candlesticks, keys and locks, kitchen utensils, tableware, smoking utensils, etc.

19. Textile section: old gold brocade, fabric fragments from antiquity, etc.

20. Clothing and ornamentation section: official uniforms, daily clothes, mountain dwellers' clothes, clothes for women, hair ornaments such as combs and hairpins, umbrellas and woven hats, rain coats, containers [*inrō*], purses [*kinchaku*], sandals and clogs, etc.

21. Leatherwork section: various kinds of leatherworks and old leather cloth with dyeing patterns

22. Coin and paper money section: old gold, silver, and ancient coins, paper money, etc.

23. Metalwork section: various vessels and items made of copper, brass, copper alloy with tin and lead [*shakudō*], bronze, pure gold [*shikon*], iron, tin, etc.

24. Ceramic section: pottery and porcelain from various countries, etc.

25. Lacquerware section: various vessels made of metal powder sprinkled lacquer decoration [*makie*], lacquer inlaid with mother-of-pearl, red lacquer carvings [*tsuishu,* Ch. *tihong*], etc.

26 Measuring tool section: balance, a pair of scales, measuring rod, dry and liquid measures, Japanese abacuses, and other ancient tools

27 Section of utensils used in tea ceremony, incense-smelling ceremony, and flower arrangement: charcoal brazier, tea kettle, and utensils used in tea making such as tea bowls, utensils used in incense-smelling ceremony such as incense containers and incense burners, utensils used in flower arrangement such as flower vases and flower vessel stands

28 Amusement section: *go* board game, *shōgi* board game, *sugoroku* pachisi, *kemari* football, board games [*yasasuguri*], pitch-and-toss with arrows and a pot [*tōko*], toy bows, throwing fans, poem cards [*karuta*], etc.

29 Section of toys for children such as *hina* dolls and carp banners, other human figures: dolls protecting small children [*hōko*], dolls protecting small children [*amagatsu*], dolls displayed for the girls' festival [*hina*], wooden dolls, earthenware dolls, Nara dolls, and others; and various toys for children's play

30 Old Buddhist statues and implements section: Buddhist statues, cylindrical containers of sutras, five ornaments for the altar consisting of an incense burner and a pair of flower vases and candlesticks, bells hung under the eaves at the four corners of a building roof [*hōchaku*], and other old Buddhist items

31 Fossil section: fossils of animals, bones, horns, and tusks of animals, seashells, etc.

The above objects are presented regardless of their origin in or outside Japan, from the age of the gods [*jindai*] to the recent past[4]

On the one hand, this list can be seen as a rather splendid taxonomic chart of the world of things past, insofar as efforts have been made to list all kinds of things in such a way that no item could slip through this net of preservation. At the same time, though, it creates a kind of dazzling confusion similar to that which Foucault found in Borges's Chinese encyclopedia—although the scale of confusion is much smaller in this case. In addition to the sheer number of categories, there are more than a few sections whose ordering seems unreasonable, or whose content unclear. For instance, take the example of (3), the stone arrowhead and stone ax section. Within the field of present-day archaeology, the items listed under this section are considered to be stone implements. However, the terms used here, such as "stone arrowheads" (*sekido*), "stone axes" (*raifu*), "stone rods" (*hekirekichin*), and "spoon-shaped scraper stones" (*tengunomeshigai*) are hardly ever used today. Even more confusing, however, is the fact that the relationships among the thirty-one sections are left unexplained. It could be the case that the Meiji government deployed the term *kokikyūbutsu* in this edict to produce the sense that an actual condition was shared among the objects that they deemed worthy of preservation. In other words, there was no firm and concrete category of *kokikyūbutsu,* which the government could then further subdivide into thirty-one sections. This makes it easier to understand a document whose systematic characteristics are otherwise difficult to grasp.

To further my point, I suggest that the way of framing things as *kokikyūbutsu* alone is a novel method. To assert this new category convincingly to the public, the government needed to emphasize the significance of the "objects of *kokikyūbutsu*" at the beginning of the document.

> The objects of *kokikyūbutsu* are profitable to no small extent in order to examine the vicissitudes of times old and new, and the development of laws and customs. Naturally, because of the unfavorable practices of disparaging the old and competing for the new, these objects have become lost or destroyed, and this is a lamentable situation. We should carefully preserve various objects of *kokikyūbutsu,* as classified in the attached paper, stored for generations in each region, regardless of their size.
>
> However, authorities concerned should write down the names of the items and their owners in detail and submit [the list].[5]

That is, the Meiji government saw social utility in *kokikyūbutsu* items, because they could help to "examine . . . the vicissitudes of times old and new, and the development of laws and customs."

How, then, was this edict calling for the preservation of *kokikyūbutsu* put into effect within its own time? Naturally, the specific items that were to be preserved had to come first. Let us first survey the activities and thoughts regarding the world of things past around the time this edict was issued, as the policies of the Meiji government changed dramatically and rapidly throughout the period. With such understanding, we will be able to arrive at a more contextualized analysis and interpretation of this *kokikyūbutsu* edict.

THE MEIJI GOVERNMENT AND THE WORLD OF THINGS PAST

One of the first major shifts brought about by the Meiji government was the way in which the environment around the world of things past was brought into a close relationship with various systems of the nation. During the previous Tokugawa period, the shogunate promoted the "study of local products" (*bussangaku*) for their social utility. But the scale and content of such activity around things past changed greatly in Meiji. Generally, three significant changes took place: (1) they became objects that ought to be preserved legally, (2) they became objects that ought to be exhibited for the public, and (3) in order to be exhibited, they became objects that ought to be researched in order to discover more objects. We can chronologically identify specific movements and acts at the very beginning of the Meiji government. The *kokikyūbutsu* edict can be positioned as the starting point of these changes.

The following brief survey of the movements of museums and exhibitions in the early half of the Meiji period reveals how governmental policies changed over the fifteen years after the Grand Council of State issued its *kokikyūbutsu* preservation edict in the fifth month of 1871. Established as the Bureau of Local Products under the South School of Daigaku (*Daigaku nankō*) in 1870, the administrative body of this office underwent various dramatic moves: to the Ministry of Education in 1871, to the Home Ministry in 1875, to the Ministry of Agriculture and Commerce in 1881, and finally to the Imperial Household Ministry in 1886. Save for the final 1886 shift to the Imperial Household Ministry, these changes can be seen as the process of framing *kokikyūbutsu* within the government's policy to encourage industry. In particular, the change in managerial hands from the Home Ministry to the newly established Ministry of Agriculture and Commerce in 1881—which coincided with the second Domestic Exposition for the Promotion of Industry—was decisive (see appendixes, table 1).

In the twelfth month of 1869 (Meiji 2), the Kaisei School (Kaisei Gakko), formerly the Institute for Studying the West (Kaiseijo) of the Tokugawa shogunate, was renamed the South School of Daigaku. In the ninth month of 1870, the Bureau of Local Products (*Bussankyoku*) was founded in the school. In the fifth month of 1871, an exhibition of local products (*bussankai*) organized by the South School of Daigaku took place at the Shōkonsha Shrine in the Kudan area of Tokyo, which had been renamed from Edo in 1869.[6] Although this exhibition was small in scale—only lasting seven days, from the fourteenth to the twentieth days of the fifth month—it came to serve as the forerunner for many exhibitions that would take place later. Throughout the Meiji period, exhibitions came to carry significant weight as the critical mechanism by which to display objects to the general public.

Just before this exhibition, in the fourth month of 1871, Daigaku (part of the Ministry of Education), submitted a proposition to the Grand Council of State asking for the preservation of *kokikyūbutsu*.[7] The edict of *kokikyūbutsu*, issued in the fifth month of 1871, was both a response to and elaboration of this proposition. The Grand Council's edict was submitted after the end of the exhibition at the South School of Daigaku, on the twenty-third day in the fifth month. It is important to note here that the proposition by Daigaku included specific suggestions such as the construction of *shūkokan,* which means a building for gathering past things—virtually a museum. We will explore this topic in depth in chapter 2.

In the seventh month of 1871, the Ministry of Education was established, following the closure of Daigaku. Just two months later, this new ministry established the Museum Bureau (*Hakubutsukyoku*). And in the third month of 1872, the Ministry of Education hosted an exhibition at the Yushima Seidō, a Confucian temple in Tokyo, which marked the first instance that the Meiji government used the term *hakurankai,* or exhibition. This neologism would become the commonplace term for exhibitions in Japanese. In the second month of 1872, in addition to these activities organized by the Ministry of Education, the Central Council [*Seiin*] of the Grand Council of State used this term to establish the Exhibition Bureau (*Hakurankai Jimukyoku*) within the council. This office was established because the Meiji government had officially decided to participate in the Vienna World Exposition (Weltausstellung Wien), scheduled to begin in 1873. The exhibition organized by the Ministry of Education in the third month at the Yushima Seidō, then, can be understood as a preview of what the Japanese exhibition in Vienna would look like. In fact, one of the two golden fishlike ornaments (*shachihoko*) that stood on the tower of Nagoya Castle was shown at the Yushima Seidō in 1872, while the other was displayed in Vienna in 1873.[8]

Parallel to these new initiatives, in the eighth month of 1872 the Ministry of Education began extensive research on treasures in old temples and shrines in the central part of Japan.[9] It was during this research that the door of the Shōsōin, the eighth-century imperial repository inside of Nara's Tōdaiji Temple, was opened for the first time since 1833.[10] This research would later be remembered as the inspection conducted in the year of *jinshin* (*Jinshin kensa*).[11]

In the third month of 1873, the Exhibition Bureau under the Grand Council of State absorbed the Museum Bureau of the Ministry of Education. From April 15 to July 31, an exhibition organized by the Ministry of Education was held at its newly built museum (*Hakubutsukan*) located in the Uchiyamashitachō area of Tokyo. In May, the Vienna World Exposition began. In 1874 (Meiji 7), another exhibition was held at the same museum in Uchiyamashitachō from March to June, while in May, a calligraphy and painting exhibition took place at the Taiseiden Hall of the Yushima Seidō, which was used as a secondary location for the exhibition.[12]

In March 1875 (Meiji 8), the Exhibition Bureau under the Grand Council was moved into the Home Ministry and its name changed to Museum (*Hakubutsukan*). At this point, then, there were two institutions called *hakubutsukan,* a building in Uchiyamashitachō and a bureaucratic office at the Home Ministry. In the same month, a research team revisited Shōsōin, and then its registration was transferred to the museum from Tōdaiji Temple, where the Shōsōin had been originally located since the eighth century. In April 1876, the Museum was renamed the Museum Bureau (*Hakubutsukyoku*). A month later, in May, Philadelphia's Centennial International Exhibition opened; the Meiji government participated in this exposition.

In August 1877 (Meiji 10), while the Satsuma Rebellion continued, the Home Ministry held the first Domestic Exposition for the Promotion of Industry (*Naikoku kangyō hakaurankai*) in Tokyo's Ueno Park.[13] Such expositions, the domestic version of world expositions, took place five times between 1877 and 1903, serving as the major advertising pillar for the Meiji government to advance its industrializing policies. The Meiji government also participated in the Paris Universal Exposition (Exposition Universelle) of 1878.

Around this time, construction of the new museum in Ueno Park designed by the British architect Josiah Conder (1852–1920) had begun. By the time of its completion in January 1881 (Meiji 14), the museum had already started to move from Uchiyamashitachō into this new location.[14] In March 1881 the second Domestic Exposition for the Promotion of Industry took place in Ueno Park, and on this occasion the ground floor of the new museum building was used as a gallery for fine art.

In March 1881 the Home Ministry and the Finance Ministry jointly organized the second Domestic Exposition for the Promotion of Industry. Just a month after the opening, though, the sections promoting industry and agriculture in the Home Ministry and the Commerce Bureau (*Shōmukyoku*) of the Finance Ministry were transferred and merged to begin the new Ministry of Agriculture and Commerce. In the process of this reconfiguration, the Museum Bureau of the Home Ministry was also transferred to this new ministry. Here we can see how the Meiji government attempted to house all of its departments for the encouragement of industry under one roof. Then, in March 1882 (Meiji 15), the Home Ministry's building designed by Conder in Ueno Park was reopened as the Museum of the Ministry of Agriculture and Commerce.[15]

Under the direction of the Ministry of Education, a new project to explore and research temples and shrines in the western region of Japan began in June 1884. Advisers such as Ernest F. Fenollosa (1853–1908) and Kanō Tessai (1845–1925) joined the project under the direction of Okakura Kakuzō (also known as Tenshin, 1863–1913), an official of the Ministry of Education. The well-known narrative of the "discovery" of the Guze Kannon statue (an Avalokiteśvara of the seventh century) at the octagonal Hall of Dreams inside Hōryūji Temple in Nara constituted a part of this research.[16]

In July 1885 (Meiji 18), Shōsōin, which had been under the jurisdiction of the Home Ministry since 1875, was transferred to the management of the Library Office (*Zushoryō*) of the Imperial Household Ministry. In March 1886 (Meiji 19), the jurisdiction of the museum in Ueno Park, which had been administered by the Museum Bureau of the Ministry of Agriculture and Commerce, moved to the Imperial Household Ministry.

Looking back chronologically, the first Domestic Exposition for the Promotion of Industry in 1877 was a great watershed for evaluating *kokikyūbutsu*. Certainly the positive reception of items from Japan at the 1873 Vienna World Exposition (the first time the Meiji government participated in such an event) encouraged the government. The slogan for the government's policy of promoting industry was "considering the past to benefit the present" (*kōkorikon*), and with this, the Meiji government forged a direction for industrialization in which things past became the object of study to utilize as models and sources for new products. In other words, these decisive moments trace an almost entirely opposite trajectory from the Grand Council's edict of 1871, in which the purpose of preserving *kokikyūbutsu* was understood as "examin[ing] the vicissitude of times old and now and the development of laws and customs."

In these processes of changing directions, the group of objects understood as *kokikyūbutsu* were re-evaluated and vetted according to the utility prescribed by the government's policies. It is worth highlighting here that the term *bijutsu,* a contemporary Japanese term for art, was also coined around the same time. Although this term consists of two Chinese characters, it was a complete neologism, without any reference to usages in Chinese vocabulary. The term appeared for the first time in the Japanese translation from the original German official documentation concerning the terms and conditions for the Vienna World Exposition of 1873. The government published the translation of this instance as "Guidelines for Exhibiting Objects at the Vienna World Exposition" (*Ōkoku uīnfu hakurankai shuppin kokoroe*), and attached it to the edict by the Grand Council of State in the first month of 1872, a year before the Vienna exposition, to solicit submissions of objects to the exposition.[17] While this usage of the term *bijutsu* did not limit itself only to visual arts but also included to music and poetry, it is telling that an exhibition that served to promote the government's industrialization policies played the role of the midwife for the term.

As if grafting onto its industrialization policy, the Meiji government introduced another new direction for things past. This direction played an instrumental role, particularly in the latter half of the Meiji period. The crucial moment arrived in March 1886, when the administrative responsibility of the museum designed by Conder in Ueno Park was transferred from the Museum Bureau (then under the Ministry of Agriculture and Commerce) to the Imperial Household Ministry. This series of shifts gave the museum an important role in charting the cultural landscape of the latter half the Meiji period and beyond. In September 1888 (Meiji 21), the Imperial Household Ministry established the Provisional Bureau for the Inspection of National Treasures (*Rinji Zenkoku Hōmotsu Torishirabekyoku*). In May 1889, the ministry issued an edict for the establishment of imperial museums in Tokyo, Nara, and Kyoto. In October 1890, it established an academy system of imperial artists (*teishitsu gigei'in*), accelerating its process of consolidating infrastructure. In June 1897 the Law for the Preservation of Old Shrines and Temples (*Koshaji hozonhō*) was enacted. Needless to say, these actions are clearly distinct from the policy of promoting industry. The Imperial Household Ministry established its new systems from 1886 on in the context of a growing reception and advancement of the concept of *bijutsu;* in this sense, it also came to play a role in embellishing and lending weight to the modern emperor system of Japan.[18]

This shift in policy development between the late 1880s and early 1890s emerged in parallel with the establishment of major political infrastructure: the implementation of the cabinet system (1885), the promulgation of the imperial constitution (1889), and the establishment of the Diet (1890), to name a few. In the context of education, Imperial University (Tiekoku Daigaku) was founded in 1886, while in 1877 (Meiji 10), Tokyo Medical School (Tokyo Igakkō), the former East School of Daigaku, and Tokyo Kaisei School (Tokyo Kaisei Gakko), the former South

School of Daigaku, had merged to become the University of Tokyo. In 1885 the University of Tokyo absorbed Tokyo Law School (Tokyo Hōgakkō) under the auspices of the Ministry of Justice and the Technical Art College (Kōbu Daigakkō) of the ministry of technology, thereby consolidating to become a general university, which was reestablished as the Imperial University (Tiekoku Daigaku) in the following year. In this way, some institutions of higher education run by the government were integrated into the comprehensive administration of the Ministry of Education. Various governmental systems that were reconfigured through merges and political changes came to determine the direction of historical development from this point on.[19] The same can be said about the preservation policies of *kokikyūbutsu*. While there had been important modifications, its basic structure centering on the Imperial Household Ministry would be maintained for the next sixty years, until the end of the Pacific War.

ORDINARY EVENTS

In surveying the movements and activities regarding the world of things past through the lens of government in the first half of the Meiji period, the following remarks can be made. The world of things past—which had been positioned as *kokikyūbutsu* that would help to examine "the vicissitudes of times old and new"— was folded into the government's policy of industrialization, and then became a mechanism to reproduce the almost spiritual values that would maintain Japan's modern emperor system. After Japan's defeat in the Pacific War, the world of things past was repositioned as a zone of cultural protection, which could then play an important role in Japanese cultural policy. In other words, after 1945, the world of things past stood in to provide evidence of the nation's history and the culture of its citizens, thereby replacing subjects of the empire. It was only in this context of the postwar cultural climate that the government brought forth the term "cultural properties" (*bunkazai*) to describe certain objects.

Even examining only the Meiji period, the environment surrounding the world of things past changed repeatedly. In retrospect, it is clear that almost all systems—from the legal framework for protection to the infrastructure of exhibitions and museums—and all conceptual manipulations that supported them, including various terms and neologisms, were constructions initiated and led by the Meiji government. To put it differently, the systems and language that reconfigured the world of things past were produced through the monopoly of the Meiji government.[20] It goes without saying that in this process, the government looked at "universal" systems and language used by developed civilizations in Europe and deployed them as their model.

However, if we pay attention solely to the changes of the Meiji government's policies, we will only see one side of the historical metamorphosis. The changes in the world of things past also encompassed various aspects that cannot be easily grasped by the analysis of government policies. Certainly the actions of the Meiji government were a significant factor, but at the same time, we should examine things that were excluded from the scope of policies—things that came to be eliminated in the process of implementing these policies, or things that were rendered obscure as a result of this implementation. Only then, I believe, can we view the shifting conditions of the world of things past more holistically, and only then we can interpret such changes critically.

To put it simply, the world of things past became classified and hierarchical. In every instance where the meaning of an object changed in response to an outside motive, the entire world of things past reverberated in response. In this way, objects were sifted through and re-evaluated for their utility against a new set of standards. On the one hand, some objects later became designated as "national treasures" (*kokuhō*), thereby receiving the highest recognizable value. Still, other objects were deemed useless and became buried under many objects in the corner of curio shops. These might be extreme examples, but I wonder: What happened to objects that went up and down in the hierarchical order that was established, and what kind of position did they receive as a result? Did this hierarchical system resemble a pyramid in which objects were placed systematically from top to bottom? Or did it more closely resemble a mountain range, in which multiple peaks and ordering systems existed in parallel? In any case, the things that remained on the sifter received attention. Shouldn't we pay close attention to the objects that fell through the cracks, and see where they went?

In the same vein, we should also pay close attention to the worlds that the government actively excluded or ignored through its policies. We should also consider the worlds that had been outside the one constructed and supported by the government, but which were later absorbed into it. To give one example, consider the world of antique collectors, which had existed from the prior Tokugawa period. Because the range of their activities covered surprisingly large historical areas, and because their activities tended to bypass the social hierarchies of the Tokugawa period, the social changes brought about by the Restoration did not affect this group significantly during the early years of Meiji; they continued to pursue their activities as they had done before. In fact, because the Restoration so dramatically overhauled the structures of basic sociopolitical systems, the early Meiji period proved to be an opportune time for these collectors: They could now seek out objects in various collections that had once been off limits.

In the entry of the eighth month of 1868 of the *Chronicles of Edo* (*Bukō nenpyō*, 1882), the writer Saitō Gesshin (1804–78) included the heading "Things that are popular and prevalent these days." The first item following the heading was "curio shops."[21] From this record, we can ascertain that in the early days of Meiji, or at least until the mid-1880s, the activities of these collectors were not folded into the policies of the Meiji government, nor were collectors prohibited from carrying out such activities. On the contrary, it seems that the government supported their collections and proactive pursuits, and in some instances we can detect the deliberate, collaborative approaches that certain collectors took to work with government officials. Although it is tempting to suggest that the realms of the official and the private were definitively mixed in such activities, I would simply prefer to say that, at least in these early days of Meiji, it would be a difficult task to draw a distinct line separating the two.

However, by the time the structured understanding of the official and the private sectors became prevalent and accepted in the late 1880s, collecting was seen as a normal practice and stopped receiving much scholarly or historical consideration. To be more precise, even if its existence was acknowledged, its meaning went unconsidered. In this way, the existence and activities of collectors were written up as the merely anecdotal, inserted between the major tides of historical events. As a consequence, the rich and expansive world of things past that had existed before bureaucratization came to be gradually forgotten. One reason for this is surely that many histories are written from the perspective of the official or the bureaucrat. If we take the position of these forgotten collectors, it is not difficult to imagine that the policies related to the world of things past proposed by the government would have felt to them as if an intruder with muddy shoes had walked into a *tatami* room in which they had gathered peacefully. While the activities of these collectors were understood as normal practices, what kind of view would we gain if we saw this period from their perspective? What kind of cultural and political panorama would we see?

Similarly, we should also pay closer attention to the opposite of successful policies and programs—plans that were lost, deemed failures, and left behind. As we have already seen, the policies of the Meiji government included various twists and turns. In each of these turns, some policies and ideas were thrown out, with the individuals who promoted them following close behind. Far more than elucidating the differences between the official and private sectors, I argue that an analysis of failures and setbacks will illuminate the contradictory qualities of specific governmental policies and the systems that they produced.

If we return to the point of departure of my argument and consider the historiographical concern outlined above, it becomes clear that my methodology is the opposite of a teleological approach, in which a researcher retroactively projects various values that support a particular order of the present into the past in the hope of finding the origin of the present order and values. Such a teleological method seeks out elements and values that guarantee their continuity to the present. Grafting such instances onto one another, this method only produces a genealogical tree that develops along a temporal progression. As a result, elements and values that are discontinuous with the present order, and those that are buried or thrown out, are rendered as anomalies—dwarfed branches stemming out from nodes on the main trunk of the genealogical tree. In other words, they are left outside the field of investigative vision, as elements that were left behind or were merely transitional. The resulting historical diagram produced by such a methodology accepts the order of the present as natural, inevitable, and universal. What is more, this methodological approach reconfirms the present order as a fait accompli, and fabricates another fiction that reproduces the established values of the status quo.

For example, if one were to take the 1871 edict on the preservation of *kokikyūbutsu* simply as the origin of administrating the protection of cultural properties, it would provide a basis upon which to understand the present-day system of the protection of cultural properties as the inevitable outcome of a natural progression—and as a practice that simply ought to be, without any questions. In this way, it becomes almost impossible to imagine that the system might, in fact, be a contingent product of its time.

The approach I take in this book is antithetical to this teleological method. In short, I aim to explore the unexamined potentialities of discontinuous elements. That is to say, I pay close attention to failed attempts and to elements or values that have been buried, abandoned, or otherwise forgotten because they are discontinuous with the present-day order. Analyzing these failed experiments lets us see the pressing issues of an age with greater clarity. Observing the failed attempt to clear a bar makes it easier to understand the height of the bar and where it was set.

By patiently digging up cases, factors, and values that have remained unexamined, and by unearthing experiments that have been forgotten, we will be able to see just how the classified and hierarchized world of things past was layered and accumulated. Boring into these deposits of history would, I hope, bring forth the issues and potentialities of this world. This approach would, then, illuminate the fact that the present order is constituted historically, rather than on the basis of a universal value. It would also yield a clear view of the twists and turns that actually structure the present order.

THE INSTRUMENTAL ACTIVITIES OF TAKAMURA KŌUN

What historical reality, then, met the Grand Council of State's edict on *kokikyūbutsu* in the fifth month of 1871? What were the concrete phenomena or objects that this edict was designed to preserve? Let us re-examine this edict from the perspective of the methodology outlined above.

Many scholars have identified the anti-Buddhist movement (*haibutsu kishaku*) as a reason for the government to issue this edict.[22] In fact, since the 1868 Edict on the Separation of Shintoism and Buddhism (*shinbutsu bunri rei*), more than a few notable temples became the targets of deliberate physical attacks and theft while the anti-Buddhist movement grew in force.[23] In some cases, even if a temple did not face immediate physical violence, it lost its financial basis from which to maintain and manage its affairs, when these temples had previously enjoyed the support of the Tokugawa shogunate and local domainal governments. As a result, properties and buildings within these institutions deteriorated and rotted over time. Sometimes these objects were brought to the market to be exchanged for modest sums.[24]

The generally accepted interpretation of the edict of preservation of *kokikyūbutsu* holds that the Meiji government was deeply concerned with the financial and physical conditions of Buddhist temples. To be sure, some elements of the situation after the 1868 Edict on the Separation of Shintoism and Buddhism correspond to this interpretation. The 1871 edict situated the meaning of *kokikyūbutsu* as "profitable" to the activity of examining, but immediately after this phrase also noted: "Naturally, because of the unfavorable practices of disparaging the old and competing for the new, these objects have become lost or destroyed, and this is a lamentable situation." Although the separation of Shintoism and Buddhism is not directly mentioned in the text, perhaps the government could not publicly mention it by name in this preservation edict. This line of thought might offer an explanation for the vagueness of the language of the 1871 edict, especially in the way that it referred to certain "unfavorable practices of disparaging the old and competing for the new," which had produced "a lamentable situation." But is this really the case?

There is an insightful recollection by Takamura Kōun (1852–1934), a famed sculptor of Buddhist icons, that helps us to think about the actual condition of this time more concretely. Let me quote a section from it and imagine this specific situation in the past.

> The situation in which Shintoism and Buddhism became mixed and jumbled grew rather serious [after the issue of the separation edict] because [we had to] assign this to Shintoism and that to Buddhism. Like some kind of natural disaster, this approach protected Shintoism and destroyed things belonging to Buddhism. Various things that belonged to the side of Buddhism in attendant forms became the target of destruction at this time. Things like sutras that consisted of multiple volumes were thrown into rivers or burned in the fields. Many fine things were destroyed in a frenzy. There is even a ridiculous tale that during the height of this movement, especially in places like Nara and Kyoto [where many significant and historical temples are located], the pagoda of Kōfukuji Temple was put on the market at an absurdly low price and nobody even came forward to buy it. At that time, however, this situation wasn't regarded as ridiculous because the times were radically changing. Everything was understood as a natural and inevitable force, and nobody found it strange.[25]

This quote is taken from *Recollecting the Bakumatsu and the Restoration* (*Bakumatsu ishin kaikodan*, 1929) by Takamura Kōun. He was one of the apprentices of the noted Buddhist icon sculptor Takamura Tōun (1826–79) of the city of Edo. Kōun's description of the blasé attitude toward the destruction of temple property should be read as the frank testimony of someone who experienced the changes of the time. It is well known that Kōun later taught woodcarving at Tokyo School of Fine Arts (Tokyo Bijutsu Gakkō) and became an imperial artist. His son, Takamura Kōtarō (1883–1956), also became a famous poet and sculptor. In 1874, at the age of twenty-three, Kōun finished his apprenticeship with Tōun. In his memoirs, just before describing the effect of the edict on the separation of Shintoism and Buddhism, Kōun vividly tells the story of an incident that took place during his apprenticeship. This story, which I will recount below, deals with "rescuing" Buddhist statues from Rakanji Temple—literally, a temple of Arhats. The story involves two sets of sculptures: one hundred statues of Avalokiteśvara located in one of the structures, known as Sazaedō, inside the precinct of Rakanji Temple, and a gathering scene of Buddha's first disciples, also known as the five hundred Arhats, which were located in the main structure of Rakanji Temple.

Also within the famous Rakanji Temple in Edo stood Sazaedō, a building containing one hundred statues of Avalokiteśvara (J. Kannon, Ch. Guanyin) were lined up along a corridor.[26] This set of statues was particularly well known among the public; many of the statues were produced by prominent sculptors of Buddhist icons and had been donated by various individuals. As Sazaedō had already been deteriorating due to weather, and the temple had difficulty maintaining it, it was finally decided to turn the building over to a demolition contractor, thereby sealing the cruel fate of the building and its statues.

This temple stood in the area of Honjo Itsutsume (present-day Ōjima in Kōtō ward, Tokyo).[27] It was a Zen Buddhist temple founded in 1695 by a Zen monk of the Ōbaku sect, Shōun Genkei (1648–1710).[28] Trained as a Buddhist sculptor in Kyoto prior to becoming a monk, Shōun produced five hundred wooden sculptures of Arhats (J. *rakan,* Ch. *luohan*) by his own hand for the temple. Rakanji enjoyed a great deal of popularity not just because of these sculptures, but also because of Sazaedō itself.[29] The structure of this building was unique in that it was built with two inner corridors that formed a double helix, which led visitors on a path up and down the corridor, worshiping the one hundred Avalokiteśvara statues one after another. Sazaedō was named after a turban shell (*sazae*) because of the resemblance in their inner structures; it was also known as Sansōdō, meaning "hall that is circled three times."[30]

When the Sazaedō was to be demolished, a "raw metal broker" was to purchase the one hundred statues of Avalokiteśvara. Kōun noted: "This kind of raw metal broker was not a hardware store. It was a person who purchased used metals to resell them. There were two kinds of metal brokers: those who bought used metal products such as pans, pots, and kettles; and those who dealt in gold and silver. The latter was a higher-quality broker, and this is the kind who bought the hundred statues of Avalokiteśvara. The statues had been colored skillfully and decorated with gold leaf, and the broker had bought them became of this."[31] The broker's scheme was to burn the wooden statues and salvage the gold from the ash. The broker's shop was located at the foot of the Makurabashi Bridge in Honjo, and one of Tōun's friends saw that "the one hundred statues of Avalokiteśvara were tied together tightly and placed inside straw rice bags or straw charcoal sacks, each having three or four bodies packed together. The limbs and legs of statues that were broken off, or came off, were tied with thick straw ropes and left outside."[32] This friend, who happened to witness the scene, set off at once to tell Tōun of the situation; while he was not at his workshop, Kōun was. Upon hearing of the situation, Kōun could not bear to sit still, and went directly to the metal broker. Tōun's workshop at this time was located in the Komagata area of Asakusa in Tokyo, just a stone's throw from the Makurabashi Bridge. Once Kōun reached the shop, though, the broker paid no attention to him. In the meantime, Tōun had returned to his workshop, and when he heard what was happening, he immediately came to the metal broker's shop. Luckily, Tōun convinced the broker to let him buy the five best statues. By the time they had rented a cart and transported the five Avalokiteśvara statues back to their workshop in Komagata, the sun was already setting. Kōun recounts that he successfully pleaded with Tōun to give him one of Shōun's statues; from that time on, this statue served as Kōun's guardian Avalokiteśvara.[33]

The story of how five Avalokiteśvara statues were rescued amid a storm of anti-Buddhist activity is all the more intriguing for Kōun's own skillful narration. It is not difficult to imagine that many such events, with different degrees of intensity, took place around this time. One can also say that it was quite lucky that this case was experienced and later recounted by a figure such as Takamura Kōun, who went on to become a noted sculptor. However, we must be mindful of the fact that the first edition of *Recollecting the Bakumatsu and the Restoration* was published in 1929.

In fact, the time of its publication coincided with the sixtieth anniversary of the Meiji Restoration, an anniversary that gave rise to many books recalling this time. Within a month of its publication, Kōun's book was already in its fourth printing.[34] According to a note by the novelist Tamura Shōgyo (1874–1948) included at the end of the volume, he started to write down Kōun's spoken recollections in November 1922, along with Takamura Kōtarō, Kōun's son.[35] The fact that this year marked Kōun's seventieth year probably inspired the project. Still, fifty years stood between the time of the incident and the time of the retelling. We should note that Kōun may have added information to his account that he learned later, or he may have reinterpreted his story to fit the framework of this later time.

THE EDICT AND THE REALITY

I have already noted that in 1897 the Meiji government implemented the Law for the Preservation of Old Shrines and Temples. Under this new law, certain things of the past became objects of legal protection. It is plausible, though, that Kōun reframed the "rescue" of the Avalokiteśvara statues within the cultural climate of 1922—a time by which people generally accepted the belief that the government ought to protect things of the past.

In the section "Recollecting the Bakumatsu and the Restoration," which immediately precedes the story of the rescue, Kōun vividly recalled repercussions of the separation of Shintoism and Buddhism. It is not surprising, then, that the rescue story is generally understood as a concrete example of the consequences of the anti-Buddhist movement. Because the story is based on Kōun's own experience and is told skillfully, it is hard to interpret it otherwise. However, I think that the story can be re-interpreted in a way that connects it to the government policy of preserving *kokikyūbutsu*. In March 1929, the same year that Kōun's *Recollecting the Bakumatsu and the Restoration* was published, the Law for the Preservation of National Treasures was implemented. Even without the knowledge of details of the law, many readers of Kōun's book would have encountered it in the context of this legislation.[36] Not only that, it is also possible that Kōun himself retold the story with the Meiji preservation laws in mind, or indeed that the interviewers themselves edited Kōun's stories to fit with the contemporary legislative context.

We must, then, trace the histories of Rakanji Temple around the time of the Restoration, and get a clearer sense of the temporality of this rescue. Two primary sources provide a solid starting point for this: (1) *The Far East*, an English-language newspaper published by John Reddie Black (1827–80) in Yokohama, and (2) *Illustrated Notable Places of Tokyo* (*Tokyo meisho zue*, 1877), which contains an introductory remark dated October 1876, published by Okabe Keigorō.[37] In the second volume of *Illustrated Notable Places of Tokyo,* the section on the eleventh main ward contains a description of Rakanji Temple. We learn that the decisive year of its deterioration was 1874, since the description notes that "the temple deteriorated after the Restoration, and its annexed temple building was removed. Then all the Buddhist sculptures inside the building were moved to the main temple hall, and the site of the building was designated to become a graveyard in 1874 (Meiji 7)."[38] Takamura Kōun had completed his eleven-year-long apprenticeship in March of that year. *The Far East* was a biweekly newspaper that featured photographic images on albumen paper that were pasted directly onto the page. In the 16 July 1872 issue it included two photographs: one of the exterior of the main building of the Rakanji Temple, the other of the interior of what appears to be the same building.[39] The first photograph shows a structure (presumably the central structure of Rakanji) that has lost its east and west wings (fig. 1). In the photograph of the interior of the remaining structure, some of the wooden statues of the five hundred Arhats are shelved in a disorderly manner (fig. 2). The former grandeur of the monastery compound, which can be seen in a woodblock print in volume VII of *Illustrated Famous Places of Edo* (*Edo meisho zue*, 1834–36) by Saitō Gesshin, is nowhere to be seen in these photographs.[40] According to *Illustrated Famous Places of the Great Japan* (*Dainihon meisho zue,* 1908), the temple buildings were destroyed in the Ansei earthquake of 1855. It also notes that "because the Arhat halls of the east and west [wings] were destroyed [by the earthquake], the statues [of Arhats] were moved to Sansōdō." Furthermore, it notes, "when the Sansōdō collapsed during the first years of Meiji, all statues [of Arhats in the Sansōdō] were moved to the [remaining] main hall."[41] As noted earlier, Sansōdō is the alternate name of Sazaedō, the double-helix structure. To summarize the description from this book, the east and west wings extending from the central structure of the main building collapsed

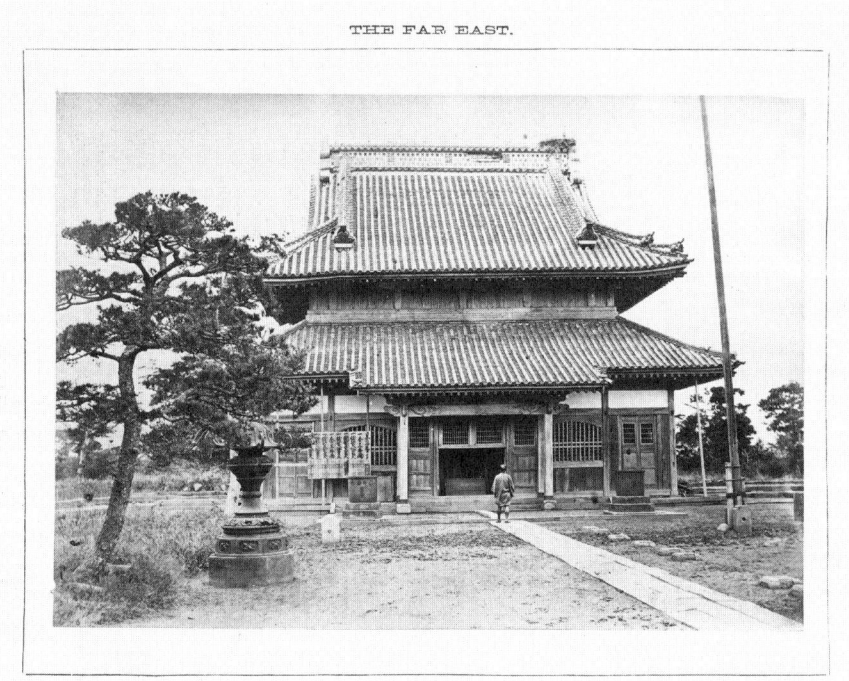

FIG. 1.

Temple of Five Hundred Gods at Yedo, from *The Far East*, 16 July 1872.

Albumen print, 19.3 × 13.5 cm. Los Angeles, Getty Research Institute, 2652-854.

---

as the result of the Ansei earthquake, and thus the statues of five hundred Arhats were transferred to Sazaedō, and when Sazaedō collapsed, they were then moved again to the remaining central structure of the main temple building. We can gather from this that what Okabe's *Illustrated Notable Places of Tokyo* referred to as an "annexed temple building" that was removed was Sazaedō. The photograph of the interior published in *The Far East* in 1872 aligns with this temporal progression of the temple. We can thus ascertain from these documents that Sazaedō, in which the hundred statues of Avalokiteśvara had been originally installed, was demolished before July 1872.

While the time of Kōun's rescue is clearer—it happened sometime before 1872—its relationship to the *kokikyūbutsu* edict of 1871 becomes more ambiguous. Of course, it is possible that Kōun's rescue of the statues happened immediately after the edict was issued in the fifth month of 1871. However, as a matter of probability, it is more likely that the event took place before, rather than after, the edict. In 1871, Kōun was twenty years old. It is not particularly strange that in 1922, after turning seventy, either Kōun himself or the interviewers Takamura Kōtarō and Tamura

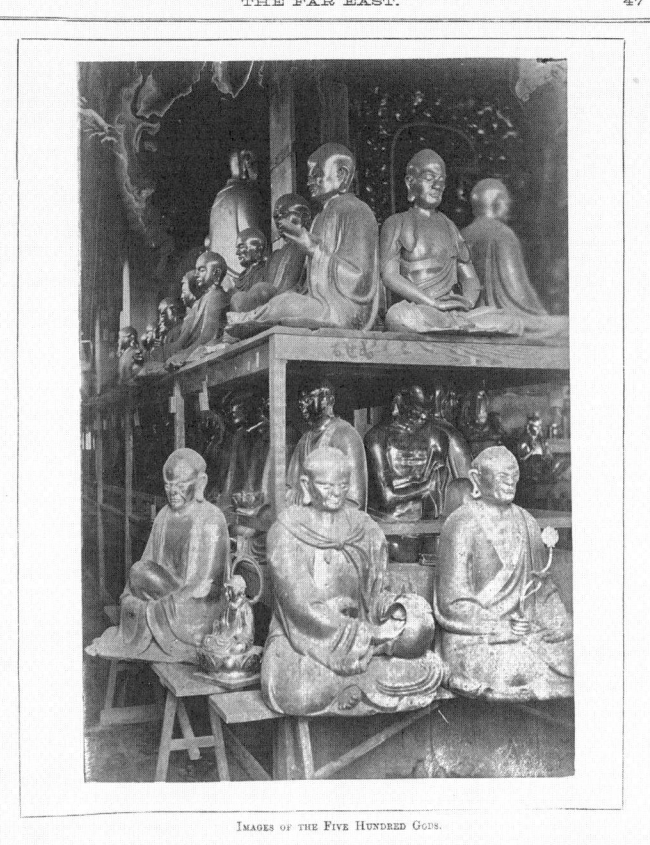

FIG. 2.

Statues of some of the Five Hundred Gods, from *The Far East,* 16 July 1872.

Albumen print, 19.3 ×13.5 cm. Los Angeles, Getty Research Institute, 2652-854.

Shyōgyo would have re-interpreted the event to fit the preservation policies set by the government after the Restoration. I suggest, though, that the content of Kōun's story becomes enriched and multilayered by distancing the event from the preservation of *kokikyūbutsu*. While it may feel like a detour, let us re-read Kōun's story again in light of the 1871 edict in order to illuminate another aspect of this policy.

First, let's look at the event from the perspective of Kōun and Tōun, both of whom played the role of protagonists here. Their motivations had little to do with the significance of *kokikyūbutsu*. While the 1871 edict declared that the purpose of preserving *kokikyūbutsu* was to examine the "vicissitude of times old and now and the development of laws and customs," they were rather more interested in the statues because of their position as practicing Buddhist sculptors. Let us attend to Kōun's description again.

According to Kōun, the Rakanji Temple—which housed the statues of five hundred Arhats and one hundred Avalokiteśvaras—was "the only place in the Tokyo area where I could train myself [as a sculptor]." He added, "Because the statues of five hundred Arhats and one hundred statues of Avalokiteśvara [at Rakanji Temple] were made in the Genroku period (1688–1704) and after, they were not appropriate for the study of ancient sculpture. But as a place to observe and gain an understanding of eminent and skilled craftsmen of woodcarving in the later period, there was no place finer than Rakanji Temple." He remembered that during his apprenticeship he would "walk in the morning taking rice balls for lunch, study various aspects [of the sculpture all day] in the temple," and "after the sunset, walk on back home."[42] Here are some more crucial aspects from Kōun's recollections: "The statues of one hundred Avalokiteśvara are about to be burned. They will be ashes. What use could their ashes be? . . . These statues . . . which have burned themselves into the back of my eyes, which have served as my only teacher, are about to be burned."[43] He continued: "This thought made me feel helpless, nostalgic, cruel, and disappointed. I just wanted to go to the site." When he reached the shop of the raw metal broker, he found "among the Avalokiteśvara statues, one with very refined techniques of *hosokane* made by the Buddhist sculptor in Kyoto Shichijō Sakyō. Then there was another piece skillfully carved by another famous carver, nicknamed Chōbei the Long-Nosed Goblin [*Tengu*]. Then I saw a piece by Shōun Genkei, the Zen monk of Rakanji Temple."[44] These accounts reveal that Kōun's motivation in rescuing these statues was to save works by the illustrious carvers that came before him. It would be reasonable to assume that Tōun's interest also stemmed from similar concerns. For Kōun and Tōun, then, there was a sense of shared identity as woodcarvers with the people who made the works they saw at Rakanji Temple. At the very least, their gaze toward these statues bore little relation to the distanced and analytical gaze that one would have wished to examine "the vicissitude of times old and now" and "the development of laws and customs" as expressed in the 1871 edict.

There is a sequel to this story. As I noted earlier, Kōun received one statue by Shōun Genkei from Tōun, and protected this Avalokiteśvara as his own guardian icon. Later, however, Tōun sold the remaining four statues they had rescued. According to Kōun, although the destination of one is unknown, two were sold to merchants, and one was sold to a brothel in Yoshiwara, an officially sanctioned brothel area.[45] The fact that Tōun sold off these four statues should not invalidate the motivations that led Kōun and Tōun to rescue them in the first place, and it seems that Kōun recounted this sequel so honestly because he was sure it would not dishonor his teacher. It also seems that the known purchasers, the merchants and the brothel, bought the statues because of their religious affiliation. Kōun became an independent workshop owner in 1874. Although Kōun prefaced his recollections by noting that the events took place during the years of his apprenticeship, we have already ascertained they must have taken place before 1872. In light of this timeline, I find it impossible to conclude that Kōun and Tōun acted in the way they did because they recognized an "artistic" value in these statues. Although it bore little structural economic resemblance to the modern art market, then, there was a social custom through which objects like Buddhist statues could be exchanged for money. Indeed, Tōun paid the raw metal broker in exchange for the five statues, and Kōun also gave some money to his master Tōun for the statue of Avalokiteśvara by Shōun Genkei.

When part of the infrastructure of a society changes radically, the values that such systems supported waver with it. When the Meiji government introduced the strict separation of Shintoism and Buddhism into the syncretic fusion of Shintoism and Buddhism (*shinbutsu shūgō*) that existed during the Tokugawa period, it directly affected the economic and moral systems that had supported the infrastructure of Buddhist temples. To wit, the decision to dismantle Sazaedō was primarily a financial one. Still, the conditions that led to burning the one hundred Avalokiteśvara statues for their precious metal were more complicated. While the financial motivations here are clear enough, the act of burning a Buddhist sculpture itself required some general level of acceptance. Here we can witness the shift in a broader moral evaluation of Buddhism. The edict of the separation of Shintoism and Buddhism brought on a multiplicity of socioeconomic confusions and moral fluctuations. This is why innumerable objects later designated as *kokikyūbutsu* came to be "lost or destroyed" in the conditions that the 1871 edict bitterly described. Even so, we must recognize a slight but significant gap between the rhetoric of the edict and the actual conditions of society at that time.

Of course, I am not arguing that this edict had no practical effect. One tends to interpret the incident told by Kōun as a historical example of how ordinary people took it upon themselves to preserve things of the past. Alternately, we can interpret the story by noting that it is more likely that Kōun retold the story fifty years later in the context of the preservation of things past, or that his interviewers edited their transcription with a particular perspective along the lines of this context. However, once we look at the story in light of the assumptions of these actors, we can see another aspect of this story. The action taken by Kōun and Tōun had nothing to do with the edict of preserving *kokikyūbutsu*. In fact, it is difficult to imagine that this edict would have become a common topic of discussion among ordinary people.

The edict of the separation of Shintoism and Buddhism shook the world of things past on an unprecedented scale. As a result, many things fell through the sifter—and wound up on the market. Kōun's story reveals that some fortunate objects found new owners or affiliations. To put it somewhat abstractly, the order of the world of things past was shaken until it became liquefied and absorbed into the lives of ordinary people. While the five wooden statues of Avalokiteśvara rescued by Kōun and Tōun were forced out of their original home, they found new homes with Kōun or the wealthy merchants. The depth of the concern of these ordinary folks, it seems, deserves closer attention.

SECTION 2: WORKING WITH THINGS

KOKIKYŪBUTSU AND EXHIBITIONS

As we will see in the following analysis, it seems that the government had envisioned another more concrete effect of the 1871 edict on the preservation of *kokikyūbutsu*. A 1973 publication, *One Hundred Years' History of the Tokyo National Museum: Material Part* (*Tokyo Kokuritsu Hakubutsukan hyakunenshi: Shiryōhen*) contains numerous significant documents concerning the policies and approaches of the Meiji government. Two types of material from this publication are of particular interest to this project.

The first document relates to the sales of *kokikyūbutsu*. This report, written by Daigaku and submitted to the Grand Council of State, dates from the sixth month of 1871, one month after the edict was issued. It noted that while the edict was issued in the fifth month by the Grand Council: "[T]here are people who have misunderstood this edict to be a ban on sales of *kokikyūbutsu,* even though the intention of the edict was only to intervene in the habit of disparaging the old and competing for the new. For this reason, there is no need to think one cannot sell things in case it is inconvenient to keep them. We therefore would ask [the Grand Council] for a further edict clarifying this intended meaning."[46]

In other words, although the previous edict on *kokikyūbutsu* was not a direct ban on sales of these items, some portion of the general public took it to be such a prohibition. Considering this situation in the report, the Daigaku asked the Grand Council for further assurance that the edict was not a ban on sales of *kokikyūbutsu*. It is difficult to ascertain from this document alone the extent to which this request was informed by the question of ownership, a concept that was up for debate within the ongoing effort to write new civil laws at the time. However, the last line of this report, which reads, "we have already conveyed this point verbally [i.e. that the edict is not a ban on selling] to the chief official Sasaoka of the city of Tokyo," indicates that in reality there was a certain amount of confusion about the 1871 edict among ordinary citizens.

Of course, Takamura Kōun's rescue of the Avalokiteśvara statues included a sale. His master Tōun bought the five statues from the raw metal broker and sold one to Kōun, and the rest to merchants and a brothel. Without these transactions, the rescue could not have been completed. While it is not possible to consider the unfolding histories of the modern art market here, it is likely that sales of things past were accepted as part of everyday activity. It is precisely for this reason that a misunderstanding regarding the prohibition of sales of *kokikyūbutsu* would create such confusion—and that, in turn, a second edict to clarify the status of such sales was necessary. The report by Daigaku suggests that a ban on selling might, in fact, have been proclaimed in Tokyo.

In light of all this, the crucial point of the 1871 edict on preservation is the fact that those who wrote this report at the Daigaku took the government's intention to be "to intervene in the bad habit of disparaging the old and competing for the new." How does this interpretation relate to the motivation to either permit or ban the sales of objects? As the 1871 edict itself noted, "the objects of *kokikyūbutsu*" "have become lost or destroyed" because of "the unfavorable practices of disparaging the old and competing for the new." This is similar to the phrase used in the report, "to intervene in the bad habit of disparaging the old and competing for the new." This habit brings about the "loss and destruction" of things past. At the very least, the sales of these objects would prevent their "loss and destruction." To sum up, we may conclude that the 1871 edict did not have anything to do with the commercial trade of *kokikyūbutsu,* and that, therefore, the government allowed owners to sell their properties.

Another primary document worth considering is a series of papers that cataloged *kokikyūbutsu*. These documents were submitted either to the Ministry of Education or to the Finance Ministry by prefectural governments across the country between the seventh month of 1871 and the ninth month of 1872. These documents were submitted in response to the section of the 1871 edict that requested prefectural governments to "write down the name of the items and their owners in detail and submit [the list]." As such, each prefectural government had researched and cataloged the items held within their respective precinct under the category of *kokikyūbutsu*.[47] Reports from thirty-three prefectures are printed in *One Hundred Years' History of the Tokyo National Museum: Material Part,* attesting to the fact that temples and shrines as well as individual collectors were called upon to compile the report.[48] While the scale of these investigations is unclear, the phrase "treasures belonging to shrines, temples as well as all classes of people" [*shaji shimin shozō kata hōmotsu*] is frequently deployed in the documents.

Among these documents, there is a report from Inba prefecture (the northern part of present-day Chiba prefecture) that accompanied a notice the Grand Council of State had sent to the local government in the second month of 1872. According to this notice, "this time the officials of the Finance Ministry will be sent to all regions around the country in order to examine and compile a record of not only the holdings of each prefecture, but also all treasures belonging to shrines, temples, and all classes of people. Let each prefecture be aware of the gist of this notice, and henceforth notify shrines, temples, and all others within their jurisdiction."[49] Based on these documents alone, it is difficult to ascertain whether the treasures of each prefecture were actually listed at this point. But what is certain is that these notices were sent to each prefecture; it can easily be imagined this helped to realize successful research on the *kokikyūbutsu* of each prefecture in later years.[50]

Ultimately, it seems that the edict issued in the fifth month of 1871 had the clear and practical objective of producing a list that would contain the treasures of each prefecture and the names of their owners. The aim of the next notice, issued in the second month of 1872, seems to have been even more concrete. As noted in the previous section, in this month the Central Council of the Grand Council of State established the Exposition Bureau within their institution, in response to the government's decision to participate in the Vienna World Exposition of 1873. We can easily imagine how these lists sent from each prefecture of "all treasures belonging to shrines, temples, and all classes of people" could be transformed into the checklist of a display at the world exhibition.

This is not to say that the government already had their participation in the Vienna World Exposition in mind when they issued the edict on the preservation of *kokikyūbutsu* in 1871. However, the fact that this edict was issued on the twenty-third day of the fifth month—just three days after the closing of the exhibition at the Shōkonsha Shrine in Kudan organized by the South School of Daigaku—deserves more careful consideration. In the third month of 1872, the Museum Bureau under the Ministry of Education would hold another exhibition at the Yushima Seidō. It is not hard to imagine a close practical relationship between this edict and the structure and administration of exhibitions, which started taking place more frequently. Put differently, it would be superficial and one-sided to interpret the 1871 edict on the preservation of *kokikyūbutsu* as merely an idealized origin point of the governmental preservation policies of old things that exist in our present day. I contend that this 1871 edict developed in a way inextricably bound up with the new practices and ideas around exhibitions (like the Exhibition of Local Products) in early Meiji. Re-examining the 1871 edict from this perspective, we can see how the thirty-one sections of *kokikyūbutsu* came to constitute an understandable tapestry of the world of things past.

THIRTY-ONE SECTIONS OF *KOKIKYŪBUTSU*

Now we can re-examine the list of thirty-one sections again. The first noticeable element of this list is the fact that old architectural structures, which would later come to be major objects of preservation, are not included. In *Recollecting the Bakumatsu and the Restoration*, Takamura Kōun noted regarding the deteriorating Rakanji Temple that "if the main temple hall had been preserved to this day, although it was a fairly recent construction, it would certainly have been designated as one of the Architectural Structures under Special Protection and served as a wonderful example of a building."[51] As noted earlier, the Law for the Preservation of Old Shrines and Temples was implemented in 1897. The system of National Treasures was born out of this, and the category of Architectural Structures under Special Protection (*tokubetsu hogo kenzō butsu*) was introduced within this system. For someone familiar with the histories and laws of preservation systems, the lack of a section on architecture in the 1871 edict would seem odd.

In number 17 on the list, "Carriage and palanquin section," both wheeled carriages and palanquins were listed. While their sizes are nowhere near the scale of architectural buildings, these items are comparatively larger than items listed in other sections. I raise the question of scale because almost everything else on the list was small enough to be collected and admired by individuals alone. In other words, the list did not contain anything else monumental in size. For instance, let us try to imagine the scale of objects under number 30, the "Old Buddhist statues and implements section." While this section included "Buddhist statues," we can presume that these were under-life-size statues, rather than the enormous principal Buddhas found in temples.

The wooden statues of Avalokiteśvara that Kōun and Tōun rescued give some helpful indications here. Although these statues were produced after the Genroku period (1688–1704), the government would certainly have understood these statues to fall within the limits of preservation since the edict applied to objects produced "from the age of gods to the recent past." Of the five statues rescued in this event, the one by Shōun Genkei that Kōun purchased from Tōun is still in the collection of the Takamura family. It is about 92 centimeters tall (approximately 3 feet), and it would be fair to imagine that the other statues in the group of Avalokiteśvaras at Sazaedō were equally small.[52]

Considering the lack of large-scale objects among the listed *kokikyūbutsu,* we could also interpret the list as being motivated by a desire to collect objects that would be attractive on the market. Here, the role of collectors comes to the fore.

This seems to be an apt place to introduce one of the primary protagonists of this book, Edward Sylvester Morse (1838–1925). He arrived in Japan for the first time in June 1877. While he is well known in Japan for his discovery of the prehistoric shell mounds in Ōmori, he also left some significant statements in his archaeological reports on these remains. He published two such reports: *Shell Mounds of Omori,* and its Japanese translation by Yatabe Ryōkichi (1851–99), *Ōmori kaikyo kobutsu hen.* Both were published in 1879 (Meiji 12) by the University of Tokyo. Yatabe had become the first professor of botany at the University of Tokyo. A notable quote reads as follows: "There is no other country in the world where so great a number of gentlemen interested in archaeology can be found as in Japan."[53] Morse must have been surprised by the number of the "gentlemen interested in archaeology" in Japan. What kind of people did Morse have in mind with this phrase?

Today, the term *archaeology* calls to mind a department or field of study within the humanities at institutions of higher learning. However, we must remember that 1877 was the year that the University of Tokyo was founded, and thus the institution had just started playing a role as the cradle in which modern disciplinary fields would develop. Thus, it is not appropriate to imagine the denotation of Morse's use of the term *archaeology* as the academic field and department in the contemporary sense. Could it be that Morse used this term in a broader sense? It appears that Yatabe had understood this broader meaning when he chose the Japanese term *kōkoka* to translate the phrase "gentlemen interested in archaeology." Here, we can begin to see a more concrete group of individuals associated with Morse.

Morse also published his recollections of days in Japan as *Japan Day by Day* (1917). In this book, there is a section that gives a better sense of Morse's impression of the Japanese collectors he met:

> Through Ninagawa, I have learned many interesting things about collectors and collections. It was interesting to find that for hundreds of years these people have had their collections and crazes for collecting. He said that the Japanese have never specialized so much in their collecting as foreigners, and, I judge from what I have learned, were never so systematic or scientific and generally not so curious nor so exact as to the age and locality of the objects. Among Ninagawa's friends he specified the following as the kinds of objects they collected: pottery, porcelain, coins, swords, kakemono (pictures), pieces of brocade, stone implements, and roofing tiles. The collections of brocade are mounted in books like postage stamps, the pieces three or four inches square; he had seen specimens four or five hundred years old. Bits from the robes of famous men were highly esteemed. The tiles are considered very interesting objects; he had seen roofing tiles a thousand years old. He did not know of anyone collecting armor. A few collect shells, corals, and the like. There are many books treating of all the kinds of objects above mentioned.[54]

Here, Morse described the vast range of objects that collectors were accumulating. Along with these items, he informs us of the existence of publications on these collections. We can take this report, and the comment that "there is no other country in the world where so great a number of gentlemen interested in archaeology can be found as in Japan," as a direct observation based on the reality he experienced. I would suggest further that the sentence from *Shell Mounds of Omori* was conversely based on the group of collectors he described in *Japan Day by Day*.

At the beginning of the quoted section above, a fellow named Ninagawa is mentioned. This name first appears in the previous section in *Japan Day by Day*, in which Morse wrote: "I have lately become acquainted with a celebrated antiquarian, Ninagawa Noritani [sic], and have visited him at his house. He is the author of a book on the various kinds of pottery in Japan, illustrated by lithographic plates."[55] As they were of the same generation, Morse seems to have established an amicable friendship with Ninagawa Noritane (1835–82); they would continue to foster their friendship through the collection and study of ceramics. As we will see in the next chapter, Ninagawa was also one of the key figures behind the preservation policies of the early Meiji government.

The Japanese translation of Morse's *Japan Day by Day*, *Nihon sonohi sonohi*, is also suggestive for my argument. Its translator, Ishikawa Kin'ichi (1895–1959) was a newspaperman and a skilled translator. Ishikawa was the first son of Ishikawa Chiyomatsu (1860–1935), a zoologist who was one of Morse's students.

In translating Morse's phrase "a celebrated antiquarian, Ninagawa Noritani," Ishikawa chose the term *kōkosha* to render the English word *antiquarian*. In Ishikawa's view, the Japanese term *kōkosha*, as well as the English term *antiquarian*, designated people who admired, collected, and studied things past. As mentioned above, in Yatabe's translation of *Shell Mound of Omori,* he did not literally translate the phrase "gentlemen interested in archaeology" but rendered it as *kōkoka*, nearly the same term as Ishikawa's *kōkosha*.[56] My argument here is that Yatabe's evocation of *kōkoka* was closer to the term Morse deployed to introduce Ninagawa: antiquarian. Needless to say, Yatabe was also familiar with the activities and collections of people like Ninagawa, as Morse was. I want to posit, then, that the term *kōkoka* used by Yatabe encompassed the meaning of *antiquarian*.[57]

ANTIQUARIANS ENTER THE STAGE

I want to attend to another aspect of Morse's quote above: the interrelationships among collectors. Morse noted that Ninagawa "did not know of anyone collecting armor." In other words, Morse knew that there were armor collectors, even if Ninagawa did not seem to know them personally. Ninagawa had a truly wide circle of collector friends, and from Ninagawa's point of view Morse was part of this group. In fact, he had given Morse many ceramics.[58] Certainly the personality, commitment, and popularity of an individual played a significant role in creating and maintaining such a circle of friends. Moreover, we should imagine here that a world of friendship existed among collectors, regardless of differences in what they collected.[59]

How did these collectors perceive the 1871 edict on the preservation of *kokikyūbutsu*? When we compare the objects of their collections and the thirty-one categories listed in the edict, we can see a precise correspondence between the two.

In the collectors listed by Morse, there are a total of eleven categories: "pottery, porcelain, coins, swords, kakemono (pictures), pieces of brocade, stone implements, and roofing tiles," "armor" whose collectors Ninagawa didn't know, "shells," and "coral." All of these fit neatly within the attendant note of thirty-one sections of the 1871 edict. Pottery and porcelain would belong to the ceramic section (24), coins to the coins and paper money section (22), swords and armor to the weaponry section (7), *kakemono* to the old calligraphy and painting section (8), and pieces of brocade to the textiles section (19). In *Japan Day by Day,* Morse noted: "The collections of brocade are mounted in books like postage stamps, the pieces three or four inches square; he [Ninagawa] had seen specimens four or five hundred years old. Bits from the robes of famous men were highly esteemed." This probably referred to an album of precious textile fragments on whose leaves small pieces of gold brocade and satin damask were pasted. The description of the textile section (19) also includes "old gold brocade and fabric fragments from antiquity, etc." Here, Morse added an explanation in which he invoked philately to explain albums of textile fragments, thus helping to explain the practice clearly to his English-speaking audience.

In addition, the "stone implements" described in *Japan Day by Day* correspond to the stone arrowhead and stone ax section (3), and "roofing tiles" to their eponymous section (6). In the brief explanation of that section, the document noted "famous things and old tiles in general regardless of fame," which indicates that certain roofing tiles were well known among collectors. Morse probably thought readers in Europe and America might find it hard to understand that roofing tiles could become the object of a collection. In fact, he added a note here: "The tiles are considered very interesting objects; he [Ninagawa] had seen roofing tiles a thousand years old."

The last items from *Japan Day by Day,* "shells" and "coral," belong to the final section of the 1871 edict, the fossil section (31): "fossils of animals, bones, horns, and tusks of animals, seashells, etc." This section does appear odd among others on the list, as it does not quite fit squarely into the category of *kokikyūbutsu*. I am not flagging this as odd in the belief that this section actually belongs to natural history; such an interpretation would be the product of a modern understanding of the natural sciences that draws a sharp boundary between natural things and artifacts. Rather, I think it is odd because it is difficult to imagine how this section would actively support the intentions of the edict, that is, to "examine the vicissitudes of times old and now and the development of laws and customs."

When we compare sections 1 to 30 against the fossil section, it becomes evident that the latter does not quite match up with the rest of the list in terms of the purpose of the edict. This section does not fit the supplementary description at the end of the list, which specifies a chronological range "from the age of the gods to the recent past." Why include fossils, then? I contend that the fossil section was included because collectors were interested in "fossils of animals, bones, horns, and tusks of animals, seashells" and the like around the time of this edict. In this way, the fossil section is related to the overall intention of the 1871 edict on the preservation of *kokikyūbutsu*.

Thus, all the objects of collecting that Morse noted in *Japan Day by Day* can be found in the thirty-one sections of the 1871 edict. In other words, it is possible to interpret the list of the 1871 edict as an attempt to capture all kinds of objects that had been (and were currently being) collected by collectors. The 1871 edict was written with a view to the activities of collectors at that time. Certainly, then, we can see why the edict was not intended to ban the sales of *kokikyūbutsu*.

THE WORLD OF THINGS PAST

Let me summarize my argument thus far. While the edict issued in the fifth month of 1871 on the preservation of *kokikyūbutsu* has generally been regarded as the origin of the governmental policy for the protection and preservation of things of the past, this understanding is framed through later knowledge of preservation policies. In other words, it is an interpretation enabled by retroactively casting present values onto the past. On the other hand, there is also an interpretation of this edict that puts it in direct dialogue with the anti-Buddhist movement that resulted from the new governmental policy of the separation of Shintoism and Buddhism. While the historical reality into which the edict was introduced was certainly affected by this policy, interpreting the 1871 edict solely within this context would result in a simple and reductive pairing of destruction versus protection, loss versus preservation. Such an approach would only produce an understanding centered on the values of the government's preservation policy. At the very least, this position cannot account for the fact that the edict did not impose any restrictions on sales of *kokikyūbutsu*. In short, interpreting the edict from the position of anti-Buddhist activity occludes the edict's productive side.

This edict came with a note that read: "Authorities concerned should write down the names of the items and their owners in detail and submit [the list]." The most concrete and important role of the edict was condensed in this short request. The government might have intended to list and catalog various *kokikyūbutsu* located within each prefecture. Then, of course, exhibitions are part of the overall picture here. We could interpret the thirty-one sections of the 1871 edict as items that could have easily turned into exhibition items at such occasions, and in actuality, this list was used to evaluate objects ahead of the 1873 Vienna World Exposition.

Furthermore, we must not forget the roles of collectors who were accumulating objects listed in this edict. Their collections, too, could have become exhibition items for public display. In order to rally collectors together, the government had to group objects under the name of *kokikyūbutsu* with the intention of examining "the vicissitude of times old and now and the development of laws and customs." Here, in this productive aspect of the government's effort, we can begin to see the omens of radical changes in the world of things past. Not so much a starting point, this edict actually functions like a vivid cross-section of these changes.

Certainly the examples and quotes used here are limited. However, these materials, including the edict itself, function like a film negative, projecting the vast world of things past that existed then. To put it differently, when we trace the contours of the very actuality which this edict affected through concrete phenomena, we come to see an unexpectedly rich world of the things past. The analysis of the width and depth of this world is the subject of the following chapters.

NOTES

1   Combining existing vocabulary, the Meiji government coined the term *kokikyūbutsu*, literally "old vessels" (*koki*) and "ancient things" (*kyūbutsu*), for the preservation of these objects.

2   Tokyo Kokuritsu Hakubutsukan, *Tokyo Kokuritsu Hakubutsukan hyakunenshi* (Tokyo: Tokyo Kokuritsu Hakubutsukan, 1973), 39.

3   Tokyo Kokuritsu Hakubutsukan, *Tokyo Kokuritsu Hakubutsukan hyakunenshi*, 40.

4   Tokyo Kokuritsu Hakubutsukan, *Tokyo Kokuritsu Hakubutsukan hyakunenshi*, 39–40.

5   Tokyo Kokuritsu Hakubutsukan, *Tokyo Kokuritsu Hakubutsukan hyakunenshi*, 39.

6   The meaning of *Shōkonsha* is "shrine to beckon the soul [of the war dead]." The shrine later became known as Yasukuni Shrine.

7   Daigaku was the successor of the Institute of Confucian Learning (Shōheikō) of the Tokugawa shogunate.

8   *Shachihoko* are a pair of roof-edge ornaments for donjon, shaped like a fish with a tiger-like head and dragon's dorsal fins, usually covered with gold scales.

9   Specifically, this research covered the regions of Tōkai and Kinki.

10 In the Japanese lunar calendar, 1833 was the fourth year of Tempō.

11 According to the Chinese sexagenary cycle, 1872 was the year of *ren* (J. *jin*) of the ten heavenly stems and *shen* (J. *shin*, the year of the monkey) of the twelve earthly branches.

12 This exhibition was known as *Shōheizaka shogakiai*.

13 Fomented by rebels of the ex-Satsuma domain, war against the Meiji government broke out in February 1877 in Kyūshū, the southernmost main island of the Japanese archipelago. See Augustus H. Mounsey, *The Satsuma Rebellion: An Episode of Modern Japanese History* (London: John Murray, 1879).

14 The land in Uchiyamashitachō on which the old museum stood was given to the Ministry of Foreign Affairs. In 1883 a government-owned accommodation for foreign guests known as Deer-cry Hall (*Rokumeikan*), also designed by Josiah Conder, was built on this land, where the Imperial Hotel in Tokyo is now located.

15 This museum was so badly damaged by the Great Kanto Earthquake of 1923 that it was abandoned. The building was later disassembled, and the new Tokyo Imperial Household Museum designed by Watanabe Jin (1887–1973)—the present-day main building of the Tokyo National Museum—was constructed on the same site in 1937.

16 The details of this narrative can be found in Earnest F. Fenollosa, *Epochs of Chinese and Japanese Art: An Outline History of East Asiatic Design* (London: William Heinemann, 1912), 1:50–52. The Hall of Dreams is known as *yumedono*.

17 Aoki Shigeru and Sakai Tadayasu, eds., *Bijutsu* (Tokyo: Iwanami Shoten, 1989), 403–5.

18 Takagi Hiroshi, *Kindai tennōsei no bunkashiteki kenkyū* (Tokyo: Azekura Shobō, 1997), 284–308.

19 Nakayama Shigeru, *Teikoku daigaku no tanjō: Kokusai hikaku no naka de no Tōdai* (Tokyo: Chūō Kōronsha, 1978), 16–25.

20 Satō Dōshin, *"Nihon bijutsu" tanjō: Kindai nihon no "kotoba" to senryaku* (Tokyo: Kōdansha, 1996), 32–66, 170–88. See also Satō Dōshin, *Modern Japanese Art and the Meiji State: The Politics of Beauty,* trans. Hiroshi Nara (Los Angeles: Getty Research Institute, 2011), 44–65.

21 Saitō Gesshin, *Zōho bukō nenpyō,* ed. Kaneko Mitsuharu (Tokyo: Heibonsha, 1968), 222.

22 See Satō, *"Nihon bijutsu" tanjō,* 179.

23 *Shinbutsu bunri rei* is the general name for a series of edicts concerning the separation of the two religions, beginning with an edict issued on the seventeenth day in the third month of 1868.

24 For records of various actions taken by temples, many are recorded in the forms of letters and dialogue in Murakami Senjō et al., eds., *Meiji ishin shinbutsu bunri shiryō* (Tokyo: Meicho Shuppan, 1970).

25 Takamura Kōun, *Bakumatsu ishin kaikodan* (Tokyo: Iwanami Shoten, 1995), 154.

26 One of the eight bodhisattvas, Avalokiteśvara (Ch. *Kuanyin*, J. *Kannon* or *Kwannon*) is believed to embody compassion to save and protect all sentient beings. See Damien Kwan, *A Dictionary of Buddhism* (Oxford: Oxford University Press, 2004).

27 The proper name of Rakanji Temple is Ten'onzan Rakanji Temple.

28 The year of founding in the Japanese lunar calendar is Genroku 8.

29 Sazaedō was also the subject of Katsushika Hokusai's *Turban Shell Hall of the Temple of Five Hundred Arhats*, from the series *Thirty-Six Views of Mount Fuji*, ca. 1830–32.

30 The temple moved to the present land in the Meguro area of Tokyo in 1908 and was renamed Gohyaku Rakanji. To this day, Shōun's statues are housed in this temple.

31 Takamura, *Bakumatsu ishin kaikodan*, 158.

32 Takamura, *Bakumatsu ishin kaikodan*, 158.

33 Takamura, *Bakumatsu ishin kaikodan*, 158–67.

34 Sakai Tadayashu, "Kaisetsu," in Takamura, *Bakumatsu ishin kaikodan*, 453.

35 Tamura Shōgyo, "Tamura Shōgyo no kotoba," in Takamura, *Bakumatsu ishin kaikodan*, 449.

36 I have consulted the republished text from Iwanami Library here, and it is possible that the reader of this library series might read this text with the Law for the Protection of Cultural Properties (*Bunkazai hogohō*), issued in 1950.

37 Takahashi Tsutomu, *Yomigaeru rakan tachi: Tokyo no gohyaku rakan* (Tokyo: Tōyō Bunka Shuppan, 1981), 199–205.

38 Okabe Keigorō, "Tokyo meishō zue," in Ichiko Natsuo and Suzuki Ken'ichi eds., *Edo meisho zue jiten: Shintei Edo meisho zue bekkan* (Tokyo: Chikuma Shobō, 1997), 2:170.

39 The newspaper *The Far East* used the date in the Gregorian calendar; *Far East* 3, no. 4 (16 July 1872). See Kaneyuki Shinsuke, Aoki Yūsuke, and Tsunoda Mayumi, "Edo no kenchiku, toshikeikan to shashin shiryō: *The Far East* keisai shashin yori," *Kenchiku shigaku* 35 (September 2000): 65–72, 77.

40 Gesshin had taken over this publishing enterprise from his grandfather and father.

41 *Dainihon meisho zue* (Tokyo: Tōyōdō, 1908), 61:33.

42 Takamura, *Bakumatsu ishin kaikodan*, 156.

43 Takamura, *Bakumatsu ishin kaikodan,* 160.

44 *Hosokane* is presumably identical with the traditional *kirikane* technique, in which thin gold leaf is used to depict the drapery patterns of Buddhist icons. The sculptor Shichijō Sakyō worked at the Kyoto studio Shichijō Bussho. Takamura, *Bakumatsu ishin kaikodan,* 163.

45 Takamura, *Bakumatsu ishin kaikodan,* 156–68.

46 "Daigaku jōshin," dated on the twenty-eighth day of the sixth month in Meiji 4 (1871), Tokyo Kokuritsu Hakubutsukan, *Tokyo Kokuritsu Hakubutsukan hyakunenshi: Shiryōhen* (Tokyo: Tokyo National Museum, 1973), 606–7.

47 In some of the reports, the term *treasure* (*hōmotsu*) was used instead of *kokikyūbutsu*.

48 The content of these catalogs themselves is omitted in the volume.

49 The attached document to that of Inba prefecture, dated the seventeenth day of the sixth month in 1872, sent to the Ministry of Finance. See Tokyo Kokuritsu Hakubutsukan, *Tokyo Kokuritsu Hakubutsukan hyakunenshi: Shiryōhen,* 609.

50 Tokyo Kokuritsu Hakubutsukan, *Tokyo Kokuritsu Hakubutsukan hyakunenshi: Shiryōhen,* 606–9.

51 Takamura Kōun, *Kōun kaikodan* (Tokyo: Banrikaku Shobō, 1929), 568.

52 Takahashi, *Yomigaeru rakan tachi,* 342.

53 Edward S. Morse, *Shell Mounds of Omori* (Tokyo: University of Tokio, 1879), iv.

54 Edward S. Morse, *Japan Day by Day: 1877, 1878–79, 1882–83* (Boston and New York: Houghton Mifflin, 1917), 106–7.

55 Morse, *Japan Day by Day,* 106.

56 While the syllable *sha* from *kō-ko-sha* by Ishikawa means "person," *ka* from *kō-ko-ka* by Yatabe, literally meaning "house" or "family," often represents a person who devotes himself to something special, in particular arts, sports, sciences, and the like. The first and second syllables of both words have the same pair of characters, meaning "to have affinity for" and "the past."

57 The section above that introduced Ninagawa in *Japan Day by Day* appears just after the section describing events of February 1879. His *Shell Mounds of Omori* was also published in the same year. According to Ninagawa's diary, it was on 6 January 1879 that Morse came to visit Ninagawa's house. According to an article written by a Ninagawa descendant, the Ninagawa family keeps his diary (unpublished) and it ascertains the exact date when Ninagawa first met Morse. See Ninagawa Chikamasa, "Mōsu no Nihon tōki korekushon to Ninagawa Noritane," *Jinruigaku zasshi* 87, no. 3 (March 1979): 314.

58 Ninagawa, "Mōsu no Nihon," 321.

59 The activities of these collectors constitute one of the major pillars of this book, and we shall return to this topic in chapters 4 and 5.

CHAPTER 2

"The Past and the Present" and "The New and the Old"

SECTION 1: TWO PARADIGMS

NINAGAWA NORITANE'S *ILLUSTRATED BOOK OF PAST THINGS: CERAMICS SECTION*

We have learned a little bit about Ninagawa Noritane in the previous chapter. Edward Morse, in *Japan Day by Day*, mentioned Ninagawa as a famous "antiquarian."[1] In *Japan Day by Day*, Morse described Ninagawa as "the author of a book on the various kinds of pottery in Japan, illustrated by lithographic plates."[2] Morse went on: "These plates, though rather roughly done and colored by hand, are far more characteristic of the pottery than the most perfect chromolithographs one sees in French and English publications on similar subjects."[3] Morse was referring to *Illustrated Book of Past Things: Ceramics Section* (*Kankozusetsu tōkinobu*, 1876–80), which was published in seven volumes. Given its position within the chronologically ordered *Japan Day by Day,* this entry can be dated between the end of February and the beginning of April of 1879 (Meiji 12). By the time Morse wrote this entry, then, five of the seven volumes of Ninagawa's book had been published. As Morse made clear, the exceptional quality of this publication was its accurate and detailed lithographic illustrations. Volumes one to five were accompanied by a small booklet that contained the French translation of the texts, called *Kwan-ko-dzu-setsu, notice historique et descriptive sur les arts et industries japaonais par Ninagawa Noritané, art céramique*. These pamphlets were published by H. Ahrens & Co., a publisher located in the Tsukiji area of Tokyo. Takamura Kōun mentioned this publisher in his book *Recollecting the Bakumatsu and the Restoration* (*Bakumatsu ishin kaikodan*, 1929). He wrote that at the end of 1877 (Meiji 10) or the beginning of 1878, he received a commission from "a famous business house in Tsukiji, Kyobashi ward, called Ahrens & Co. that was owned by a German" to produce a pair of dolls depicting Chinese children in wood.[4] The commission was from Germany, and the work would be used as a pair of lampstands. Considering that Ninagawa's *Illustrated Book of Past Things: Ceramics Section* was going to be sold among products such as these, it appears that H. Ahrens & Co. was exporting a wide range of manufactured goods from Japan. Hinrich Ahrens, the founder of the business, passed away at the young age of forty-four from cholera in 1887 (Meiji 19), but even after his death, Ahrens & Co. continued to be one of the most successful companies of German origin in Meiji Japan.[5] It seems that Ninagawa published his books with the understanding that they might be read in Europe or the United States, and the fact that Morse admired the finished illustrations in Ninagawa's book indicates that this was hardly a far-fetched ambition.

"THE PAST AND THE PRESENT" AND "THE NEW AND THE OLD"

We will return to Ninagawa's publication and examine its illustrations in depth in chapter 5. For the time being, I want to focus on its text. Taking into account the argument thus far, Ninagawa's introduction to volume 1, published on 8 March 1877 (Meiji 9), is particularly compelling. In this text, Ninagawa issued a pointed warning against the general trend of disregarding things from the past for the sake of pursuing the new. While it is somewhat long, let us examine the deft rhetoric Ninagawa employed in this text. The operative and decisive conceptual tools here are the two pairs of binary concepts: first, "the new and the old," and second, "the novel and the ordinary." In addition, he overlays another set to these two sets, "the past and the present."

> Yesterday's new becomes today's old, and today's novel becomes tomorrow's ordinary. Studies become more detailed every day, and manufacturing becomes more refined every month. The force of today's prosperous world is like a constant stream of water that never ceases. Under this force, the general population is unable to escape from pursuing the new and the novel and hating the old and the ordinary. From the large-scale effort of the government to the smaller-scale changes in each small and individual object, even the rare items are denigrated into the dust, and this worries me. Even if this propensity of society is natural, the thought that leads to such actions is nothing but shortsighted and superficial, without much consideration of its intention and consequences. Needless to say, it is important to examine and clarify the new and the novel, but it is similarly important to preserve the old and the ordinary. It is important because by looking at other civilizations, we come to see the barbaric state of our own, and by considering the past, we come to learn what is needed in the present. These are the urgent obligations for governance today. And it is historical books that connect the two.

However, to gain confirmation, no method is surer than to observe actual objects, rather than taking a detour to examine the historical time by consulting historical books.[6]

First, Ninagawa compares "the new" and "the old," and then overlays on top of this binary "the novel" and "the ordinary."[7] In this way, he combines the two and posits a binary of "the new and the novel" against "the old and the ordinary," a standard against which values can measured—and in which new things are valued highly, and old things not valued at all.

Under this standard, all old items—ranging from those that serve as a reminder of past governments and powers to rare items that attest to humble phenomena—become neglected and effectively buried. While Ninagawa claims that this tendency is inescapable because it is part of a broader societal tendency, he says it is rooted in shortsighted thinking and a basic lack of consideration. Ninagawa says it goes without saying that new and rare items are in demand. However, old and ordinary items should be carefully preserved all the more because of this situation. Ninagawa's desire to preserve the old and ordinary comes from his belief that one of the government's urgent duties is to understand its own condition by looking at "advanced" civilizations and by comprehending the present specifically in relation to the *past*. Although the reasons for making this a governmental duty may seem complicated, they signal a dynamic turn in Ninagawa's rhetoric.

Here, Ninagawa insists that one must simultaneously "examine and clarify the new and the novel" and "preserve the old and the ordinary," and then attempts to recognize "the old and the ordinary" as having the same value as "the new and the novel." After establishing this point, he continues to advocate "looking at other civilizations … to see the barbaric state of our own" and "considering the past … to learn what is needed in the present" as "the urgent obligations for governance." Judging from the context, these two actions for the governance indicated here run parallel to the sentence immediately before. To "look at other civilizations" is to highlight the advanced civilizations of the West, which serve as the sources of "the new and the novel." (This also includes selecting what of these places would be introduced to Japan.) Similarly, in order to "consider the past to learn what is needed in the present," "the old and the ordinary" must be preserved in such a way as to be able to make a comparison. That is to say, if the pair of "the old and the ordinary" is dismissed, the methods and tools to consider the old would also be lost at the same time. To summarize, Ninagawa insists that "the new and the novel" should be considered on the same level as "the old and the ordinary." By demonstrating the content of the two "urgent obligations for governance," he buttresses his claim through the concrete examples that follow in the volume.

When we analyze the content of Ninagawa's claims, it appears that his approach to "the new" and "the old" are fair. However, as he admits that the need to "examine and clarify the new and the novel" is important, the value of "the new" has generally been accepted already. Ninagawa's point is to assert in this general admission that the value of "the old," too, needs to be acknowledged. The significant point is that Ninagawa is trying to assert the equality of the positions of "the old" to the level of "the new."

When we interpret Ninagawa's argument in this manner, the critical move he makes in the last section of the quote is compelling. In expressing "the urgent obligations for governance today" and articulating the need "to recognize the present by considering the past" as an example, he deploys the concept of "the past"—instead of "the old"—and its counterpart, "the present." By contrasting them as a pair, "the past" and "the present" form a symmetrical dichotomy without a hierarchical relationship of value between the two. Here we witness the refined technique of Ninagawa as a rhetorician.

The episode I discussed in the previous chapter, of the rescue of the statues of Avalokiteśvara from Sazaedō, helps to explain the ramifications of this pairing of "the past and the present." Although the works at this temple were produced in the Genroku period and after, Kōun noted: "As a place to observe and gain an understanding of eminent and skilled craftsmen of woodcarving in the later period, there was no other place finer than Rakanji Temple."[8] Kōun's words made no distinction between "the new" and "the old," or between the works by "eminent and skilled craftsmen" of bygone eras and the works he himself was making. It would not be possible for the two sculptors to appreciate and admire the craftsmanship of prior generations if their works were posited as "the old." Indeed, in that case the very act of learning from this craftsmanship would become meaningless. To put it differently, Kōun shared a sense of continuity and identification with the Buddhist sculptors of both the past and the present, and this sense allowed him to find value in the works from the past and use them as meaningful learning devices. In Ninagawa's argument, this relationship appears as one between "the past and the present." The past gives the present its meaning, and in valuing the past, the present is what throws it into relief. The phrase "to recognize the present by considering the past" should be interpreted with this sense of "the past and the present" in mind.

However, general trends in society had replaced the relationship between "the past and the present" with that between "the new and the old." In a certain sense, there is little difference between the two pairs, as they are both grounded in a temporal evaluation. However, when "the new and the old" overlaps with "the novel" and "the ordinary" and creates another set of binaries, "the new and the novel" against "the old and the ordinary," the difference becomes starker. As Ninagawa noted, people pursued "the new and the novel" continuously while paying no attention to "the old and the ordinary." The slogan of "civilization and enlightenment" (*bunmei kaika*) enabled the rise of this asymmetrical set of values, which Ninagawa called "the force of this prosperous world," similar to "the constant stream of water that never ceases."[9] What was considered "the new" here included many kinds of products, institutions, systems, technologies, and ideas brought by civilization and enlightenment, as well as the exchange of people and human resources that brought these over to Japan.

Thus, things past were doomed to fall into the position of "the old" that confronted "the new" brought by civilization and enlightenment. Or, rather, the perspective of "the past and the present" itself was placed squarely on the side of "the old." This change in perspective led not only to a change in value systems, but to a larger overhaul of the ways in which society looked at things. Certainly the popularized slogan of "civilization and enlightenment" was in the process of changing society. But these changes were not brought about because the items and things within the world changed, but rather because the framework from which perspectives were constructed changed. In a sense, this was a paradigm shift. Or, to borrow the language of Foucault that I discussed earlier in the book, we could also note that it was a change in episteme.

Clearly Ninagawa made attempts to deal with this unprecedented situation. In the introduction to his *Illustrated Book of Past Things: Ceramics Section,* he attempted to raise the status of "the old and ordinary" to the same level as "the new and novel," and then to posit "the old and ordinary" in comparison to "the past and the present." This new configuration enabled him to eliminate the asymmetry between "the new" and "the old." We can characterize Ninagawa's effort by saying that he attempted to push the contrasting pair of "the new and the old" into the paradigm of the symmetrical dichotomy of "the past and the present" in order to rebalance the relationship between "the new" and "the old."

THE ANTIQUARIANS' CRISIS

The replacement of the harmonious pair of "the past and the present" with the more polarizing binary of "the new and the old" brought about an enormous crisis among antiquarians. When "the past and the present" came to be marginalized under the popularized slogan of civilization and enlightenment, things past came to be categorized under "the old and the ordinary." Beyond crucial taxonomic shifts in collectible objects, the act of collecting things past was itself on the verge of being pushed to the side of "the old." For those antiquarians who had skillfully dealt with various changes since the Meiji Restoration, the time had come to face the new paradigm brought by the wave of civilization and enlightenment. How could they best withstand this new paradigm? They were, in short, facing up to a problem they had never experienced before. Ninagawa's claims, articulated through his tactful rhetoric, formed one such response to the crisis.

How, then, did the antiquarians deal with this issue in concrete terms? Did they merely accept the paradigm of "the new and the old," did they try to overcome it, did they look for ways to strike a compromise with it, or did they turn their back to it? Of course, there were other possibilities. Perhaps some tried to respond consciously to it, while others let time pass by without becoming aware of the problem. In this regard, the introduction to Ninagawa's *Illustrated Book of Past Things: Ceramics Section* conveyed the core of the problem clearly and succinctly. Even judging from this attitude alone, it seems that Ninagawa engaged this new problem in a conscious and positive manner. While Ninagawa's attitude might not correspond to the generalized response of all antiquarians, he represents an important example of one kind of response. Let us explore this response further through the example of Ninagawa.

THE 1871 DAIGAKU PROPOSITION

Here, I want to compare Ninagawa's case with the proposition that Daigaku submitted to the Grand Council of State regarding the building of a *shūkokan* in the fourth month of 1871 (Meiji 4). As noted earlier, the edict issued by the Grand Council of State on the protection of *kokikyūbutsu* (old and ancient objects) was a response to this proposition, which included a series of programs that would deepen the relationship between the protection of *kokikyūbutsu* and policies on the encouragement of industry over the coming decades. When we examine its content in relation to the binary opposition of "the new and the old," the contours of Daigaku's claims emerge clearly. At the same time, we can discern certain concrete problems that antiquarians faced.

While the document speaks to the sense of crisis regarding *kokikyūbutsu* from a similar point of view as Ninagawa, it provides more details and makes clear the thinking that became the basis for the edict:

> Since the Boshin War, many unrivaled treasured rare items are being lost. How can we protect them? It is a regrettable situation. Particularly in recent days, mistaken reports circulate without a full understanding of the practices of the West, that in European countries people are swept up by the ideas of enlightenment. Thus, only new and novel items are treasured. Based on this misunderstanding, an evil practice of disparaging the old and embracing the new thereby emerged. Consequently, no attention is paid to the destruction of *kokikyūbutsu* that have been stored over generations. It is said that some of these objects are destroyed already. It is regrettable in the extreme that small artifacts that could help the examination of the past are being lost day by day.[10]

The edict issued by the Grand Council of State is somewhat vague in its explanation of the crisis of *kokikyūbutsu*, referring only to "the unfavorable practices" of "disparaging the old and competing for the new." (See chapter 1, section 1.) The proposition by Daigaku, though, offers a more detailed history that leads back to the Boshin War (1868–69) as a cause for the loss of "the unrivaled treasured rare items."[11]

Here, elements of the paradigm of the new and the old crisscross each other. Because of the general tendency to disparage the old and embrace the new, the loss of *kokikyūbutsu* does not receive fair attention. Similarly, Ninagawa also raised the issue of "pursuing the new and the novel and hating the old and the ordinary." The origins of such tendencies brought about by civilization and enlightenment reside in Europe. This proposition, moreover, notes that it is a mistake to think that only "the new" is respected in Europe. In other words, the proposition insinuates that in European countries, the value of the items belonging to "the old" is also acknowledged.

This proposition continues: "Every European country establishes a *shūkokan* [literally, a building for assemblies of things past] because it takes on a mission to examine laws, things, and institutions of the bygone, as well as the development of times old and now." This sentence was adopted almost piecemeal in the text of the 1871 edict, which reads: "The objects of *kokikyūbutsu* are profitable to no small extent in order to examine the vicissitudes of times old and new, and the development of laws and customs" (see chapter 1, section 1). Although the 1871 edict did not mention *shūkokan*, the mission of the *shūkokan* seems to have been replaced by the significance of "the objects of *kokikyūbutsu*" in the 1871 edict. This proposition also employs the phrase "the past and the present," but here the concept did not carry the positive resonance of Ninagawa—it was, instead, paired with "the bygone."

What needs to be underscored here is that the thought of "examin[ing] laws, things, and institutions of the bygone, as well as the development of times old and now" itself belongs to "the new" because the *shūkokan,* whose primary responsibility is to execute such examination, is itself embedded within a European system. The term *shūkokan* refers to something close to what we now call a museum: It functioned largely as a repository or archive, but also exhibited parts of its own collection. In other words, the proposition to build the *shūkokan* was part of a broader claim to introduce a European system to Japan, which was clearly grounded in the concept of "the new" brought about by the widely propagated idea of civilization and enlightenment. Here we can see the way of thinking that tries to assimilate "the old" into the dichotomous binary of "the new and the old," as something from the distant past, without any possibility of affecting present.

How does this proposition relate to Ninagawa's claims, and how do they differ? Ninagawa tried to re-insert the asymmetrical values of the new and the old dichotomy into the thinking framed by the past and the present. The proposition by Daigaku, too, was aimed at correcting the imbalance of values that existed between the new and the old. In this respect, there are commonalities between the two. However, even if both demanded a broader recognition of the value of the old, Ninagawa's thinking relied heavily on the temporal continuity that grounds the paradigm of "the past and the present," while Daigaku's proposition sought to enhance the binary opposition assumed in the configuration of the "new and the old." Naturally, they came to different conclusions. As I noted briefly earlier, from the early years of Meiji on Ninagawa's career was centered around drafting government policies regarding the preservation of *kokikyūbutsu*. It is not a surprise, then, that the logic presented in the proposition of Daigaku overlaps with that of Ninagawa. However, as we will see in chapter 4, this difference in thought cast a shadow over the later part of Ninagawa's career.

To fold "the old" into the binary opposition construed as "the new and the old" and still maintain a balance in value between the two required providing a stable sense of meaning that could function within this binary opposition. In other words, it was necessary to evaluate the old through the logic that defined the new. In order to accomplish this, the proposition by Daigaku took three concrete steps: (1) it brought in the idea of *shūkokan* from the European system, (2) it deployed the framework of *kokikyūbutsu,* and (3) it introduced the logic of "examin[ing] laws, things, and institutions of the bygone as well as the development of times old and now."

Within the binary of the new and the old proposed by Daigaku, the objects that antiquarians such as Ninagawa collected could be seen to belong to the old. This is how Daigaku's proposition aimed to redefine the old, to give them new value so as to produce a balanced relationship within the dichotomy of the new and the old. Certainly one could describe this approach simply as governmental. When and if the policies based on this way of thinking were to be implemented, antiquarians would be forced to choose between the two: to accept it or to reject it. For those antiquarians, then, the ramification of facing the new was, I assert, to accept this very situation of facing two stark choices.

SKETCHING ILLUSTRATIONS

The main point of the proposition by Daigaku was to establish a *shūkokan*. After Daigaku itself was abolished, the Ministry of Education saw out the realization of this system of the new. While it was not until 1873 (Meiji 6) that the Ministry of Education established the Museum, just a month after Daigaku submitted its proposition, its South School organized the Exhibition of Local Products at Shōkonsha Shrine in Tokyo. Although this was a short-term exhibition, from the fourteenth to the twentieth days of the fifth month, we find a common function expected of museums there: that is, to exhibit objects publicly.

In this context, a public exhibition refers to the fact that the Meiji government organized it. Through exhibiting items, they aimed to attract an unspecified number of spectators, rather than a select few. At the same time, this idea of the public also gave antiquarians a new challenge: whether to join the public or to take the side of organizers by providing the government with their objects. In chapter 4 we will see that while many antiquarians (including Ninagawa himself) enthusiastically took the side of the organizers, this did not necessarily secure their future position.

Let us return to Daigaku's proposition, which noted that the institution faced a mountain of work at the present, and would thus find it difficult to start work on the construction of a *shūkokan* immediately. For this reason, in the latter half of the proposition it detailed an alternative plan, which was later foregrounded in the edict on *kokikyūbutsu* issued the following year. An important section of this plan reads as follows:

> We suggest that for the time being we issue an edict to each prefecture. It should ask to list not only treasured objects that have been passed down through generations, but also what appear to be small artifacts that could help the examination of the past because these items should be protected as much as possible. Further, these items should be given to specialists who would depict them pictorially. We also ask that these pictures be compiled and collected. If our current condition persists for over a year, many unrivaled treasured objects that have been passed down through generations might become mostly destroyed, some to the extent that their shapes are unrecognizable. This would result in a regrettable and unspeakable situation. For this reason, a prompt response is desired. Such is proposed.[12]

What is particularly noteworthy here is the proposal that certain officials be appointed exclusively to pictorially represent these treasured objects, and that the illustrations be preserved and collected. While this is quite a practical suggestion, the edict by the Grand Council of State did not include it; perhaps it was thought too difficult to implement. Yet the Ministry of Education itself would, in fact, put this plan into effect, when it began surveying the treasures kept in the shrines and temples of the Tōkai and Kinki regions in the following year, 1872 (Meiji 5). As noted earlier, this led to the re-opening of the doors of the Shōsōin Repository in Tōdaiji Temple for the first time since 1833. Ninagawa was a central member of this project, which also enlisted the painter Kishi Kōkei (1839–1922), the photographer Yokoyama Matsusaburō (1838–1884), and a pioneer of oil painting in Japan, Takahashi Yuichi (1828–1894), in order to visualize the treasures.[13] The functions and meanings given to the act of picturing itself are worth exploring.

Daigaku's proposal considers the act of protecting "small artifacts that could help the examination of the past" together with the act of picturing and collecting them. It is only when both actions are taken that this activity can stand in for the construction of a *shūkokan*. According to the proposition, at a *shūkokan* one would examine "the development of times old and now" as well as "laws, things, and institutions of the bygone." For this purpose, "*kokikyūbutsu* that have been stored over generations" are indispensable as "small artifacts for the examination of the old." To picture such items was regarded as a method of recording. Moreover, there seems to be a special relationship between objects and illustrations beyond that of documentation.

The previous quote by Ninagawa from his introduction is helpful to shed light here. Toward the end of the quote, he noted, "And it is historical books that connect the two. However, to gain confirmation, no method is surer than to observe actual objects, rather than taking a detour to examine the historical time by consulting historical books." "The two" in this sentence is articulated in the phrase that comes immediately before, "by considering the past, we come to learn what is needed in the present." In other words, Ninagawa claimed that one should rely on "historical books" in order to unlock the present by thinking through the past. However, this reliance on historical books was somewhat of a detour when "actual objects" were at hand. Ninagawa's logic, therefore, prioritized examination of actual objects.

Moreover, in Ninagawa's logic we see how the act of picturing things reveals deeper layers. Couldn't he be positing script against pictures when he made the comparison between "historical books" and "actual objects"? In fact, he noted the superiority of "actual objects" over "historical books" in his book *Illustrated Book of Past Things: Ceramics Section,* which included the introduction translated at the beginning of this chapter. This book is a work in which Ninagawa observed "actual objects" "to gain confirmation."

To put it differently, the illustrations reproduced in *Illustrated Book of Past Things* are not merely documentation. Things deteriorate eventually—with this premise, illustrations can serve the same function as the things themselves. The proposition by Daigaku warned that if the present condition was unchanged, "unrivaled treasured objects that have been passed down through generations might become mostly destroyed, some to the extent that their shapes are unrecognizable." Things and their illustrations are connected through the act of picturing. These two do not form a hierarchical relationship; instead, this process creates a complementary relation between them.

PICTURING THINGS

Let us return to the position of the antiquarians. I assert that for them, the act of collecting items, picturing them, and editing volumes constituted a set of actions that provided them with the self-definition of their role. During the Tokugawa period, illustrations of various kinds were produced, and many were published. Although these illustrations numbered fewer than those of *materia medica,* it is notable that many illustrations of things past were published. Recall here that in *Japan Day by Day,* Morse made note of the passion of the Japanese for collecting and listed various objects that were collected. He immediately followed this description by noting: "There are many books treating all of the kinds of objects above mentioned."[14] Here I suggest that Morse was referring to collections of illustrations, rather than to books of explanatory essays or more casual writing. At the end of the introduction to his *Illustrated Book of Past Things: Ceramics Section,* Ninagawa noted: "Over the last twenty years, I have sketched what I saw and heard and accumulated it in a box. While working officially for the government, I found time to add one or two thoughts along with the illustrations. I spent the remainder of my salary to publish this book."[15] This reveals how significant the activity of picturing things was to antiquarians.

Here, too, the binary opposition of "the new and the old" was at work. As I noted earlier, Morse highly regarded Ninagawa's illustrated book. He wrote: "These plates, though rather roughly done and colored by hand, are far more characteristic of the pottery than the most perfect chromolithographs one sees in French and English publications on similar subjects."[16] Lithographic technology was introduced during the Bakumatsu period, and by the time Ninagawa's book was published this technology had been developed and refined further. However, what Morse called "chromolithographs" had not yet been popularized. This is one of the reasons why Ninagawa's illustrations were hand colored. In describing them as "roughly done," Morse was not referring to a kind of technological underdevelopment, but rather to the coarse-grained finish on the illustrations. This lithographic technique, which was beginning to be used around this time, produced the impression of gradation on the surface of objects.[17] Without this context, Morse's comment that the illustrations are "far more characteristic of the pottery than the most perfect chromolithographs" makes little sense.

In this description, Morse was probably referring to the depiction of the pottery's shape and surface texture in the illustrations. He uses the word "characteristic" here. What makes this comment particularly astute is that it embodies the qualities that Ninagawa himself desired in illustrations when he said: "No method is surer than by observing the actual objects." Here we can find the instantiation of an equal and symmetrical relationship between the illustration and the thing, rather than a relation that subordinates the former to the latter. Moreover, what grounds this relationship is Morse's skill to describe things as if they were standing directly in front of him—a description that was, itself, enabled by the newly introduced technology of lithography. Here we find Ninagawa's response to the challenge brought on by the paradigm of the new and the old: The old illustrated antiquarian books were dressed up with the new technology.

SECTION 2: A NEW DISCIPLINE

TRANSLATING "THE STUDY OF THINGS PAST"

Along with the governmental edict on *kokikyūbutsu* and Ninagawa's *Illustrated Book of Past Things,* we should also consider the role of the subject of archaeology in this context. My question is: What kind of challenges did the acceptance of this new disciplinary framework create for the antiquarians? The acceptance of such a framework that belonged to "the new" enabled them to find not only a relation to the new but also the new significance in their collections and act of collecting, both of which were regarded as the old.

From around 1873, the Ministry of Education published a series of books titled *Encyclopedia (Hyakka zensho).* As one can imagine from the title, the publication was a series of translations aimed at enlightening the reading public. Among this series is a volume from 1878 titled *The Study of Things Past* (*Kobutsugaku*)," translated by Shibata Shōkei (1850–1910). This volume was published around the same time as Ninagawa's *Illustrated Book of Past Things: Ceramics Section*. Shibata's volume is noteworthy as one of the earliest publications on the discourse of archaeology as a Western academic discipline.[18]

This *Encyclopedia* series, which consisted of ninety-two volumes, is a translation of the fourth edition of *Chambers's Information for the People*, a two-volume book that was compiled by brothers William Chambers (1800–83) and Robert Chambers (1802–71) and published between 1856 and 1858.[19] The central figure behind the Japanese translation project was Mitsukuri Rinshō (1848–97), who worked at the editorial bureau of the Ministry of Education. Mitsukuri assembled a group of men who were familiar with English and used a method of divided translation, in which each member of the team was assigned a set of articles from the original volumes to translate.[20] It appears that the payment was rather lucrative.[21] It also appears that translating articles on less familiar topics like psychology produced many headaches for the team. Furthermore, it seems that articles were assigned to translators without much consideration of their knowledge of or interest in the subject.[22]

After the translation of each article was completed, the Ministry of Education published each one as a separate volume, sometimes combining two articles into one volume. However, the ministry did not see out the completion of the series, and the publisher Maruzen continued the project, using the fifth edition (1874–75) of *Chambers's Information for the People*; in the end, ninety-two volumes were published. Maruzen published the completed *Encyclopedia*—three hardcover volumes and twelve paperback volumes—between October 1883 and October 1884. In addition, an index was released in January 1885. In April 1883, after Maruzen announced that the publication would be sold only through advance orders, the *Encyclopedia* secured a thousand orders.[23] Apart from this Maruzen edition, the Ministry of Education also reconfigured the ninety-two volumes into twenty and published them through the publisher Yūrindō between 1883 and 1886.[24]

The Maruzen edition of the *Encyclopedia* contains an unsigned foreword that introduces the original publication by the Chambers brothers. Oddly enough, no mention of the original is found in the edition by the Ministry of Education and Yūrindō. The Maruzen foreword notes:

> The title of the original on which this translation is based is *Information for the People*. To enlighten the people about things and phenomena of the world, two Englishmen, William Chambers and Robert Chambers, compiled and wrote this book. The body of the text begins with astronomy and ends with rules for home economics. It includes approximately ninety-two articles. Although the articles lack details, they are enough to give a general sense of the thing discussed.[25]

The foreword mostly suggests the contents of the series, including academic and technical categories like astronomy, geology, architecture, and printing technology, as well as on systems and customs like "Military and Naval Organizations," "Clothing and Costumes," and "Christian Churches." It also includes categories on history, geology, folklore, and practical subjects such as the history of Great Britain and Ireland, the history of Rome, Africa-Oceania, and Scandinavian mythology. The expansive contents listed under these categories make clear that absolutely everything "about things and phenomena of the world" is included in this series. To be sure, a didactic book like this must provide such a summary.

However, it is difficult to answer a critical question: To what extent did general readers understand the contents of these vast and broad categories? The foreword gave readers a warning: "Examining these volumes thoroughly, there are cases where different translations are provided for the same original term."[26] In translating a term in English, the *katakana* syllabary, one of the three writing scripts in Japanese generally used to render foreign terms, is deployed for phonetic transcription in some cases, whereas the same word also sometimes appears as a compound of Chinese characters, a translation effort that entails more semantic interpretation. The foreword explains this difference away by claiming that "each translator provides different renderings in Japanese"—but the difference in translators would not seem to be at issue. Even considering the varying levels of linguistic abilities of the translators, the instability of the translated terms themselves signals a deeper problem.

For example, the famously vexing volume on psychology was published in 1878 under the Japanese title *Jinshinron* (a literal translation in English would be "theory of human mind"). The original English title was *The Human Mind,* and the content of the original corresponds to a discipline that was then called "mental philosophy." By contrast, when the Ministry of Education published a translation of *Mental Philosophy, Including the Intellect, Sensibilities, and Will,* in 1875–76 (first published in 1862) by Joseph Haven (1818–74), the translator Nishi Amane (1829–97) translated "mental philosophy" into Japanese as *shinrigaku*. This word is still the term used in Japanese today for psychology. Similar observations can be drawn across this field. For example, one of the seminal concepts, "consciousness" was rendered differently by Nishi and the translator of *The Human Mind*.[27] While certain scholars have argued that Nishi's translation is in fact superior, the superiority of these translations has less to do with the skill of the translator and more to do with the course of later history.[28] In general, translated terms that an influential actor used repeatedly remain in the discourse, while others came to be forgotten.

The case of *Jinshinron* allows us to compare to another translation by Nishi, and there are plenty of similar cases among the translations of concepts during this period. In fact, precisely the same can be said in the case of *kobutsugaku* (the study of things past), originally "archaeology" in Chambers' book. The original English title was rendered as *kobutsugaku,* but the Japanese term *kobutsugaku* eventually receded in the background while the term *kōkogaku* became prevalent. It is obvious, but when a translator does not have the appropriate term for the original in her vocabulary, or when this process of pairing is difficult, translated terms fluctuate. The stability of a translated term is thus deeply connected to the reception of the concept underpinning it.

This project of publishing the translated *Encyclopedia* should be understood as another practice of the Ministry of Education's enlightenment campaign around this time. While it might have been a coincidence, the inclusion of archaeology in this context is noteworthy for our analysis. The proposition by Daigaku issued in the fourth month of 1871, which we have examined in this chapter, argued that "*kokikyūbutsu* that have been stored over generations" should be understood in terms of "the new." Here, the world of things past as redefined in Daigaku's proposition overlapped with the field of archaeology. We can easily imagine, then, that the world of things past overlapped with the realm of archaeological study. In the seventh month of Meiji 4 (1871), Daigaku was dismantled and the Ministry of Education replaced it. It is this new ministry that led the *Encyclopedia* project.

THE SIGNIFICANCE OF THE STUDY OF THINGS PAST

As we have seen, in 1877 the Ministry of Education published a book called *Kobutsugaku*; the title of this book was a translation of the English term *archaeology*. However, the content of this book explains a much different sense of European archaeology than the one that we are familiar with today. Because it was written as a general introductory book, it lacks detail and depth, but the scope of the discipline is rendered in a more expansive and inclusive way. Let us look at the beginning of this volume, as it explains precisely how this study emerged.

> Archaeology [*Kobutsugaku*]: The meaning of this English term in its etymology is clear. This study includes a vast number of things. In recent years, its use has been limited to discussions of ancient arts in Greece and Rome. However, because the etymological meaning of the term includes the thorough examination and explanation of various ancient events and phenomena, this term today is used with the understanding of this meaning. Today, the term is used based on the broadest sense of the word—the term archaeology [*kobutsugaku*] has come to encompass science, based on the examination of ruins and relics that provides the outlines of the past through deduction.[29]

What is critical here is that "the term is used based on the broadest sense of the word." Insofar as a study is based on "ruins and relics of the past," or involves speculation on "the outlines of the past," it belongs to the discipline of archaeology. The point here is an assumed universality unconfined to the study of Greek and Roman objects. This phrase immediately recalls the proposition by Daigaku in 1871: recall that it noted that the principal task of a *shūkokan* is "to examine laws, things, and institutions of the bygone, as well as the development of times old and now," through consultations of "small artifacts that could help the examination of the past." Wouldn't this match up precisely with the discipline of archaeology as described in the *Encyclopedia*? Moreover, this discipline did not confine the object of study to prehistoric relics and ruins, nor did it distinguish between articles excavated and those handed down.

In the latter half of the second paragraph, the universal characteristics of archaeology or *kobutsugaku* and its wide-ranging objects of study are articulated.

> However, archaeology is not a newly constructed discipline of modern invention. All people passionately struggle with a desire to think and know the unclear and uncertain future. The desire to pursue the time before the present is a natural feeling that causes this. Therefore, even since human beings have existed, we can only say that the seed to pursue this study has always been in our minds. Furthermore, archaeology occupies a critical spot in the study of the past. Supported by the studies done by scholars of anthropology and philology, archaeology constitutes a large part of science. For this reason, when one reviews the books of civilized nations, one always finds clear evidence that people have pursued the study of archaeology. Therefore, it is as if this study flourishes and advances when one enters a time of great progress in civilization and arts.[30]

After this quote, the text refers to the Renaissance, and posits "the revival of letters in the sixteenth century" as an exemplary period of such flourishing. The archaeology that this text describes, therefore, is a mode of historical thinking grounded in objects. In other words, the text describes a mode of study in contrast to the study of history based on script—precisely the way Ninagawa articulated his logic in the introduction to his *Illustrated Book of Past Things: Ceramics Section*. This logic holds that while historical books must certainly be consulted to think about the past, it is much more direct to explore actual objects, rather than taking a detour through textual materials. This way of thinking, to champion actual objects over written records, is expressed in the *Encyclopedia* as the very study of archaeology.

What I want to question here is not the influence of the *Encyclopedia*'s volume on archaeology.[31] Instead, my question is: What kind of challenges did the acceptance of this new disciplinary framework create for antiquarians? The acceptance of such a framework that belonged to the new enabled them to find a way in which their collections and the act of collecting itself—both of which had been regarded as the old—could belong to the new. It seems to me that they would have welcomed this state of affairs. In reality, they all faced broader issues and questions due to the introduction of the binary of "the new and the old": their particular interpersonal networks they had nurtured among themselves, the way of thinking they mastered in illustrations, and the new system of museums and exhibitions were all questions floating in the air.

To think in chronological terms, in the same year of 1877 (Meiji 10) that the volume on archaeology was published, the Ministry of Education also founded the University of Tokyo by merging Tokyo Medical School, the former East School of Daigaku, and Tokyo Kaisei School, the former South School of Daigaku. In 1886 (Meiji 19), higher specialized education run by the government was streamlined when the Ministry of Education established the Imperial University, with the University of Tokyo serving as its mother institution. Even without the activity of Edward S. Morse at the University of Tokyo, it is certain that archaeology would have been absorbed into the academic system. The emergence of archaeology, with its appearance of a European field of study, would come to draw a clear and visible border between professional and amateur spheres. Or rather, it is more accurate to say that the binary opposition between professionalism and amateurism emerged for the first time when the academic system was introduced. This course of events would eventually seal the antiquarians' fate, setting up a fall that could be compared to that of the dinosaurs in the Mesozoic era.

NOTES

1   As we saw in the previous chapter, in the Japanese translation of Edward Sylvester Morse's *Shell Mounds of Omori* (*Ōmori kaikyo kobutsu hen*) (Tokyo: University of Tokyo, 1879) (Meiji 12), translator Yatabe Ryōkichi rendered "antiquarian" as *kōkoka*. In the Japanese version of Morse's *Japan Day by Day,* translator Ishikawa Kin'ichi had used the term *kōkosha*. Ishikawa's translation of Morse's *Japan Day by Day* bore the Japanese title *Nihon sonohi sonohi* and was published by the Association for the Promotion of Scientific Knowledge in 1929 through the support of the Keimeikai Foundation. At the time of Morse's stay in Japan, the term *kōkoka,* used by Yatabe, was probably more popular than the term *kōkosha,* deployed by Ishikawa. Fujikawa Haruto, "Kaisetsu," in Edward S. Morse, *Nihon sonohi sonohi,* trans. Ishikawa Kin'ichi (Tokyo: Heibonsha, 1970), 257.

2   Edward S. Morse, *Japan Day by Day: 1877, 1878–79, 1882–83* (Boston and New York: Houghton Mifflin, 1917), 2:106.

3   Morse, *Japan Day by Day,* 2:106

4   Takamura Kōun, *Bakumatsu ishin kaikodan* (Tokyo: Iwanami Shoten, 1995), 129–36.

5   Dirk van der Laan, "Bakumatsu Meijiki no Doitsu shōsha," in Yokohama Archives of History, ed., *Yokohama kyoryūchi to ibunka kōryū: Jūkyū seiki kōhan no kokusai toshi o yomu* (Tokyo: Yamakawa Shuppansha 1996), 87–88.

6   The French translation of this section uses *sciences* for "studies" and *arts* for "manufacturing." Ninagawa Noritane, *Kanko zusetsu tōkinobu* (Tokyo: Ninagawa Noritane, 1876), 1:1.

7   Etymologically speaking, the Chinese character for *ordinary* can be traced to mean "old," but when contrasted to the character for *the novel,* the same character takes on the negative meaning of "ordinary."

8   Takamura, *Bakumatsu ishin kaikodan*, 156.

9   John Dower describes this popularized slogan as follows: "This evocative phrase went far beyond just frills and fashions, however, and was explicitly associated with the progressive values of Western 'civilization' and the European Enlightenment. Fukuzawa Yukichi, Meiji Japan's most prolific interpreter of Western values and practices, offered a concise interpretation of what 'civilization and enlightenment' entailed. The strength and progress of the great Western nations, he argued, rested on science; and scientific accomplishment, in turn, required a spirit of free inquiry among the general populace. Thus, it followed that liberal and progressive values were not simply moral and political ideals; they were also part and parcel of creating a 'rich country, strong military' capable of assuring national independence." John W. Dower, "Throwing Off Asia I," in *Visualizing Cultures*, https://visualizingcultures.mit.edu/throwing_off_asia_01/pdf/toa1_essay.pdf.

10 Tokyo Kokuritsu Hakubutsukan, *Tokyo Kokuritsu Hakubutsukan hyakunenshi: Shiryōhen* (Tokyo: Tokyo Kokuritsu Hakubutsukan, 1973), 605–6.

11 A civil war that broke out in 1868, named after the breaking year of *bo* (Ch. *wu*) of the ten heavenly stems and *shin* (Ch. *chen*, the Year of the Dragon) of the sexagenary cycle. Satsuma, Nagato, and allied domains fought with the shogunate forces supported by the rest of domains during the war.

12 Tokyo Kokuritsu Hakubutsukan, *Tokyo Kokuritsu Hakubutsukan hyakunenshi: Shiryōhen*, 605–6.

13 Takahashi had previously worked at the Bureau of Pictorial Studies, known as the Institute for Studying Western Learning during the shogunate.

14 Morse, *Japan Day by Day,* 2:107. Although this sentence reads awkwardly in contemporary usages and grammar of English, this is an exact transcription of the published diary by Morse.

15 Ninagawa, *Kanko zusetsu tōkinobu*, 1.

16 Morse, *Japan Day by Day,* 2:106.

17 The technique is called *suname*, literally "sand-like grain."

18 Saitō Tadashi, *Nihon kōkogakushi* (Tokyo: Yoshikawa Kōbunkan, 1974), 87–89.

19 The first edition of the books had been published between 1833 and 1835.

20 Maruzen Kabushiki Gaisha, *Maruzen hyakunenshi: Nihon kindaika no ayumi to tomoni* (Tokyo: Maruzen, 1980), 193–203.

21 The task seems to have paid so well that Ishii Kendō (1865–1943), in his book *Origins of Things Meiji*, cited an episode from Mitsukuri's biography under the section "Fee-Hired Translation of the Encyclopedia."

22 Ishii Kendō, *Meiji jibutsu kigen* (Tokyo: Chikuma Shobō, 1997), 4:333–35. As it happens, Shibata had studied in Germany, and his area of expertise was organic chemistry. Fukukama Tatsuo, *Meiji shoki hyakka zensho no kenkyū* (Tokyo: Kazama Shobō, 1968), 345.

23 Tsukasa Tadashi, ed., *Maruzen shashi* (Tokyo: Maruzen, 1951), 62–63. Considering the volume and the price, this project should be regarded as a success.

24 Maruzen's edition is twice the trim size of the version published by the Ministry of Education, and was in a two-column format. Yūrindō's edition retained the full text used by the ministry and was published in twenty volumes.

25 "Reigen," in William Chambers and Robert Chambers, eds., *Hyakka zensho* (Tokyo: Maruzen Shōsha Shuppan, 1883), 1.

26 Chambers and Chambers, *Hyakka zensho*, 1.

27 Nishi rendered the term *consciousness* as *ishiki*; this remains the current term in Japanese, while the translator of *Jinshinron* rendered the same term as *jikakuryoku*, literally the "force of self-awareness."

28 Fukukama Tatsuo, *Meiji shoki hyakka zensho no kenkyū* (Tokyo: Kazama Shobō, 1968), 229–30.

29 The original text reads: "The term *archaeology*, though sufficiently definite and comprehensive in its original meaning, was confined, until a comparatively recent period, to the study of Greek and Roman art. The word, however, literally signifies the description of ancient things; and it has now been universally adopted in its largest sense to give name to the science which deduces history from the relics of the past." William Chambers and Robert Chambers, *Chambers's Information of the People,* new ed. (London and Edinburgh: W. & R. Chambers, 1833–35), 2:721.

30 The original text reads: "Archaeology, however, is no newly discovered science. It has its origin in the natural cravings of the human mind to master the secrets of the mysterious past, no less than of the mysterious future: it forms an essential branch of the historian's studies: it enters largely into the inquiries of the ethnologist, or investigator of the various races of the human family: and into those of the philologist, or analyser of their numerous languages. We accordingly find evident traces of an archaeological spirit in the literature of every civilised nation; and generally it exhibits the strongest symptoms of development during periods most marked by rapid progress in the arts of civilisation." Chambers and Chambers, *Information of the People*, 2:721.

31 In fact, Ninagawa's logic had been presented about a century before him by the eighteenth-century antiquarian Tō Teikan (1732–97). In the section "Antiquities Passing for Generations" of his *Antiquarian Journal* (*Kōko nichiroku*), (Kyoto: Sasaki Sōshirō, 1797), Tō insisted, "however small, the objects should be prized and treasured by those [antiquarians] to examine the past." He also noted, "As for the things by which the past should be examined, one should keep all and not throw anything away, even if they are such things as a piece of paper, a half sheet of pages, a deserted tray, or a broken roofing tile. One should make a copy of them without exceptions. I would hope to make up a deficiency of books by these things" in the introduction of Tō Teikan, *Commentary on Illustrations of Six Kinds* (*Rikushu zukō*, transcribed copy). The logic of Tō was ahead of that of Ninagawa as well as that of the proposition of 1871 by Dagaku. The antiquarians in the early Meiji years probably understood the European discipline of archaeology in accord with this logic. Saitō, *Nihon kōkogakushi*, 47–54.

CHAPTER 3

The Season of Exhibitions

SECTION 1: LOOKING AT THINGS

EXPOSITIONS ACCORDING TO FUKUZAWA YUKICHI

Conditions in the West (*Seiyō jijō*, 1866), written by Fukuzawa Yukichi (1834–1901) is an exemplary publication from the Bakumatsu period that details various Western things including institutions, laws, customs, and histories. In 1898 (Meiji 31), Fukuzawa himself noted, in the introduction to the first volume of *The Complete Works of Fukuzawa Yukichi,* that "*Conditions in the West* was the most widely read and popular book I have written."[1] At the beginning of a short preface to the first volume of *Conditions in the West,* Fukuzawa sharply critiques the attitude that would study science and technologies such as geology, military science, and the art of navigation only from a practical point of view. He asserted that if someone "only studies languages and technologies of the West" and "does not explore the politics and customs in each country," then, even if they were to absorb Western sciences and technology thoroughly, "it will be not only useless but harmful to the country, since one would not be able to return to the duty of administrating the country."[2] He further elaborates that concerning efficiency, no method comes close to reading history books to "observe the politics and customs in each country." True to his words, *Conditions in the West* begins with an elaboration on twenty-five categories: from "the politics and customs" that ground political and economic infrastructure in the West to other social systems such as schools, hospitals, newspaper and technological advancements such as steam engines, the telegraph, and gaslight. Of course, the categories of museums and expositions are also included in this list.

In the entry for museums, Fukuzawa begins rather simply by noting that "museums are established to broaden the scope of people's knowledge by collecting products, things past, things rare from around the world and displaying them." He then lists types of museums known by a specific term based on the kind of collection they hold. He touches briefly on a mineralogical museum that collects minerals and rocks from around the world, and a zoological museum that exhibits taxidermied animals, fish, and insects. He then adds more examples of specific museums, namely a zoo that nurtures living animals, fish, and insects; a botanical garden that holds plants, flowers, and grasses from every corner of the world; and a medical museum, a type of museum that is solely dedicated to the art of medicine, which dissects human bodies and collects skeletons.

The entry of expositions follows this immediately. He observed:

> As noted in the previous entry, each country established museums that collect objects from around the world, old and new. However, arts and crafts of each nation develop daily, and new inventions follow. There is always something new. For this reason, it often happens that what was considered a rare and precious item in the past belongs to the stale today, and that a clever item yesterday becomes useless today. Therefore, in metropolitan cities of the West, they organize the assembly of products to gather together notable products, useful instruments, old and rare items through notification and show these to people from around the world. These are called expositions [*hakurankai*].[3]

Fukuzawa lists various exhibited items and claims: "When surveying the expositions, it is possible to say that everything one needs to conduct life is there. [Expositions] assemble millions of objects under one roof, place them in a row, and exhibit them to the people for five to six months.... After the exposition is over, the objects are sold by bidding."[4] He then comments on the Paris Exposition (Exposition Universelle) of 1867, which was scheduled for the following year. The Tokugawa shogunate, then still in power, would send a delegation to this exposition.

Fukuzawa astutely noted that the role of museums is to "broaden the scope of people's knowledge." If we replace the objects of knowledge with newly invented technologies and unknown local products, this description would fit neatly into the exposition he is referring to. Regarding the relationship between museums and expositions, Fukuzawa does not miss the vital point. Although various countries in the West "established museums that collect articles from the around the world, old and new," the advancement of technology and industry continues to produce new products. For this reason, "in metropolitan cities of the West, they organize the assembly of products" to display them to the people in expositions. In other words, Fukuzawa posits expositions as the extension of the inspiration that gave rise to museums.

The first world exposition, known as the Great Exhibition or the Crystal Palace Exhibition, took place in 1851 in London. In *The Politics of Expositions: Imperialism, Commercialism, and Popular Entertainment* (*Hakurankai no seijigaku: Manazashi no kindai,* 1992), sociologist Yoshimi Shun'ya claims:

> With the assumption of layered processes such as the transition from the age of discovery to the age of museology, and the development in systematization and democratization of museums, zoos, and botanical gardens, the age of museology emerged at a time when each European country took it upon themselves to produce the space for a museological gaze as an ideological instrument of capitalism. Expositions totalized the systems of visuality that had developed in museums, botanical gardens, and zoos, within the format of a great spectacle that revolved around the axis of industrial technologies.[5]

It is also possible to place the relationship between museums and expositions on the same plane of contemporaneity. Seen this way, we can start to see that when the historical unfolding from museums to expositions was taking place, they developed a mutually supportive relationship. In *Origins of Things Meiji* (*Meiji jibutsu kigen,* 1908), the author Ishii Kendō noted that "our museums developed unanimously as one with the expositions and exhibitions."[6] By using the phrase "unanimously as one," Ishii means that they formed an intimate relationship to one another and that their development, too, was inseparable. If this is the case, then it underscores the characteristics of the Meiji period, in which the relationship between museums on the one hand and expositions and exhibitions on the other evolved simultaneously.

Although this is not limited to museums and public displays, Fukuzawa's own experience of the West grounded these sorts of claims. He was a member of two overseas delegations of the Tokugawa shogunate, one sent in 1860 (Man'en 1) to the United States, and the other in 1862 (Bunkyū 2) to Europe. The level and quality of the knowledge he accumulated through reading books and from limited direct contacts with the Dutch who came to Nagasaki paled in comparison with the knowledge and observation that he gained through his own experience in Europe and the United States. However, a mere assemblage of knowledge and observation based on personal experience could not provide a bird's-eye view of the whole, so he needed an intellectual process through which to digest these experiences and present them systematically. Through a repetition of this process, Fukuzawa's own actual experience provided a firm basis to demonstrate this knowledge and observation with persuasiveness, and the accumulation of his knowledge systematized through the intellectual process formed a body of knowledge that was, in fact, appreciated by many in public.

THE EXPERIENCES OF OVERSEAS DELEGATIONS DURING BAKUMATSU

After the Tokugawa shogunate abolished the seclusion of the country in 1854, the experiences of members of overseas delegations sent to the United States and Europe were crucial to the process of expanding the knowledge of things Western. It is not difficult to imagine how the encounter with unknown "politics and customs" like museums and expositions affected the experience and knowledge of many delegation members, including Fukuzawa Yukichi. In the early Meiji period, institutions whose aim was public display emerged in Japan, and these new beginnings brought about great changes to the world of things past. The observations of delegation members in the Bakumatsu period conveyed their initial experience and responses toward these unknown things and systems in the West. At the same time, the confusion and puzzlement in response to the unknown in some way anticipated the experiences of the general public of the Meiji period when museums and expositions first appeared before their eyes.

The 1860 delegation to the United States was the first diplomatic delegation that the Tokugawa shogunate dispatched to the West. The immediate purpose of this delegation was to exchange and ratify the Treaty of Amity and Commerce between the United States and Japan. The official group consisted of sixteen main members. The three leaders were Shinmi Masaoki, the Lord of Buzen, who served as the chief delegate; Muragaki Norimasa, the Lord of Awaji, who was the deputy chief delegate; and Oguri Tadamasa, the Lord of Bungo, who served as the inspector. Under these leaders, officials from the bureaus of foreign services (*Gaikoku kata*) and the accountant (*Kanjō kata*), as well as supervisors and medical doctors, joined the official group. In addition to these official members, each member brought at least one or more attendants for themselves. Including the kitchen staff in this group, it became a rather large party of seventy-seven individuals. They left Shinagawa Bay on the eighteenth day of the first month in Man'en 1 (February 1860), on the naval frigate *Powhatan,* which had been sent by the United States. The shogunate warship *Kanrin Maru* was dispatched separately on the next day from Uraga port, with the charge of protecting the delegation. Among those on board were Kimura Yoshitake, the Lord of Settsu and the magistrate for the military ship; Katsu Kaishū, the captain; and officers and sailors sent by the US Navy as crew members. The *Kanrin Maru* traveled via Hawaii to San Francisco, then returned to Uraga port on the fifth day of the fifth month of the same year. Fukuzawa was on the *Kanrin Maru* as an attendant of the magistrate Kimura.[7]

The plan for the delegation to the United States was originally underwritten by Iwase Tadanari, who belonged to a reformation group promoting treaties with foreign countries. However, as a consequence of an incident in which the Tokugawa shogunate failed to receive an imperial sanction for concluding a treaty with the United States, Ii Naosuke, a strong advocate for the conservative faction of the Tokugawa shogunate, became chief minister in 1858, after which a group led by

Iwase lost their positions.[8] In the end, according to historian Matsuzawa Hiroaki, the delegation consisted of those "petty officials and mediocre talents" who, "although given higher titles, only carried out orders from the shogunate without the ambition or intellect to understand the unknown world." However, there were many among this group who volunteered and applied in order to explore "the situation of barbarian countries," and took on the role of attendant or servant to the officials of the delegation.[9]

One such person was Tamamushi Sadaiyū Yasushige (1823–69), a clansman from the Sendai domain, who applied to become an attendant for Shinmi Masaoki. His *Journal of a Voyage to the United States* (*Kōbei nichiroku,* after 1860) offers a glimpse of his ambition.[10] For instance, the difference in eating habits on board presented a challenge; it seems that he was turned off by the smell of oil in the food on the ship. But Tamamushi claimed this could be overcome by becoming familiar with the unfamiliar. He noted that "to have difficulty with the foreign food and drinks is the opinion of a frog in a well" and that "volunteers would suffer from these differences without fail."[11] For those volunteers who persevered through such conditions, rather than simply rejecting difference, this kind of experience could create an opportunity to broaden their understanding. The object of their exploration, the concept of "the situation of barbarian countries," emerged from the China-centric notion of *huayi* (J. *kai*) or "civilized (China) and uncivilized (the rest of the world)," originating in Confucianism. However, Matsuzawa claims that as they interacted with other crews on the warship, their acute sensibility and the patient work of the intellect eventually brought them to "reflect on and modify concepts of the West and of Japan," which were also based on an ethnocentric notion of "civilized and uncivilized."[12]

On the other hand, the book that deputy delegate Muragaki Norimasa left behind, *Diary of a Delegate to the United States* (*Kenbeishi nikki,* 1898), evinces little of the fresh sensibility and flexible intellect that we find in Tamamushi's notes. For instance, on the last day of the third month in 1860 (Man'en 1), Muragaki and others were invited to a musical recital at the White House in Washington, DC. Upon taking the tour of the White House, Muragaki noted, "it resembles a great hall of our temples without a resident priest. At times, there are heads made of white stone displayed above the lintel. They are said to be the heads of successive presidents, and they remind me of execution sites in our country."[13] It is probably reasonable that the members would associate these Western busts, which they had not seen before, with the heads of executed criminals.[14] Even then, when we compare Muragaki's writing with that of Tamamushi, it is difficult to overlook the rigidity of the former when confronted with unknown things and phenomena.

Tamamushi's *Journal of a Voyage to the United States* not only details the events of each day, it also provides information about each place and city he visited in separate categories, ranging from geological characteristics, customs, weather, and vegetation to currency and commodity prices.[15]

After leaving San Francisco, the group landed in Panama, then traveled to Washington, DC, sailing along the Atlantic coast. As the Panama Canal was not yet constructed, the group traveled by train to reach the Atlantic. Naturally, this was the first time they had been on a steam locomotive. Tamamushi created an entry on steam engine trains in his journal and began by writing: "Steam engine trains have three hundred horsepower. There are four big wheels in front, four smaller wheels in the rear, and the engine is placed on the wheels. The steam is created in the rear through fire, and there is a chimney in the front." He then described in detail the working of the steam engine, the appearance of the railroad tracks, the operation of the trains by drivers, the structure of trains, and the interior of passenger carriages. The entry ends with a frank description of his experience.

> Once the car begins to speed up, one cannot recognize the trees on both sides of the carriage. The sound of the carriage is noisy, like loud thunder. Two men sitting face to face cannot hear their own conversation. However, when the train runs in flat areas, it is possible to sit quietly and comfortably, so much so that one can write letters. On occasion, when one opens the glass window, a cool breeze comes in, and no matter how hot it may be outside, one is compelled to forget this heat because of the wind. One must marvel at the detailed and complicated workings of the train.[16]

Passengers on a moving train are unable focus their eyes on a close object passing by the window, and in fact, some members of the delegation expressed their strange experiences on the train in the form of Chinese poetry.[17] It appears that an overwhelming initial experience does not appeal so much to intellectual analysis as to to all five human senses, urging the person toward a sensuous reaction.

A book by Osatake Takeki, *To the Barbarian Countries: Tales of Overseas Delegations in Bakumatsu* (*Iteki no kuni e: Bakumatsu kengai shisetsu monogatari,* 1929), is well-known as an interesting nonfiction work produced by weaving together several records of the members of delegations. However, it is also fascinating because it allows us to imagine the varying degrees of intellect and sensitivity of each member. We can see that on the one hand, the impact of the initial experience was so strong that Muragaki Norimasa, the deputy chief delegate, imagined sculpted busts as severed heads. On the other hand, a reaction like that of the deputy also demonstrates a threshold that distinguishes the flexible intellect and rich sensibility of some members from the stiffness and dullness of the rest.

MUSEUMS AND EXHIBITIONS IN THE BAKUMATSU PERIOD

After the group led by Shinmi Masaoki arrived in Washington, DC, to exchange and ratify the Treaty of Amity and Commerce between the United States and Japan, they visited the Patent Office on the second day of the fourth month.

Tamamushi Yasushige described the experience of the day in *Journal of a Voyage to the United States* in the following manner:

> The group visited the Patent Office, in other words the office of expositions.... Once we walked up to the third floor, we saw layers of shelves on the left, right, front, and back, displaying taxidermies of birds, animals, fish, and insects. Their forms were maintained as if they were alive. In addition, the room also displayed various household goods, numbering in the tens of thousands. Included among them were items from my country, probably brought to the US by Beruri a few years ago. We looked at three items: clothing for the female attendants in the castle, straw sandals, and smoking pipes.[18]

Tamamushi was impressed with the taxidermies of the animals and fish. He was also surprised to see items they used daily and were thus familiar. The figure of Beruri he names here is Admiral Matthew Calbraith Perry (1794–1858), the commander of the East India squadron of the US Navy, who visited Uraga in 1853 (Kaei 6) and the following year. The next room showcased various types of machinery. Tamamushi noted:

> Passing through this room and entering the next, we saw many prototypes of machines. The number of these, too, was difficult to count. Therefore, if one observes one machine, it would be impossible to observe others, and if we looked at all of them together, we couldn't ask questions about each of them. We could only stare in blank amazement. In addition, we saw American men and women in the crowd; when we identified an item to take a close look, people gathered all around us, we hardly had a moment to stand. We observed the machines, but we ourselves were observed by the crowd.[19]

This group felt amazement and confusion when they came face to face with these unfamiliar objects in Washington, DC, and anticipated their first experience of an exposition. The next delegation to Europe, in 1862 (Bunkyū 2), went to experience firsthand the Great London Exposition, also known as the International of 1862. Within the space of an exhibition, there is a particular type of gaze that diligently stares at the objects within the space. Tamamushi felt some surprise to find this gaze directed at his own delegation, but as museums and public exhibitions began to appear in Meiji Japan, his group would come to practice this type of gaze themselves.

On the seventh day of the fourth month, the attendants and servants were permitted to explore on their own, and they visited Washington's Smithsonian Institute. Established in 1848, the institution is today one of the world's largest museums that includes a research section. Tamamushi was surprised by its size even in 1860. He wrote, "Within a half *chō* walk [around sixty yards] from the entrance of a park, there is an enormous house, four or five stories in height. Its name is Smithsonian Institute."[20]

He continued to describe his experience as the group entered the building:

> We first entered a room on the second floor used for delivering religious sermons. The front of the room was occupied by a high wooden stage, around which a few hundred long benches were installed. Next to it was a small room, with depictions of human figures hung on each of its four walls. At the center of the room was a wooden figurine of a naked body with his private parts covered by a leaf. This figurine is said to have lived before President Washington founded the country. After seeing this room, we entered another room where a set of writing materials was installed, along with a photographic portrait. It probably depicts a person who lived in this house, and this image is used to preserve his likeness and shape. After leaving this room, we moved to a room to the left, where a globe and various curios from around the world were displayed. On one side there was a large mirror. When one walks in front of it, one's reflection is enlarged ten times; this was quite strange. From there, we moved to the floor below, where dozens of high shelves had been installed to display rare birds, strange animals, as well as household goods from all over the world. A few dozen items from our country were displayed, including swords, Japanese halberds, shields, smoking pipes, and clothing. Compared to the Patent Office, there were more items from Japan here.[21]

It appears that they observed exhibited items eagerly from room to room. At the end of this tour, they saw four or five mummies and were utterly shocked by the sight. Tamamushi noted, "there were dried and condensed human corpses. Including the old and young, there are about four or five bodies. When looking at these, our hearts beat quickly.... We did not have time to examine the other few thousand items, but each one of them surprised us." On the way back, a dark cloud appeared, and lightning began: "All was pitch dark. Lightning flashed in every direction, and it was already four o'clock in the afternoon." Their day out in the afternoon had lasted into the evening.

The writings by members of the delegation from 1860 were only collections of fragments of experiences. However, as Tamamushi's entry on trains attests, their experiences came to be reconstructed as a broader body of knowledge as time passed. The Tokugawa shogunate sent a sequence of overseas delegations: in 1862 (Bunkyū 2) a group led by Takenouchi Yasunori, the Lord of Shimotsuke, traveled to Europe; in 1863 (Bunkyū 3) another group led by Ikeda Nagaoki, the Lord of Chikugo, visited France; and in 1865 (Keiō 1), a group led by the Magistrate of Foreign Service, Shibata Takenaka, also traveled to France.[22] Their experiences and anecdotal observations were passed down through words, and some of their records were eventually copied in writing. These observations and experiences rippled outward, and the gradual accumulation of such information spurred on a rapid growth in knowledge about the West. Between 1860, when the first delegation was sent to the United States, and 1866, when Fukuzawa Yukichi's *Conditions in the West* was published, these once-informal observations had become systematically catalogued and constructed as knowledge.

One Hundred Years' History of the Tokyo National Museum: Material Section (*Tokyo Kokuritsu Hakubutsukan hyakunenshi: Shiryōhen,* 1973) includes many sections related to museums taken from the diaries and other writings by the members of the overseas delegations.[23] A portion of Tamamushi's *Journal of a Voyage to the United States* is included, and certain other writings are worth noting. *Essay of Ten Kinds by Hōan* (*Hōan jusshu,* 1869), written by Kurimoto Joun (1822–1897), is one such example. Kurimoto played a significant role in the diplomatic relations between the Tokugawa shogunate and the French government. He was sent to France in the sixth month of 1867 (Keiō 3) as a special envoy, arriving in the eighth month. In the same year, the shogunate had sent another delegation led by the chief delegate Tokugawa Akitake, a younger brother of the shogun Tokugawa Yoshinobu, to participate in the International Exposition of 1867, which Fukuzawa noted in *Conditions in the West*. This delegation had arrived in the third month.

Kurimoto stayed in Paris for nine months, until the third month of 1868, when he returned to Japan as the Tokugawa shogunate was being dismantled. *Essay of Ten Kinds by Hōan* was published in 1869 (Meiji 2), and its second volume, *Memories Recalled by the Window at Dawn* (*Gyōsō tsuiroku,* 1869), is a collection of his observations during his time in Paris.[24] In this volume, Kurimoto praises Napoleon III's skill at governance, and lists the Paris International Exposition as one of the reasons for his positive endorsement. "The most compelling reason why I respect Napoleon is the series of events he organized around the exposition. Overturning the existing agreements between lords and the emperor, the exposition expands the field of knowledge. By displaying new products that exist in this cosmos, ordinary objects become instruments to examine the old, delighting perception and lifting the spirits. Finally, the exposition attracts world leaders, thereby assembling them within his own reign. He has brought them all unknowingly to Paris. What a clever technique it is!"[25] Kurimoto was cognizant of the political dimension of expositions. Regarding museums, he wrote: "What are referred to as *musées* are places that are designed to examine the old by collecting vessels, toys, stone figures, encaustic painting, outer stone coffins, minerals from pre-historic ages, bones, and skeletons of strange beasts. They are established by the government, and open to the people. Their visitors feel pride because of the splendidness of the objects, which entertain the ears and eyes of the visitors, thereby stimulating knowledge and wisdom. This is one aspect of good governance."[26] Here, too, Kurimoto found what he took to be another benevolent effect of Napoleon's skill as a governor, while developing an awareness of the political aspect of museums.

In 1869, Murata Fumio (1836–91) published the book *Record of Things Seen and Heard in the West* (*Seiyō bunken roku*). Murata had traveled to England along with clansmen from Saga domain in 1865 (Keiō 1) as a stowaway. Upon returning to Japan, he worked for the Meiji government for a brief time, but soon established *Marumaru chinbun,* a satirical newspaper, in 1877 (Meiji 10). As if following Fukuzawa's example, Murata described in his book various aspects of the West according to geography, law, customs, and conventions. In the third volume of the first part, "Geography of the United Kingdom," he wrote about the British Museum. Murata referred to the museum as a "treasure house," noting that "while there are many treasure houses in London, the British Museum is the most gorgeous and splendid of all." After introducing the department of printed books, the department of antiquities, the department of drawings and prints, the department of botany, the department of zoology, and the department of mineralogy, he summarized the general condition of the institution:

> Various items from around the world are collected, and incredible numbers of them are rare. By making boxes and doors with glass plates to avoid dust, and by using medical liquor to protect against decay, the collected things are preserved very effectively. Thus, they very effectively accumulate and house these items. The museum makes clear the details of how Westerners pay attention to encyclopedic study. The popular saying in Japan that Westerners are only absorbed in things new and novel, and throw away old things and remains, is not the case. Almost all people who are interested in encyclopedic study can enter this house and examine these objects.[27]

Murata's observation that Westerners did not in fact ignore the past is particularly noteworthy; it would be repeated two years later in the proposition by Daigaku to build the *shūkokan.*

Experiences of the West in the Bakumatsu period expedited the growth in knowledge around museums, expositions, and exhibitions. Of course, the opportunity to set foot in the West was limited to a very few. Still, as the observations made by this select group developed into more systematic forms of knowledge, the ground for the arrival of museums and public, large-scale exhibitions in Japan was being prepared.

KAICHŌ SHOWS AND EXHIBITIONS

Insofar as they involved displaying objects and inviting the public to observe them, the exhibitions that began to be organized in the Meiji period appear surprisingly similar to events known as *kaichō* shows that took place frequently during the Tokugawa period. Both exhibitions and *kaichō* shows created an extraordinary festive space, since a significant number of people gathered together at a specific site. Furthermore, to the degree that the size of the crowd measured their success, both strived for the same goal. It is not surprising, then, that their methods of attracting crowds were similar.

However, when we consider the paradigm of "the new and the old" in relation to these two, the situation changes completely. In his book *Art as Spectacle: The Age of Oil Painting Teahouses* (*Bijutsu to iu misemono: Aburae jaya no jidai,* 1992), art historian Kinoshita Naoyuki makes a significant observation pertinent to our discussion. He notes that "spectacles [*misemono*] are the home where art exhibitions grew up."[28] *Misemono* is a general term used for various types of entertainment hosted during the *kaichō* shows. According to Kinoshita, the relationship between spectacles (*misemono*) and art exhibitions was "intimately intertwined in that they relate to the types of status that Japanese people have given to art in modern society. The formation of disdain toward spectacles and the formation of modern art are in fact two sides of the same coin."[29] Historically, spectacles and *kaichō* shows formed an inseparable relationship, and a similar observation can be made about *kaichō* and exhibitions. Despite or because of this, public exhibitions in Meiji highlighted their differences from *kaichō* shows and spectacles, or pretended to have no relation at all to them—as if they had an aversion to their close relative.

Comparing similar things brings the characteristics of each into sharp relief. Let's start with *kaichō* shows. Historian Hiruma Hisashi's essay "Kaichō Shows in the City of Edo" (Edo no kaichō, 1973) provides both detailed analyses and a general summary of *kaichō* shows, and as such helps us to grasp its critical aspects. Although *kaichō* took place throughout the Tokugawa period all over the country, the city of Edo, present-day Tokyo, was the best known for these shows. In other words, *kaichō* are inseparable from teeming metropolitan areas. According to Hiruma, during the two hundred years from the mid-seventeenth century onward, 1,565 *kaichō* were recorded in Edo alone. By a simple calculation, this amounts to a little more than seven *kaichō* per year. Hiruma divides this period into three separate stages, and notes that its heyday was during the middle stage, approximately in the eighteenth century.[30] There were two types of *kaichō*: the in-house show (*igaichō*) and the traveling show (*degaichō*). In the case of the former, the temple exhibited treasured items, such as its images of Buddha; such an event was a special occasion on which the temple opened its doors to show the public its treasures. Traveling shows rented out the precincts of other temples and used it as the site of a *kaichō*. Those rented temples were referred to as lodging temples (*shukuji*). In this case, the event was open generally for sixty days, with certain exceptions in which ten to thirty extra days were allowed. Of the 1,565 *kaichō* shows recorded in the city of Edo, 824 were in-house shows and 741 were traveling shows. In Hiruma's first stage, the number of traveling shows was slightly greater, but from the middle stage on, the number of in-house shows increased steadily, and by the last stage, this trend had become even more apparent. These shifts also attest to the development of Edo itself.[31]

Kaichō shows took the form of pious monetary contributions so that temples could repair damaged parts of their structure or rebuild temple buildings. The Magistrate of Temples and Shrines (*Jisha bugyō*) evaluated the applications submitted

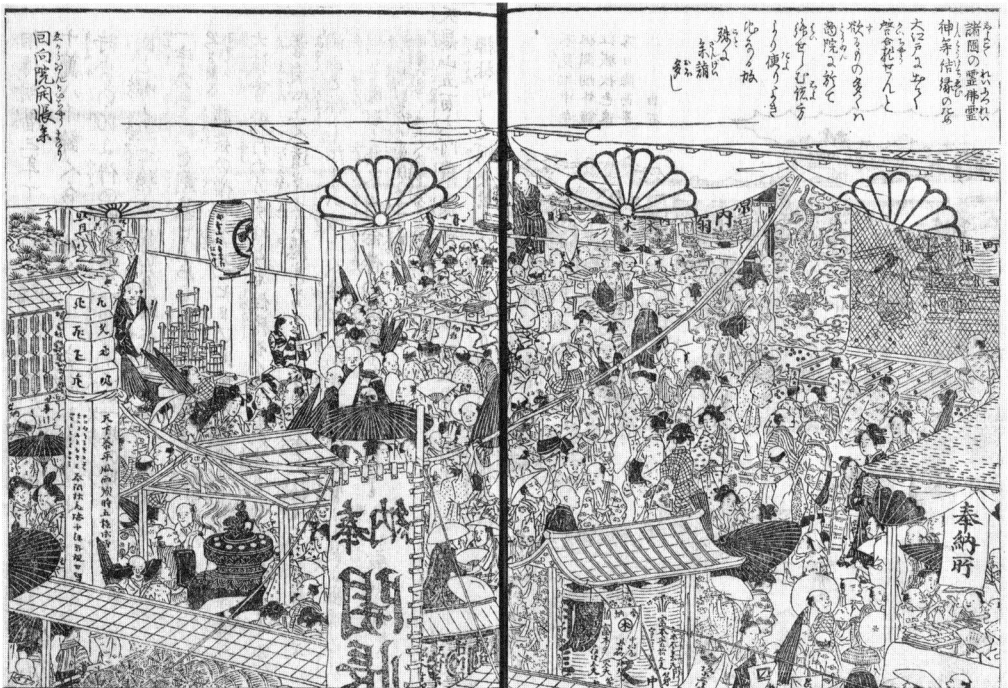

FIG. 3.

Hasegawa Settan (Japanese, 1778–1843). A scene of the *kaichō* show at Ekōin (*Ekōin kaichōmairi*), from *Edo meisho zue*, vol. 7, 1836. Woodblock print, 25.5 × 32.5 cm. Tokyo, Kokuritsu Kokkai Toshokan, 000007277957.

---

from temples and shrines and granted permissions for these shows accordingly. In a sense, it functioned as an aide to the Tokugawa shogunate's policy on temples and shrines. To maximize potential contributions, *kaichō* were expected to bring in large crowds. Over seventy percent of traveling shows took place around areas of Edo such as Honjo, Fukagawa, and Asakusa where many lodging temples were concentrated. Among temples in these areas, Ekōin Temple in Honjo, located at the east end of the Ryōgoku Bridge over the Sumida River, offered the most number of lodging temples on its grounds. Along with Ekōin Temple, the Eitaiji Temple in Fukagawa, Yushima Tenjin Shrine, and Gokokuji Temple in Otsuka were frequent sites for traveling shows.[32] The seventh volume of *Illustrated Famous Places of Edo* (*Edo meisho zue*, 1834–36), compiled by three generations of editors including Saitō Gesshin (1804–78), includes an entry on the Kokubusan Ekōin Temple (fig. 3). One of the illustrations, captioned "A scene of the *kaichō* show at Ekōin," describes the scene as follows: "This is the temple that many visit in the great Edo to make ties with various sacred Buddhas and gods of various provinces. Because the temple is conveniently located to travel from various directions, this temple attracts a particularly large number of worshipers."³³ It then illustrates a chaotic scene of a traveling show at the temple.

The third volume of *An Account of the Prosperity of Edo* (*Edo hanjō ki*, 1832–36) by Terakado Seiken (1796–1868) also includes an entry on *kaichō* shows. From the start, Seiken observed *kaichō* with a sense of irony. "Although gods are sacred and Buddhas are holy, Amitabha would lose the shine on its halo and the gods would be hard to make out unless one worships them with money.... It is still hard to tell today whether gods bless the people of Edo with prosperity or whether it is the people who bless the Buddhas with prosperity."³⁴ In other words, do the gods (*kami*) and Buddhas bring merit to the people who bring them money or is it the other way around—that the money people give extends the prosperity of the gods and Buddhas?³⁵

An Account of the Prosperity of Edo also includes a valuable testimony, namely the transcript of a speech by an orator who held forth on the sanctity and provenance of the exhibited treasures to the audience.

> The holy treasure is to the left. Turning the corner to the left, I now see a row of treasures on display. There is a person sitting next to the treasures and explaining the connections among them. Boasting aloud, he says: "The holy cane resting before you is the very cane used in the seventh year of Intō, when there was serious drought. Wells all over the country were exhausted. People were suffering from thirst. Feeling pity for the people, the great master Kōbō began an incantation, took this cane and stabbed at the soil with it. How holy! Each spot touched by this cane became a spring at once. Praying to this cane once would thoroughly eliminate all bad events and disasters. This was the oath of the great master." He then immediately rolls up the veil covering the cane. Urging people on, he shouts: "Come closer now, and worship."³⁶

The story of the holy cane belonging to the great master Kōbō is a preposterous story, and the audience then would have recognized that. The name of the era, Intō, is itself a creation of the author, Terakado Seiken. However, regardless of the content of the orator's speech, the behavior and gestures of the orator are probably based on the author's own observation.

In Enkōan Kōriki Takanobu's *A Record of Kaichō Shows of Holy Treasures of Ryūkōji Temple* (*Ryūkōji reihō kaichō ki*, 1826), the author pictured this exact scene (fig. 4). In the illustration, the treasures are placed on the central stage, while the people who came to visit the *kaichō* show crowd the space in front. Next to the treasures on display, a man wearing a very formal type of kimono stands facing the center of the crowd. He is depicted with a small pole in his right hand, and is about to lift a curtain veiling a hanging scroll. A large label attached to the hanging scroll appears just underneath, and reads: "Authentic calligraphy by the hand of the founder." The face of the man is directed toward the crowd. Similar to the earlier

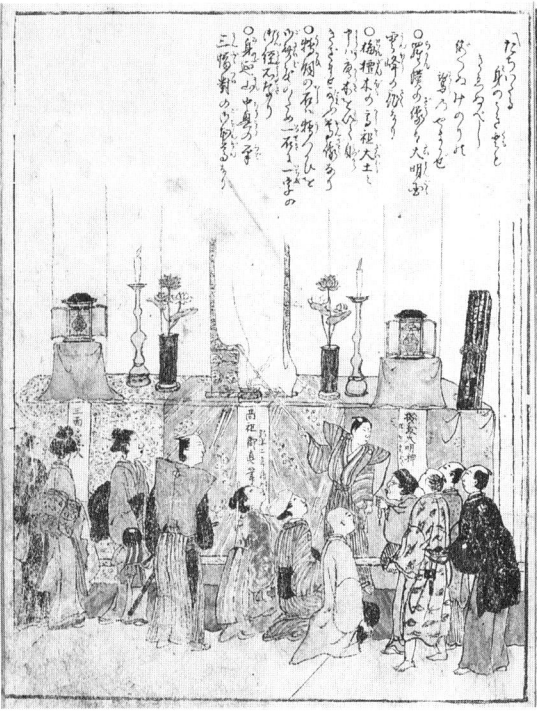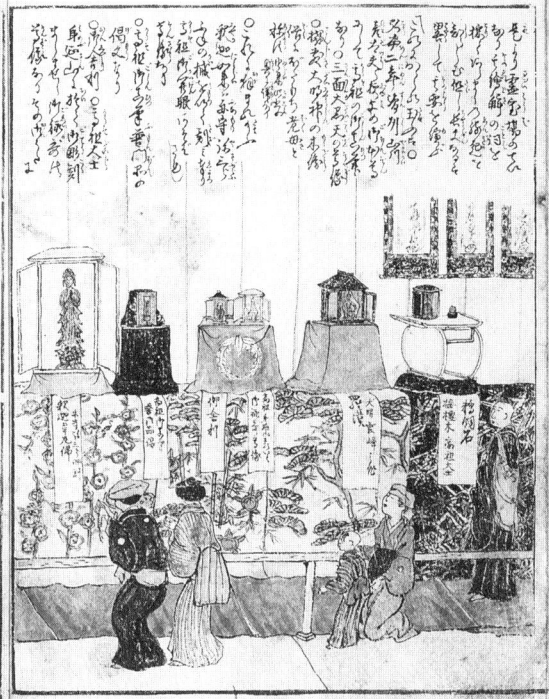

FIG. 4.

Enkōan Kōriki Takanobu (Japanese, 1756–1831). Reihō, visitors, and the orator in *A Record of Kaichō Shows of Holy Treasures of Ryūkōji Temple* (*Ryūkōji reihō kaichō ki*), 1826. Woodblock print, 25.6 × 35.6 cm. Nishio, Iwase Bunko Library, 145–46.

---

case from *An Account of the Prosperity of Edo,* this man was also probably shouting to the crowd: "Come closer now, and worship." An old woman standing to the right of the man is shown holding Buddhist prayer beads in both of her hands, and is indeed about to pray.

This record is based on a show that took place in Nagoya in 1826 (Bunkyū 9). It depicts a scene of a traveling *kaichō* show using Genjōji Temple as a lodging temple, displaying treasures of Ryūkōji Temple.[37] Although it is not an example based on the city of Edo, this illustration vividly shows the conditions of *kaichō*. The treasured items were placed on a stage, which was covered with a beautiful textile, and the crowd filled the space. A scene almost exactly the same as this *kaichō* was also depicted in multicolor woodblock prints for the exhibition organized by the Ministry of Education at the Yushima Seidō in the third month of 1872 (Meiji 5)—save for one significant difference (fig. 5). In this later illustration, the orator disappears. In the public display spaces that emerged in the Meiji period, sound came to be excluded.

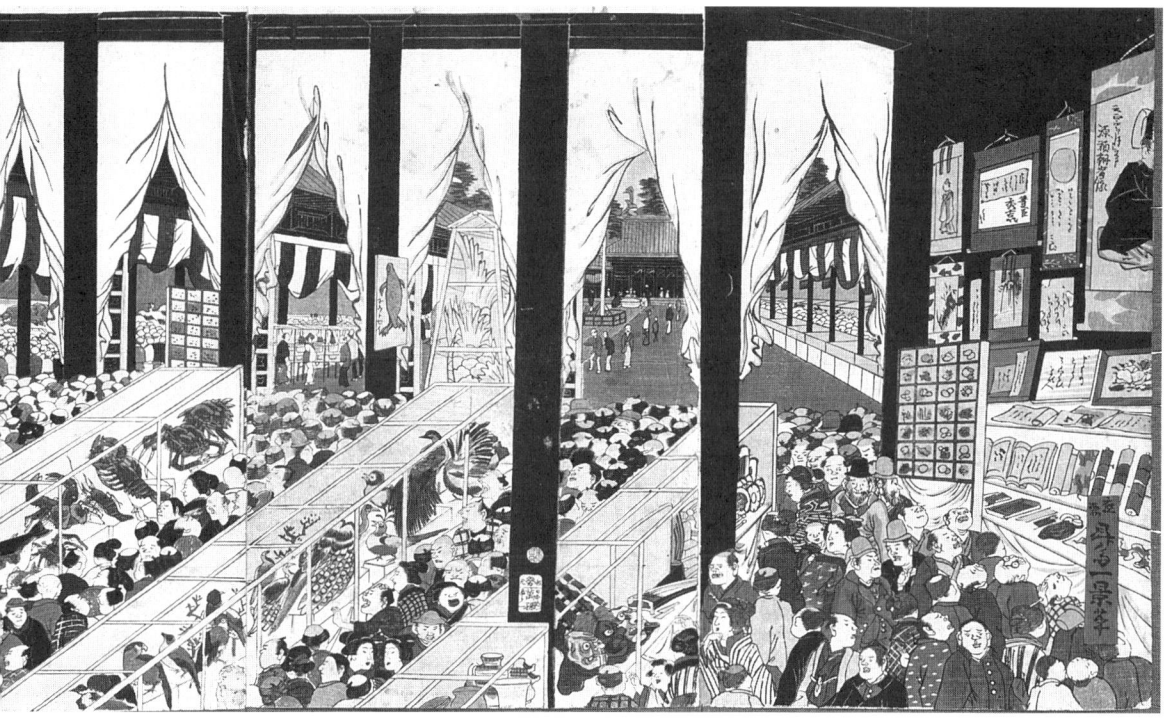

FIG. 5.

Shōsai Ikkei (Japanese, active ca. 1851–74).

"Crowds of People at the Exposition" (*Hakurankai shojin gunshū no zu*), triptych, 1872. Multicolor woodblock prints, 36.5 × 24.8 cm. Edo-Tokyo Hakubutsukan, 94200064.

THE PLEASURES OF *KAICHŌ* SHOWS

An Account of the Prosperity of Edo also detailed the prosperity of *kaichō* shows. It noted, for example, "This spring, *kaichō* were held in nineteen places. The statue of *Acala* (*fudō*) from Narita-san Shinshōji Temple was displayed in Fukagawa, following previous instances."[38] This entry refers to the traveling show of Shinshōji Temple in Narita that was held at Eitaiji Temple in the Fukagawa district, beginning in the third month of 1833 (Tenpō 4). Terakado Seiken also noted in detail a puppet theater performance of "Water Margin" (Ch. *Shuihu zhuan*) at the Tomigaoka Hachimangū Shrine, which shared the precinct with Eitaiji Temple. These *kaichō* events attracted *misemono* spectacles, theatrical performances, a sumo tournament held for pious contributions, and teahouses, all of which helped to attract crowds.

Saitō Gesshin, the author of *Illustrated Famous Places of Edo*, was also known for books such as *Records of Annual Events in Edo* (*Tōto saiji ki*, 1838) and *Chronicles of Edo* (*Bukō nenpyō*, 1850). In addition, his diary included accounts of his own visits to *kaichō* shows. According to the diary, Gesshin often went with his family members to *kaichō*, where he would see a *misemono* spectacle or stop by a restaurant. While he wrote about the quality or price of the food, he never commented specifically on the relative merits of *kaichō*. According to Hiruma, "for the children, or even for adults, visits to *kaichō* were only an excuse to see *misemono* spectacles, make votive offerings, or eat and drink at teahouses and restaurants."[39] One literati writer of the day, Yanagisawa Kien (1708–58), also noted that men often went to *kaichō* sites in order to visit nearby pleasure quarters.[40]

Some argued that the prosperity of *kaichō* shows stemmed from spectacles. The Buddhist monk Jippōan Keijun wrote about a traveling *kaichō* at the Tomigaoka Hachimangū Shrine in Fukagawa in 1821 (Bunsei 4).[41] He noted here that, aside from the cases of the traveling *kaichō* of Zenkōji Temple in Shinano domain and Seiryōji Temple in the Saga area of Kyoto, people did not go to *kaichō* in order to look and pray at principal images of Buddha. He wrote, "[I]n recent years, it is not the Buddhist treasures at *kaichō* events that are popular. Except for the cases of Zenkōji Temple and the Seiryōji Temple, what is popular are various types of *tsukurimono* (huge craftworks), voluminous votive offerings, and rare objects."[42] Evaluations of these events spread, such that Jippōan noted that "rumors vary among people, and human minds are constantly changing, like men and women in affairs. From those in highest ranks to the lowest, buzz is enough to propel people to travel to the sites of *kaichō,* however far they must travel."[43] Jippōan extracted a kind of crowd psychology in these events. "Therefore, to visit *kaichō* when using spectacles and *tsukurimono* as a foil is, in short, the same as going to a spectacle then offering prayer incidentally."[44] He complained that the relationship of master and servant between *kaichō* and spectacles was in the reverse order.

Although numerous spectacles in Edo became widely popular, most of them began as shows that took a gamble on attendance numbers for the *kaichō* shows. Hisashi Hiruma's "*Kaichō* Shows in the City of Edo" notes two exemplary cases: "the Flying Sacred Treasure" (*tonda reihō*), a spectacle held at the *kaichō* in the Sensōji Temple in Asakusa in 1777 (An'ei 6), and "the Great Buddha of Raincoats" (*kappa daibutsu*) at the *kaichō* in the Kaianji Temple in Shinagawa in 1793 (Kansei 5).

"The Great Buddha of Raincoats" was a spectacle of a giant Buddha created by assembling pieces of raincoat textiles; its height was said to measure about nine meters.[45] Shiba Zenkō (1750–1793), a well-known writer of popular novels, had turned this famous spectacle into the topic of a satirical story that was published as *The Origin and History of the Great Buddha of Raincoats* (*Kappa daibutsu ryaku engi,* 1793). In *Art as Spectacle* Kinoshita Naoyuki notes that these spectacle shows focusing on craftsmanship were particularly popular during the Bunsei period (1818–30), and lists several examples. In particular, the exhibit at the Shitennōji Temple in Osaka in the second month of 1819 (Bunsei 2) was so large that the nirvana of Buddha in reclining position made of bamboo measured about thirty meters long. Ichida Shōshichirō produced this enormous figure; afterward, he continued to make large figurines out of bamboo. In the fourth month of 1819, he showed a standing Shakyamuni measuring about eighteen meters tall inside the precinct of Taiyūji Temple in the Kitano area of

Osaka. He then traveled to Edo, and his works became quite popular. The popularity of these figures reached such a point that in the fifth month of 1827 (Bunsei 10) in Edo, an official notice for merchants and artisans (*machibure*) was issued prohibiting such giant craftworks. According to Hiruma, the ban noted that "in recent years at *kaichō* events in shrines and temples, many people congregate and do not stop quarreling when huge craftworks are presented within their precinct.... Such spectacles deviate from the intention to worship gods and Buddhas."[46] This ban attested to the popularity of "huge craftworks" in the context of spectacles.

On the other hand, the name "the Flying Sacred Treasure" at the 1777 *kaichō* show of Sensōji Temple in Asakusa referred to the objects for a spectacle that used dried foods such as salmon, sardine, and cod, in combination with utensils like soup bowls, to represent various statues of Buddhist icons (fig. 6). The Japanese name of the spectacle, *tonda reihō,* is a pun, in which *flying* (*tonda*), was a homonym for

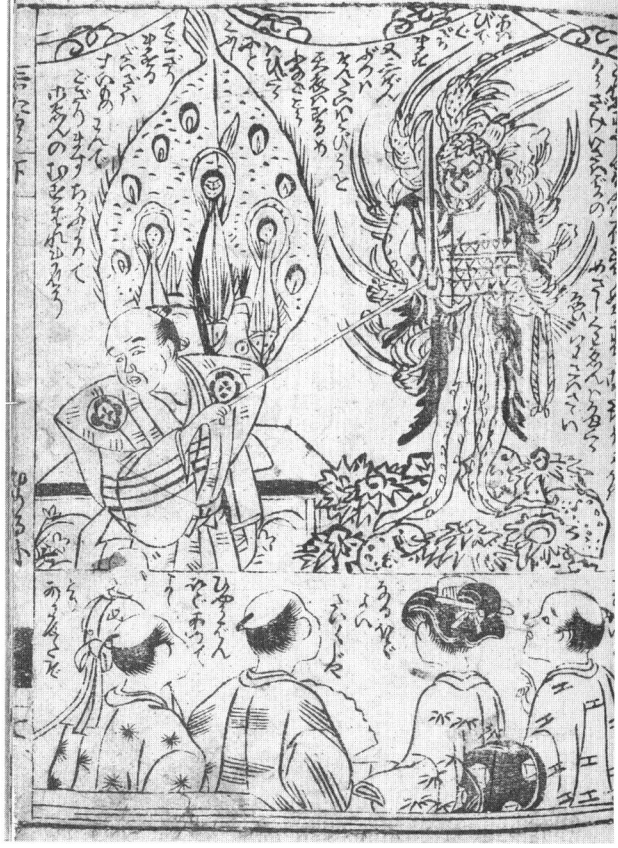

FIG. 6.

Torii Kiyotsune (Japanese, active mid-eighteenth century). *The Flying Sacred Treasure* (*Tonda reihō*), in *Mitsutakararishō no wakatake,* 1777. Woodblock print, 17.5 × 13 cm. Tokyo, Tokyo Metropolitan Central Library Special Collection Room

absurd. The title suggested a double meaning of "an absurd treasure of the sacred." Spectacles of a similar nature were called "buffoonery *kaichō*" (*odoke kaichō*), and they spread to various cities in the country.⁴⁷ The presentation of "the Flying Sacred Treasure" played with the phenomenon of *kaichō* itself, using the aesthetic strategy of unexpected juxtapositions. Essayist Asakura Musei noted in 1928:

> The entrance to the the "Flying Sacred Treasure" spectacle imitated the gates of a temple. Inside the gate, items were displayed like the treasures at *kaichō* shows. An orator in formal kimono with a pole in his hand pointed to each holy treasure and explained, "Here we are lucky to have an appearance of *Acala*, the face of which is made of dried salmon, his Buddhist clothes of dried surf clams on skewers, his fiery halo of spiny lobster shells, and a pedestal of turban shells and abalone shells. As for the triad of Buddha, the sacred bodies are made of flying fishes, the drapes of dried squid and crucian carps, the halos of dried cods and abalones, and the pedestals of soup bowls. Come to see up close now, so you can connect yourself to Buddha!"⁴⁸

In the case of both "the Great Buddha of Raincoats" and "the Flying Sacred Treasure," the connections between spectacles and *kaichō* ran deep.

On the other hand, Hiruma noted: "Once *kaichō* shows began to attract crowds for spectacles rather than for the miracles brought by Buddhist icons, the entertainment area started to break away from the *kaichō*." According to Hiruma, two areas that established themselves as entertainment areas early on were Okuyama in Asakusa and Hirokōji in Ryōgoku.⁴⁹ The 1827 prohibition of "huge craftworks," in the form of an official notice for merchants and artisans, also claimed that these manufactured objects were not appropriate for sites that ought to be spaces of worship. The popularity of *kaichō* and the prosperity of spectacles were inseparable, but the question was whether the authority of gods or Buddha was to be brought to the forefront or kept in the background.

As we have seen, Jippōan Keijun thought that visiting *kaichō* shows because of an interest in spectacles rather than in sacred works was almost the same as offering a prayer in passing. He elaborated on this theme further: "If a statue of a Buddha at a *kaichō* show were to speak, it would murmur and complain that changes of time and mentality are inevitable in this corrupt world. Even if spectacles (*misemono*) are what attract people to visit *kaichō*, they would still pray to the principal image of Buddha and chant the holy name of Buddha at least once. No matter how confused these priorities may be, such acts might still tie these people to Buddhas."⁵⁰ In this instance, the subtle nuances of religious life among the people of Edo can be acsertained.

After their zenith in the mid-Tokugawa period, *kaichō* shows in Edo became less popular around the Bakumatsu period in the mid-nineteenth century. Although there were some signs that *kaichō* might regain their popularity, the tidal waves of the anti-Buddhist movement and civilization and enlightenment ensured that this never came to pass. In particular, advancements in transportation like the spread of railroads made it possible for the people to travel to shrines and temples more easily. This reduced the significance of the traveling *kaichō*. In contemporary Japan, according to Hiruma, the remnants of *kaichō* "can be felt ever so slightly in the exhibitions of notable treasures organized at museums and the galleries of department stores."[51] His perspective suggests that as long as we understand *kaichō* during the Tokugawa period as a form of contributions for pious purposes, there is no equivalent today. However, if we examine *kaichō* without consideration of the role of faith, the present-day events in which treasures of shrines and temples are exhibited can be understood as an updated format of *kaichō*. Here, Hiruma paid particular attention to the affinity between expositions and museums on the one hand, and *kaichō* and spectacles on the other.

Returning to Fukuzawa's impression of the exposition, with which I began this chapter, one could quickly point out contrasting elements between *kaichō* shows and exhibitions at a core level: for example, the purposes of exhibition, their formats and structures, the unspoken restraints that organized them, as well as the manners expected of the audience. The goal of the museums, to borrow Fukuzawa's words from *Conditions in the West,* was "to broaden the scope of people's knowledge." Expositions shared the same purpose. On the other hand, *kaichō* events took place as a kind of contribution for pious purposes like donations to renovate and restore temples and shrines; their objective was thus primarily religious in nature.

SECTION 2: SHOWING THINGS

EXHIBITIONS IN TOKYO

The City of Edo was renamed Tokyo (literally, "east capital") following the collapse of the Tokugawa shogunate. The name change took place in the seventh month of 1868 (Keiō 4). Fewer and fewer people were attending *kaichō* shows; in their place, exhibitions and museums began to emerge within the city. As a result, spectacles as entertainment were left to survive on their own. The kind of interdependence that resulted from sharing profit and support between spectacles and *kaichō* shows could not, however, be maintained in the relationship between spectacles and exhibitions or museums. Generally, an easy way to highlight the values of the new, such as museums and expositions, was to emphasize the difference between these things and their older counterparts. Spectacles, then, were treated as a paradigmatic example of the past. It is also worth noting here that drawing too much attention to these differences might well have revealed certain affinities between these newer forms of display and *kaichō* themselves.

In *Origins of Things Meiji,* Ishii Kendō noted in a section called "The Origins of Exhibitions": "Between 1871 or 1872 and 1877, exhibitions were a major trend in the city and the country. As one element of civilization and enlightenment (along with preaching, cutting off top-knots, building schools, horse carriages, and rickshaws) exhibitions had a time of extreme popularity."[52] As noted in the section "The Meiji Government and the World of Things Past" in chapter 1, after the Meiji Restoration, exhibitions began on a small scale with the Exhibition of Local Products that took place in the fifth month of 1871. This exhibition, within the precinct of Shōkonsha Shrine in the Kudan area, was organized by the South School of Daigaku. The next year, an exhibition by the Ministry of Education organized by the Museum Bureau took place at the Yushima Seidō (a Confucian temple in Tokyo). In 1873 an exhibition by the Ministry of Education took place at the museum in Uchiyamashitachō in April, and the Vienna World Exposition, in which the Meiji government participated for the first time, opened in May. In March of the following year, another exhibition took place at the museum in Uchiyamashitachō, and in May, the calligraphy and painting exhibition took place at Taiseiden Hall of the Yushima Seidō, which served as the supplementary pavilion for the exhibition. In May 1876 Philadelphia's Centennial Exposition began, and in 1877 (Meiji 10) the first Domestic Exposition for the Promotion of Industry took place in Ueno Park (see appendixes, table 1).

The first Domestic Exposition of 1877 was a version of the Vienna Exposition organized by the Meiji government, its confidence brimming after its positive reception in Vienna. While *kokikyūbutsu* had dominated the majority of exhibitions up to this point, this show foregrounded the government's policy of encouraging industry, serving as a model for later expositions. Ishii Kendō noted that "after the first Domestic Exposition for the Promotion of Industry, the number of the government officials who had experienced exhibitions abroad increased, and these events came to be well organized, in terms of both content and appearance."[53] Such domestic expositions realized the government's ideal form of public display. Their thinking around educating and persuading the public is well represented in the following example: "The main aim of the Domestic Exposition for the Promotion of Industry is to support the progress in various sectors of engineering and industries and to increase profit through local products and foreign trade. It is not to provide an occasion for pleasure by securing a site for entertainment."[54]

Thus began the section of "Advice to Visitors" (*kanja chūi*) included at the beginning of the *Guide to the Site of the Domestic Exposition for the Promotion of Industry in 1877* (*Meiji jūnen naikoku kangyō hakuran kaijō annai*).[55] The term *kōgei* (industries) here is closer to the meaning of "engineering" rather than to a kind of craftwork centered on manual labor, in the present use of the word. According to this brochure, the aim of the exposition was to promote the use of resources for financial gain. Based on their success in Vienna, the organizers must have been aware of the possibility of acquiring foreign currency through trade. What I want to underscore here is the latter half of this excerpt: the claim that the exposition is not a "site for entertainment" at which visitors can find "an occasion for pleasure." Clearly, this was a reference to spectacles (*misemono*).

This guidebook was a brochure published by the administrative office for the Domestic Exposition for the Promotion of Industry within the Home Ministry. It is interesting to note that sets of Chinese characters are glossed, with a reading in Japanese words (*yamato kotoba*) to make them understandable to ordinary people who might not have been able to read the Chinese characters. This quote also demonstrates that the Meiji government tried to remind visitors of the distinction between expositions and spectacles. In addition to this, the very fact that this entry appears at the beginning of the official guidebook published by the government itself is intriguing. It highlights that a primary concern of the organizers was to push viewers away from the attitude that the exposition was to be enjoyed in the same way as a spectacle. The section continued: "To summarize the benefit of expositions, they offer the opportunity to survey millions of items from across the country in one site, without having to make an effort to travel a long way. Through this, people will be able to distinguish between superior and inferior items, as well as differences or similarities between them. In addition, each visitor will be able to learn about experiments and achievements in engineering and industry."[56] The phrase "the opportunity to survey millions of items from across the country in one site" dovetails with "traveling" *kaichō* shows. However, the text goes on, "if one tried to obtain the benefits of an exposition through any other means (such as reading or traveling)," one could never recreate this experience even if one spent a lifetime or a fortune. The organizers emphasized what a rare opportunity an exposition brought to visitors. They then concluded: "Indeed, expositions are aimed at supporting the progress of various sectors of engineering and industries, including the actual profit that is otherwise difficult to gain as shown here. However, it is up to each visitor to maximize the practical uses and apply them in his own way."[57]

According to this view, expositions had the merit of developing the practical uses of monetary value. This led to the claim that the site of an exposition was different from that of a spectacle, which was "a site for entertainment." Further, the guidebook claimed that the point of the exhibition was to learn "how to compare things." In order to exercise this, the brochure listed five categories of comparison: "clarifying the materials of a thing," "judging the quality of its production," "measuring the benefit of its use and its function," "knowing the merit of its effect in society," and "thinking whether its price is appropriate." The booklet continued that it was the job of the judges at the exposition to decide the relative merits of the displayed items, and therefore they had the responsibility to maintain their fairness. However, it also claimed that "all visitors entering the site are expected to assume the same attitude as these judges." This section concluded with a remark that although expositions were organized through the "encouragement of the government," whether it succeeded or turned into "a kind of spectacle [*misemono*] site" was "up to the general visitors and how they use perception to observe the displayed items."[58] Thus, the guidebook sent out a warning to its readers—that is to say, to potential visitors to the exposition.

CONFUSIONS AROUND EXPOSITIONS

Regardless of this clear explanation of the exposition's goals, the extent to which people understood it is an entirely different story. Takamura Kōun's *Recollecting the Bakumatsu and the Restoration* includes a famous anecdote that allows us to imagine this situation. The episode refers to the Domestic Exposition for the Promotion of Industry in 1877, when his master Takamura Tōun received the first prize for the wooden sculpture of Avalokiteśvara in a white robe (*byakue Kannon*)—a work that Kōun had actually carved.

According to Kōun, this took place in April of 1877. Because this was the first time such an exposition had been organized, he noted: "Those in charge from the government came to solicit participants, going to various small businesses and shops of craftsmen. They explained things such as the aim of the exposition, and provided detailed attention to help shops apply to display articles at the exposition. They didn't mind answering questions, and encouraged people to participate. They visited many places and looked after those people who might potentially submit to the exposition."[59]

These governmental officials probably visited Tōun and Kōun and explained that the aim of the exposition was to "support the progress in various sectors of engineering and industries and to increase profit through local products and foreign trade," as described in *Guide to the Site of the Domestic Exposition for the Promotion of Industry in 1877*. The officials probably emphasized as well that the exposition was not an occasion of spectacles. Even after such explanations were given, it is not surprising that Kōun still noted, "But nobody in public was clear about precisely what this exposition was. It was unclear to the point of being funny. Today it is well known, again to the point of being funny, but at that time, we didn't understand what it was in the slightest."[60]

Most people did not understand what an exposition was before they experienced it for themselves. In this regard, the brochure guide to the exposition was not as useful as the government expected.

Expositions could not happen without people to submit works; this is why officials from the government went door-to-door to commercial and craft businesses. Kōun noted, "Even when these officials came and solicited our participation, people seemed to find it bothersome." His master Tōun was no exception. Kōun remembered: "We asked the officials what kinds of things we should submit, and they answered that anything was fine, as long as a sculptor produced it. They suggested that we could submit the kind of thing we usually make. Based on this conversation, my master decided to send a statue of Avalokiteśvara in a white robe."⁶¹ Kōun then undertook the job of making the statue under his master's direction.

The completed statue of Avalokiteśvara was about thirty centimeters tall, and was made of sandalwood. According to Kōun, it was "a work carefully and attentively carved over much time, with great effort." It was a work that "was made to be a decorative figure as in other common styles," and was therefore not a novelty in any way. The opening ceremony for the exposition took place on 21 August 1877. About midway through the exposition period, a call was sent to Tōun, Kōun's master, saying that the submitted work had been selected for the Ryūmon prize, and asking him to attend the award ceremony. Neither Tōun nor Kōun knew of this award, or about any such distinction, for that matter. In fact, they could not even tell if this prize was awarded to particularly excellent—or dismal—work. On the day of the ceremony, Tōun went to the exposition site in Ueno in his full formal kimono.⁶² According to Ishii Kendō, the award ceremony took place on 20 November. In addition to six honorary awards, which included one for Kikuchi Yōsai in painting and the Nagasaki Kōransha Company for porcelain, 336 people received the Ryūmon prize, while 611 received the Hōmon prize (second prize, the phoenix crest), and 918 received the Kamon prize (third prize, the flower crest).⁶³

Following this ceremony, according to Kōun, "The exposition in the tenth year of Meiji closed. The general public, who at first didn't know what an exposition was at all, began to understand the general gist of what it was. Among those who submitted work, some may have at first been confused and found the event bothersome, but at last they came to accept it, thinking: 'I see—expositions are a quite useful convenience.'"⁶⁴ This experience is similar to that of those samurai who joined the overseas delegations with an aspiration during the Bakumatsu.

The *Guide to the Site of the First Domestic Exposition for the Promotion of Industry in 1877* had explained that what was important was to learn and practice "how to compare things." Although it was the responsibility of the judges at the exposition to determine the relative merits of the things on display, the guidebook also asked visitors to the exposition to "assume the same attitude as these judges." Having things compete against each other would make people understand the principle of competition through the space of the exposition. Thus, even if the appearance of expositions and spectacles was similar, there was a critical difference between the two. It is not difficult to imagine that conferring awards at the exposition made this point clear and memorable to the public. In addition, the guidebook claimed, "it provides the opportunity to survey millions of items from across the country in one site, without having to make an effort to travel a long way." Isn't this quite similar to the *kaichō* shows of the past? Using their familiar experiences of spectacles and *kaichō*, people began to find new ways to enjoy expositions. As the government had planned, the first Domestic Exposition for the Promotion of Industry in 1877 was a turning point in this regard.

PLEASURES OF EXHIBITIONS

As we saw earlier, Ishii Kendō characterized exhibitions in *Origins of Things Meiji* by stating that "between 1871 or 1872 and 1877, exhibitions were a major trend in the city and the country." As the phrase "the city and the country" indicates, many prefectures organized their own notable exhibitions around this time. Exhibitions organized by prefectures began in 1871, the same year as the Exhibition of Local Products organized by the South School of Daigaku, with the Kyoto Exhibition in the tenth month, and the Nagoya Exhibition in the eleventh month. Kyoto in particular saw a number of private companies organize exhibitions.[65] While the sections of prefectural governments charged with promoting industry and agriculture sometimes took the lead in organizing exhibitions, it was more common for local exhibition companies to take on this task. The scale of these exhibitions varied, but a decade on from the mid-1870s more than eighty exhibitions were recorded all over the country (see appendixes, table 1).[66] This number must be taken seriously.

The contents of these events were as varied as their scale. For example, let us examine an exhibition that took place in the city of Matsumoto in Chikuma prefecture (present-day Nagano prefecture) in 1873 (Meiji 6). This exhibition was organized by the Matsumoto Exhibition Company (*Matsumoto hakuran kaisha*) and ran for thirty days from 10 November at the main palace of Matsumoto Castle. Situating the exhibition at the castle—which was only accessible to a limited number of people during the Tokugawa period—was a sure-fire way to attract a large crowd. Further, this exhibition also had a section for entertainment. Ishii Kendō also wrote about this event in *Origins of Things Meiji*: "As exhibitions were becoming more popular, there was an event called the 'supplementary exhibition' [*tsuketari hakurankai*], which added a new flavor to it; this model has continued to the present day. The content of this event is the same as so-called 'entertainment' [*yokyō*] in the present, consisting of performances of popular shows."[67]

The small booklet *Regulations for the Matsumoto Exhibition in Chikuma Prefecture* (*Chikumakenka Matsumoto hakurankai kisoku*, 1873) lays out various regulations. An entry titled "supplementary exhibition" is included in the latter half, and it lists its general outline in ten sections. The first explains its purpose, noting: "On the other side of the exhibition, we have selected many novel spectacles so that visitors can alleviate their sense of depression [*utsuketsu*] and expand their energy outwardly [*shinki wo nobashi*] in order to add to this exposition. For this reason, it is called a 'supplementary exhibition.'"[68] Realistically, the "supplementary exhibition" was nothing other than entertainment whose aim was to attract more customers.

The second entry outlined the specific programs that were included. First, there were exhibitions of animals and plants, followed by sections referring to the following types of performances: a calligraphy and painting display including on-site performances of making works (*bunboku*, section IV); storytelling of past events and anecdotes (*enshi*, section V); and a theatrical performance. The description of the theatrical performances reads: "These are performances of the legacies of various individuals: those possessed by loyalty and filial piety, chaste and strong-minded women, virtuous and wise men. This will lead to virtue in those children of farmers and uneducated women who do not know the existence of these values, opening their tiny eyes like those of elephants."[69]

Four more sections follow: horse racing (*keiba*, section VII); a polo-like sport with horses (*gekikyū*, section VIII); a sword-crossing performance (*gekiken*, section IX); and acrobats "performing a variety of curious feats on a rope with a pole" (*torojutsu*, section X). Through theatrical performance (section IV), it appears that by performing the roles of individuals who ought to be exemplars for women and children in villages of the countryside, the organizers intended to use these performances as a method to instill high morals and virtue in its audience. The organizers attempt to justify these performances on the grounds of moral enlightenment, but this is only because the essential function of the exhibitions themselves was to enlighten. In reality, the relationship between the main exhibition and the supplementary exhibition bears more than a striking resemblance to the relationship between *kaichō* and spectacles in the Tokugawa period; "supplementary exhibitions" were effectively spectacles (*misemono*).

I also want to bring in an example of an exhibition from Kanazawa City dating from 1872 (Meiji 5). Using the Kenroku'en Garden as the exhibition site, it took place between the sixteenth day of the ninth month and the sixteenth day of the tenth month. The organizers published three volumes of the *Catalog of the Kanazawa Exhibition* (*Kanazawa tenrankai hinmoku*, 1872) in woodblock prints. These volumes provided descriptions of the items displayed at the exhibition, as well as the distinguishing characteristics of the event.[70] The first twenty-one items listed in this catalog were owned by the Maeda family, the feudal lords of the Kaga domain during the Tokugawa period. These items speak to the collection of a wealthy lord: among other lavish utensils and works, they included a set of four hanging scrolls of "birds and flowers of four seasons" attributed to Lü Ji from Ming dynasty China, lacquerware inlaid with mother-of-pearl, a celadon flower vase, and an incense burner in bronzeware. A taxidermied peacock and a reptile known as a *tōda,* which had been pickled in a bottle, were also displayed. (A *tōda* is a sacred snake that produces a cloudy fog, then plays around in it.) These items reflect the taste of hobbyists of encyclopedic studies, particularly the feudal lords during the Tokugawa period.

After the collections of the Maeda family, the catalog listed the following: fifty-one items under the miscellaneous category, twenty-nine swords, 136 items under "gold and jewel work, including shells and minerals," forty-one items under "copper and tin work," thirty-five pieces of lacquerware, twenty-six pieces of textiles, forty-six items of woodwork and bamboo carving, and 287 items of painting and calligraphy. Clearly, paintings and calligraphy included the largest number of items on display. Starting with entries of flower arrangements and "sugar confectionary in the shape of a pair of red snappers," the miscellaneous category included particularly curious objects such as "two mythical spheres of foxes," the bones of a snake, a falcon, and a tiger's head, as well as the horn of a killer whale. Further mysterious objects included "the tail of an imaginary ape," "the hand of a thunder beast" representing an imaginary animal coming down with a thunderbolt, and a six-legged and a three-legged frog. The category of "gold and jewelry, including shells and minerals," which contained the second-largest number of items, included decorative objects and handicrafts made of crystals, agate, jade, and amber, *bonseki* stone ornaments, ink slabs, as well as old coins from Japan and China and oval gold coins of varying sizes. Although it also included gold and silver coins from Western countries, which were rare, all of these items had very little to do with the commercial or industrial sectors. Instead, most of the objects that were displayed were closer to collector's items, or to ornaments for the alcove of a Japanese home where scrolls and the like would be displayed. In addition, on dates ending in one or six, *noh* and *kyogen* performances took place; the titles of the plays and the names of the actors were listed in the third volume of *Catalog of the Kanazawa Exhibition*. This list also informs the reader about the other forms of entertainment that took place, including a tea ceremony, live displays of calligraphy and painting, and the demonstration of a telegraph machine.

This catalog also stated explicitly that some of the exhibited items were for sale, noting: "Those items submitted by people who admire the items and are not willing to pass them on to others are marked with the term 'owned,' and those submitted by people who are willing to make the most of the item by selling it at a reasonable price are marked with the term 'exhibited.'"[71] It seems as if this event was more in line with expositions. However, examining the catalog, one finds only a few items marked as "exhibited." Here it is difficult to detect the kind of attitude that was present at the Domestic Exposition for the Promotion of Industry of 1877 in Tokyo, which clearly aimed to stimulate commercial and industrial activity. Instead, this exhibition in Kanazawa, with its various cultural performances, again brings to mind the close relationship between *kaichō* and spectacles.

Naturally, there were various other regional exhibitions, each with their own particular characteristics. While some regional exhibitions took after Matsumoto and were held at a castle from the Tokugawa period, in most cases the site was a famous temple or shrine.[72] It is also noteworthy that many exhibitions took place in castle towns that had been ruled by wealthy daimyos during the Tokugawa period: the cases of Nagoya in 1871, and Kanazawa and Wakayama in 1872, are fitting examples. Here, we can see that exhibitions were not just held in places that could attract a significant number of visitors; cultural capital accumulated from the Tokugawa period also played a significant role.

SECTION 3: THINGS CHANGE

WORLD EXPOSITIONS AND *MISEMONO* SPECTACLES

The intimate relationship between exhibitions and spectacles (and their close affinity to *kaichō* shows) was not limited to regional exhibitions alone. Even with their at times global scope and commercial aspirations, expositions also shared some qualities with this earlier form of display. The Vienna World Exposition (Weltausstellung Wien) of 1873 was the Meiji government's first experience of a world exposition. In addition to the golden fishlike *shachihoko* ornament from the tower of Nagoya Castle mentioned previously (fig. 7), various other noteworthy items were shown in Vienna. These included a life-size model of the Great Buddha of Kamakura and the great paper lantern from the Kaminarimon Gate of Sensōji Temple (fig. 8). According to *Origins of Things Meiji* by Ishii Kendō, the lantern was "a reproduction of the great lantern at the Kaminarimon Gate in Asakusa, three *ken* (5.45 meters) in diameter, with a great dragon flying in clouds painted on its surface. When hung, six men could easily enter the lantern."[73] Regarding the Great Buddha, Ishii wrote: "After many deliberations, a carpenter was ordered to make a wooden mold of the

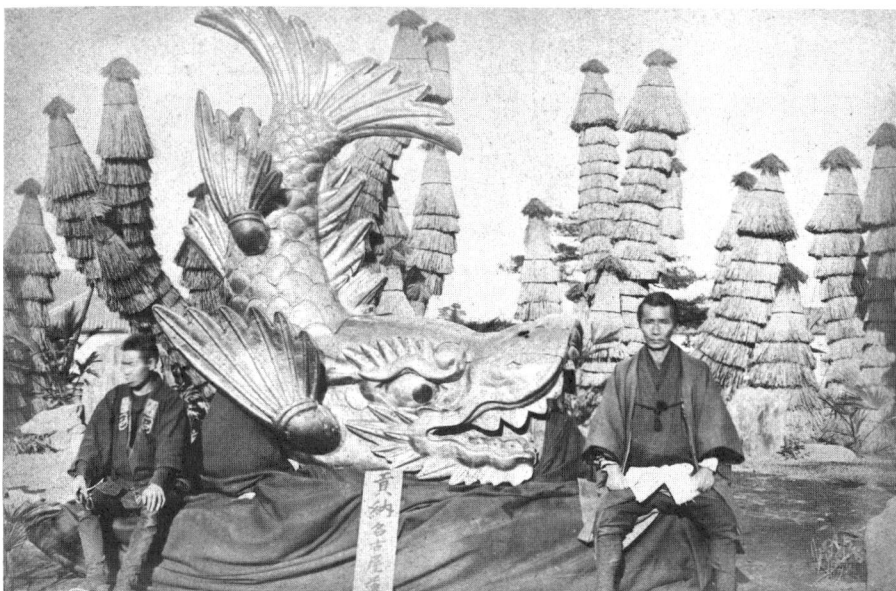

FIG. 7.

Yokoyama Matsusaburō (Japanese, 1838–84).

The golden fishlike *shachihoko* ornament from the tower of Nagoya Castle (Nagoyajō no kinshachi), from *Photographs of Submissions at the Vienna World Exposition in Austria* (*Ōkokuifuhakurankai shuppinsatsuei*), 1872. Albumen print, 11 × 17 cm. Tokyo Kokuritsu Hakubutsukan, E0068123.

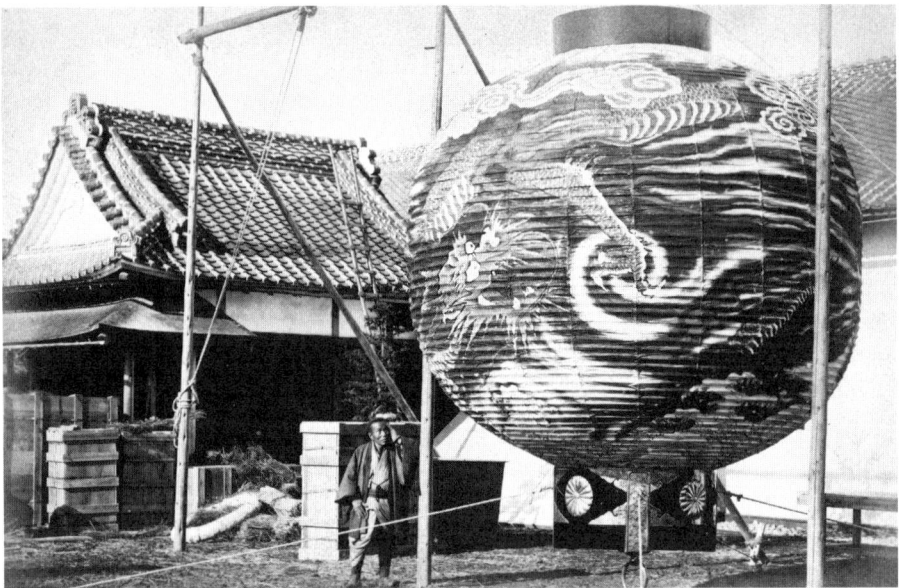

FIG. 8.

Yokoyama Matsusaburō (Japanese, 1838–84). The Great Paper Lantern from the Kaminarimon Gate of Sensōji Temple (Daichōchin), from *Photographs of Submissions at the Vienna World Exposition in Austria* (*Ōkokuifuhakurankai shuppinsatsuei*), 1872. Albumen print, 11 × 16.9 cm. Tokyo Kokuritsu Hakubutsukan, E0068125.

Great Buddha, on which he pasted up paper and varnished it with lacquer after removing the mold... the plan was to display it in the open air to demonstrate the durability of Japanese paper and lacquer."[74] In *Art as Spectacle,* Kinoshita Naoyuki demonstrated that this replica of the Great Buddha was the work of Nezumiya Denkichi, a famed woodcarver and papier-mâché maker. Kinoshita finds it important that the replica was life size.[75] When the papier-mâché of the Great Buddha was finished, according to Ishii, it was then taken apart and shipped in sixty-two large boxes, but "unfortunately, when the boxes were being unpacked, a fire that was caused by the carrier's inattention burned all of its torso, so during the exposition only the head was displayed. Still, the display was very well received."[76] The policy of the government, as seen in this case of the Great Buddha and the great lantern from Sensōji Temple, was to display large and old objects.

The life-size papier-mâché of the Great Buddha, indeed, recalls the series of "huge craftworks" that became a craze at spectacles during the Bunsei period (1818–30). This included the enormous "Great Buddha of Raincoats" and an enormous Buddha in Nirvana made of baskets in 1819 by Ichida Shōhichirō. While an official notice banned these monumental handicrafts from spectacles in 1827, it appears that the Meiji government promoted such "huge craftworks" at the Vienna World Exposition of 1873.

Two officials working for government expositions, Tanaka Yoshio (1838–1916) and Hirayama Narinobu (1854–1929), edited a volume called *Proceedings of Participation in the Vienna Exposition* (*Ōkoku hakurankai sandō kiyō*, 1897). There, they note that they were also advised by Alexander von Siebold (1846–1911) to make "gigantic objects."[77] The work of Gottfried Wagener (1831–92) at the Vienna World Exposition is well known. Wagener, who worked as a teacher at the government-run East School of *Daigaku*, was appointed as the official advisor of the Administrative Office for the Vienna World Exposition and gave numerous suggestions in preparation. After the Vienna Exposition, he compiled a volume titled *Report on the Vienna Great Exposition: Art Museum Section* (*Ifu daihakurankai hōkoku geijutsu hakubutsukan no bu*) in February 1875, including his own article, "Report on Museums of Fine Arts and a Hundred Manufacturers." Here, he examined expositions from the 1851 Crystal Palace Exposition in London onward.[78] Wagener played a similarly important role for the government during the 1876 Philadelphia Exposition.[79]

For his part, Alexander Georg Gustav von Siebold first came to Nagasaki in 1859 (Ansei 6) when his father, the physician, botanist, and Japanologist Philipp Franz von Siebold (1796–1866), re-entered Japan. Philipp von Siebold is known for *Nippon: Archive toward a Description of Japan* (*Nippon: Archiv zur Beschreibung von Japan,* 1832–52) and other publications; he had first arrived in Japan in 1823 (Bunsei 6) as a medical officer for the office of the Dutch East India Company (also known as VOC, Verenigde Oostindische Compagnie) in Dejima, Nagasaki. Having learned Japanese, Alexander remained in Japan after Philipp was forced out of the country in 1862 (Bunkyū 2); he acquired a position at the British Embassy until 1870. During this time, he traveled along with Tokugawa Akitake as a member of the delegation sent by the Tokugawa shogunate to participate in the 1867 Paris Exposition. Siebold continued to thrive within the Meiji government, as his linguistic abilities allowed him to help revise international treaties.

In *Proceedings of Participation in the Vienna Exposition,* he was listed as the "person in charge of receiving foreign visitors." Wagener was listed as the "person in charge of examining the provenance of exhibits and other items and advising on techniques."[80] This text also noted: "According to a proposal by Baron Alexander von Siebold, a German foreign employee, it was decided that one or two enormous objects would be displayed. Since the customs of the Far East are rare sights in Europe, it is necessarily the case that visitors there would pay attention to what we submit. It was also decided that we would submit golden fishlike ornaments, a papier-mâché of the Great Buddha of Kamakura, a scale model of a pagoda at Tennōji Temple in Yanaka, a large *taiko* drum, and a great paper lantern; we would also build a garden, a Shinto shrine, and a shop."[81] From this, we can imagine the content of Siebold's suggestions. The government also sent a model for the pagoda of Tennōji Temple in Yanaka, as well as a large drum. One of the fishlike ornaments from Nagoya Castle was also submitted based on this idea.

While Alexander von Siebold was familiar with European matters, he was also well informed about circumstances in Japan, having lived there since 1859. He had probably heard of or seen *kaichō* shows and spectacles. If he had advised the government based on his familiarity with such entertainments, Siebold would most likely have thought about things like a papier-mâché of the Great Buddha of Kamakura or the great lantern of Kaminarimon Gate at Sensōji Temple.

A similar example can also be found in the case of the 1867 Paris World Exposition. According to Yoshimi Shun'ya, at this event "a merchant from Edo named Shimizu Usaburō opened a Japanese-style teahouse on the exhibition grounds; it became popular through the service provided by geisha. Top spinner Matsui Gensui and many other entertainers went abroad and performed at the exposition."[82] Shimizu Usaburō (1829–1910) was born into a sake-brewing family in Hanyū (present-day Saitama prefecture) and was said to have studied under Mitsukuri Genpo (1799–1863) at the Institute for the Study of Barbarian Books, an office the Tokugawa shogunate established in 1856 (Ansei 3). For the Paris Exposition he was appointed as the general representative of the exhibitors.[83] During his stay in Paris he became an assistant to the Japanologist Léon de Rosny (1837–1916). Shimizu published the Japanese newspaper *Rumors at Large* (*Yo no uwasa*), which used lithographic technology incorporating his own handwriting.[84] In Osatake Takeki's *To the Barbarian Countries: Tales of Overseas Delegations in Bakumatsu* (*Bakumatsu kengai shisetsu monogatari: Iteki no kuni e,* 1989), Rosny is described as "someone who was knowledgeable of the Japanese language, and absorbed in things Japanese. He lived his life in Japanese style, drinking matcha tea, smoking fine-cut tobacco in a Japanese pipe, and reading Japanese books such as *Chronicles of Japan* [*Nihongi*] and *Unofficial History of Japan* [*Nihon gaishi*] by Rai Sanyō (1780–1832). He had more than ten publications on Japan, including a Japanese-French dictionary, and was a teacher of Japanese at a language school."[85] Shimizu returned to Japan in the fifth month of 1868 (Keiō 5), bringing with him a type printer and a lithographic printer, among other things. He also wrote a memoir of this time, "On the Beginnings of Type and Lithographic Printers" ("Sekiban oyobi insatsu kikai no ranshō ni tsuite," 1901).[86]

One could say that Shimizu Usaburō, with his knowledge of the West, and Alexander von Siebold, with his experience of the Bakumatsu transition in Japan, stood in contrasting positions. It is rather curious, then, that these two shared similar approaches to expositions. Siebold had, in fact, traveled with the Tokugawa shogunate's delegation to the 1867 exposition in Paris. It is fair to imagine that the thought behind Siebold's suggestions for the Vienna Exposition came in part from the popularity of the teahouse and the performances that Shimizu had orchestrated there. As we have seen, various forms of entertainment were made available at *kaichō* shows in Edo in *expectation* of a large crowd: spectacles, theatrical performances, sumo tournaments, and teahouses operated there precisely because they knew crowds were already flocking to the site. By contrast, in Paris and Vienna the spectacle shows and teahouses were included in order to *attract* visitors. Here, the close and intertwined relationship between *kaichō* and spectacles was brought directly into the context of world expositions.

In *The Politics of Expositions: Imperialism, Commercialism, and Popular Entertainment,* Yoshimi Shun'ya cites a newspaper article published in 1890 which noted that "among ordinary people, those who regard expositions as similar to spectacles (*misemono*) are relatively large in number."[87] Yoshimi then pays close attention to the fact that even in this article, published a month before the opening of the third Domestic Exposition for the Promotion of Industry in Ueno in April 1890, there was "a great gap" between governmental approaches to the expositions and the ways in which the public received them. In fact, he noted that "because the continuity with the *misemono* practices from the Tokugawa period was maintained, expositions were received relatively easily by the Meiji public from early stages."[88] We can position the practices brought from *misemono* spectacles to the world expositions by Shimizu Usaburō and Alexander von Siebold within the logic of Yoshimi's argument.

At the same time, it is worth pointing out the fact that people at the Paris and Vienna expositions accepted the Japanese teahouse, acrobatic performances, with tops, a life-size papier-mâché of the great Buddha of Kamakura, and the great lantern of the Sensōji Temple. In other words, could it be possible that the idea of expositions, which nominally originated in Europe, shared a certain logic with *kaichō* shows and spectacles? Expositions were extraordinary, ceremonial spaces in which a large crowd came to a specific area for a particular period. Regardless of their differing purposes, expositions, spectacles, and *kaichō* practices during the Tokugawa period all produced a particular kind of festive space. If we approach these phenomena diachronically, and narrate a history that begins with *kaichō* and leaves them behind as we move toward exhibitions and expositions, we will miss certain connections between them. It is only when we position *kaichō,* spectacles, expositions, and museums synchronically that we begin to see the elements that are shared among them.

GLASS CASES

In April of 1874 (Meiji 7), writer and journalist Hattori Bushō (1841–1908) published the book *New Tales of Tokyo Prosperity* (*Tokyo shin hanjō ki,* 1874–76). This title followed the format of another popular book from the Tokugawa period, Terakado Seikan's *Tales of the Prosperity of Edo* (*Edo hanjō ki,* 1832–36). Hattori and his book were well received, and by 1876 a total of six volumes had been published. In 1874, two different books with similar titles were published: *An Account of Prosperity by Enlightenment in Tokyo* (*Tokyo kaika hanjōshi*) by popular literature author Hagiwara Otohiko (1826–86) and another book of the same title by the writer Takamizawa Shigeru (d. 1875); both of these were published in four volumes. A few more books with similar titles appeared after *New Tales of Tokyo Prosperity,* but none of them sold particularly well.[89] In the third volume of Takamizawa's book, though, there is an illustration captioned "A View of an Exhibition" that described the smaller-scale practice of exhibitions. This illustration depicted the exhibition organized by the Ministry of Education at the museum in Uchiyamashitachō in March 1874 (fig. 9).⁹⁰

The image depicted the exhibition room in single-point linear perspective. It appears that the room had skylight windows in the ceiling, and that the room was large and well lit. In particular, the tall exhibition cases along the sides of the room and the two rows of display cases positioned parallel to them in two straight lines stand out. These cases used sheets of glass. In the text of the book, Takamizawa

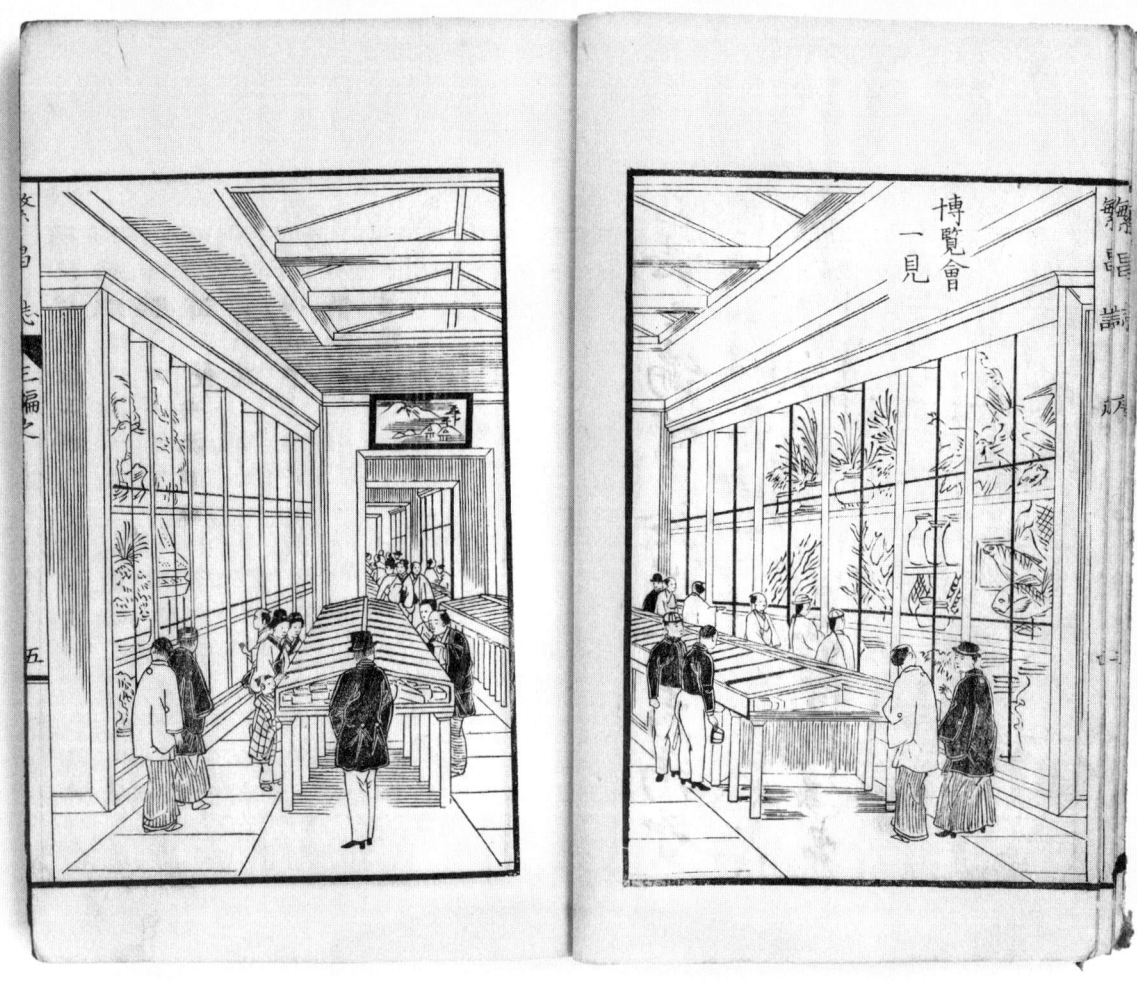

FIG. 9.

Takamizawa Shigeru (d. 1875). *A View of an Exhibition (Hakurankai ikken)*, from *An Account of Prosperity by Enlightenment in Tokyo (Tokyo kaika hanjōshi)*, 1874. Woodblock print, page 22.3 × 15.1 cm. Tachikawa, Kokuritsu Kokugo Kenkyūjo, W193/Ta43/3.

wrote: "In front, the shouldered palanquin with wicker roofing [*Ajiro no katakoshi*] was displayed, with a stone sculpture next to it. This stone was white, and depicted the emperor of Austria. In addition, there were several types of maps of the greater Tokyo area. Turning left at this point, one saw continuous glass display cases."[91] Turning left to the exhibition room, one probably encountered a scene similar to the one depicted in the illustration.

In 1869, Murata Fumio, who later founded the satirical magazine *Marumaru chinbun*, published the book *Record of Things Seen and Heard in the West*. There he noted that at the British Museum in London, various rare things from around the world were displayed, and that "by making boxes and doors with glass plates to avoid dust, and by using medical liquor to protect against decay, the collected things are preserved very effectively. Thus, they very effectively accumulate and house these items." Actually, sheets of glass in display cases were one of the most particularly symbolic products of civilization and enlightenment. There is a set of photographs depicting scenes from the exhibition by the Ministry of Education at Yushima Seidō, a Confucian temple in Tokyo, in the third month of 1872 (Meiji 5). Among these images are numerous impressive cases built for this occasion. Indeed, these cases used sheets of glass covering the front (fig. 10). One of the pair of golden fishlike ornaments from Nagoya castle, too, was displayed inside of a glass case with complicated wooden framing at this site in the open air (fig. 11).

Edward Morse arrived in Japan in June 1877 and visited the museum in July, leaving an account of this visit in *Japan Day by Day*. He noted: "I examined another museum in Tokyo, an industrial art museum, and there saw many models of their coal mines, bridges, dams, and models to show how they protect their river embankments from erosion.... In this museum were collections sent from the South Kensington Museum—English porcelain and pottery. The cases were gracefully made and the glass was French plate. The halls were finished in cedar."[92]

The *Guide to the Site of the Domestic Exposition for the Promotion of Industry in 1877*, from which I have already quoted, helps us to understand that the "industrial art museum" Morse visited in 1877 is, in fact, the museum in Uchiymashitachō that Takamizawa Shigeru had referred to in his *Account of Prosperity by Enlightenment in Tokyo* of 1874. The *Guide* contains a supplementary article that introduces other facilities related to the domestic exposition in Tokyo, in which a "museum" is mentioned with a description of the facility: "Located at lot number 1, Uchiyamashitachō. The Museum Bureau of the Home Ministry administers it.... There are eight exhibition rooms in the museum.... This museum stores many valuable and refined items that the South Kensington Museum donated."[93] When Morse visited the site in 1877, he undoubtedly entered the same exhibition room illustrated in Takamizawa's book, identified some of the exhibits donated by the South Kensington Museum, and saw that the glass plates used for cases in the room were Frenchmade.

The plan for the exhibition in 1874 at the museum in Uchiyamashitachō had been to exhibit items obtained at the Vienna Exposition (either through sales or exchange) the previous year. However, the French ship *Neil,* which contained the first shipment of these items, sank off the coast of the Izu peninsula.⁹⁴ Although the plan for the exhibition had to be changed because of this accident, the exhibition opened in March of the same year. *The Catalog of Displayed Imported Objects* (*Hakuraihin chinretsu mokuroku,* 1874), published for this exhibition, reveals that many items obtained in Vienna managed to escape a watery demise.⁹⁵ It might have been that the French-made glass sheets were imported to create new display cases at this point, and that the new cases were the ones depicted in *An Account of Prosperity by Enlightenment in Tokyo.*

Either way, it is important to note that these glass display cases were a requirement for both the museum and the exhibition. It is easy to imagine that they needed high-quality glass to show the objects inside without distortion, and that the organizers decided to order French glass on these grounds. But we should consider why it was important to insist on glass for the display cases. Here, we can begin to see some of the significant differences between *kaichō* shows and spectacles of the previous period in comparison to the newer forms of museums and exhibitions.

Sano Tsunetami (1822–1902), from the Saga domain, is known as the father of the Japanese Red Cross Society. More important to this study is the fact that Sano thrived in various practices of display both at home and abroad; these projects served as a kind of billboard for the industrializing policies of the Meiji

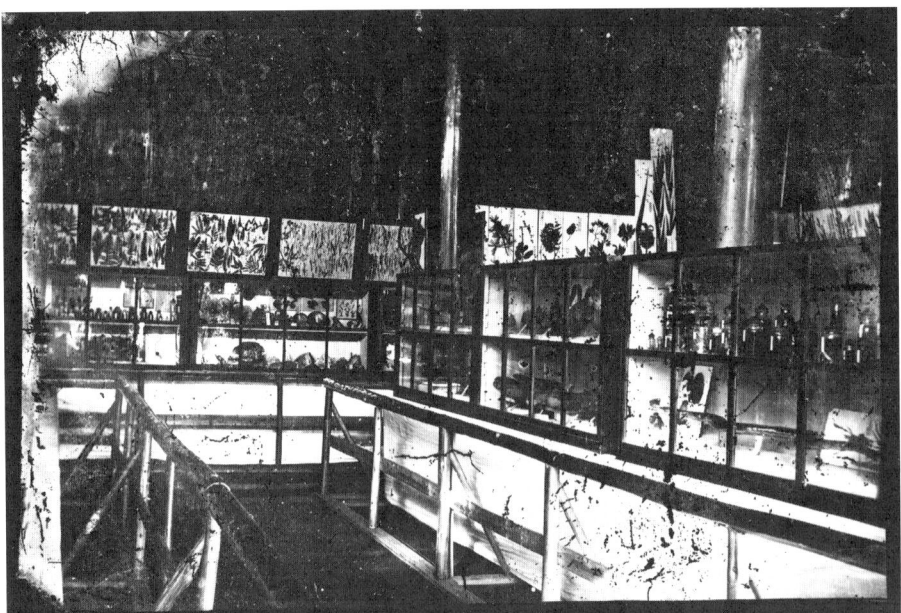

FIG. 10.

Inside the *Daiseidō* at Yushima Seidō at the 1872 Exhibition, 1872.

Albumen print, 7.6 × 10.8 cm. Edo-Tokyo Hakubutsukan, 91214187.

government. At the Vienna Exposition, he worked as the deputy director of the Exposition Bureau within the Central Council of the Grand Council of State. In the entry of the first volume of the "Museum section" in *Report on the Vienna Exposition,* Sano's stance toward the display techniques and museum is clearly stated at the beginning:

> The purpose of the museum is to develop knowledge and skills of people by learning through perception. Now then, what touches the minds of people when observing objects stems most frequently and impressionably from the power of visual perception. Think of the fact that when people speak different languages, and are thus unable to communicate emotions and intent, hand gestures enable

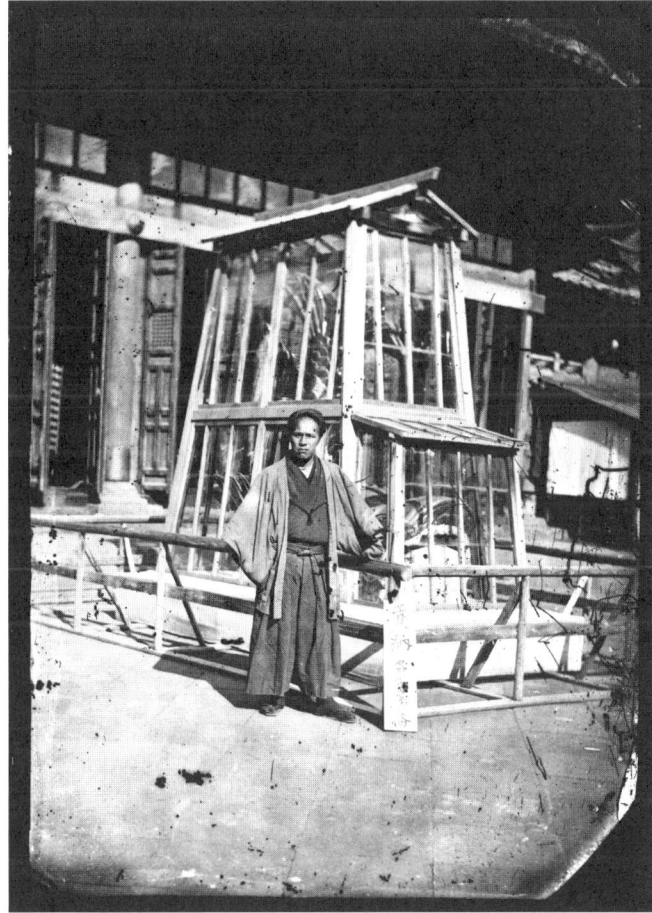

FIG. 11.

Display of the golden fishlike ornament from Nagoya Castle at the 1872 Exhibition, 1872. Albumen print, 7.8 × 10.9 cm. Edo-Tokyo Hakubutsukan, 91214192.

general principles to be understood between them. So it cannot but depend on the power of the eye that one can understand the way to produce and use a thing through its form and appearance alone, or to cause a feeling of love and hate to well up on the basis of the beauty or ugliness of a thing. As ancient people have said, one eyewitness is better than a hundred hearsays. Learning through the eye is the most effective and accessible way to develop people's wisdom and advance arts and industries. This is the reason why recently in Western countries, each country competes to construct museums, to demonstrate to its people rare objects and necessary items from across the world, let their citizens examine them as they wish, and by this guide and encourage them.[96]

What Sano was seeking in museums also fitted into his vision of display practices: "Expositions share the same purpose as museums, in that they are also based on the intent to bring out enlightenment of the people that would then serve as a resource for national wealth. In short, a world exposition is nothing but the expanded and enriched form of a museum, held over a short time. In other words, these two are not mutually exclusive."[97]

Giving a privileged position to perception entails suppressing or eliminating other sensory faculties. In *An Account of Prosperity by Enlightenment in Tokyo*, Takamizawa Shigeru reported on the interior of the museum in Uchiyamashitachō in 1874 (Meiji 7). He noted, for example, "everywhere, there is a notice not to touch the objects" (see fig. 9).[98] This prohibition of touching is nothing other than the elimination of the tactile sense from viewers' experience. A similar prohibition appeared in a set of regulations compiled for the exhibition of 1873.[99] The same document includes another notable entry: "Inside the museum, going up and down on wooden clogs or low clogs is prohibited; only shoes, sandals woven from straw, and sandals with leather soles are permitted."[100] This regulation was probably issued in consideration of the sound wooden clogs make on wooden floors. This extraneous sound made by viewers inside the museum became a target.

At *kaichō* shows during the Tokugawa period, orators who would explain to the visitors the histories of the displayed objects played an integral role. In *An Account of the Prosperity of Edo,* Terakado vividly recorded the acts of orators at "traveling" *kaichō*. The appearance of an orator wearing a formal kimono was depicted in an illustration of Kōriki Enkōan's *A Record of Kaichō Shows of Holy Treasures of Ryūkōji Temple* (see fig. 4). At spectacles, too, orators were indispensable. However, in Meiji display practices and museums that aimed to maximize the effect of "learning through perception," the roles of orators were nowhere to be found. Not only that, audible sounds came to be removed from the sites as being noise; it was understood as an obstacle to the process of "learning through perception." The superiority of visual perception thus came to suppress the auditory sense. The transparent and non-distorting sheets of glass used on the display cases then, can be, understood as the metaphor of the eye, of which much was expected here.

NECESSARY THINGS AND UNNECESSARY THINGS

The rise of expositions, exhibitions, and museums saw a shift from offering money to enter a *kaichō* show, or paying an admission fee to enter a spectacle, to purchasing tickets. This represents a dramatic shift in the format and infrastructure of entertainment. However, the expectations for and dependence on "the power of visual perception" at museums and public display sites also paved the way for a much more fundamental change, which was related to the process through which meaning was ascribed to the exhibited objects themselves. Yoshimi Shun'ya explained this change: "Expositions provided the space of gaze in which, according to the transparent taxonomic order, all things that could be 'discovered' on the earth were ordered as signs. When positioned in this space, whether it was an object or a person, all things were equally symbolized."[101] The same argument can be made of museums. What, then, did the process of "symbolization" look like in actuality?

In general, the goals that Sano Tsunetami laid out in *Report on the Austrian Exposition* in 1875 (Meiji 8) were actualized in the 1877 Domestic Exposition for the Promotion of Industry. In the text "Advice to Visitors" included in the *Guide to the Site of the Domestic Exposition for the Promotion of Industry in 1877,* the key point visitors had to keep in mind was "to compare articles." In addition, it also noted that while "it is the principal duty of judges to decide the relative merits of the items," it also asked that "all visitors entering the site are expected to assume the same attitude as these judges."[102] For the visitors to decipher the "relative merits of the displayed items," it was necessary for them to use the function of "the power of visual perception" carefully. That the *Guide* concluded in the last section that the success of the exposition was "up to the general visitors and how they use perception to observe the displayed items" spoke directly to a significant reliance on "learning through perception." The fact that the text spoke of the potential failure of an exposition in terms of becoming "a kind of spectacle (*misemono*) site" emphasized the idea that spectacles, like *kaichō* shows, were things of the past. By doing so, the organizers were able to insist that nothing could be further from exposition sites—where "learning through perception" through "the power of visual perception" took place—than *kaichō* shows and spectacles, in which miscellaneous noise and quarrels were commonplace.

At the same time, the practice that the *Guide* extols—"to compare articles" and judge the "relative merits of the items" through "the power of perception"—entailed much larger issues concerning the exhibited objects. First, there was the issue of the conditions under which comparisons and judgment of relative merits was possible. Second, there was the question of what these comparisons and judgments would bring to the exhibited objects. A brochure titled *Guidelines for Exhibitors to the Domestic Exposition for the Promotion of Industry in 1877* (*Meiji jū nen naikoku kangyō hakurankai shuppinsha kokoroe,* 1877) was published by the Exposition Bureau for those who submitted items to the expositions. The content of the second article from this publication is particularly intriguing, as it indicates concretely where the problems lay. "Even if it is rare, objects such as deformed birds, animals, insects, fish, as well as old roof tiles, comma-shaped beads from ancient times, calligraphy, and paintings and the like should not be submitted at this exposition. In general, submissions ought to be necessary things in the lives of people with a prospect of further improvement and flourishing, or objects that could be sold more widely within the country. Objects the submitter intends to sell abroad, or objects with outstanding craftsmanship and ideas worth considering, are the priorities of this exposition."[103]

Most suggestive here is the list of prohibited objects at the beginning of the section. At the 1872 exhibition in Kanagawa that we analyzed earlier, items such as the dried bodies of a three-legged or six-legged frog were included in the miscellaneous category. These two examples correspond to the deformed animals listed at the beginning of this document. What were the reasons for their prohibition? There must have been numerous excuses. From the point of view of the principles behind exhibition practices, though, it was because these objects were all highly individuated in and of themselves, making it difficult "to compare articles" through "the power of perception." It could have been possible to compare the three-legged frog to the six-legged frog, but what kind of merit could be drawn from such a comparison? As long as the comparison did not yield a meaningful interpretation, even with "the power of perception," judging the relative merits of the two was meaningless.

The basic condition that made it possible "to compare articles" through "the power of perception" was the fact that articles stood on equal footing with each other. The three-legged frog existed without establishing any connection to other things at the exhibition; so long as individual things insisted on their inherent value, it was impossible to make comparisons among them. In other words, it was necessary for certain commonalities to exist in tandem with differences in order for things to be compared. That is, there had to be a common denominator between the articles to be compared. Unless such a common ground could be guaranteed, the act of comparison would be meaningless.

Thus, a second requirement for judging the "relative merits of articles" was a standard of evaluation. At the Domestic Exposition for the Promotion of Industry of 1877, the government stated that one of its aims was "to support the progress in various sectors of engineering and industries and to increase the profit through local products and foreign trade." What suited this aim were the "necessary things in the lives of people." The prohibited things at the beginning of this section, namely rare articles, were deemed unnecessary. Following this logic, the world of objects was divided into necessary and unnecessary things. The standard to draw this dividing line between the two became precisely the standard for judging the "relative merits of articles." The text listed two kinds of rare articles, deformed creatures and "old roof tiles, comma-shaped beads from ancient times, calligraphy, and paintings and the like." The former did not meet the first condition of standing on equal footing with other objects, while the latter failed to meet the second condition of necessity to "the lives of people."

What, then, did the practice of comparing articles by judging the relative merits of things through "the power of visual perception" bring to the exhibited things? One effect was that things came to be understood as a representation of something else. For example, commodities fulfill the first condition of sharing the same footing with other objects, and each one can easily be substituted by something similar. This is possible because one object is only a representative example of a larger group of objects and its classificatory category. In other words, an object comes to represent something other than itself. This is precisely the process of "symbolization" that I discussed earlier in this section. In other words, the process of symbolization entailed a display of things as a sample, as an example, or as a representation of something else.

A second effect was that items became inseparable from their status as representations. By being displayed in public, objects became exemplary demonstrations of the standard itself. At the same time, the second condition of necessity to life also called for the careful selection of objects. Here, it's not only the case that "necessary things in the lives of people" were distinguished from unnecessary things, but also that the very selection on the basis of this standard demonstrated the standard itself to the public. The production of value entails distinguishing objects that do not meet a standard from those that do. This process was not based on a simple binary selection or multiple choice. Instead, it asked a fundamental question about the object itself: whether it possessed any inherent value.

It seems to me that that the effect of objects becoming representations and objects of selection was also inseparable from the mode of viewing objects through "the power of visual perception." Yet there is another crucial issue lurking here.

Let us examine the category of "old roof tiles, comma-shaped beads from ancient times, calligraphy, and paintings and the like," which was prohibited alongside deformed creatures. It is striking to note that the proposition to establish a *shūkokan* issued in 1871 by Daigaku understood objects like "old roof tiles, comma-shaped beads from ancient times, calligraphy, and paintings" as *kokikyūbutsu* (see chapter 2). In addition, the proposition recognized these objects as significant "articles for the examination of the past." This document, which deployed *historical* function as its criterion of judgment, regarded these objects as "necessary things." Although the criteria of the 1871 proposition and the 1877 regulations differ, the logic by which objects are judged to be necessary or unnecessary is the same. By the time of this later document, objects like "roofing tiles and comma-shaped beads from ancient times, calligraphy, and painting" had fallen out of favor, and were considered merely as rare, unnecessary things.

Such things that were deemed unnecessary demonstrate the standards of the selection process in general. In other words, if they were presented in this context, these objects signified a specific, absent past. In the end, the Domestic Exposition for the Promotion of Industry of 1877 demanded that the exhibited objects be representatives, samples, and examples of products and commodities.

As we have seen, there was an enormous distance between the *kaichō* shows and spectacles on the one hand, and museums and public displays on the other. Within the space dominated by "the power of visual perception" at the museums, exhibitions, and expositions, the world of things past sooner or later began to fluctuate widely, and underwent a significant transformation. As we will examine in chapter 5, the category of *kokikyūbutsu* emerged as a new concept that contained the possibility of transforming things past into objects that represented a past extending beyond their own specificity. This concept thus enabled the sifting of things past, and created a standard of value based on "articles for the examination of the past." To put it differently, *kokikyūbutsu* could be the object of a judgment based on "the power of visual perception." If such an environment was prepared through the use of glass display cases, then the beginning of this history leads us back to the experiences abroad shared by the members of the overseas delegations during the Bakumatsu period.

NOTES

1   Fukuzawa Yukichi, *Fukuzawa zenshū* (Tokyo: Jiji Shinpōsha, 1898), 1:26.

2   Keiō Gijuku, *Fukuzawa Yukichi zenshū* (Tokyo: Iwanami Shoten, 1969), 1:285.

3   Keiō, *Fukuzawa Yukichi zenshū*, 1:312.

4   Keiō, *Fukuzawa Yukichi zenshū*, 1:312.

5   Yoshimi Shun'ya, *Hakurankai no seijigaku: Manazashi no kindai* (Tokyo: Chūō Kōronsha, 1992), 18.

6   Ishii Kendō, *Meiji jibutsu kigen* (Tokyo: Chikuma Shobō, 1997), 324.

7   Numata Jirō, "Bakumatsu no kengai shisetsu ni tsuite: Man'en gannen no kenbei shisetsu yori Keiō gannen no ken'ō shisetsu made," in Numata Jirō and Matsuzawa Hiroaki, eds., *Seiyō kenbunshū* (Tokyo: Iwanami Shoten, 1974), 600–607.

8   This was an incident regarding the ratification of the Treaty of Amity and Commerce with the United States, in which Emperor Kōmei refused to give the imperial sanction approving the treaty to Iwase and other leaders of the shogunate. Consequently, the shogunate was compelled to conclude the treaty with the United States without the imperial sanction.

9   Matsuzawa Hiroaki "Samazama na seiyō kenbun: 'Ijō tansaku' kara 'yōkō' e," in Numata and Matsuzawa, *Seiyō kenbunshū*, 623–24.

10 Eight volumes of manuscript by the author. For reprints, see Numata and Matsuzawa, *Seiyō kenbunshū*, 7–259.

11 In the entry of the eleventh day of the third month of Man'en 1 (1860). Numata and Matsuzawa, *Seiyō kenbunshū*, 51.

12 Matsuzawa, "Samazama na seiyō kenbun: 'Ijō tansaku' kara 'yōkō' e," 627.

13 Ōtsuka Takematsu, ed., *Kengai shisetsu nikki sanshū* (Tokyo: Nihon Shiseki Kyōkai, 1928), 1:95.

14 Kinoshita Naoyuki, *Bijutsu to iu misemono: Aburae jaya no jidai* (Tokyo: Heibonsha, 1993), 22.

15 Tamamushi would come to experience the extreme ups and downs of life after returning to Japan in 1860. He was imprisoned for supporting the position of Aizu domain, which had fought for the Tokugawa shogunate during the Boshin war. He would then commit harakiri suicide. See Numata Jirō, "*Tamamushi Sadaiyū to Kōbei nichiroku*," in Numata and Matsuzawa, *Seiyō kenbunshū*, 553–55.

16 Entry of the sixth day of the third month of Man'en 1 (1860) in the *Journal of a Voyage to the United States*, in Numata and Matsuzawa, *Seiyō kenbunshū*, 77–79.

17 Osatake Takeki, *Bakumatsu kengai shisetsu monogatari: Iteki no kuni e* (Tokyo: Kōdansha, 1989), 39–40.

18 Numata and Matsuzawa , *Seiyō kenbunshū*, 98.

19 Numata and Matsuzawa, *Seiyō kenbunshū*, 98–99.

20 Numata and Matsuzawa, *Seiyō kenbunshū*, 101. In glossing the name of the Smithsonian Institute, Tamamushi renders the name in katakana as "*sumefuriunen inshirāchūto*." Similarly to the case with the "Patent Office" entry in the original Japanese, rendered in katakana as "*patento ofuyushi*," a tireless effort of Tamamushi to render the audible English terms into script form can be sensed.

21 Numata and Matsuzawa, *Seiyō kenbunshū*, 101.

22 Numata, "Bakumatsu no kengai shisetsu ni tsuite: Man'en gannen no kenbei shisetsu yori Keiō gannen no ken'ō shisetsu made," in Numata and Matsuzawa, *Seiyō kenbunshū*, 599.

23 Tokyo Kokuritsu Hakubutsukan, *Tokyo Kokuritsu Hakubutsukan hyakunenshi: Shiryōhen* (Tokyo: Tokyo Kokuritsu Hakubutsukan, 1973), 546–53.

24 Kurimoto Joun, *Hōan jisshu* (Tokyo: Kyūsenkan, 1869). For reprints, see Shiota Ryōhei, ed., *Narushima Ryūhoku, Hattori Bushō, Kurimoto Joun shū* (Tokyo: Chikuma Shobō, 1969), 293–374.

25 Kurimoto, *Hōan jisshu*, 41v–42r; and Shiota, *Meiji bungaku zenshū* 4, 310.

26 Kurimoto, *Hōan jisshu*, 15r–15v; and Shiota, *Meiji bungaku zenshū* 4, 304.

27 Murata Fumio, *Seiyō bunkenroku* (Hiroshima: Idzutsuya Shōjirō, 1869), 3:12v–13r. For reproduction, see Murata, *Seiyō bunkenroku*, ed. Asakura Haruhiko (Tokyo: Yumani Shobō, 1987), 156–57.

28 Kinoshita, *Bijutsu to iu misemono,* 13.

29 Kinoshita, *Bijutsu to iu misemono,* 13.

30 According to Hiruma, the first stage covered from the Jōō period (1652–55) to the Genbun period (1736–41), the middle stage is from the Kanpō period (1741–44) to the Tenmei period (1781–89), and the last is from the Kansei period (1789–1801) to the Keiō period (1865–68).

31 Hiruma Hisashi, "Edo no kaichō," in Nishiyama Matsunosuke, ed., *Edo chōnin no kenkyū* (Tokyo: Yoshikawa Kōbunkan, 1973), 344.

32 The Eitaiji Temple was the attendant temple (*bettōji*) of Tomigaoka Hachimangū Shrine. Nishiyama, *Edo chōnin no kenkyū,* 428.

33 Saitō Chōshū, Natsuo Ichiko, and Ken'ichi Suzuki, *Shintei Edo meisho zue* (Tokyo: Chikuma Shobō, 1997), 69.

34 Terakado Seiken, *Edo hanjō ki,* reprinted in Terakado Seiken, *Edo hanjō ki,* reprinted in *Edo hanjō ki, Ryūkyō shin shi,* Narushima Ryūhoku, Hino Tatsuo, and Stake Akihiko (Tokyo: Iwanami Shoten, 1989), 140.

35 Among the in-house *kaichō* shows for people in Edo, the Avalokiteśvara (the bodhisattva of mercy and salvation) of Sensōji Temple in Asakusa, and the Sarasvati (goddess of learning and arts, *benzaiten*) of Enoshima Shrine in Sagami province (present-day Kanagawa prefecture) were the most popular. For the traveling shows, the four major attractions were Amitabha (Amida), bodhisattva of salvation, from Zenkōji Temple (in present-day Nagano city); Acala (Fudō), the god of fire, from Narita-san Shinshōji Temple (in present-day Chiba prefecture); Shakamuni (Shaka), the Buddha, from Seiryōji Temple in Kyoto; and the wooden portrait sculpture of the venerable Nichiren, the founder of the Nichiren sect, from Minobu-san Kuonji Temple (in present-day Yamanashi prefecture). Hiruma, "Edo no kaichō," 433.

36 Terakado, *Edo hanjō ki,* 141. The priest referred to as Kōbō in the quote is identified as Kūkai (774–835), who introduced esoteric Buddhism from Tang dynasty China and founded the Shingon sect.

37 Ryūkōji Temple is a temple of the Nichiren sect located in Katase village of the Kamakura area in Sagami domain. Tamamuro Fumio, "Edo bakufu no shūkyō tōsei," in Tsuji Nobuo, ed., *Shomin Bukkyō* (Tokyo: Shinchōsha, 1990), 71.

38 Terakado, *Edo hanjō ki,* 142.

39 Hiruma, "Edo no kaichō," 421.

40 Hiruma, "Edo no kaichō," 444.

41 This can be found in the section "Votive items in the traveling show of Narita Fudō" from his *Miscellaneous Writings on Wanderings* (1829). Daijō Keijun (1760–1832), the chief priest of Honpōji Temple in Kobinata, Edo (in present-day Bunkyō ward).

42 Jippōan Keijun, *Yūreki zakki* (Tokyo: Hōbun Shokan, 1992), 423.

43 Jippōan, *Yūreki zakki,* 423. See also Hiruma, "Edo no kaichō," 438.

44 Hiruma, "Edo no kaichō," 438.

45 One *jō,* measuring 10 *shaku,* is equal to approximately 3.03 meters.

46 Hiruma, "Edo no kaichō," 443.

47 Kinoshita, *Bijutsu to iu misemono,* 61.

48 Asakura Musei, *Misemono kenkyū* (Kyoto: Shibunkaku Shuppan, 1977), 223.

49 Hiruma, "Edo no kaichō," 444.

50 Hiruma, "Edo no kaichō," 438.

51 Hiruma, "Edo no kaichō," 472.

52 Ishii, *Meiji jibutsu kigen,* 6:303.

53 Ishii, *Meiji jibutsu kigen,* 6:303.

54 [Naikoku Kangyō Hakurankai Jimukyoku, ed.], *Meiji jū nen naikoku kangyō hakuran kaijō annai* (Tokyo: Naikoku Kangyō Hakurankai Jimukyoku, 1877), 1.

55 Glossed in hiragana as *mite no kokoroe.*

56 *Meiji jū nen naikoku kangyō hakuran kaijō annai,* 1.

57 *Meiji jū nen naikoku kangyō hakuran kaijō annai,* 1–2.

58 *Meiji jū nen naikoku kangyō hakuran kaijō annai,* 2–6.

59 Takamura Kōun, *Bakumatsu ishin kaikodan* (Tokyo: Iwanami Shoten, 1995), 123.

60 Takamura, *Bakumatsu ishin kaikodan,* 123.

61 Takamura, *Bakumatsu ishin kaikodan,* 123.

62 Takamura, *Bakumatsu ishin kaikodan,* 124–25.

63 Ishii, *Meiji jibutsu kigen,* 6:315.

64 Takamura, *Bakumatsu ishin kaikodan,* 127.

65 Maruyama Hiroshi, "Meiji shoki no Kyoto hakurankai," ed. Yoshida Mutsukuni (Kyoto: Shibunkaku Shuppan, 1986), 229–30.

66 Terashita Tsuyoshi, *Hakurankai kyōki* (Osaka: Ekisupuran, 1987), 361–67.

67 Ishii, *Meiji jibutsu kigen,* 6:318.

68 Chikuma Hakurankai Kaisha, ed., *Chikuma kenka Matsumoto hakurankai kisoku* (Matsumoto: Matsumoto Hakuran Kaisha), 1873, 6r. A volume of the printed brochure including "Hakurankai jo" by Matsumoto Hakurankaisha is dated 10 October 1973. A copy of the brochure is in the collection of the Matsumoto city archives in Nagano prefecture.

69 *Chikuma kenka Matsumoto hakurankai kisoku,* 6v.

70 The organizer deployed the term *tenrankai*, rather than *hakurankai*, to refer to their exhibition.

71 *Kanazawa tenrankai hinmoku* ([Kanazawa:] unknown, 1872), 1:1r: Hanrei. For reprints, see Tokyo Bunkazai Kenkyūjo, *Meijiki fuken hakurankai shuppin mokuroku: Meiji 4–9* (Tokyo: Chūō Kōron Bijutsu Shuppan, 2004), 156.

72 The exhibitions at Itsukushima Shrine (present-day Hiroshima prefecture) in the sixth month of 1872 and at Kotohira Shrine (present-day Kagawa prefecture) in March 1873 are exemplary in this regard. These cases underline the affinity between exhibitions and *kaichō*.

73 Ishii, *Meiji jibutsu kigen*, 6:312.

74 Ishii, *Meiji jibutsu kigen*, 6:312–13.

75 Kinoshita, *Bijutsu to iu misemono*, 28–31.

76 Ishii, *Meiji jibutsu kigen*, 6:313.

77 Kinoshita, *Bijutsu to iu misemono*, 28.

78 "The Section of Museums" in *Report on the Vienna Exposition,* published in March 1875, includes "Report by Dr. Wagener on the Establishment of Tokyo Museum," in Ueda Toyokichi, ed., *Waguneru den* (Kyoto: Hakurankai Shuppan Kyōkai, 1925), 41–62, 63–68.

79 *Report on the Vienna Exposition*, 13–19.

80 "Ōkoku hakurankai zuikō oyatoi gaikokujin shokumu buntan jin'in hyō," in "Furoku" (appendix), Tanaka Yoshio and Hirayama Narinobu, eds., *Ōkoku hakurankai sandō kiyō* (Tokyo: Moriyama Shun'yō, 1897). For reprints, see Fujiwara Masato, ed., *Meiji zenki sangyō hattatsushi shiryō*, appendix 8, no. 2 (Tokyo: Meiji Bunken Shiryō Kankōkai, 1964), 9.

81 "Shuppin no saishū," in Tanaka and Hirayama, *Ōkoku hakurankai sandō kiyō*, 1:16.

82 Yoshimi, *Hakurankai no seijigaku*, 116.

83 Ono Tadashige, *Nihon no sekihanga* (Tokyo: Bijutsu Shuppan, 1967), 41.

84 Mashino Keiko, "Nihon ni okeru sekihanjutsu juyō no sho mondai: Ninagawa Noritane *Kanko zusetsu tōki no bu* san 'Fugen' o megutte," in Machida Shiritsu Kokusai Hangabijutsukan, ed., *Kindai Nihon hanga no shosō* (Tokyo: Chūō Kōron Bijutsu Shuppan, 1998), 166–67.

85 Osatake, *Bakumatsu kengai shisetsu monogatari*, 182–83.

86 Shimizu Usaburō, "Sekihan oyobi insatsu kikai no ranshō ni tsuite," *Meika dansō* 18 (February 1897): 68–69.

87 *Tokyo Nichinichi shinbun*, 27 February 1890.

88 Yoshimi, *Hakurankai no seijigaku*, 135.

89 Ishikawa Gen, "Kaidai," in Meiji Bunka Kenkyūkai, ed., *Meiji bunka zenshū* (Tokyo: Nihon Hyōron Shinsha, 1955), 8:10–11.

90 Kinoshita, *Bijutsu to iu misemono*, 241.

91 Takamizawa Shigeru, "Hakurankai," in *Tokyo kaika hanjōshi* (Tokyo: Yamatoya Kihei, 1874), 18r–18v. For reprints, see Meiji Bunka Kenkyūkai, ed., *Meiji bunka zenshū*, 3:280.

92 Edward S. Morse, *Japan Day by Day: 1877, 1878–79, 1882–83* (Boston and New York: Houghton Mifflin, 1917), 1:149.

93 "Hakubutsukan," Appendix: "Tokyo ni aru yūeki no basho," in *Meiji jūnen naikoku kangyō hakuran kaijō annai*, 44–45.

94 Tokyo Kokuritsu Hakubutsukan, *Tokyo Kokuritsu Hakubutsukan hyakunenshi*, 91, 160–62.

95 Tokyo Kokuritsu Hakubutsukan, *Tokyo Kokuritsu Hakubutsukan hyakunenshi: Shiryōhen*, 184–93.

96 Sano Tsunetami, "Hakubutsukan bu: Hakubutsukan ichi," in Ōkoku Hakurankai Jimukyoku, *Ōkoku hakurankai hōkokusho* (Tokyo: Ōkoku Hakurankai Jimukyoku, 1875), part 3, 1r–v. For the discussion by Yoshimi Shun'ya on Sano's argument, see Yoshimi, *Hakurankai no seijigaku*, 119–21.

97 Sano, "Hakubutsukan bu," part 3, 1r–v.

98 Takamizawa, "Hakurankai," 19r.

99 "Sadame" by Hakurankai Jimukyoku, dated March 1873, a notice posted in the museum building. See Tokyo Kokuritsu Hakubutsukan, *Tokyo Kokuritsu Hakubutsukan hyakunenshi*, 94.

100 Tokyo Kokuritsu Hakubutsukan, *Tokyo Kokuritsu Hakubutsukan hyakunenshi*, 94.

101 Yoshimi, *Hakurankai no seijigaku*, 113.

102 Naikoku Kangyō Hakuran Jimukyoku, *Meiji jū nen naikoku kangyō hakuran kaijō annai*, 4.

103 Anon., *Meiji jū nen naikoku kangyō hakurankai shuppinsha kokoroe* (n.p., 1877), 22. A printed brochure bound into a volume with other brochures, the volume entitled "Meiji jū nen naikoku kangyō hakurankai kisoku chō," personally compiled by Tanaka Yoshio, an official of the Administrative Office for Expositions. The volume of brochures is in the collection of the General Library, University of Tokyo.

CHAPTER 4

Active Antiquarians

SECTION 1: PLACING THINGS SIDE BY SIDE

THE 1871 EXHIBITION OF LOCAL PRODUCTS

Each format of exhibition practice we have examined so far—*kaichō*, *misemono*, expositions, and museum exhibitions—produced a space where many people gathered for a short time within a specific site. Although these spaces were organized for different reasons, they shared the fact that they all produced an extraordinary and festive area. In addition, in each case the ability to attract a significant crowd was crucial to their success. When expositions emerged in the early Meiji period, people were aware that they were new, but they could accept them by understanding them along the same lines as *kaichō*'s paradigm of "the new and the old," which was brought about through the governmental emphasis on civilization and enlightenment, called spectacles (*misemono*) a bygone entertainment under the category of "the old"; the government worked to highlight the difference between spectacles and expositions. Through experience, people began to understand the privileged position given to visual perception in expositions and museums. Along with this assimilation of the power of perception, the significance and meanings of things that were displayed inside the glass cases also began to shift.

However, there is another context that needs to be considered in the beginnings of expositions and museums in Meiji. On the topic of an exhibition, Ishii Kendō noted in *Origins of Things Meiji* (*Meiji jibutsu kigen*, 1908): "The exhibition at the Yushima Seidō, which served as the origin of an exhibition practice, was not merely an enlarged curio gathering [*kottōkai*] or *honzō* gathering [*honzōkai*] that those *honzō* scholars [*honzōka*] had organized in the past. The Ministry of Education organized it, and thus it had a strong flavor of museums."[1]

Ishii was referring to the exhibition organized by the Museum Bureau at Yushima Seidō in the third month of 1872. He added, "This exhibition was comparable to the *bussankai* exhibits organized by the *honzō* scholars, and merely collected and showed things past and things rare in an unorganized manner."[2] Here Ishii deployed terms such as *honzō scholars*, *curio gatherings*, *honzō gatherings*, *bussankai*, and *things past* (*kobutsu*). In other words, he saw among the early exhibition practices of Meiji a continuous relationship to the study of *materia medica* (*honzōgaku*) during the Tokugawa period. Similarly, I suspect he also used terms such as *curio gatherings* and *things past* because he had antiquarians in mind.

As we explored in chapter 1, a year before this exhibition at the Yushima Seidō, the Bureau of Local Products at the South School of Daigaku organized the Exhibition of Local Products at Shōkonsha Shrine in the Kudan area of Tokyo. At the initial stage of its planning, the event was referred to as an "exhibition" (*hakurankai*).[3] If we situate this fact as a kind of ancestral return, then, Ishii's observation of the early exhibitions as the extension of the study of *materia medica* in the Tokugawa period was astute. The Exhibition of Local Products was smaller in scale and shorter in duration. It began on the fourteenth day of the fifth month and lasted seven days. The Shōkonsha Shrine had been completed just two years prior as a place to commemorate those who had lost their lives fighting in the imperial forces against the shogunal forces in the Boshin War.[4]

A manuscript of the catalog of exhibited items in the 1871 Exhibition of Local Products, "Catalog of the Gathering of Local Products in the Year of *Shinpi* of Meiji" (*Meiji shinpi bussankai mokuroku*) sits today in the collection of the Tokyo National Museum. It lists not only the name of each item but also its taxonomic classification and the name of its exhibitor.[5] According to this catalog, the main three categories were "Mineral," "Plant," and "Animal." In addition to these, there were sections for "Measuring and Scientific Instruments," "Internal and Surgical Medical Instruments," "Ceramics," "Items of the Past," and "Miscellaneous." "Mineral" consisted of three subcategories: "Fossil" section, "Stone and Soil" section, and "Ore" section. In the list of items there are objects with the same name, or cases in which a similar item appears repeatedly. If we count each exhibited item on its own and ignore such repetitions, "Mineral" contained the greatest number of items, with 808. The "Plant" category included 512 items, separated into subcategories of "Austrian Plant section," "Tree" section, and "Grass" section. The "Animal" category contained 698 items, with subcategories of "Birds," "Fish," "Shellfish," "Insects," and "Reptiles" sections, showing a systematic structure. The total number of items submitted to these three categories came to 2,018, while the total number for the entire exhibit came to 2,347. In other words, the three main categories accounted for 86 percent of the total items, and thus served as the central part of this event. As the name Exhibition of Local Products indicates, this event was much closer in content to the Tokugawa period gathering of the same name (*bussankai*) than to exposition practices from abroad.

At the same time, there were certain aspects here that only could have emerged through the Restoration. The "Animal" category made a notable distinction between "Live Animals" and "Skeletons and Illustrations" in one group, and "Taxidermy" in another. In the "Bird" and the "Fish" sections, too, a similar separation was made, with "Caged Birds" and "Live Fish" in one group, and "Taxidermy" in another. Just as members of overseas delegations during the Bakumatsu were surprised to see taxidermy in museums, seeing displays of taxidermy was a novel experience for many. Shifting our focus to items outside of the three main taxonomies of mineral, plant, and animal, we note numerous novel items, although their total number was limited to 329. Of particular note are the thirteen items under "Measuring and Scientific Instruments" and twenty-one under "Internal and Surgical Medical Instruments." In addition to a microscope, a telescope, and a barometer, it contained a "model of solar system rotation." In "Internal and Surgical Medical Instruments," the items displayed included instruments for surgery and dissection, a model of the human anatomy, models of eyeballs and of male and female sexual organs, and a set of models of fetuses in pregnancy from the first to the ninth months. In numerical terms, "Ceramics" contained the most, with 130 exhibited items. These included ceramics produced in various areas across the country, rather than select rare pieces from the past. In *Conditions in the West* (*Seiyō jijō*, 1866), Fukuzawa Yukichi noted that expositions "gather together notable products, useful instruments, old and rare items through notification and show these to people from around the world"; such aspects can be seen in the 1871 Exhibition of Local Products.

Would it be fair to characterize this event as consisting of elements of both the new and the old? Such an equivocal interpretation would, I think, ignore the historical tides of time. The exhibitions of local products, a type of exhibition practice known as *bussankai* that had taken place since the Tokugawa period, must have also faced the issues emerging from the paradigm of "the new and the old." Sooner or later, such a gathering would have been labeled as "the old" under these circumstances. How, then, did organizers of such gatherings respond to this issue?

PROFILES OF THE EXHIBITORS: TANAKA YOSHIO AND ITŌ KEISUKE

Characteristics of the earlier exhibitions of local products are also apparent in the exhibitors. According to the catalog mentioned above, among the 2,347 items exhibited at this event, only 462 were owned by the government. Including one item submitted by the Ministry of Technology, the number of government-owned items thus came to less than 20 percent of the total. In other words, individuals submitted over 80 percent of the items exhibited. Among them, Tanaka Yoshio submitted the highest number to the event, with 752 objects. After Tanaka, the following individuals submitted overwhelmingly large numbers of items: Itō Keisuke with

341, Takemoto Yōsai with 319, and Uchida Masao with 348. The catalog noted that Uchida donated 344 of these items, almost all of them to the government. In total, forty individuals participated in this event by submitting their personal belongings. Let us examine the most important among them.

Tanaka Yoshio (1838–1916), whose quantity of submissions dwarfed the number of those belonging to the government, was in the position of an organizer, as he was an official employed by the Bureau of Local Products at the South School of Daigaku. He was born in Iida, Shinano domain (present-day Iida city in Nagano prefecture), and studied under Itō Keisuke, a scholar of *materia medica* based in Owari domain. Accompanying his teacher, Tanaka moved to the city of Edo when Itō was appointed as an official of the learning of local products at the Institute for the Study of Barbarian Books in 1861.[6] The following year, Tanaka was appointed the assistant official at the Institute for the Study of Barbarian Books. Tanaka was sent to Paris for the Paris Exposition, in which the Tokugawa shogunate participated, and he actively helped the administrative office of exhibited items. To find items for the exposition, Tanaka collected insects from the domains of Sagami, Suruga, and Shimousa (present-day prefectures of Kanagawa, Shizuoka, and the north part of Chiba), and tried producing specimen samples in the Western style. The Institute for the Study of Barbarian Books was renamed the Institute for Studying the West under the Tokugawa shogunate, which was taken over by the Conglomerate of Garrisons (Chindaifu) in 1868 and then absorbed under the new Meiji government. Tanaka remained in his position then, and was later appointed as the official adviser at the Institute for Studying the West. For a while, Tanaka took part in the construction of the Institute of Physics and Chemistry (Seimikyoku) in Osaka with Mitsukuri Rinshō, but in the ninth month of 1870, he returned to Tokyo when the Bureau of Local Products at the South School of Daigaku was established. When Daigaku was abolished in the seventh month of 1871, Tanaka moved to the newly established Ministry of Education. In the first month of 1872 he was appointed as the official advisor for the Vienna Exposition of 1873 and traveled there. When the Museum Bureau moved from the Ministry of Education to the Home Ministry and then the Ministry of Agriculture and Commerce, Tanaka moved to these different ministries. He played significant roles at the 1876 Philadelphia Centennial International Exposition and the series of Japan's Domestic Expositions for the Promotion of Industry that began in 1877 in Tokyo. At the same time, he founded associations such as the Society of Agriculture of Greater Japan and the Society of Fisheries of Greater Japan, and took part in the improvement of plant breeds.[7] Tanaka collaborated with the scholar of *materia medica,* Ono Motoyoshi (1843–90), and in 1874 published *Newly Revised Illustrated Explanations of Plants and Trees of Japan* (*Shintei sōmoku zusetsu*). This publication added new Linnaean names to Iinuma Yokusai's twenty-volume *Illustrated Explanations of Plants and Trees of Japan* (*Sōmoku zusetsu,* 1856). For the publication of the revised edition of the original volumes, Tanaka received advice and proofreading help from Paul Savatier (1831–91), a botanist who came to Japan in 1866 to work as a medical officer at the ironworks in Yokosuka operated by the Tokugawa shogunate.[8] In addition to these activities, Tanaka edited and published numerous didactic books and translations such as *Useful Botany Illustrated* (*Yūyō shokubutsu zusetsu*, 1891).

Returning our attention to Tanaka as an exhibitor in 1871, most of his submissions fall under the three main categories of mineral, plant, and animal, reflecting his engagement with the study of local products that began in his study of *materia medica*. Particularly notable are 204 items under the "Stone and Soil" section, 86 items under "Ore," and 122 items under "Seeds, Fruits, and Pressed Leaves of Trees," in which domestic and foreign plants useful for food and medicine were collected. Tanaka also submitted 119 items, including products from Europe and America, to the "Ceramics" section; these items accounted for almost all of the 130 items in this section. The breadth of his interests, which included industrial products, is impressive. In addition, he submitted ten stone implements such as stone axes, stone arrowheads, and "spoon-shaped scraper stones" to the "Items of the Past" section.

More than anything, Tanaka's quality as a collector is epitomized by a series of personal scrapbooks he made. He gave a proper title to each of these books, such as "Album of the Found and Gathered," "Album of the Found and Gathered in Foreign Countries," "Album of Wide Knowledge," and "Album of Encyclopedic Knowledge." Inside each of these albums are items of various kinds that interested Tanaka, from an announcement flyer and a commodity label to a train timetable and a menu card of a restaurant.[9] In particular, the ninety-eight volumes of "Album of the Found and Gathered," which Tanaka began at the age of twenty-one in 1859 and continued until his death in 1916, are a highlight of this work.[10] One could argue that the attitude of this collector over half a century from the Bakumatsu on sustained a particular consistency.

Itō Keisuke (1803–1901), who submitted 341 items to the event, served as Tanaka's mentor and was a central figure in the study of *materia medica* in Owari domain (the western part of present-day Aichi prefecture). He had studied natural history under Philipp Franz von Siebold in Nagasaki in 1827. As Itō was leaving, Siebold gave him a copy of *Flora Japonica* by the Swedish botanist Carl Peter Thunberg (1743–1828), and Itō published his translation of this book as the three-volume *Nominal Differentiations in Western* Materia Medica (*Taisei honzō meiso*, 1829). This translated book marked the first publication that applied the Linnaean taxonomic system to plants in Japan. In 1861 Itō was appointed as the official for the study of local products at the Institute for the Study of Barbarian Books in Edo, but resigned from the position in the twelfth month of 1863 and returned to Nagoya, leaving his responsibilities at the institute to his disciple Tanaka. In 1870 he moved again to the city now known as Tokyo, when he responded to a request from the Meiji government to work for Daigaku. In the seventh month of the following year, he became an employee of the Ministry of Education. In 1877 Itō became a Special Professor at the Faculty of Science at the newly established University of Tokyo. In 1880 he took charge of the botanical garden in Koishikawa.[11]

After arriving in Japan in June 1877, Edward Morse soon met Itō Keisuke through the introduction of David Murray (1830–1905), who had been a superintendent of educational affairs for the Ministry of Education.

> The other afternoon a distinguished old Japanese by the name of Ito called on Dr. Murray, and I had the honor of being presented to him. He is an eminent botanist and was president of a Japanese Botanical Society in 1824. He had come to bring to Mrs. Murray the first lotus in bloom. He was in full Japanese dress, though he had abandoned the queue. I regarded him with the greatest interest, and thought how Dr. Gray and Dr. Goodale would have enjoyed meeting this mild and gentle old man, who knew all about the plants of his country.[12]

Morse introduced Itō in a favorable light, and added a sketch of Itō sitting on a chair. Itō studied *materia medica* under Mizutani Hōbun (1779–1832) of the Owari domain. Mizutani was the leader of a group of scholars of *materia medica* known as the Shōhyakusha, and after Mizutani's death Itō had led their collective activities. Morse must have meant Shōhyakusha when he referred to "a Japanese Botanical Society." The Dr. Gray of this section most probably refers to Asa Gray (1810–88), who studied Japanese botany. When Morse discussed collectors in Japan, he also included Itō by noting, "Dr. Ito, the famous botanist, whom I have already mentioned in the early pages of the journal, has a large collection of plants."[13]

The items Itō submitted to the Exhibition of Local Products centered on the mineral category. In its subsection "Fossils," he submitted twenty-six items, including "a fossil of a flounder, from Utsumi village in Chita county, Owari province." Under the "Stone and Soil" section, he submitted 253 items, including "a crystal from Mount Suishō in Kokura, Buzen domain" (the eastern part of present-day Fukuoka prefecture and the northern part of Ōita prefecture). This outnumbers Tanaka Yoshio's submission to the same section, which included 204 specimens. Tanaka's scrapbook, "Album of Encyclopedic Knowledge," includes a piece of an ink rubbing of the flounder fossil. In the "Ore," section, Itō submitted fifty-three items, including "a stone of sulfur from Mount Ontake." In the categories of "Plant" and "Animal," he submitted only one item each, which were "dried pressed leaf herbariums of trees and plants from India" and "a tusk of a walrus," respectively. Morse had noted Itō's vast plant collection, and considering that his disciple Tanaka had submitted items in each category, we can easily imagine that Itō only submitted a small fraction of his collection to this exhibition.

In addition, Itō submitted seven items under "Items of the Past," which included "comma-shaped beads," "stone axes," and "stone arrowheads" from prehistoric times. While Itō studied under Siebold in Nagasaki, he had written a short essay titled "On Comma-Shaped Beads" in Dutch for Siebold, who was collecting materials on Japan. Itō's own collection of these items was also well known. It included about 270 stone implements mostly consisting of stone arrowheads; the collection is contained in nine small wooden boxes, measuring about twenty centimeters wide. Each stone arrowhead is wrapped in *mino* paper, on which the domainal names of their origin, such as Shinano, Mino (the south part of present-day Gifu prefecture), and Hida (the north part of Gifu prefecture), were inscribed in india ink. These are telling historical examples of how these items were collected. Itō also was a member of the editing team for *Products of Japan* (*Nihon sanbutsu shi*, 1873–77), published by the Ministry of Education in eleven volumes. In one of the volumes, titled "Part of Mino Region" published in 1876, Itō contributed illustrations of stone implements such as stone axes, stone rods, stone arrowheads, and "spoon-shaped scraper stones" under the "Mineral" section. Itō used items from his own collection for the productions of these illustrations.[14] Although it is difficult to identify precisely which items from his own collection were submitted to the Exhibition of Local Products in 1871, these facts more than suffice to help us imagine the vastness of the type and quantity of objects in Itō's collection.

Gatherings in the interest of local products and *materia medica* and gatherings of calligraphy and paintings had been practiced since the Tokugawa period. These forms of collective exhibitions, in which participants displayed their own items, required a central figure who instigated the gathering: the "meeting sponsor" (*kaishu*). In the case of gatherings of calligraphy and painting, in addition to the sponsor, there were roles for those who assisted the sponsor and contributed to gatherings by submitting items from their own collections. These included roles such as "meeting assistant" (*kaiho*), "steward" (*shitsuji*), "leading member of the meeting" (*kaikan*), or "assistant" (*hojo*). They could consist of five or six members, or sometimes even more than one hundred. There are said to have been gatherings of such a large scale that they attracted over a thousand participants.[15] The announcement flyers for these gatherings inform us of various types and formats to gatherings of calligraphy and paintings, and in most cases, they were organized by a central figure, a "meeting sponsor," supported by "assistants," "a secretary" (*kanji*), or "a tutor" (*kōken*), a group collectively numbering between one to a dozen, and who were in turn assisted by over a few dozen "assistants."[16] The number of members in the organizational committee reflected the scale of the gathering.

A similar structural format was also deployed in the case of exhibitions of local products. When we review this basic historical format of the exhibition practice, we can discern the central figure at the Exhibition of Local Products in 1871 by focusing on the number of submitted items. With an overwhelming number of 752 items, the role of Tanaka Yoshio was akin to that of a meeting sponsor. Rather than submitting the entirety of his collection, Itō Keisuke, Tanaka's mentor, focused on the category of "Mineral" to maintain the balance among the three main categories of mineral, plant, and animal. For this reason, Itō played a role similar to that of a tutor of his disciple.

At the time of the 1871 exhibition Tanaka was an official working for the Bureau of Local Products at the South School of Daigaku, but surprisingly, he was also a notable collector who was able to submit a large number of items from his own collection. While 462 items owned by the government were distributed evenly among the three main divisions, it is difficult to say that they formed the core of the exhibition in comparison to the total number of exhibited items. Rather, the fact that over eighty percent of the items belonged to private collections is worth exploring. It is reasonable to assert, then, that the Exhibition of Local Products in 1871 was organized in accord with the basic structure of local product gatherings, which were orchestrated by individual collectors who responded to an invitation to display their collections. The exhibitors and visitors at this exhibition most likely were familiar with this continuity in the structural format. Along with Itō Keisuke, Takemoto Yōsai and Uchida Masao also submitted over three hundred items each. From this point of view, these two figures also played a role of the "leading member of the meeting" or the "steward" for the gathering. Indeed, their submissions were concentrated on the three categories of mineral, plant, and animal that Tanaka had excelled in, and for this reason, Takemoto and Uchida served fitting roles as assistants to Tanaka in the role of the meeting sponsor. The remaining thirty-six exhibitors provided from one to a few dozen items and, therefore, can be seen as playing the role of assistants.

PROFILES OF THE EXHIBITORS: TAKEMOTO YŌSAI AND UCHIDA MASAO

Most of the 319 items submitted by Takemoto Yōsai consisted of items in the section "Plants on Trays [*bonshu*]" under the "Plant" category. These were bonsai, or potted dwarf trees. Takemoto provided seventy-three to the "Tree" section of "Plants on Trays," and 196 to its "Grass" section. In the former instance, his submissions were notable for their focus on subtropical trees originating in Ryūkyū and Annam, whereas in the case of the latter, most items were plants for appreciation such as lilies, orchids, and cacti.[17] Indeed, Takemoto was a well-known skilled gardener from the Bakumatsu period, among other things creating new breeds of morning glory.[18] In the "Animal" category, Takemoto submitted a Pekinese dog and a guinea pig under the "Live Animals" section, and seven items such as koi, crucian carp, and goldfish to the subsection of "Live Fish" under the "Fish" section. In all of these cases, Takemoto was the only exhibitor who submitted items to the subsections of live animals and fish. In total, thirty-nine items were submitted to the subsection of "Birds in Cages" under the "Bird" section, and Takemoto submitted thirty-six of these. Among them were rare and foreign birds such as parrots and the like, "a quail from Choson" that "was imported during the Keiō period (1865–68)," and a *tojukei* pheasant from India that was "imported in 1870."[19] Takemoto's submission concentrated on the categories of plant and animal. Most of the items that Takemoto submitted were objects to be appreciated or items for hobbyists; in this sense, there is a stark contrast here between the items Tanaka Yoshio submitted, which were mostly edible or contained medicinal qualities.

Takemoto Yōsai was originally from the direct vassal class of the shogun (*hatamoto*). Between 1861 and 1864, he served twice as magistrate of foreign affairs (*gaikoku bugyō*), handling decisive diplomatic issues such as the Namamugi Incident.[20] In the third month of 1868, Takemoto was dismissed from the work of *rusui* and did not work for the new Meiji government after the Restoration.[21] One of the reasons Takemoto's name became recognizable was the invention of Takemoto ware, which he developed in collaboration with his heir, Takemoto Hayata (1848–92). It seems natural that his interest in plants would expand to an interest in plant pots and bonsai pots. The father-son team, who had lost their stipend from the Tokugawa shogunate after the Restoration in 1867, started a ceramic business the next year, for which they hired ten potters at their residence located in Takada village of Kita Toshima county (present-day Takada area of Toshima Ward). Their business stood within a plot of land measuring around 3.28 acres, or four thousand *tsubo*. They mostly produced export goods such as ceramic vases and jars with the brand name Gansui'en, and this endeavor was quite successful. I have already discussed Shimizu Usaburō, who became well known at the Paris Exposition when he opened a Japanese teahouse. Takemoto learned a method of casting vessels using plaster molds from Shimizu that enabled mass production of complicated shapes of porcelain. In 1873 their factory was burned completely, and the business was forced to close. However, Takemoto Hayata restarted Gansui'en, and, around 1877, made an upright circle kiln at his factory. This kiln made it possible to use a casting process using plaster molds, the process his father Yōsai was unable to accomplish. Hayata continued to submit works in Takemoto Ware to Domestic Expositions for the Promotion of Industry, and received numerous rewards.[22]

At the Exhibition of Local Products in 1871, Takemoto Yōsai submitted many pottery pieces to the ceramics section in addition to the section of "Plants on Trays." More specifically, I am referring here to two entries: "one hundred and thirty items of pottery pieces," and "twenty-eight items of homemade pottery." The term "homemade" here needlessly points to the fact that these were Takemoto Ware pieces bearing the Gansui'en brand. These entries suggest they had already a large collection of ceramics, probably to use in *bonsai* or for other potted plants. Among the 119 ceramic items submitted by Tanaka Yoshio, two are noted as coming from "the kiln of Gansui'en," indicating the proximity of the relationship between Tanaka and Takemoto. In addition, Takemoto organized a "small Exhibition of Local Products" in the tenth month of 1871 at Gansui'en, followed by a gathering for foreigners titled "Exhibition" at the same site in the next month. In the third month of 1872, he organized a "small Exhibition of Local Products" at the Denpōin temple in Asakusa.[23] Although the details of these exhibitions and their scale are not known, they attest to Takemoto's effort to link his interest and hobby to a business.

Along with Takemoto, Uchida Masao is another person who befits the role of the "head of gathering." Out of 348 items he submitted, Uchida donated 344 to the government. Among the donated items, 316 items were exhibited under the "Shellfish" section under "Animal." Because of these submissions, the number of items submitted under "Animal" came to almost the same as those under "Plant," thereby providing a sense of equilibrium among the main categories of minerals, plants, and animals. Among those under "Shellfish" section were four kinds of shellfish that were of French origin; this was probably a by-product of Uchida's experience studying in Holland before the Restoration. Uchida also submitted five specimens of taxidermied animals such as a porcupine and a pangolin. Under the subsection "Taxidermy" in the bird section, he submitted a parrot, a peacock, and a set of "twenty-seven kinds of rare birds from various countries," totaling twenty-three donated items. In addition, he brought in three items he did not donate, such as "a bird belonging to the genus of *Gallus* from Himalayan mountains" with the scientific name "*Rohohorus impeanius*."[24] Unlike Takemoto, who submitted items to "Live Animals" and "Birds in Cages," all of Uchida's submissions to the animal section were taxidermies, which he acquired while he was traveling in Europe. His submissions to the shellfish section were probably shells, not live shellfish. In addition, among the items submitted by Takemoto under the subsection of "Plants on Trays" of the "Grass" section, we find "*gasteria,* belonging to the genus of *Aloe,* an item brought back by Mr. Uchida." This entry reveals not only the relationship between Uchida and Takemoto but that Uchida brought back rare plants from Europe. It is also noteworthy here that under "Miscellaneous," Uchida submitted "framed oil paintings, seven by Westerners."

Like Takemoto, Uchida Masao was also from a family of the vassal class directly retained by the shogunate. After studying at the Institute of Confucian Learning, Uchida learned navigational skills and languages at the Nagasaki Naval Training Center, after which he became an assistant to a professorial instructor at the Warship Training Center in Tsukiji, Edo. He then received an order from the Tokugawa shogunate to study abroad in Holland and left in the sixth month of 1862. The shogunate delegation totaled nine: five members from the Warship Team, or shogunate navy, including Enomoto Takeaki, Akamatsu Noriyoshi, and Uchida; Tsuda Mamichi and Nishi Amane from The Institute for the Investigation of Western Books (Yōsho shirabesho); and another two medical students, Itō Genpaku and Hayashi Kenkai. Uchida, whose stipend was fifteen hundred *koku,* the most substantial allowance among the members, became the supervisor of this group. Although the ostensible purpose of the trip was to absorb naval technology and knowledge while the Dutch constructed a warship that the Tokugawa shogunate had ordered, Uchida remembered that he hardly learned anything about the navy. Instead, already having developed a discerning eye and a skill for sketching, he went to sketch landscapes and customs of various places. He researched oil painting by studying under a painter on site, and had made some progress by the time he returned. Such stories were passed on by Uchida's close friend, and a member of the student group, Akamatsu Noriyoshi (1841–1920). According to Akamatsu, when they visited the South Kensington Museum (renamed the Victoria and Albert Museum in 1899) Uchida was impressed with the jewelry and other items looted from the Qing dynasty displayed there. Akamatsu also recalled stories that revealed Uchida's hobby in antiquities.[25]

Uchida returned to Japan in the third month of 1867 and was ordered by the Tokugawa shogunate to work as an official at Bureau of the Inspection of Schools (Gakko torishirabe goyō kakari) along with Mitsukuri Rinshō and Fukuzawa Yukichi.[26] After the Restoration, Uchida worked at Daigaku and the South School of Daigaku, and became an intermediate professor of the Ministry of Education (*Monbu chū kyōju*) in 1871. In the fourth month of 1872, Uchida was appointed as an official in the sixth rank of the Ministry of Education, with a concurrent post in the Museum Bureau of the ministry. In the eighth month of the same year, he participated in the inspection of treasures known as *Jinshin*. Uchida resigned from public positions in July 1873. Beginning in 1870, he published *Concise Topography of the World* (*Yochi shiryaku*, 1870–77), which consisted of eleven parts in twelve volumes. This was a didactic book that surveyed geography, climate, customs, and histories of various countries in Asia and Europe. Along with *Conditions in the West* by Fukuzawa, and *The Story of Self-Made Men in the Western Countries* (*Saigoku risshi hen*, 1870–71), a Japanese translation by Nakamura Masanao of Samuel Smiles' *Self-Help*, *Concise Topography of the World* was one of the most widely read books of that time. The photographic images Uchida had collected during his study in Europe were used as the basis for the variety of illustrations in this book.[27] Although the publication of *Concise Topography of the World* was temporarily suspended with his passing in February 1876, its publication was completed in 1877.

The total number of items submitted by Tanaka, Itō, Takemoto, and Uchida at the exhibition of local products in 1871 comes to 1,760. This means that over three-quarters of the items on display came from these four collections. What is particularly significant here is the fact that both Takemoto and Uchida were from vassal-class families, or the former retainers of the shogun, while both Tanaka and Itō worked for the Institute for Studying the West operated by the Tokugawa shogunate. As historian of science Nakayama Shigeru has noted:

> Although various systems set up by the Tokugawa shogunate were supposed to be completely dissolved by the Meiji Restoration, many educational institutions set up by the shogunate surprisingly continued to operate. The Institute of Confucian Learning, which was central to study of Confucianism; the Institute for Studying the West, which taught Western studies in general; and the Institute for Medical Studies, which taught Western medicine were all temporarily closed. However, immediately after the restoration, these institutions

reappeared with new names, such as Shōhei School, Kaisei School, and the Medical School. These were exceptional institutions in which certain continuities were maintained before and after the Restoration, especially in regards to the people and their structures.[28]

In 1861, Itō Keisuke worked in the Institute for the Study of Barbarian Books as an official for the study of local products; this institute was renamed the Institute for the Investigation of Western Books when the building moved away from the Kudan area in the fifth month of 1862. It was renamed again in the eighth month of 1863 as the Institute for Studying the West. In 1868, the Institute for Studying the West was taken over by the Conglomerate of Garrisons and became known as the Kaisei School. While some members of these institutions, such as Nakamura Masanao and Nishi Amane, left the Institute for Studying the West and relocated to the Shizuoka area in order to follow the last shogun, Tokugawa Yoshinobu, others like Tanaka Yoshio continued to work for the same institution under the new government.

Tanaka Yoshio left a fascinating essay, "Narrative of My Career," which includes his recollection of the time around the downfall of the Tokugawa shogunate:

> General society became noisier around the fourth year of Keiō, a year of *boshin*, which then became the first year of Meiji. But since my task was to engage the works that I had been asked to do, I looked into the encouragement of industry related to the Bureau of Local Products, and cultivated various plants; I was never involved in worldly affairs. In the fifth month of the same year, a civil war began in Ueno. Even then, as we were told it was dangerous to be outside, we observed the battle from the watchtower with professors, like guards. After the Ueno war ended, things in Edo changed dramatically. I received an order from the government on the eighteenth day of the sixth month and became an official advisor to the Institute for Studying the West. Since the Institute for Studying the West was to be continued under the new government, we, the employees became advisors at the Institute for Studying Western Learning.[29]

In May 1912 an exhibition titled *Commemorating the Seventy-Sixth Birthday of Mr. Yoshio Tanaka* was held in Akasaka, Tokyo. His speech at this event was later published as "A Talk on Experience by Mr. Yoshio Tanaka" in its commemorative publication. It is not strange that given the fact his recollection took place more than forty years after the revolutionary days, the emotional fluctuation he might have experienced at that time was left out from this account. Even then, the kind of indifference Tanaka and his colleagues at the Institute for Studying the West showed toward society at large is quite surprising. It might be the case, as Nakayama asserted, that institutions such as the Institute for Studying the West and the Institute for Medical Studies that were responsible for translations and medical practices "already had the propensity of a technician who would perform non-politically regardless of the regime of the time under which they were practicing."[30] It also might be the case, as Nakayama noted, that "the training of talented persons that are fluent in languages of the West, or those who are equipped with skills of Western medicine, were seen a matter of great urgency by the new government."[31] What I want to highlight here is the fact that the 1871 Exhibition of Local Products organized by the South School of Daigaku is situated at the extension of the continued accumulation of knowledge and information, in particular the knowledge manifested in Western learning and the study of local products at the Institute for Studying the West. Through this institution, these practices were carried out from Bakumatsu into the new Meiji era. Seen this way, it becomes possible to understand the seemingly contradictory elements within the exhibition. That is to say, individuals like Takemoto Yōsai—a former retainer of the shogun who turned his back on the new political body—played significant roles at this exhibition organized under the Meiji government because this exhibition was itself constituted through the continuation of broader epistemological practices.

PROFILES OF THE EXHIBITORS: MATSUURA TAKESHIRŌ AND KASHIWAGI KAICHIRŌ

Here, I want to consider two additional vital collectors who submitted items to the Exhibition of Local Products in 1871.

First, there is Matsuura Hiroshi, better known as Matsuura Takeshirō. He began wandering in various provinces of Japan at the age of sixteen, and is known today as the person who named the northern main island of the Japanese archipelago as Hokkaido. His energetic explorations took him around Ezo, the land of the Ainu, and northern frontiers, and resulted in numerous recorded materials. In 1869 (Meiji 2), he became an official of the Pioneer Office (*Kaitakushi*) of the new government and participated in selecting the names for entire provinces and counties within the island. However, Matsuura became disillusioned with the policies of the new government and resigned from the position the following year. He was also known as an eminent collector. A one-mat room, a study that measures one-tatami mat size, which he completed at his home in Kanda Gokenchō in Tokyo in 1886, perfectly exemplifies this. He solicited donations from his friends across the country for notable historic pieces of wood, with which he built his study. Among the sixty-six donors who responded to Matsuura's call soliciting wood scraps was Ninagawa Noritane, a figure we have explored already in chapter 2.[32] Matsuura also published two volumes of illustrated catalogs of his collection *The Pleasures of Scattering Clouds* (*Hatsuun yokyō*, 1877), which we will examine in the next chapter. The breadth of Matsuura's interest toward things past demonstrated in this set of catalogs is impressive, as his collection encompassed items such as stone implements, comma-shaped beads, socketed bronze spearheads, bronze wares, old seals, old coins, and the like.[33]

Matsuura's submission to the Exhibition of Local Products in 1871 were items he acquired in Hokkaido: in the "Fossils" section under the category of "Mineral," he submitted a fossil of a shell of "a kind of enormous nautilus" and in the section of "Items of the Past," four stone implements that included a stone arrowhead. Of these four, Matsuura wrote about three of them, specifically "a whetstone for a stone ax," "a handsaw for a stone ax," and "an unfinished stone ax" in *The Pleasures of Scattering Clouds*.[34] These three items seem to be a unit that was famous within Matsuura's collection. The "Catalog of the Exhibition of Local Products in the Year of *Shinpi* of Meiji" offers brief explanations of these items, noting that the whetstone and the handsaw were stone implements used to make a stone ax. In his aforementioned volume of *Part of Mino Region,* Itō Keisuke had also introduced these accounts as Matsuura's view of the stone implements.[35] Itō had visited Matsuura's home in Kanda with his disciple Tanaka Yoshio in the sixth month of 1862.[36] Since this visit took place immediately after Tanaka had become the assistant official at the Institute for the Study of Barbarian Books, it might have been the case that Itō was introducing Tanaka to his old friend Matsuura. Edward Morse, too, visited Matsuura in the winter of 1882, and noted, "I visited Matsura [sic] Takashiro, an antiquarian of some note, who received me very kindly."[37] Morse was shown a collection of comma-shaped beads strung together on a long thread, noting that Matsuura had "the largest collection of these objects in Japan."[38]

Kashiwagi Kaichirō was another famous collector who was as well-known as Matsuura Takeshirō. He submitted "a fossil of fish teeth" under the fossils section and "ninety-six items including comma-shaped beads, stone axes, stone arrowheads, stone daggers" under "Items of the Past." If we ignore the listing order of "Miscellaneous," both Matsuura and Kashiwagi submitted items only to the first and the last sections at the exhibition.[39] That their submissions were limited to the sections at the beginning and end appears to have been intentional. Moreover, it seems that these two had a sense of rivalry between them as collectors. Once Matsuura borrowed an old hand-scroll of Buddhist sutras from Kashiwagi, and returned it to him after cutting out a section in the middle. But Kashiwagi had weighed his scroll before lending it to Matsuura, thus was able to expose Matsuura's theft at once.[40]

Kashiwagi Kaichirō also had an extended relationship with the administration of the Museum. From 1874 to 1883, he worked at the Exposition Bureau, then at museums under the administrations of the Home Ministry and the Ministry of Agriculture and Commerce.[41] He authored a section on gold lacquer in the seventh chapter, on lacquerware, in *Histories of Material Crafts* (*Kōgei shiryō*) by the historian Kurokawa Mayori, which was published by the Museum Bureau in 1878. He participated in the second research of treasures at the Shōsōin in Tōdaiji Temple in Nara along with Ninagawa Noritane in 1875. Even before this, Kashiwagi accompanied the *Jinshin* survey in 1872, which opened the doors of the Shōsōin for the first time since the Tenpō period (1830–44) to sketch the old and ancient items held at the repository.[42]

Although Kashiwagi is said to have studied pictorial skills under the Tani Bunchō disciple Suzuki Gako (1816–70) and tea ceremony through the Sōhen school of tea ceremony, his family business was as a master carpenter who, for generations, were in charge of building and repairs (*kobushin gata*) under the Tokugawa shogunate. Kashiwagi built numerous houses in the *sukiya* style, as well as teahouses including the Zenkyoan. This teahouse was built in 1880 at the residence of Masuda Takashi, an entrepreneur of the Mitsubishi conglomerate, practitioner of the tea ceremony, and collector, located in the Gotenyama hills of Shinagawa, Tokyo.[43]

Kashiwagi also had a discerning critical eye. In the winter of 1882 Edward Morse visited this antiquarian. According to him, Kashiwagi "has the rarest collection of old Japanese coins, ancient pottery a thousand and more years old, rare pictures, and many other things. Every object in the room was old and rare."[44] Morse was invited to a warehouse with earthen walls. Inside, on each wall, Kashiwagi had placed bamboo frames from which textile was hung, transforming the interior into an entirely cloth-covered space. Morse introduced this technique in *Japan Day by Day* when he described "the way the Japanese convert a large, cold, barny room of a fireproof building into a pleasant place to live in."[45] Prior to this, Morse also mentioned Kashiwagi's warehouse in his *Japanese Homes and Their Surroundings*, published in 1886. He included sketches by his own hand of the interior of the warehouse, as well as of the bamboo frames, noting, "[a] loft above, to which access was gained by a perilous flight of steps, was filled with ancient relics of all kinds,—stone implements, old pottery, quaint writing-desks, and rare manuscripts" (fig. 12).[46] Kashiwagi was literally living surrounded by his collection.

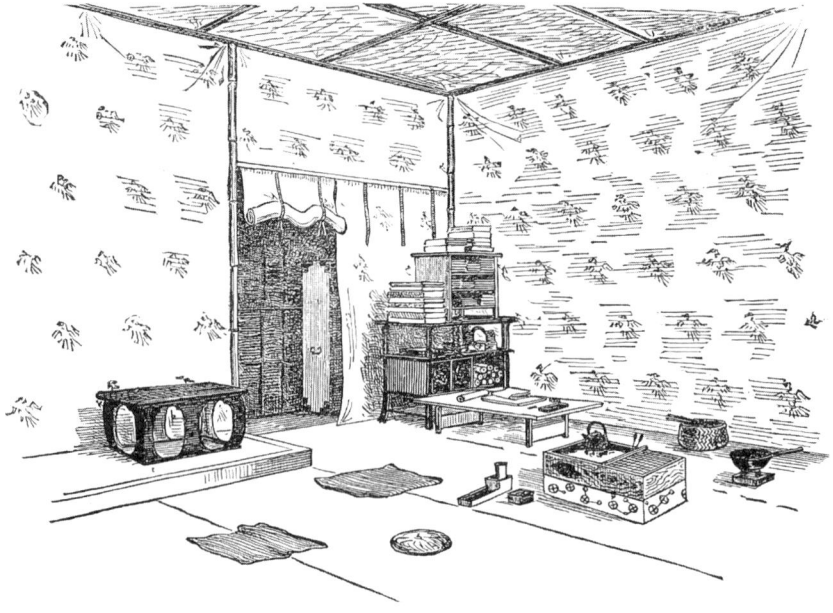

FIG. 12.

Edward S. Morse (American, 1838–1925). Illustration showing room in Kura fitted as a library, Tokyo, from Edward S. Morse, *Japanese Homes and Their Surroundings*, 1886.

At the Exhibition of Local Products in 1871, Kashiwagi submitted a fossil and stone implements. In the quotes by Morse above, he mentioned old coins, pottery, and paintings as objects among Kashiwagi's collection. In regards to ancient coins, his collection is said to have included rare types of a coin from the Nara period (*Wadō kaichin*) and those from the Edo period (*Kan'ei tsūhō*), respectively nicknamed "hane Wadō" and "*reisho Kan'ei*."[47] Regarding porcelain, his collection included three celadon flower vases of the "turning-bottom" type (*shimokabura hanaike*) made in the Southern Song dynasty. This particular type of celadon was one of the most treasured items among imported celadons. Among his paintings, there were two out of four scrolls of the *Tales of the Buddhist Hells* and a set of *The Tale of Genji* scrolls.[48] Both scrolls date back to the late Heian period in the twelfth century, and Kashiwagi would later hand these to Masuda Takashi. It is noted that the scroll of *The Tale of Genji* in his collection was the scroll that "an individual named Ninagawa bought."[49] The Ninagawa mentioned here is probably Ninagawa Noritane. Yet another story about Kashiwagi involves an item exhibited at a calligraphy and painting exhibition at Shōheizaka at the Confucian Shrine Taiseiden Hall in Yushima, Tokyo in May of 1874. He was said to have promised to purchase a fragment of a set of hand scrolls of *Frolicking Animals* from the twelfth century submitted at this exhibition but was outbid by Ninagawa.[50] In 1884 Kashiwagi published *Ranking List of Notable Yamato-e Picture Scrolls* (*Yamatoe meikan kurabe*), a ranking of old hand scroll paintings.

The catalog of antiquities *The Pleasures of Scattering Clouds* by Matsuura Takeshirō includes a few woodblock images based on illustrations by Kashiwagi Kaichirō. His profession, family business, interests, hobbies, and collections blended as a whole, whereby none of these categories could alone describe his true value. Matsuura, too, shared a similar characteristic. These two individuals represent a typical antiquarian of this period.

PROFILES OF THE EXHIBITORS: MACHIDA HISANARI AND NINAGAWA NORITANE

There are a few other exhibitors to the 1871 Exhibition of Local Products that I want to explore. One of them is Machida Hisanari. Unlike others noted in this chapter, Machida was born into a notable family of the Satsuma domain (present-day Kagoshima prefecture). Through a domainal order, he joined a covert study-abroad program in the United Kingdom from 1865 for three years, and he served as a supervisor of the group, which consisted of seventeen members. During his study-abroad period, the 1867 Paris Exposition took place. While the Tokugawa shogunate sent their own official delegation to this exposition, there was a controversy over the separate participation of the Satsuma and Saga domains. Machida accompanied the Satsuma delegation to Paris and experienced the exposition for himself. After the Restoration, he became a senior secretary in the Ministry of Foreign Affairs after serving as a magistrate of the Nagasaki court. In the ninth month of 1870, he became a senior secretary of Daigaku. One of his colleagues at this post was Katō

Hiroyuki (1836–1916), who came to work for the new government from the Institute for Studying the West, operated by the Tokugawa shogunate. Katō would later become the president of Tokyo University and Tokyo Imperial University. Machida and Katō managed the South School of Daigaku as senior secretaries of Daigaku. Here I want to revisit the proposition of the fourth month of 1871 by Daigaku to build a *shūkokan*. At the beginning of the text, it included the phrase, "[r]egarding a great important matter of building *shūkokan,* the Ministry of Foreign Affairs has already submitted a preposition."[51] It appears that Machida, who had just changed his position from a senior secretary in the Ministry of Foreign Affairs to a senior secretary of Daigaku, had played a role in composing this proposition. When the Museum Bureau was established under the Ministry of Education in the ninth month of the same year, Machida's title changed to include both positions: "an administrator at the Ministry of Education and the Museum Bureau." In the first month of 1872, he and Tanaka Yoshio became official advisors for the Vienna World Exposition. In the *Jinshin* survey, which began in the fifth month of the same year, he played a central role in the research of treasures at old temples and shrines in the Tōkai and Kinki regions. After this, Machida focused his work on museum administration. When the Museum was moved under the umbrella of the Home Ministry in March 1875, then renamed as the Museum Bureau in April 1876, Machida became its first director. Even after the museum of the Home Ministry was transferred to the Ministry of Agriculture and Commerce, he continued to thrive as a central figure of the museum. In October 1882, he resigned from the director position and temporarily returned to a role within the Museum Bureau. In March 1885 he became a member of the Chamber of Elders, but resigned from the post suddenly in December 1889 and became a Buddhist priest.[52]

Katō Hiroyuki, Machida's colleague as the senior secretary of the Ministry of Education, also submitted items to the Exhibition of Local Products in 1871. He presented a school atlas and a "milk-sucking device made of rubber, large and small, two items" to the "Miscellaneous" section. Contrary to this, Machida submitted three kinds of birds including "a male and a female turkey" under the subsection of "Birds in Cages," "two kinds of Satsuma ware" and "two kinds of *Cochin* ware" under the "Ceramics" section, and two further items, "stirrups made by Dōzen" and an "inkstone made of a roofing tile of Rojōmon gate," under the "Items of the Past" section. One item submitted by Katō was a teaching map in an educational setting, and the other entry probably was a feeding bottle with a rubber mouthpiece. Both items were European products, displayed with the intent of "civilizing" their audience. On the other hand, the small number of items Machida submitted evokes Takemoto Yōsai with his submission of birds in cages, while also suggesting a deep interest in things past. The historian Shigeno Yasutsugu (1827–1910) authored a text inscribed on a commemorative stone dedicated to Machida that notes, "you have long been knowledgeable about the old and a brilliant thinker with a great discerning eye."[53] Another historian, Okanoya Shigezane (1835–1920), who was of the same generation as Machida, relayed an insightful episode. According to Okanoya, Machida took notice of a large vacant space behind the Hall of Great Buddha at Todaiji Temple in Nara. Okanoya recounted, "as Machida was such an antiquarian, he came to consult with me and said 'once we dig that abandoned land, some things might be unearthed. I want to dig some things up.'" Machida then negotiated with the temple, purchased the land, and hired laborers to dig the area. They excavated five or six pieces that appeared to be old iron nails of a large size. Pleased with the result, Machida then returned the land to the temple. Once, when an old *biwa* lute appeared on the market, he sold his house to purchase it. According to Okanoya, "nobody was as fitting as Machida to be a director of a museum when it came to things past."[54] These anecdotes reveal Machida to be a passionate antiquarian.

Another individual involved in the museum and expositions is Ninagawa Noritane, a figure whose work we have explored already (see chapter 2). Ninagawa submitted sixteen items to the Exhibition of Local Products in 1871. Among them, eleven were under the "Items of the Past." While his contribution of items such as stone axes, stone arrowheads, and old coins were similar to those of other exhibitors, what distinguished Ninagawa's submission were items such as an old saddle, old mirrors, old archer's wrist protectors, old bamboo wrapping mats from Hōryūji Temple, "beads of decorating ornaments hung from a ciborium" from Hōryūji Temple, and "a lampshade hat woven with rush from Tōdaiji Temple."[55] The fact that some of Ninagawa's items originated from historic temples like Hōryūji and Tōdaiji is a telltale sign of his interest. The rush-woven hat *ayaigusa,* characterized by the wide brim and protruding top, was originally used for hunting. Under "Miscellaneous," he also submitted a "reproduction of an *ayaigasa* hat in the old style," which seems to have been a reproduction of this original hat. Ninagawa, born in 1835, passed away early at the age of forty-eight in August 1882. According to Morse, who attended Ninagawa's funeral service, the cause of his death was cholera.[56] In August 1932, fifty years after his passing, an exhibition took place at Okazaki Public Hall in Kyoto to commemorate Ninagawa's life. Along with items cherished by Ninagawa, several reproductions of treasury items from temples, including Hōryūji, Tōdaiji, and its repository Shōsōin were displayed.[57] Considering the compilation of his *Illustrated Book of Past Things: Ceramics Section* referred to in chapter 2, a series of comprehensive catalogs of Japanese ceramic works based on his collection, as well as the reproductions of old treasures, it appears Ninagawa's interest was not limited to collecting alone.

At this commemorative event of 1932, a volume titled *Documents in Memory of Ninagawa Noritane* (*Ninagawa Noritane tsuibo roku,* 1933) was published, in which the historian Inokuma Nobuo (1882–1963) wrote an essay titled "Traces of Ninagawa Noritane." Inokuma wrote:

> From a young age, he [Ninagawa] was inclined to cherish things past. Every day at playtime, he fiddled with soil and caressed roofing tiles. When he became mature, he read Japanese and Chinese books on wide-ranging topics and

studied a series of strange texts lined up horizontally like a crab walk [referring to Western languages]. He also visited numerous eminent gentlemen in the East and West and examined treasures far and near. He was so devoted to expanding the range of his experience and deepen the content of his knowledge that he forgot to eat in the morning and to sleep at night. Spending many years like this, Ninagawa finally established himself as an outstanding individual.[58]

In an essay by Tanaka Yoshio published in the same book, he described Ninagawa's personality by noting: "Taking extra care for the preservation of things past, even his own house was readily equipped to prevent fires. His character was simple hearted and unpretentious. He was frugal and sometimes walked around wearing a lampshade hat woven with rush. When it came to food, he was not particular. It should be said that he was a rather extraordinary individual."[59]

Since this account comes from one of his closest colleagues, the words sound convincing. It could be that the hat he wore regularly is the same hat he submitted to the 1871 Exhibition of Local Products as the "reproduction of an *ayaigasa* hat in the old style."[60] When wearing this type of hat, one puts the topknot of one's bundled hair within the protruding central top. According to Morse, "Ninagawa not only always wore the queue, but his outer garment was slit as if he still carried the two swords," thus wearing the lampshade hat was convenient.[61] Incidentally, the famous portrait photograph of Ninagawa was a result of Morse's action (fig. 13). He noted, "[o]ne day I actually abducted him, carrying him in my jinrikisha, against his protestations, to a photographer, and had his picture made, the first and only one he ever had."[62] The photograph was taken on 15 July 1879, and Ninagawa does not have a topknot in this image.[63]

The ancestors of Ninagawa Noritane can be traced back to the court family of Miyaji Ason Iyamasu in the late ninth to early tenth centuries. Miyaji held the official title of senior vice-president of the Imperial Household Ministry (*Kunai taifu*), and was a maternal grandfather of Emperor Daigo (r. 897–930). For generations, the Ninagawa family owned the land in the Yamashina and Daigo areas of Yamashiro province (present-day Kyoto prefecture).[64] Later, the family fell when Ninagawa Sadanaga followed the order of his master Akechi Mitsuhide, a feudal lord who unsuccessfully rebelled against his master Oda Nobunaga, but Sadanaga's grandson Sadatsune resurrected the family name when he took the role of a low-ranking employee (*kunin*) at Tōji Temple in Kyoto. From this point on, Sadatsune took up his residence in the south of Kyoto, Hachijō Ōmiya, and became the restorer of the Ninagawa family of Kyoto.[65] Those of the *kunin* position belonged to a large temple compound, and worked on miscellaneous jobs such as the collection of land tax. The Ninagawa residence in Kyoto was noted and illustrated in Morse's *Japanese Homes and Their Surroundings*.[66]

In the sixth month of 1869, Ninagawa moved to Tokyo, where he took a position as "a general affairs official of Bureau of Institutional Investigation" for the

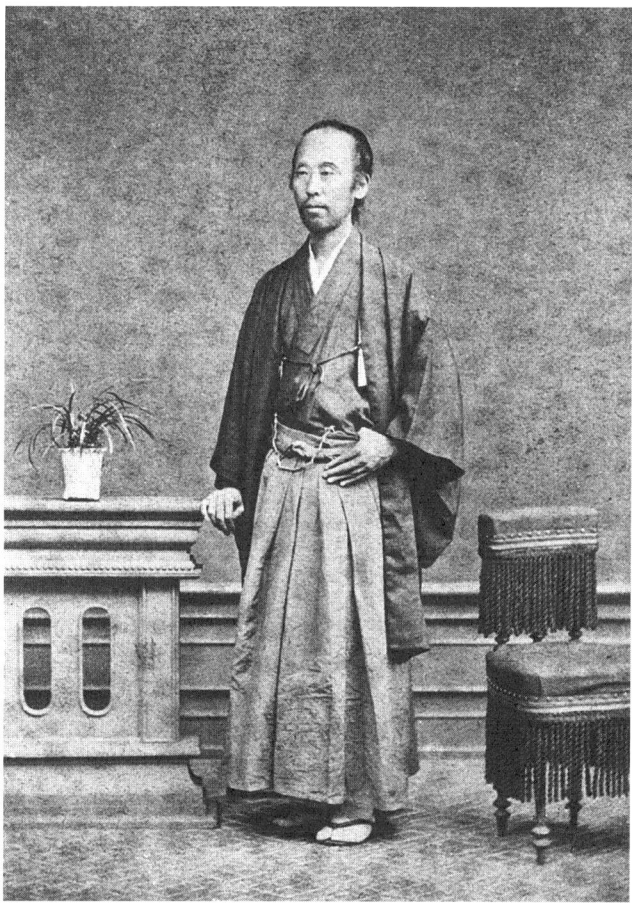

FIG. 13.

Ninagawa Noritane, from Ninagawa Daiichi, ed., *Ninagawa Noritane Tsuiboroku*, 1933.

Tokyo Bunkazai Kenkyūjo, J03/5.

Meiji government. In the seventh month of 1870, he was promoted to provisional second secretary of the Grand Council of State (*gonnoshōshi*), then to the second secretary of the same office (*shōshi*) in the ninth month. However, in the seventh month of 1871, the Bureau of Institutional Investigation was abolished to reform the Grand Council of State, and all were dismissed from their positions. Ninagawa returned to Kyoto following this change. In the tenth month of the same year, he returned to Tokyo to serve the role of an eighth rank in the Ministry of Foreign Affairs (*gaimu dairoku*). In the twelfth month, he was asked to take on another concurrent role as an officer in charge at the Museum Bureau within the Ministry of Education.[67] The first exposition in Kyoto took place during the tenth month of 1871, and according to Tanaka Yoshio, Ninagawa worked tirelessly for this event.[68]

During the *Jinshin* survey the following year, which included the opening of the Shōsōin of Tōdaiji Temple, he traveled to the Tōkai and Kinki regions and played a central role in the research on treasures along with Machida Hisanari and Uchida Masao. In the directory of the Museum Bureau at the Ministry of Education, dated March 1873, Ninagawa is listed as "Ninagawa Noritane, eighth rank, responsible for attending to the old and ancient items, and accumulating and editing publications on the histories of institutions."[69] In the same month, the Museum Bureau was absorbed into the Exposition Bureau, and in two years, this office was transferred to the Home Ministry. In the directory published in May 1875 by the Museum Bureau (now under the Home Ministry) Ninagawa is listed as "an officer in charge of antiquities, in the eighth rank, employed by the Home Ministry," under the "historical research" section. Ninagawa began a printing business in January 1876 at Gakukōsha, a part of his large residence that he had renovated. His house was located in Marunouchi Dōsanchō (present-day 2-chōme, Ōtemachi, Chiyoda Ward, Tokyo), which used to be the official residence of the magistrate of construction and repairs of the Tokugawa shogunate. Ninagawa bought a set of printing machines for this business. He published the first volume of *Illustrated Book of Past Things: Ceramics Section* in March of the same year. In January of 1877, he resigned from the Museum Bureau.[70] His close relationship with Morse through collecting and studying ceramics, therefore, took place after this point.

Three figures I have explored in this section—Machida Hisanari, Ninagawa Noritane, and Tanaka Yoshio—although their origins and backgrounds differed, all played crucial roles in early exhibitions and museum activities by promoting them. While Tanaka, a student of Itō Keisuke, played a central role in the study of local products, Machida and Ninagawa thrived in the areas centering on things past. However, all three of them began to fade from the world of exhibitions and museums between 1877 and 1887. The earliest instance was marked by the resignation of Ninagawa in January 1877; this was followed by Machida's departure as the director of the Museum Bureau under the Home Ministry in October 1882. Tanaka filled in as the director of the Museum Bureau after Machida's departure, while also serving as the head of the Bureau of Agriculture under the Home Ministry. But in June of 1883, Tanaka transferred to become a member of the Chamber of Elders. Although he was asked to perform the role of an agent of museum administration, he in effect retired from the front line of the museum field.[71] Kashiwagi Kaichirō also retired in 1883.[72] According to the directory of the Museum Bureau under the Home Ministry, his name is listed as "Kashiwagi Kaichirō, in the fourteenth rank" under "the section on historical research" as "an official in charge of antiquities." Kashiwagi was positioned below Ninagawa, who was in the eighth rank.[73] Ninagawa passed away in August 1882, and two months later, Machida resigned from the director of the Museum Bureau.

Tanaka Yoshio, who outlived both Ninagawa and Machida, passed away at the age of seventy-nine in June 1916. After moving away from museums and expositions, he became active in the context of the Society of Agriculture of Greater Japan and the Society of Fisheries of Greater Japan. Because of his background in the study of *materia medica*, he was able to find a new trajectory for himself in the field of study of local products. What is worth noting, however, is the fact that the timing of the retirement of these figures overlapped with the time when expositions became absorbed into industrializing policies. More specifically, this period runs from the First National Industrial Exposition in 1877 to the mid-1880s. After the second Domestic Exposition for the Promotion of Industry opened in March 1881, the Museum Bureau under the Home Ministry was transferred to the newly established Ministry of Agriculture and Commerce, marking a decisive moment from which the direction of museum administration could not return.

A GALAXY OF INDIVIDUALS—UNTIL THE 1872 EXHIBITION

Let us return to the Exhibition of Local Products in 1871. There are still a number of fascinating figures among the exhibitors.

Based on the content of submitted items, there are those who submitted new objects from the West. We have already discussed Shimizu Usaburō, also known by his shop's name Mizuhoya, who was active at the Paris Exposition of 1867. Shimizu submitted two entries, one under the "Ore" section called "Thirty-Six Elements," and the other under "Ceramics," "Ceramics, Sèvres ware in France, four items," and "Ceramics after French production methods, ten items." This list reveals that Shimizu was exploring the methods of making French ceramics.

Under "Internal and Surgical Medical Instruments," the physician Matsumoto Ryōjun (1831–1907) submitted the "skull of a Western man." He was the director of the School of Western Medical Science operated by the Tokugawa shogunate, backing the shogunate side with his students during the Boshin War. During the war, he was arrested in the Aizu domain for attending to injured soldiers. Later, he was pardoned of this crime and was employed by the Ministry of Military Affairs from 1871. He became the first surgeon general and resigned from his position at the Ministry of the Army in 1877. Another exhibitor, Ichikawa Seiryū (1822–79), submitted "Western *shōgi*" (a set of chess pieces) under the "Miscellaneous" section. Ichikawa traveled to the West as a servant to the deputy chief delegate, the Lord of the Iwami domain Matsudaira Yasunao, with the 1862 delegates to Europe led by the Lord of the Shimotsuke domain, Takenouchi Yasunori. Ichikawa authored *A Confused Account of a Trip to Europe, Like a Fly on a Horse's Tail* (*Oba'e ōkō manroku*). His submission was probably an item he brought back from this trip.

Earlier, we discussed the pioneer of oil painting, Takahashi Yuichi, in relation to the *Jinshin* Survey of 1872. At the Exhibition of Local Products in 1871, he submitted one entry listed as "framed oil paintings" under the "Miscellaneous" section. Although their titles are unknown, there is a letter from Takahashi to Tanaka Yoshio in which Takahashi asked Tanaka to enter two oil paintings he owned, and four of his own paintings, to the exhibition.[74] We have already noted two items submitted by Katō Hiroyuki, a colleague of Machida Hisanari. Katō, too, belonged to this circle of these exhibitors.

On the other hand, there were many exhibitors of things past at this exhibition. Most of these individuals belonged to the group of nativist scholars.[75] Sakakibara Yoshino (1832–82) is one such figure. Sakakibara submitted a "reflecting, mirror-like stone [*kagami ishi*]" under "Stone and Soil" section. Born into a merchant family in Nihonbashi area of Edo, he worked at the Shōhei School after the Restoration. After taking a role of the immediate assistant professor at *Daigaku*, he became a senior secretary at the Ministry of Education in 1871.

Yokoyama Yoshikiyo (1826–79) also submitted five entries under "Items of the Past" that included "a boxful of comma-shaped beads, cylindrical beads, stone arrowheads, etc.," and other jade works and stone implements. Yokoyama served as a lecturer at the Institute of National Learning (Wagakukōdansho) under the Tokugawa shogunate. After the Restoration, he was employed at the Shōhei School. He then served as a general affairs official of the Bureau of Institutional Investigation, and in the ninth month of 1870, became a second secretary of the Grand Council of State. While he authored many books such as *History of Institutions of Japanese Rice Fields* (*Nihon denseishi*, 1926) and *Consideration of Ancient Pottery* (*Kodai tōkikō*), he also translated *Robinson Crusoe* by Daniel Defoe into Japanese from a Dutch translation, and published this in 1857. He was also an avid collector of old vessels, old coins, and old calligraphy and paintings, and published the two volumes of the catalog of his collection, *Illustrated Catalog of Appreciating the Past* (*Shōko zuroku*), in 1871 and 1876.[76] He also had extensive engagements with public exhibitions. According to one of Ninagawa's diaries, *A Path along Nara* (*Nara no sujimichi*), there was a plan to open an exhibition in the tenth month of 1871 organized by Machida, Ninagawa, and Yokoyama, although this plan was never materialized.[77]

Another nativist scholar, Kimura Masakoto (1827–1913), submitted three entries to the "Items of the Past" section: "an old mirror, published in *Illustrated Catalog of Appreciating the Past*," "an old copper sealing stamp, same as above, letter of svastica from India," and stone axes. Kimura and Yokoyama must have been old acquaintances, since at least 1863 when Kimura became an assistant to the director at the Institute of National Learning. After the Restoration, Kimura worked for the new government and was well known as a specialist of the anthology of ancient *tanka* poems, *Manyōshū*.

The nativist scholar Kurokawa Mayori (1829–1906) was another exhibitor at the exhibition of 1871. He submitted two entries under "Items of the Past": an "old bamboo wrapping mat" and a "silver *gyotai*." *Gyotai*, literally a "fish bag," was a form of tallying originally in shape of a bag decorated by shapes of fish that signified the status of officials of the court. The fish-shaped ornaments were made of either silver or gold. In 1869, Kurokawa worked first as a general-affairs official in charge of the investigation of prefectural schools. He then worked in the Ministry of Education, followed by a seat in the Chamber of Elders. In June 1877, he became the deputy chief of the historical records section at the Museum Bureau of the Home Ministry, replacing Ninagawa, who had retired from the position in January of the same year.[78] In 1879, Kurokawa authored *Consideration on Cave Habitation* (*Kekkyokō*), and *Consideration on Ancient Stone Implements* (*Jōdai sekkikō*) under a series of the Museum Bureau, *Series on Encyclopedic Studies* (*Hakubutsu sōsho*).

There is one additional exhibitor to mention here. Kanda Takahira (1830–98) submitted "Illustrations of comma-shaped beads, cylindrical beads, stone daggers, stone arrowheads, etc.," under "Items of the Past." Kanda was exceptional in this group, in the sense that he was a not a nativist scholar but rather a scholar of Western studies. In 1862, he was dispatched as a professor to the Institute for the Study of Barbarian Books, taught mathematics such as algebra, and became the director at the Institute for Studying the West. After the Restoration, he worked for the new government, serving among many roles as a general-affairs official of the Bureau of Institutional Investigation. In the eleventh month of 1871, he became the governor of Hyōgo prefecture. He also participated in the founding of the Meiji Six Society (*Meirokusha*) in 1873.[79] Kanda collected many illustrated catalogs of stone implements and submitted some to this exhibition.[80] In addition, he was a passionate collector of actual stone implements, and as I will elaborate in chapter 5, he published an illustrated book, *Notes on Ancient Stone Implements, etc., of Japan* (*Nihon taiko sekkikō*, 1886). In 1887, Kanda became the first president of the Anthropological Society of Tokyo, a society founded by the anthropologist Tuboi Shōgorō (1863–1913) and others.

These capture the main lineup of the exhibitors to the Exhibition of Local Products in 1871. Here it is helpful to compare this briefly to the Yushima Exhibition organized by the Museum Bureau under the Ministry of Education in the following year. The exhibition at the Yushima Seidō began on the tenth day of the third month. It became a very popular event, and the initial duration of twenty days was extended much longer, with the exhibit finally closing at the end of the following month.[81] In terms of the exhibitors and submitted items, the unpublished manuscript "Draft of a Catalog of Exhibited Items at the Exhibition in the year Meiji 5 ("Meiji gonen hakurankai shuppin mokuroku sōkō") is a helpful resource.[82] According to this document, the exhibitors consisted of seven official institutions, including Kanagawa prefecture, four Buddhist temples, and 148 individuals. Thus, the number of exhibitors was greatly expanded compared to the Exhibition of Local Products we examined. While it was the first time that names of the temples appeared as exhibitors, the number of individuals overwhelmed the list. The same could be said about the items submitted. Of 617 items submitted, there were forty-five from official institutions. Among these forty-five items, nineteen were from the imperial properties, fifteen were from the Ministry of Religious Education, and seven were from the Imperial Household Ministry. Although these submissions are notable, they made up less than ten percent of the total number of items.

On the other hand, there was a considerable difference from the previous year in terms of the content of the exhibited items. Unfortunately, the "Draft of a Catalog of Exhibited Items" did not include established categories. If we look to the three categories from the previous year (mineral, animal, and plant) for some guidance, about seventy items fall under these. This number reflects a little over 10 percent of the total items, creating quite a contrast to the Exhibition of Local Products of 1871, where the total of items under these categories constituted over 86 percent. In fact, at the Yushima exhibition, the vast majority of submitted items fall under the category of "Items of the Past." The popularity of the Museum Bureau's exhibition lent itself to reproduction in broadsheet color woodblock prints. A triptych of woodblock prints, *Assemblage of Rare Things of the Past and the Present* [*Kokon chinbutsu shūran*] by Ichiyōsai Kuniteru, took the format of showing exhibited items (Plate 1). These images make palpable the greater numbers of things past compared with animals or plants. At the same time, the total number of items at this exhibition, 617, did not even come to a third of the total of items at the 1871 Exhibition of Local Products, 2,347. This difference should be understood in relation to the size of the items that were submitted. One reason for the tendency to exhibit larger items at the Yushima exhibition was the edict regarding the preservation of old and ancient objects issued by the Grand Council of State. This edict was issued only three days after Exhibition of Local Products closed. At the Yushima exhibition, Tanaka Yoshio did not submit any items; instead, Machida Hisanari and Ninagawa Noritane took the roles as the sponsors of the meeting.

There are a few overlapping exhibitors between this exhibition and the previous year's exhibition: Machida Hisanari, Uchida Masao, Ninagawa Noritane, Matsuura Takeshirō, Kashiwagi Kaichirō, Itō Keisuke, Sakakibara Yoshino, and Kimura Masakoto. While the previous event included forty individual exhibitors, the Yushima exhibition included 148 names, signifying a vast increase in the number of new exhibitors. Among them was Fukuba Bisei (1831–1907). He submitted a total of fifteen items that included stone implements and comma-shaped beads, along with items of the past such as three prehistoric "bell-shaped bronze vessels" and two "one-million pagodas."[83] Fukuba was from a vassal family of the Tsuwano domain (southwestern part of present-day Shimane prefecture) and became active as a bureaucrat in the new government, especially in implementing policies advocated by the Ministry of Divinities. Meanwhile, the former feudal lord of the Fukuoka domain, Kuroda Nagahiro, submitted the King of Na gold seal, which was accidentally excavated in Shikanoshima island off Kyūshū (present-day Fukuoka prefecture). It is noted that when Kuroda visited Machida in 1872 and showed him this gold seal, Machida was greatly surprised.[84] Also, Sawa Nobuyoshi (1835–73) submitted seven items, including the fragments of *Commentary of Zuo on Spring and Autumn Annals* (Ch. *Chunqiu Zuoshizhuan*, J. *Shunjūsashi den*) from the Jin dynasty China, which had been passed down within the aristocratic family of Nakahara, who for generations held the title of the major external secretariat of the Council of

State in the imperial court. Sawa was the minister of Foreign Affairs when Machida became its senior secretary in 1869. In short, these individuals had ongoing relationships with Ninagawa and Machida.

Among former retainers of the shogun, notable was Narushima Ryūhoku (1837–84), who was born into a Confucian family serving as the shogun's lecturer. He had held critical positions throughout the Tokugawa period. He submitted 160 kinds of ancient coins to the exhibition of 1872. Narushima became a well-known author through the publication of *New Chronicles of Yanagibashi* (*Ryūkyō shin shi*, 1859), a reportage on the Yanagibashi gay quarter, and he was also known as a collector of old coins.[85] After the Yushima Seidō exhibition, he traveled to Europe along with the twenty-second abbot of the Higashi Honganji division of the True Pure Land sect of Buddhism, Ōtani Kōei (1852–1923). Narushima's diary from this trip, *Diary of a Journey to the West* (*Kōsei nichijō*, 1884), is scattered with episodes of Narushima seeking out old coins at the various cities he visited.[86] He later thrived in the context of printed media, mostly through the platform of the *Chōya shinbun* newspaper. He then published the first volume of his numismatic study, *Catalog of Coins: Meiji New Edition* (*Meiji shinsen senpu*, 1882). Although there was no submission from Takemoto Yōsai who, like Narushima, did not pursue a governmental position after the Restoration, there were a few items from Ōtsuki Bankei (1801–77). Ōtsuki was the second son of Ōtsuki Gentaku, a physician of Western medicine from the Sendai domain (present-day Miyagi prefecture). He was imprisoned during the Boshin War, but was released only in 1871 and had just arrived in Tokyo. Among the five items he submitted were items that had a strong relation to the Sendai domain, such as "an undamaged roofing tile from remains of Tagajō Castle," the site of the eighth-century capital of Mutsu province located in present-day Miyagi prefecture, and "an old bow made of a zelkova tree" whose former owner was said to be Fujiwara Hidehira, the late twelfth-century lord of the Mutsu and Dewa provinces (present-day six prefectures of Tōhoku region). A younger brother of the last shogun, Tokugawa Akitake, submitted a "*xuanwu* bell" (Ch. *xuanwu*, J. *genbu*), a small bell decorated with the shape of the black turtle-snake that, in Taoist tradition, defends the north.

In addition, three individuals working in paintings and calligraphy submitted items to this exhibition: Kanō Tadanobu (1823–80), the tenth chief painter of the Kobikichō branch family of the Kano school, also known by the pseudonym Shōsenin; Sumiyoshi Hirokata (1835–83), known by the official title *naiki*, the internal secretariat of the Ministry of the Center in the Imperial Court and a direct descendant of the Sumiyoshi school of *Yamato-e* painting; and Kohitsu Ryōetsu, the twelfth head of the Kohitsu family of connoisseur in calligraphy and paintings.[87] Tsuda Sen (1837–1908), the father of Tsuda Umeko and a scholar of Western studies, also participated.[88] According to the essay "Narrative of My Career" by Tanaka Yoshio, Tsuda and Tanaka had been friends since the Bakumatsu period. After accompanying Tanaka to the Vienna World Exposition of 1873, Tsuda was later baptized as a Christian and founded the Girl's Elementary School in 1874, a predecessor of Aoyama Jogakuin (Aoyama Women's School, present-day Aoyama Gakuin University). Tsuda submitted three items, including "a piece of marble from America, the stone used to build the United States Capitol." There were quite a few items from Western civilization at this Yushima exhibition that the Exhibition of Local Products in 1871 would have categorized as miscellaneous.

So far, we have explored two exhibitions that were organized by the new government, by focusing on the exhibitors. They came from wide-ranging backgrounds and held different interests. While many were involved with the Institute for Studying the West operated by the previous Tokugawa shogunate, many were newly hired employees of the new Meiji government after the Restoration. We should also be mindful of the fact there were employees of the former shogunate who refused to work for the new government. What is surprising is the fact that these exhibitions were constituted by people with such varied backgrounds and interests. Furthermore, there was an invisible thread that connected these people. For instance, many of the exhibitors I have discussed here were at the Bureau of Institutional Investigation established in 1869: namely, Ninagawa Noritane, Kanda Takahira, Katō Hiroyuki, Yokoyama Yoshikiyo, and Fukuba Bisei. When the Civil Law Assembly took place at the Bureau of Institutional Investigation in the ninth month of 1870, Mitsukuri Rinshō and Akamatsu Noriyoshi were at the Assembly.[89] Akamatsu was particularly close to Uchida Masao. There was, for instance, the thread of interpersonal relationships. Various other threads at unexpected junctures connected the individuals involved in the early practice of exhibitions. There was also another act of collecting that bound them together above and beyond their social standings.

SECTION 2:
THINKING ABOUT THINGS

A DISCIPLINE OF ORIENTING THINGS:
THE STUDY OF NAMES AND THINGS OR
THE SCIENCE OF MEDIATING NAMES AND THINGS

If we were to connect the myriad interests of the individuals we have explored so far to a single disciplinary field, we could surmise that this would be a field centered on the study of individual objects through intellectual activity. To put it simply, this is a field that directly engages with things as objects of study. This field also takes a practical form called collecting tied to individual interests. At the same time, the practical aspect of their activity also had a public form of engagement, in which collections were displayed at events that enabled exhibitors to expand their interest and knowledge with other attendees; in this sense, they served as pragmatic public forums. They were referred to in general as exhibitions of local products (*bussankai*), of *materia medica* (*honzōkai*) and of calligraphy and painting (*shogakai*). The series of exhibitions in early Meiji, instigated by the Exhibition of Local Products in 1871, was conceived as a new form of these pre-existing public engagements and was accepted among these individuals as such.

Furthermore, the object of individual interests in the disciplinary field crossed over the line between natural and man-made objects. Certainly their interests were focused on specific objects, and there were different spheres of collecting, an act that served as an extension of their interests. Edward S. Morse called individuals such as Matsuura Takeshirō, Kashiwagi Kaichirō, Ninagawa Noritane antiquarians, while he referred to Itō Keisuke as a botanist.[90] Although the term *botanist* was translated as "*shokubutsugakusha*" in the Japanese version, it would probably be more fitting to have translated it in Japanese as "*honzōka*," or "a scholar of *materia medica*." But the issue is not as simple as finding an equivalent term, because to group these figures under a single classificatory category is not even possible. Morse had been, I suspect, very aware of the complexities of the situation. As the submitted items to the Exhibition of Local Products revealed, their collections encompassed a surprising variety of items. Itō's collection, in this sense, was exemplary. The breadth of their interests, like their collected items, crossed over many fields of study, making it difficult to fit them into one category. What we should explore, therefore, is the manner in which this field of inquiry existed. To use today's terminology, it might be called transdisciplinary. This field crossed over between natural and man-made things, rather than segregating its interests into a separated and individuated field like *materia medica*.

Let us return to the time before the Bakumatsu period and survey the disciplines that were oriented to the study of things. The first notable interpretation comes from Shirai Mitsutarō (1863–1932), a botanical scholar of the early twentieth century. Shirai was about a generation younger than Morse. Although it is lengthy, I will quote a full paragraph here because it is crucial for our discussion. The "mentor" at the beginning of this quote refers to Kaibara Ekiken (1630–1714), a scholar of *materia medica* whose great works include *Materia Medica in Japan* (*Yamato honzō*):

> At the time when the mentor was active, there was no encyclopedic study [*hakubutsugaku*] as we know it today. The encyclopedic study of today is vastly different from the encyclopedic study to which he was accustomed. In his time, there were, instead, three subjects: the study of *materia medica* [Ch. *bencaoxue*, J. *honzōgaku*], the study of names and things [Ch. *mingwuxue*, J. *meibutsugaku*], and the study of local products [*bussangaku*]. What the mentor called "encyclopedic study" encompassed all three subjects. The study of *materia medica* focused on the examination of medicinal objects used by the medical doctors trained in Chinese medicine. In other words, it was a subject related to physicians. The study of names and things compared and researched the names of

things and actual objects. These scholars sought to explain names and their relationship to actual things such as animals, plants, and other products that appear in myriad books. This was a necessary study, because even if one read about various objects and things in books, one could not have been said to have understood the book if one did not know what the actual thing was. I think the study of names and things was necessary in the past as much as it is today. There are people today who read and compose poetry using the names of things without knowing the actual things. This is not a permissible situation. For this reason, it is imperative to study the actual existing things earnestly; in other words, a study of actual things is necessary. Then there was the study of local products. This referred to the section of geography books dealing with different countries, detailing where the products are produced or what kinds of products are available. It is, in a sense, a kind of study of names and things, with an emphasis on the encouragement of industry. Today this field is often called the study of merchandise [shōhingaku], an advanced form of the study of local products.[91]

It is best to understand Shirai's description here as referring to the broader Tokugawa period, rather than limited to "the time when the mentor was active." Striking in this quote is the fact that Shirai seems to see the three fields of study as one group. The first field, the study of *materia medica,* is based on the medicinal pursuit of things for healing and curing illnesses. Among the objects of study were plants, animals, and minerals, and the field's purpose was to inquire into their medical efficacy. The next category of scholarly activity, the study of names and things, may be less clear. Shirai noted it was a study that "compared and researched the names of things and actual objects." The objects of study were not limited to natural objects such as animals and plants. Indeed, Shirai added that this study helped to clarify the nature of things that are used when "read[ing] and compos[ing] poetry." Compared to this, the study of local products is clearer in its definition. It studied the products and special products of local areas. Although Shirai says that the study of local products is "a kind of study of names and things," it seems difficult to ascertain the common thread among the three. Let us leave Shirai's understanding for now, and consult another interpretation of the fields of study attached to things. Aoki Masaru (1887–1964), a scholar of Chinese literature, proposed an alternate definition of the study of names and things.

Aoki's interpretation is articulated in a section called "Introduction to the Study of Names and Things" in his book *On the Study of Names and Things in China* (*Chūka meibutsukō,* 1959). He traces the development of the field in China and identifies its beginning as "the study of names and things as exegetics of *xungxue*," which took place during the fifth to the third centuries BCE in the Spring and Autumn periods, followed by "the independence of the study of names and things" at the end of the Eastern Han dynasty, 25–220 CE. This phase is followed by "the developments of the study of names and things" taking myriad forms in the Sung dynasty and beyond, finally arriving at "the study of names and things as evidential research (Ch. *kaozhengxue*)" during the Qing dynasty (1616–1911). In the afterword to a reprinted edition of Aoki's *On the Study of Names and Things in China* in 1988, Chinese philosophy scholar Togawa Yoshio wrote a concise summary of Aoki's thought. According to Togawa, the innovation of Aoki's thought lay in the fact that he saw *mingwuxue* (J. *meibutsugaku*) as an independent field of study, rather than a combination of three fields of study as proposed by Shirai.

> The term *mingwu* [J. *meibutsu*] was used in ancient times, as noted in *Rites of Zhou*, which characterized the term as "the name and its colors and shapes." That is, the term *mingwu* referred to the names of things and their shape and characteristics. The pursuit of this *mingwu* constituted a part of exegetics [Ch. *xunguxue*], which developed in ancient China. After the Eastern Han dynasty, the field of *jingxue* [J. *keigaku*, annotated interpretations of classical Confucian texts] included the exegetic aspect, which focused on interpreting ancient texts, and the *mingwu* aspect, which focused on the explanation of animals and plants in regard to their names, shapes, taste, and medicinal properties. After the Song dynasty, these two aspects became independent as *xiaoxue* [J. *shōgaku*, exegetics of classics] and *mingwuxue*. The former developed into the study of ancient texts and linguistics, which involved the explorations of character shapes [Ch. *tizhi*], the meanings of characters [Ch. *xungu*], and the pronunciations of characters [Ch. *yinyun*], while the latter developed into vast philological inquiries constituted by the studies of institutions, rules, and customs [Ch. *lixue*], the study of archaeology [Ch. *gegu*], the study of *materia medica* [Ch. *bencao*], the study of horticulture [Ch. *zhongshu*], the study of topography [Ch. *wuchan*], and encyclopedic studies [Ch. *leishu*].[92]

The term *mingwu*, literally "names and things," referred to the relationship between the name and the thing and the attributes inherent in the object, while the term *mingwuxue* (J. *meibutsugaku*) pointed to a broader field that connected names to things or to a field that served to bridge names and things. In other words, it was a field of study whose goal was to match names and things accurately, and developed accordingly to achieve its aim. Aoki's stance is that *mingwuxue* developed from the exegetic studies of classic texts. That is, *mingwuxue* was initially concerned with philological and hermeneutic aspects, and then diverged from it. This logocentric pursuit, based on the interpretation and annotation of original texts, can be characterized as an exploration that took the name of a thing as a starting point and tried to clarify the actual thing that corresponded to the name. In other words, although this discipline began with names, it also encompassed the possibility of acting in the opposite direction from exegetic annotations: to start with things and move toward names. This potential of reversal anticipated another discipline which would look at things directly in order to identify their names and articulate their characteristics. The "developments of the study of names and things" after the Song dynasty in Aoki's view emerged, in particular, from this opposite direction that began with things and moved toward names. Certainly, there is no limit to the world of things that surrounds human beings. This world includes natural things such as animals, plants, and minerals as well as man-made objects, thereby giving each thing the possibility of becoming the object of investigation in the field of the study of names and things. Aoki identified six representative branches: the study of institutions, rules, and customs (Ch. *lixue*), the study of archaeology of vessels and implements (Ch. *gegu*), the study of *materia medica* (Ch. *bencao*), the study of horticulture (Ch. *zhongshu*), the study of topography (Ch. *wuchan*), and encyclopedic studies (Ch. *leishu*).

The study of institutions, rules, and customs is more commonly known as the study of "three rites" (Ch. *sanli*, J. *sanrai*). It deals with three main texts: the *Book of Zhou* (Ch. *Zhouli*, J. *Shurai*) which included the regulations for the governmental organization of the Zhou dynasty, the *Book of Etiquette and Ceremonies* (Ch. *Yili*, J. *Girai*), which compiled rules of etiquette, and the *Book of Rites* (Ch. *Liji*, J. *Raiki*), the corpus of miscellaneous books relating to rites. These texts included the names for dresses, useful vessels and implements, food and drink, and palaces. The explanations of these entries came to constitute one of the vital aspects of the study of names and things. The study of the archaeology of vessels and implements, literally written as "assessing the past," entailed appreciating, identifying, and exploring the characteristics of vessels and implements. It is in this sense that this subject constituted a part of the study of names and things. Especially during the Song dynasty, there emerged a new trend of admiring writing implements in addition to ancient vessels and rare antiquities; since then, specialists who could hold forth on both writing implements and ancient vessels became popular. The study of *materia medica*, as Shirai had noted earlier, aimed to articulate the medicinal properties of animals, plants, and minerals. Through identifying and differentiating of properties of things, scholars of *materia medica* greatly contributed to the study of names and things. The oldest text studied in *materia medica* is *The Divine Farmer's Materia Medica* (Ch. *Shennong bencao jing*, J. *Shinnōhonzōkyō*), in eight volumes dating from the late Eastern Han dynasty (25–250 CE). The fifty-two-volume *Compendium of Materia Medica* (Ch. *Bencao gangmu*, J. *Honzōkōmoku*) by Li Shizhen, completed during the Ming dynasty (1368–1644), is considered the magnum opus of the field. The fourth item on Aoki's list, the study of horticulture, was characterized by numerous publications of illustrated catalogs whose titles began with phrases such as "the catalog of" or "the record of." The oldest title in this field was *On Bamboo* (Ch. *Zhupu*, J. *Chikufu*), attributed to Dai Kaizhi during the Jin dynasty. This field became a part of the study of names and things in its pursuit of the characteristics of specific specimens and types of plants. As for the study of local products, as Shirai had pointed out, its purpose was to study and record the products of various regions. Among topographical publications on the geography and climate of specific regions, some focused on products from the region; these can be considered an aspect of the study of names and things. The sixth category, encyclopedic studies, refers to publications in edited volumes that provided notations on ancient texts dealing with general topics. Although these publications were originally intended as reference books for composing Chinese poetry, some of these publications contained rich information that related to names and things. One exemplary publication from this group is *Collected Illustrations of the Three Realms* (Ch. *Sancai tuhui*, J. *Sansaizue*) in 106 volumes, compiled by Wang Qi and published in 1609. This title could arguably be characterized as a study of names and things itself, rather than as a mere recourse for such study. Aoki referred to these edited compilations as encyclopedic *mingwuxue*.[93]

According to Aoki, later phases of the study of names and things "developed into the discipline of evidential research (Ch. *kaozhengxue*, J. *kōshōgaku*) during the Qing dynasty, where limited numbers of names and things were extracted as objects of study."[94] He then elaborated on this development by focusing on clothing, eating and drinking, dwelling, and crafts. He concluded that the study of names and things "emerged as the exegetic study of names and things, with its ultimate goal residing in evidential research."[95] Aoki himself keenly practiced this study of names and things through evidential research on specific things, and compiled his results in *Studies on Names and Things in China*.

WORDS AND THINGS IN THE STUDY OF NAMES AND THINGS

Aoki's exposition on the study of names and things (Ch. *mingwuxue*, J. *meibutsugaku*) was based solely on materials and discussion in China, and did not include his interpretation of its development in Japan. But Aoki did use examples from the study of *materia medica*, a field of *mingwuxue* or Japanese *meibutsugaku*, including works such as *Materia Medica in Japan* by Kaibara Ekiken and *Dictated Compendium of Materia Medica* (*Honzōkōmoku keimō*, 1803–5) by Ono Ranzan, a noted scholar of *materia medica* in Kyoto. Aoki referred to works like the tenth-century *Classified and Annotated Japanese Names* (*Wamyō ruijūshō*), by the aristocratic poet Minamoto no Shitagō, and the physician Terashima Ryōan's *Illustrated Sino-Japanese Encyclopedia* (*Wakan sansei zue*, 1712), which consisted of 105 volumes, as well as Confucian scholar Itō Tōgai's twenty-six volume *Names and Things in Six Tables* (*Meibutsu rikujō*, 1714). He considered these works as examples of an encyclopedic form of *mingwuxue* in Japan. The previous quote by Shirai Mitsutarō is taken from the commemorative lecture "Kaibara Ekiken as a scholar of encyclopedic study," which was delivered in 1913 on the occasion of the bicentennial anniversary of Kaibara's death. Aoki quoted the exact section of this lecture given by Shirai at the beginning of his own "Introduction to the Study of Names and Things," noting that "pivotal points [of *mingwuxue*] were identified thoroughly here." Thus we can imagine that within Aoki's trajectory of study, he also considered developments of *mingwuxue* in Japan.

On the other hand, the Tokugawa period is distinguished for the active engagement of many scholars of *materia medica*. In particular, Li Shizhen's *Compendium of Materia Medica* was treated as the foundational text to which scholars of *materia medica* should refer, and it continued to occupy a significant position throughout the period.[96] Also noteworthy here is a different interpretation, such as one given by Mizutani Shinjō, a scholar of Chinese literature, who noted that in contrast to China, "*meibutsugaku* in Japan was nurtured through the study of *materia medica* as its womb."[97]

In Shirai's view, encyclopedic study in Japan developed with three parallel fields: the study of *materia medica*, the study of names and things, and the study of local products. Did Shirai regard the position of the study of *materia medica* as central? Given Aoki's characterization of Shirai's words that the pivotal points of *mingwuxue* were noted there, a careful reading of Shirai is necessary. Shirai stated that *meibutsugaku* is a discipline that "compared and researched the names of things and actual objects." More concretely, he noted that this field "sought to explain names and their relationship to actual things such as animals, plants, and other products that appear in myriad books." At this point, Shirai's view is similar to that of Aoki, who argued that *mingwuxue* emerged and became independent of the exegesis of classical texts. Shirai argued for the necessity of this field, asserting that "even if one read about various objects and things in books, one could not have been said to have understood the book if one did not know what the actual thing was." Even in Shirai's time, "people today who read and compose poetry using the names of things without knowing the actual things." This will not do. For this reason, he continued, "it is imperative to study the actual existing things earnestly; in other words, a study of actual things" was necessary. Indeed, this is precisely the core value of the study of names and things or *meibutsugaku*.

Following this analysis, it should be clear that Shirai's view is different from the one that argues that *meibutsugaku* bifurcated from the study of *materia medica* during the Tokugawa period. Like Aoki, Shirai views *meibutsugaku* as an entity that has a broad, expansive capacity. In other words, he claimed that *meibutsugaku* is a discipline that inquires into the tense relationship between the names of things and actual objects. Furthermore, in the latter half of the quoted section, he pushed further, asserting that this is the study of actual things. Here, he pointed to the opposite direction of *meibutsugaku* that emerged from the exegesis of classical texts, which began with names and moved toward things. That is, he promoted a form of *meibutsugaku* that begin with things and moved toward names—a field of study that literally stuck to things.

Here, it is possible to summarize the two definitions of *meibutsugaku*: one narrowly defined as centered on textual annotation and commentaries, and the other, more expansive one, which extended to all things regardless of its natural or man-made character. Aoki argues for *meibutsugaku* in this latter sense, as the structuring condition of the other two fields of study, the study of *materia medica* and the study of local products. But such claims cannot dispel the impression that in historical reality, these two types of *meibutsugaku* were practiced simultaneously. Further, such a position would not encompass the expansive ways in which *meibutsugaku* studies tried to bridge the world of names and the world of things. If we recall, Aoki noted six different areas in his book: the studies of Confucian rites, the archaeology of vessels and implements, the study of *materia medica*, the study of horticulture, topographical study, and reference books. As a premise, Aoki insisted that the study of names and things was an independent field of inquiry. In other words, Aoki observed and accepted the similarities in these interests, ways of thinking, logic, and procedures of examination. He further identified *mingwuxue* as the representative basic theory of these six areas of inquiry; this brings the significance of Aoki's view to the fore. As an example, consider Itō Keisuke's intellectual interests and the breadth of the objects in his collection. They easily defied the distinction between natural and man-made. Itō's interests, his collection, and the force that enabled such expansive thinking only becomes imaginable if we accept Aoki's argument that study of names and things is the fundamental theory running through all six areas.

We can also take another perspective, and assert that what enabled study of names and things to be so expansive as a field was a universal assumption. This assumption claims that everything in this world has a proper name of its own, and that every name is paired with a thing to which it refers. Further, the two should, fundamentally, be perfectly matched. If one imagines that the world consists of such a stable signification system, it will create a specific view of the world. This is the view that modern structuralist linguistics once criticized and called *langue-nomenclature,* the view of language considers it an inventory of names. This linguistic view claims that linguistic signifiers such as *yama* in Japanese, *montagne* in French, and *mountain* in English share the identical referent in reality. According to this view, "the world is already articulated and ordered before words."[98] In this view, names function as labels put on things that have been articulated already. The Saussurean linguist Maruyama Keizaburō claims that according to this view, "a word is merely a copy of the original, which exists a priori, and in this sense is similar to a wardrobe put on things. Put differently, a word is merely a sense-datum pointing to a specific thing or concept that has been articulated beforehand."[99] *Meibutsugaku,* too, is predicated on the view that names and things should match, and maintain this close tie in a transparent and clear relationship without any hint of doubt. On the basis of this assumption, the exegesis of classic texts and the nomenclature of the study of *materia medica* came to face the world through the same thought process.

This linguistic perspective was fostered through general grammar during the classical age in Europe. According to Nakayama Gen, a philosopher and translator of Western philosophical writings including that of Foucault:

All linguistic theory during the classical age was based on the privileged and central existence of nouns. It was a "name" upon which all linguistic theories were contingent. This preponderance was dependent upon a utopian idea that aimed to secure completely transparent language in which a name pointed to a thing without any sense of confusion. All discourses of the classical age were deployed around this "name." For two centuries, the fundamental role of linguistic discourse in the West was "to give a name to things and through its name, point out the existence of things."[100]

It is in this "general grammar" that Foucault saw in *The Order of Things* the episteme of the classical age. To point to things and name it in this world of the classical age, according to Nakayama, was not merely "giving linguistic representation to the object" but also "positioning its representation in the general tableaux."[101] This is a suggestive remark in thinking about *meibutsugaku*.

On the other hand, the cultural anthropologist Yamaguchi Masao asserted that the writing style of the essay literature known as *zuihitsu* in the Tokugawa period was demanded by a structure of knowledge that placed significance on a "mandala-like arrangement."[102] According to him, the structure of modern epistemology demands above all "a hierarchy among facts" and seeks to "specify, based on a specific paradigm, the hierarchical order among a set of facts by giving them relationships of rank and causal relations." In contrast to this, Yamaguchi claims that "the structure of knowledge in and before the Tokugawa period prioritized mandala-like arrangements over causal relations." The form of the *zuihitsu* essay, therefore, "tried to let the facts," which were arranged in a mandala-like form, "speak by themselves to distribute the facts to the mandala-like structure of knowledge already in place in the minds of its readers." According to Yamaguchi, "in the field of material as well as in biological matters, the study of *materia medica*" took the same form.[103] The "mandala-like arrangement," ordered by completely opposite structural principles of hierarchy and causal relationship, still shares fundamental elements with the "general tableau" of which Foucault spoke.[104] Both structures point to the core of *meibutsugaku*.

This idea of the mandala-like arrangement resonates with the one-mat room of Matsuura Takeshirō, made by collecting old pieces of wood through "a solicitation of wood scraps." Actual pieces collected through this were not particularly old, the majority of them dating from the Muromachi period (1338–1573) and after. But although they were relatively new, these pieces possessed "symbolic antiquity." According to Henry D. Smith, a historian of Japan, the term "old wood" (*furuku*)" itself was "an appropriate leitmotif for the structure as a whole."[105] To begin, there could not have been a relationship of hierarchical value among these wood scraps based on their antiquity. It is not that the small room was built only through collected pieces of wood scraps. Rather, some of the scraps were incorporated into larger sections of frames and walls, while others were used as decorative elements. Such mandala-like arrangements of wood scraps functioned as a device to position the one-mat room within an infinitely expanding world, and at the same time to make the interior space into a microcosm of the world.

Let me push this discussion a bit further. The arrangements of the thirty-one categories of *kokikyūbutsu* issued on the separate sheet of the edict regarding the preservation of *kokikyūbutsu* in the fifth month of 1871, too, shared a mandala-like pattern (see chapter 1). That is, this list was not a taxonomic chart, but rather the tableau that Foucault invoked. It is likely that at this point in 1871, the list encompassed things that ought to have been the object of protection. But, looking at the list from the perspective of organizing principles, it does not guarantee one of the basic principles of a taxonomic chart, "the principle of exhaustiveness," that all things are completely embraced within a particular category, and there is nothing left outside this category (see prologue). It is not guaranteed because all things under the list are regarded as having an equal value. Put differently, the list does not show how the categories themselves relate to one another. Although there is a distinctive relationship of inclusion between the names of the categories and the things included within each category, there is no demonstration of a distinction between upper and lower strata of objects among the categories themselves. The world that permeates this tableau, therefore, has no relation to the world structured by a hierarchical order.

In addition, we can also trace the thinking of *meibutsugaku* among the interests and activities of the individuals we have explored. For example, Itō Keisuke translated Carl Peter Thunberg's *Flora Japonica*, which Philipp von Siebold had presented him, and published *Nominal Differentiations in Western Materia Medica* in 1829. The primary task in this publication for Itō was to match Japanese names to the scientific names used in Thunberg's book. In 1874, Itō's disciple Tanaka Yoshio published an edited version of Iinuma Yokusai's *Illustrated Explanations of Plants and Trees of Japan* as *Newly Revised Illustrated Explanations of Plants and Trees of Japan*. The editorial work in which Tanaka was engaged was to add scientific names and family names to the botanical plants included in Iinuma's book. In other words, Tanaka's task was the reverse of Itō's. Tanaka also participated in the editorial work of the English–Japanese dictionary, *Revised and Expanded Pocket Dictionary of the English and Japanese Languages* (*Kaisei zōho eiwa taiyaku shūchin jisho,* 1866) and worked on translating names of animals, plants, and minerals by consulting Japanese and Chinese books on *materia medica* and geography, as well as English–Chinese dictionaries.[106] This was similar to the work of his mentor, Itō Keisuke.

The field of *meibutsugaku* in the Tokugawa period, particularly that of the study of *materia medica,* had a specific historical task, namely the complicated and at times tedious work of matching the names of things among different linguistic systems. Although much of this effort was directed toward matching Chinese names to Japanese names and vice versa, over this distinction of the two different names was layered another distinction between proper names (*seimei*) and popular names (*zokumei*), more colloquial or local names. Linguist Shimada Isao argues that this discursive exercise in articulating the corresponding relationships among names was referred to as the study of proper names (*seimeinogaku*).[107] Although Itō and Tanaka also worked with several European languages, the process of thinking in which they were engaged was necessarily the same as those working primarily between Chinese and Japanese. In each case, the view of language *langue-nomenclature* remained as assumed. According to this assumption, the world of things is articulated and ordered before language, and even if the names of the object differ from one language to another, the referent to which these different names point is identical.

Aoki Masaru made one other significant point in his "Introduction to the Study of Names and Things," regarding "the development of publications that included illustrations of things." According to Aoki, the illustrations depicting things such as clothing, vessels, and implements had existed since the Han dynasty within the discourses of *mingwuxue* in the books of Three Rites.[108] To articulate the relationship between names and things, illustration became a highly effective and persuasive means to demonstrate their relationship. He added that the 106-volume *Collected Illustrations of the Three Realms* by Wang Qi, published during the Ming dynasty, was the best of its kind among similar publications in its comprehensiveness "that collected notable things according to types and illustrated them pictorially."[109] Among the books listed in his introduction are those titles that begin with phrases such as "Illustrated Account of" (Ch. *tushuo*, J. *zusetsu*), "Illustrated consideration of" (Ch. *tukao*, J. *zukō*), and "illustrated catalog" (Ch. *tulu*, J: *zuroku*). Certainly many publications that bear the phrase "Illustrated books of" (Ch. *tupu*, J. *zufu*)" in the title that were written by scholars of *materia medica* during the Tokugawa period are included as examples of this kind in his bibliography. Works we have already discussed, such as *The Pleasures of Scattering Clouds* by Matsuura Takeshirō, *Illustrated Catalog of Appreciating the Past* by Yokoyama Yoshikiyo, and *Illustrated Book of Past Things: Ceramics Section* by Ninagawa Noritane, ought to be seen in this context of the illustrated explanations of notable things. The fact that Ninagawa insisted on focusing on "actual objects" rather than "historical books" in his introduction to the catalog (see chapter 2) becomes easier to understand as a type of thinking that emerged out of *meibutsugaku*. Recognizing these patterns of discursive thought also allows us to confirm the thought processes that were shared between antiquarians like Ninagawa who demonstrated a keen interest in things past, and the scholars of *materia medica* whose primary interest lay in natural things.

Let us return to exhibitions one more time. The edict for the 1872 Yushima exhibition began by noting, "The purpose of this exhibition lies in enlightening the knowledge of the people by collecting various products from the world without imposing the distinction of natural or man-made. We will correct their names, and provide explanations of their uses."[110] Similar phrases were deployed in the document titled "General Purpose of the Exhibition" that was published at the time of the Exhibition of Local Products, organized by the South School of Daigaku in the previous year.[111] What is significant in these documents is the double emphasis on collecting things without drawing any distinctions between the natural and the man-made, and the act of correcting names. These two acts constituted the core mission of the study of names and things. Another shared element between these documents, the phrases "enlightening the knowledge of the people" and "providing explanations of their uses" also stemmed from the spirit of the study of names and things on a basic level, although one could claim they were individually the roles of the study of *materia medica* and the study of local products. These early exhibition practices emerged as a new form of thinking in the field of *meibutsugaku*—and they were accepted as such.

NOTES

1   Ishii Kendō, *Meiji jibutsu kigen* (Tokyo: Chikuma Shobō, 1997), 303.

2   Ishii, *Meiji jibutsu kigen,* 320.

3   For the detail of the original plan, see Tokyo Kokuritsu Hakubutsukan ed., *Tokyo Kokuritsu Hakubutsukan hyakunenshi* (Tokyo: Tokyo Kokuritsu Hakubutsukan, 1973), 27–38.

4   Kinoshita Naoyuki, "Daigaku Nankō bussankai ni tsuite," in University of Tokyo, ed., *Gakumon no arukeorojii* (Tokyo: Tokyo Daigaku Shuppankai, 1997), 86–88.

5   Tokyo Kokuritsu Hakubutsukan, *Tokyo Kokuritsu Hakubutsukan hyakunenshi: Shiryōhen* (Tokyo: Tokyo Kokuritsu Hakubutsukan, 1973), 574–604.

6   See Maki Fukuoka, *The Premise of Fidelity: Science, Visuality, and Representing the Real in Nineteenth-Century Japan* (Stanford, CA: Stanford University Press, 2012), 165–77.

7   Iidashi Bijutsuhakubutsukan ed., *Nihon no hakubutsukan no chichi Tanaka Yoshio ten* (Iida: Iidashi Bijutsuhakubutsukan, 1999), 15–30.

8   Ueno Masuzō, *Oyatoi gaikokujin 3: Shizen kagaku* (Tokyo: Kajima Shuppankai, 1968), 81–99.

9   Isono Naohide, "Tanaka Yoshio no harimazechō to zatsurokushū," *Keiō daigaku Hiyoshi kiyō: Shizen kagaku* 18 (September 1995): 27–35. These scrapbooks are in the rare book collection of the General Library at the University of Tokyo, along with Tanaka's own collection of books.

10 Higuchi Hideo, "Tanaka Yoshio to 'Kunshūjō': Tokyo Kokuritsu Hakubutukan no hyaku nen," *Hakubutsukan nyūsu* 296 (January 1972): 4.

11 Sugimoto Isao, *Itō Keisuke*, Jinbutsu sōsho 46, new ed. (Tokyo: Yoshikawa Kōbunkan, 1988), 118–34, 188–207, 279–82. Before Itō passed away at the age of ninety-nine in January 1901, he had become the first individual in Japan to receive the doctorate of science in 1889.

12 Edward S. Morse, *Japan Day by Day: 1877, 1878–79, 1882–83* (Boston and New York: Houghton Mifflin, 1917), 1:135–36.

13 Morse, *Japan Day by Day,* 2:197.

14 Yoshida Itaru, "Itō Keisuke shūshū no sekki," *Kōkogaku zasshi* 62, no. 3 (December 1976): 1–5.

15 Kitajima Yutaka, "Owari Nagoya ni okeru shogakai ni tsuite," *Bijutsushi kenkyū* 36 (December 1998): 69–71; Robert Campbell, "Kanshō no nagare: Shogakai shi seki sono ni, Edo Kan'ōji seien gashū," *Bungaku* 8, no. 3 (July 1997): 2–3.

16 Ueno Kenji, "Shogakai annai shū," *Tochigi kenritsu bijutsukan kiyō* 6 (March 1979): 56–69.

17 Ryūkyū and Annam refer to present-day Ryukyu Islands in Okinawa prefecture and Vietnam.

18 Yokoyama Megumi, "Meiji shonen no bussankai to Takemoto Yōsai," *Toshimakuritsu kyōdo shiryōkan nenpō, fu kenkyū kiyō* 13 (March 1999): 16.

19 "Choson" (Kr. Joseon) refers to the Joseon Dynasty, which flourished between 1392 and 1897 on the Korean Pennisula.

20 In the Namamugi Incident an attending samurai of the Satsuma domain, present-day Kagoshima prefecture, killed one and injured two British men at Namamugi village near Yokohama in 1862 (Bunkyū 2) because the men riding on horseback disturbed the procession of the Lord of Satsuma to the domain from Edo. The breakdown in negotiations for compensation between the British government and the Satsuma domain caused a war between the two governments, known as the Kagoshima Bombardment, in 1863.

21 *Rusui*, literally meaning the supervisor of the Edo castle while the shogun was absent, was the highest position to which samurais of the vassal class (*hatamoto*) were appointed.

22 Yokoyama Megumi, "Takemoto Yōsai to 'Gansui-en' no sōgyō ni tsuite," *Toshima kuritsu kyōdo shiryōkan nenpō, fu kenkyū kiyō* 12 (March 1998): 7–14.

23 Yokoyama, "Meiji shonen no bussankai to Takemoto Yōsai," 17–19.

24 The scientific name is unidentified.

25 Aararenoya shujin (Akamatsu Noriyoshi), "Uchida Tsunejirō shōden," *Kyū bakufu* 3, no. 1 (January 1899): 53–59.

26 Nakayama Shigeru, *Teikoku daigaku no tanjō: Kokusai hikaku no naka de no Tōdai* (Tokyo: Chūō Kōronsha, 1978), 6.

27 Ikeda Atsufumi, "*Yochi Shiryaku* to *Bankoku Shashinchō*," *Museum* 501 (December 1992): 26–29.

28 Nakayama, *Teikoku daigaku no tanjō*, 4.

29 Tokyo Kokuritsu Hakubutsukan, *Tokyo Kokuritsu Hakubutsukan hyakunenshi: Shiryōhen*, 567. The original is in "Tanaka Yoshio kun no keireki dan" in Dai Nippon Sanrinkai, ed., *Tanaka Yoshio kun shichi roku tenrankai kinen shi* (Tokyo: Dai Nippon Sanrinkai, 1913), 19.

30 Nakayama, *Teikoku daigaku no tanjō*, 4.

31 Nakayama, *Teikoku daigaku no tanjō*, 4.

32 Henry D. Smith, *Taizansō and the One-Mat Room* (Mitaka: International Christian University, Hachirō Yuasa Memorial Museum, 1993), 21–31, 89.

33 Saitō Tadashi, "Matsuura Takeshirō no kōkogaku kan," *Nihon rekishi* 378 (November 1979), 68–71.

34 Yoshida Takezō, *Shūi Matsuura Takeshirō* (Tokyo: Matsuura Takeshirōden Kankōkai, 1964), 25.

35 Yoshida, "Itō Keisuke shūshū no sekki," 1–3.

36 Yoshida, *Shūi Matsuura Takeshirō*, 194.

37 Morse, *Japan Day by Day*, 2:365.

38 Morse, *Japan Day by Day*, 2:366.

39 A list enumerating names often shows ranks among the names in its order, in the case of which the last position of the list, or *tori*, implicitly means the highest rank.

40 A notable historian of early modern and modern Japan, Senzō Mori listed Wakaki Hayashi, Engyo Mitamura, and Chikusei Mimura as "three major connoisseurs of Things Edo." This anecdote about Matsuura and Kashiwagi was told by Chikusei Mimura to a metalsmith, Hotsuma Katori (1874–1954), and is said to be one of the strangest episodes regarding Kashiwagi. See Katori Hotsuma, "Dōkan Sanbō zakki," *Gasetsu* 8 (1937): 183–88; and Mori Senzō and Koide Masahiro, eds., *Shinpen Meiji jinbutsu yawa* (Tokyo: Iwanami Shoten, 2001), 386.

41 Ōkawa Mitsuo, "Kōshō Kashiwagi Kaichirō no keireki to sono shiteki hyōka ni tsuite," *Nihon kenchiku gakkai keikakukei ronbunshū* 459 (May 1994): 149–54.

42 Tokyo Kokuritsu Hakubutsukan, *Tokyo Kokuritsu Hakubutsukan hyakunenshi*, 79, 163.

43 Ōkawa, "Kōshō Kashiwagi Kaichirō," 149.

44 Morse, *Japan Day by Day*, 2:363.

45 Morse, *Japan Day by Day*, 2:363.

46 Edward S. Morse, *Japanese Homes and Their Surroundings* (Boston: Ticknor, 1886), 159.

47 Hirose Chika, *Yamanaka Kyōko nōto* (Tokyo: Seitōsha, 1973), 2:68.

48 Katori, "Dōkan Sanbō zakki," 188.

49 Goto Bijutsukan ed., *Donnō no me: Masuda Donnō no bi no sekai* (Tokyo: Goto Bijutsukan, 1998), 66.

50 Masuda Yoshinobu, "Kaden no 'Genji emaki': Watakushi no kokuhō," *Geijutsu shinchō* 4, no. 10 (October 1953): 129–30.

51 Tokyo Kokuritsu Hakubutsukan, *Tokyo Kokuritsu Hakubutsukan hyakunenshi: Shiryōhen*, 605.

52 Tokyo Kokuritsu Hakubutsukan, *Tokyo Kokuritsu Hakubutsukan hyakunenshi*, 26, 38–47, 85, 226. Although various guesses have been made regarding the reason of his resignation, his motivation is unclear. He then became the chief priest of Kōjōin, a sub-temple of Onjōji Temple in present-day Shiga prefecture.

53 The commemorative stone was completed in 1913 and remains standing on the grounds of the Tokyo National Museum.

54 Okanoya Shigezane, "Nara Shōsōin no hōki, tsuketari Machida Hisanari kun itsuwa," *Shidankai sokkiroku* 275 (March 1916): 20–21, 23.

55 The archer's wrist protector *tomo*, made of leather, which is put on the wrist of the left hand holding a bow. The bamboo mats, woven with bamboo fiber, are used to wrap scrolls of Buddhist sutras.

56 Morse, *Japan Day by Day*, 2:356.

57 "Shogen," in Ninagawa Teiichi, ed., *Ninagawa Noritane tsuibo roku* (Kyoto: Gotandaen, 1933).

58 Inokuma Nobuo, "Ninagawa Noritane jiseki," in Ninagawa, *Ninagawa Noritane tsuibo roku*, 24.

59 Tanaka Yoshio, "Kyoto ni okeru hakurankai no sōsetsu wa ko Ninagawa Noritane shi no yūdō ni izuru setsu" in Ninagawa, *Ninagawa Noritane tsuibo roku*, 36.

60 Aoki Shigeru, "Ninagawa Noritane ni tsuite," in Ninagawa Chikamasa, ed., *Shintei kanko zusetsu: Jōkaku no bu* (Tokyo: Chūō Kōron Bijutsu Shuppan, 1990), 63.

61 Morse, *Japan Day by Day*, 2:415.

62 Morse, *Japan Day by Day*, 2:190.

63 Reproduction of a photograph, frontispiece of Ninagawa Teiichi, *Ninagawa Noritane tsuibo roku*.

64 Ninagawa Chikamasa, "Ninagawa Noritane to *Kanko zusetsu* ni tsuite," in Ninagawa Noritane, *Kanko zusetsu fukusei ban* (Tokyo: Rekishi Toshosha, 1973), 11.

65 Sakai Seiichi, *Henreki no buke: Ninagawa shi no rekishiteki kenkyū* (Tokyo: Yoshikawa Kōbunkan, 1963), 82–94.

66 Morse, *Japanese Homes and Their Surroundings*, 64–67.

67 Ninagawa, "Ninagawa Noritane to *Kanko zusetsu* ni tsuite," 79.

68 Tanaka, "Kyoto ni okeru hakurankai," 36.

69 Tokyo Kokuritsu Hakubutsukan, *Tokyo Kokuritsu Hakubutsukan hyakunenshi*, 85.

70 Ninagawa "Ninagawa Noritane to *Kanko zusetsu* ni tsuite," 80–81.

71 Tokyo Kokuritsu Hakubutsukan, *Tokyo Kokuritsu Hakubutsukan hyakunenshi*, 229.

72 Ōkawa, "Kōshō Kashiwagi Kaichirō," 148–49.

73 Tokyo Kokuritsu Hakubutsukan, *Tokyo Kokuritsu Hakubutsukan hyakunenshi,* 173.

74 Kinoshita, "Daigaku Nankō bussankai ni tsuite," 93.

75 Throughout the book, I translate *kokugakusha* as "nativist," and *kokugaku* as "nativism." For a summary of debate surrounding the efficacy and limitation of this translation, see Mark Teeuwen, "Kokugaku vs. Nativism," *Monumenta Nipponica* 61, no. 1 (2006): 227–42. doi:10.1353/mni.2006.0023.

76 Kōda Shigetomo, "Yokoyama sensei ni tsukite," in Yokoyama Yoshikiyo, ed., *Nihon densei shi* (Tokyo: Ōokayama Shoten, 1926), 365–66.

77 Tokyo Kokuritsu Hakubutsukan, *Tokyo Kokuritsu Hakubutsukan hyakunenshi,* 46.

78 Tokyo Kokuritsu Hakubutsukan, *Tokyo Kokuritsu Hakubutsukan hyakunenshi,* 175.

79 A cultural society that Mori Arinori advocated to realize and was founded in 1873 with the original members including Fukuzawa Yukichi, Katō Hiroyuki, Nishi Amane, and Mitsukuri Rinshō.

80 Hasebe Kotondo, "Jindai ishi," *Kōkogaku zasshi* 30, no. 10 (October 1940): 6–11.

81 Tokyo Kokuritsu Hakubutsukan, *Tokyo Kokuritsu Hakubutsukan hyakunenshi,* 50–60.

82 Tokyo Kokuritsu Hakubutsukan, *Tokyo Kokuritsu Hakubutsukan hyakunenshi: Shiryōhen,* 150–60.

83 "One-million pagodas" are artifacts that date from the eighth century. An imperial order to manufacture them is understood as part of a governmental policy to govern through Buddhist principles.

84 [Anonymous], "Machida Hisanari ryakuden," a volume of manuscript in collection of the Historiographical Institute, University of Tokyo.

85 Masuo Fubō, "Kinsei kosenka retsuden dai san kai: Narushima Ryūhoku," *Hōsenka* 3 (August 1993), 90–94.

86 Narushima Ryūhoku, *Kōsei nichijō,* republished in Shiota Ryūhei, ed., *Narushima Ryūhoku, Hattori Bushō, Kurimoto Joun shū* (Tokyo: Chikuma Shobō, 1969), 117–44.

87 Kanō Tadanobu's father, Seisenin Kanō Osanobu, was a cousin of Narushima Ryūhoku.

88 Tsuda Umeko (1864–1929) is known as a forerunner of modern education for women in Japan and founded Joshi Eigaku Juku (Women's School for English Studies, present-day Tsuda University) in 1900 after studying in the United States from 1871 to 1882 and 1889 to 1892.

89 Tezuka Yutaka, "Seidokyoku minpō kaigi to Ninagawa Noritane nikki: Meiji hōsei shiryō shūi (2)," *Hōgaku kenkyū* 42, no. 8 (1969): 72–73.

90 Morse, *Japan Day by Day,* 1:136.

91 Shirai Mitsutarō, "Hakubutsu gakusha to shite no Kaibara Ekiken," in *Kōchū Yamato Honzō,* Kaibara Ekken (Tokyo: Shun'yōdō, 1932), 5; and "Honzōgaku, honzōgakushi

kenyū," in *Shirai Mitsutarō chosakushū,* ed. Kimura Yōjirō (Tokyo: Kagaku Shoin, 1985), 1:280–81.

92 Togawa Yoshio, "Atogaki" in Aoki Masaru, *Chūka meibutu kō* (Tokyo: Heibonsha, 1988), 312.

93 Aoki, *Chūka meibutu kō,* 41.

94 Aoki, *Chūka meibutu kō,* 43.

95 Aoki, *Chūka meibutu kō,* 23.

96 Ueno Masuzō, *Nihon hakubutsugaku shi* (Tokyo: Heibonsha, 1986), 42.

97 Mizutani Shinjō, "Kaisetsu," in Yuan Mei, *Zuien shokutan* (*Suiyuan shidan*), trans. Aoki Masaru (Tokyo: Iwanami Shoten, 1980), 290.

98 Maruyama Keizaburō, *Soshūru o yomu* (Tokyo: Iwanami Shoten, 1983), 131, 282.

99 Maruyama, *Soshūru o yomu,* 282.

100 Nakayama Gen, *Fūkō nyūmon* (Tokyo: Chikuma Shobō, 1996), 95.

101 Nakayama, *Fūkō nyūmon,* 95.

102 The Sanskrit mandala is, for esoteric sects of Buddhism, a tableau depicting sacred characters gathered in a geometric pattern of a harmonious cosmos, used as a principal image for esoteric rituals.

103 Yamaguchi Masao, *"Haisha" no seishinshi* (Tokyo: Iwanami Shoten, 1995), 535–36.

104 Nakayama, *Fūkō nyūmon,* 95.

105 Smith, *Taizansō and the One-Mat Room,* 25.

106 Sakurai Takehito, "Kaiseijo no yakugo to Tanaka Yoshio: Tenjiku nezumi (morumotto) no yakugo o tegakari ni," *Kokugo kokubun* 812 (April 2002), 1–3.

107 Shimada Isao, "Kaisetsu *Wakan sansai zue, jō,*" in Terashima Ryōan, *Wakan sansai zue,* trans. Shimada Isao et al. (Tokyo: Heibonsha, 1985), 2:359–62.

108 Aoki, *Chūka meibutu kō,* 35.

109 Aoki, *Chūka meibutu kō,* 41.

110 Tokyo Kokuritsu Hakubutsukan, *Tokyo Kokuritsu Hakubutsukan hyakunenshi: Shiryōhen,* 148.

111 Tokyo Kokuritsu Hakubutsukan, *Tokyo Kokuritsu Hakubutsukan hyakunenshi,* 28–29.

CHAPTER 5

Antiquarians in Nineteenth-Century Japan

SECTION 1: THINGS AND PEOPLE

EXPANDING THE STUDY OF NAMES AND THINGS

In chapter 2 we explored the publication of the 1877 volume *The Study of Things Past* (*Kobutsugaku*). This book was part of the series *Encyclopedia*, which was published in ninety-two volumes by the Ministry of Education as a civilizing and instructional book. This series was based on the two-volume *Chambers's Information for the People*, compiled by the brothers William and Robert Chambers. The title, *Kobutsugaku,* was a Japanese translation of the English term *archaeology*, which formed the title of a chapter in the original *Information for the People*. The volume explained the establishment of archaeology and noted, "Today, the term is used based on its broadest sense of the word—the term archaeology [*kobutsugaku*] come to encompass science, based on the examinations of ruins and relics that provides outlines of the past through deduction."[1] In other words, it insisted that archaeology is a broad field of study that considers history through the examination of things. This can be contrasted to the historical studies that focused on manuscripts and other text-based artifacts. The method of studying history proposed in this volume, that is, a study that resolutely placed things at the center of historical inquiry, must have appealed to those readers who were trying to understand and accept the new field of archaeology for its fresh approach to pursue the study of names and things. In the volume, in addition to the fact that the discipline emerged from historical studies of the Greek and Roman empires, the universality of this new field was asserted confidently in the claim that "the etymological meaning of the term includes the thorough examination and explanation of various ancient events and phenomena."[2]

In other words, a possibility for the study of names and things as "the new" was demonstrated through and by European language.

At the same time, the study of things past advocated here also brought with it a certain danger. This study could easily transform the objects under consideration into a representation of "outlines of the past." In other words, things could become a mere ingredient used to "deduce" the historical past, rather than the main protagonist of the historical narrative. This is similar to the case of the new concept of *kokikyūbutsu*, when the term was evoked in relation to the evaluating standard for "the examination of the past," thereby transforming objects into representations of a specific past. Despite this risk, however, I contend that this volume offered the seed of a new direction that would provide an answer to the paradigmatic shift of "the new and the old." Following this, to bet on such potential was to experiment with new directions in the study of names and things by developing existing methodologies.

Undoubtedly, the paradigm of the new and the old, which appeared after the abandonment of national seclusion in 1854, heavily shook the field of the study of names and things in similar ways to other fields of study. Attempts to expand the field of the study of names and things also indicated its concrete response to this semantic shift. We have already examined in chapter 3 how some attempted to accept the changes in the practice of exhibitions of local products by replacing them with a new device, the exposition. Although the people who implemented these changes could be categorized in many ways, such as scholars of *materia medica* or as antiquarians, they shared a foundational logic that emerged from the study of names and things. In other words, no single nominal category could group them. To avoid further confusion and misunderstanding through neologism, let me for the time being refer to this group as "they." At stake here is the concrete form—and the stance—of their activities.

In chapter 4, I noted that when we characterize their interests, thinking, actions, and theory discursively, the field is best described as a discipline centered on objects. We have also noted that in their actual practices, two forms of action were included: the more private act of collecting, and the more public act of exhibiting their collections to one another. Here, I want to consider the networked infrastructure that connected those practitioners: associations.

Edward S. Morse made a notable observation. As we saw in chapter 1, he noted in *Shell Mounds of Omori* that "there is no other country in the world where so great a number of gentlemen interested in archaeology can be found as in Japan."[3] But the number of archaeologists was not the only element that surprised him. Immediately following this, he noted that a "native Archaeological Society holds its meetings regularly in Tokio, and many of the contributions are of great value."[4] Here, it is noteworthy that Morse used the term *native* to describe those at the gatherings. He referred to such gatherings again in the introduction of the book. He noted: "With the existence of an Archaeological Society in Tokyo, consisting exclusively of

Japanese, who hold their meetings regularly, and the fact that there have already been a number of works published by native archaeologists who have figured with more or less accuracy the stone implements, ancient vessels, inscriptions and the like."[5]

In both instances, Morse's term *native* connoted "the Japanese," and pointed to the fact that "native archaeologists," or Japanese antiquarians, had been producing various illustrated books and catalogs. Following this, we can come to see the concrete meaning of his words in the preface that "many of the contributions are of great value." Morse's high regard of the antiquarians in Japan also included his appreciation of their publishing activity.

There is one more aspect I want to add regarding associations. An issue of the weekly magazine *Nature,* published on 31 January 1878, included the following: "Japan has an active archaeological society, bearing the title of Kobutzu-Kai (Society of Old Things). Its members, numbering two hundred, are scattered throughout the land, but meet once a month in Yeddo. They consist chiefly of wealthy Japanese gentlemen, learned men, and priests; the latter especially have been the means of bringing before public attention a vast number of ancient objects which have been hidden in the treasures of the temples, or preserved in private families."[6]

This article tells us of the existence of a national society named Kobutzu-Kai, a nineteenth-century spelling of *kobutsukai*. Yeddo is also a nineteenth-century rendering of Edo, renamed Tokyo in 1868. The article continued to cover what appears to be the main subject: "H. von Siebold, Attaché of the Austrian Embassy, at Yeddo, and a member of the society, has lately published a *brochure*, which will serve as a guide for the systematic archaeological study of the land."[7] It served as a type of advertisement for his brochure. We will explore Siebold in depth in the latter section of this chapter. For the time being, let us examine how Siebold himself described this association. When Siebold published a short article in 1878 in Berlin, he described his own collecting activities. According to the Japanologist Josef Kreiner, Siebold noted in this article a gathering of "archaeological study" held in December 1877 at the residence of Matsudaira Tadayuki, located in Hikawachō town in the Akasaka area (present-day Minato ward) of Tokyo, which constituted a part of their regular meetings.[8] Unfortunately, not much more can be unearthed about this gathering. However, in Morse's book *Shell Mounds of Omori,* when he mentioned "an Archaeological Society in Tokio," it is certain that he was referring to this archaeological society, that is to say the Society of Old Things.

THE LIBERTY OF ASSOCIATIONS

If we trust these articles, this society formed a large association that included a few hundred members covering all corners of the country. How did such an association come to be organized, and how was it supported?

There were a few associations during the Tokugawa period. Among them was an association known as Ibunkai, active in the city of Kyoto for over fifty years, from 1811 (Bunka 8) to the Bakumatsu period. The members regularly met to bring rare items from their collections and tell stories about these objects. Members took turns being the organizer for their gatherings. Although not all meetings were equally successful, on average about fifty members were present at regular gatherings. In the city of Edo, an association called Tankikai was well known. This association consisted of twelve literati in the city; members met once a month. The gathering was held for them to bring their own objects and entertain themselves by discussing matters concerning things past. The members included figures such as the popular novelist Kyokutei Bakin (1767–1848), the essayist Yamazaki Yoshishige (1796–1856), and nativist scholar Yashiro Hirokata (1758–1841). The painter Tani Bunchō also participated from time to time. Their gatherings began in 1824 (Bunsei 7) at a restaurant in the vicinity of Shinobazu Pond, meeting there over twenty times until 1825. The records of their gatherings remain in the form of a twenty-volume manuscript titled "Rambling Notes of Immersion in the Strange" (*Tankimanroku*). This included illustrations and explanations of objects that members brought to the gatherings such as old calligraphy and paintings, antiquities, and rare and strange objects; these volumes were circulated among members.

In terms of scale, the association called Rōsekisha was probably the largest. In the Tokugawa period, those who collected and studied stones and minerals were called *rōsekika* (literally, men who took delight in stones). The central member of this association was Kiuchi Sekitei (1725–1808), based in Omi, present-day Shiga prefecture. Kiuchi published *Records of Stones* (*Unkonshi*, 1773–1801), a comprehensive illustrated catalog in three parts consisting of fourteen volumes, between 1773 and 1801, in which he documented various types of minerals as well as wide-ranging types of stones such as stone implements and comma-shaped beads. The number of members of Rōsekisha was well beyond a few hundred, and they were based in all corners of the country. Although it is unclear when they organized their gatherings, it has been noted that Kiuchi frequently organized gatherings of Rōsekisha in Kyoto called *Kisekikai*, literally "a gathering of curious stones."[9] In regards to gatherings related to the study of *materia medica*, I have already mentioned the Shōhyakusha, whose activities were centered around Nagoya. In addition, a similar association named Shabenkai was active in the city of Edo. Its members consisted exclusively of samurais who were members of feudal lords and housemen and bannermen, and they were active until 1844, the end of the Tenpō era.[10]

Although these associations varied in size, they all gathered regularly or irregularly to conduct "show and tell" of the objects from their collections. The relationship between associations and these gathering occasions was inextricable. Early examples include a gathering of local products in 1758 that *materia medica* scholar Tamura Ransui (1718–76) organized with his disciple Hiraga Gennai (1728–79) and others at Yushima in the city of Edo. The six-volume publication *Natural Objects Categorized* (*Butsurui hinshitsu*, 1763), compiled by Hiraga, is a set of illustrated catalogs of items submitted at four different events, including the one at Yushima in 1758. In 1760, Tamura's disciple Toda Itsuki (known as Kyokuzan, 1696–1769) organized a gathering in Osaka. In 1763, a large-scale gathering of local products was held in the Higashiyama area of Kyoto. From this time on, such gatherings of local products took place in various cities in the country.[11]

The records of gatherings of painting and calligraphy were published slightly later. In Saitō Gesshin's *Chronicles of Edo* (*Bukō nenpyō,* 1850), he noted under a section called "Reports on Events during the *Kansei* Era," that "it was around this time that gatherings of painting and calligraphy began to be organized at restaurants."[12] The connoisseur Anzai Un'en's *Collected Talks on Notable Men of Calligraphy and Paintings in Recent Times* (*Kinsei meika shogadan,* 1832–44) noted, under the section of "the origins of gatherings of painting and calligraphy in Edo," that Tani Bunchō and others organized a gathering of calligraphy and painting in 1792 at the Manpachirō restaurant in Yanagibashi town of Edo (present-day Taitō ward). In Kyoto, according to the art historian Kitajima Yutaka, a series of gatherings called the "gathering in Higashiyama displaying new works of painting and calligraphy" (Higashiyama shin shoga tankankai), organized by the literati painter Minagawa Kien (1734–1807) was well known. It also began in 1792 and held shows twice a year in the spring and the fall. Minagawa organized a total of fourteen gatherings, as noted in *Kien's Collected Writings* (*Kien bunshū,* 1799). As a result, Kitajima surmises that gatherings of painting and calligraphy began in the mid-eighteenth century through the example of the literati and dilettante Kimura Kenkadō (1736–1802), who played a pivotal role in the pursuit of the study of *materia medica* and other hobbies and amusement in the Kyoto-Osaka district.[13] According to the scholar of Edo literature Robert Campbell, it is also known that Ike Taiga (1723–76) used the term *shogashūkai,* literally meaning a gathering of calligraphy and paintings, in an inscription dated 1770 on his painting. Surveying poetry in classical Chinese from this period, Campbell claims that least in the latter half of the Tenmei era (1781–88), the term *shogakai* frequently circulated as a term.[14]

If we were to emphasize an aspect of historical continuity, the Society of Old Things noted in the article in the January 1878 issue of *Nature* ought to be posited as an extension of the Tokugawa period associations surveyed above. As noted, the Rōsekisha functioned across the nation, and their activities took various forms. Were there shared characteristics among these wide-ranging activities?

The catalog *Record of Gathering* (*Bunkairoku,* 1760), a record of a gathering "to meet friends through letters," is well known as a publication based on the 1760 Exhibition of Local Products in Osaka sponsored by the scholar of *materia medica* Toda Kyokuzan (1696–1769). In this publication, a section titled "Rules of the Association" was included. One of the items noted:

> The purpose of this association, as has been notified to members, is to correct, clarify, and eliminate doubts about things submitted, especially as to whether they are real or fake. To this end, if any member holds any doubt, however

small, such doubt should be expressed, and the members shall carefully listen to them. After thoroughly discussing the matter, we shall determine collectively [whether the item is real or fake]. We hope members will express their doubts without any hesitation and explain themselves thoroughly. If our collective decision does not match with one's own opinion, please accept our decision and do not hold grudges against us.[15]

We witness here that the matter of real or fake should be decided through "collective discussion," and even when in doubt, the members would "explain themselves" without "hesitation." Therefore, it asked the members to refrain from becoming angry if resulting decision was different from what their expectation. An article such as this expresses the traits of such association clearly. In theory, the meetings of these associations strived to offer a space in which all participating members were treated equally, regardless of their class and social standing.

There is another example that I want to explore here: a collective gathering of connoisseurship to evaluate works of calligraphy and painting, including the samurai-class painter Watanabe Kazan (1793–1841). A document of their association rules, which is said to have remained as a draft, is preserved to this day. One of the articles in this document elaborated on member etiquette, noting that "this gathering is, in a word, organized with the idea to offer temporary pleasure by forgetting joy and sorrow, and to nurture our personalities." Giving concrete examples of such pleasure, it continued: "There is nothing like calligraphy and ink painting in this regard. While sitting, we can gaze a thousand miles away, or remember the faces of older generations to whom we are grateful, like our friends. There is no other way to experience these emotions. In addition, looking at the traces of a brush that had dripped the ink and stopped its motion, we can get a whiff of the ink, and become wholly absorbed in the sense of yearning."[16]

The document continued by encouraging the members: "Dear friends of similar motivation, if we dedicate ourselves together to learning, we ourselves could own" such feelings. It concluded by noting that the aim of their gathering was "to become your friends and neighbors, and to become parents to your pleasurable play and games."[17] If we read this document alone, the gathering would be easily characterized as a gathering of amateur hobbyists. There was an additional article in this document that warned the participants of an essential rule of engagement at the gathering. It asserted that the participating members should refrain from "offering lengthy descriptive explanations [of objects] with an intention of becoming intimate with other members, acting excessively subserviently to each other, interrupting others' talks, not finishing the discussions, forgetting the sense of embarrassment and continuing on to talk of one's loss, or profits, gossip of politics, or the fall and rise of people in general."[18]

This warning emerged out of their shared sense that real pleasure resided in clearing the dust of the everyday. Just as importantly, the document paid close attention to the relationships among the participants: it prohibited members from engaging in extensive and meaningless long addresses, an overtly subservient and courteous manner of speaking, and interrupting the conversations of other members. Such activities not only would mar the atmosphere of the gatherings, but also could serve to undermine the equal standing among the members. Once such a relationship is compromised, it would be difficult to speak up without hesitation. This document shares a similar logic to the rules of the *Bussankai* of 1760 in Osaka.

PLAYING A GAME, SITTING IN A CIRCLE

How did gatherings like this unfold in reality? Morse's observations are helpful here. In *Japan Day by Day,* he described a gathering of pottery connoisseurs in which he himself had participated. Although lengthy, I quote it here as it contains vivid and detailed description:

> The other night I was invited to an interesting gathering. Mr. Tanimura, a teacher of cha-no-yu, has a meeting every month of men who are interested in old Japanese pottery. It is a guessing party, and each one brings a specimen of pottery difficult to identify. These are numbered and recorded in a list by one who does not take part in the guessing contest. The method is rather curious. The party sit[s] around in a circle with candles in the middle, and each [person] has a lacquer cup with his name written on the bottom. A specimen of pottery, such as a tea-jar, bowl, or incense-box, is passed around, each in turn examines it, and then with a brush and India ink records his guess on the inside of the lacquer cup and places it face downward on the mat. When every one of the party has marked his guess, or opinion, the host records each name and opinion in a book. In this way we examined a number of old tea-jars, tea-bowls, and the like. It may be interesting to record that I got the highest number of correct attributions, and it was also gratifying to know that I was not alone when in error. A tea-jar that I called Takatori was said to be Zeze by the judge, for that was the name written on the box from which it was taken: an unsafe evidence, for the original piece in the box may have been broken or lost and another jar substituted that would fit the box—a very common practice. The two potteries closely resemble one another, however. Another piece said to be Koda, I am sure was not, as I am pretty sound on that pottery. It was interesting to meet such a pleasant party. One was a student, another a doctor, a third was an editor of a daily paper, another was a gentleman of leisure, and the host was a pottery expert. They all expressed their amazement at the quickness of my decisions, as I always put my lacquer cup down first. The others would look at the piece in turn, expressing their emotions in curious sounds, saying it was odd or troublesome, and grunt over it, and at the very last moment write their decisions. Figure 760 is a hasty sketch of the party.[19]

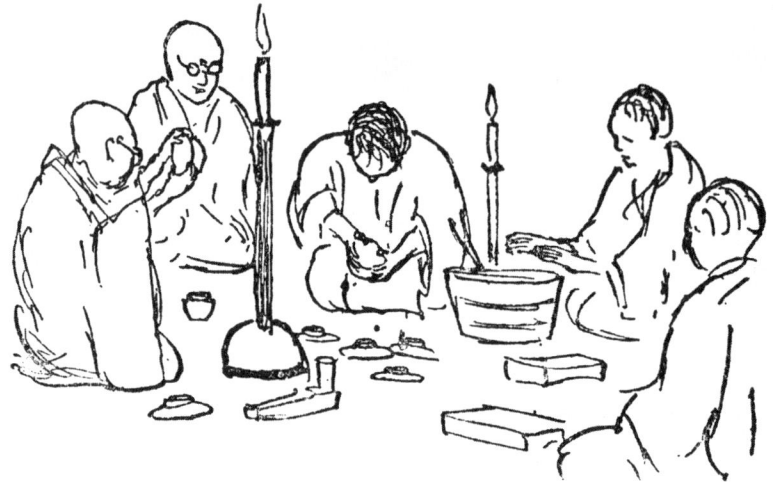

FIG. 14.

Edward S. Morse (American, 1838–1925).

Sketch of a party, from Edward S. Morse, *Japan Day by Day*, vol. 2, 1917.

We can easily imagine an expression of triumph on Morse's face. This entry was made during January of 1883 (Meiji 16) during his third visit to Japan (fig. 14).[20] Morse noted in July 1879 (Meiji 12): "Every Sunday Ninagawa has come to my house to identify the pottery I have collected during the week."[21] Morse received the know-how for the connoisseurship of pottery from Ninagawa. Ninagawa had passed away in August 1882, before the curious gathering Morse described above. For Morse, moreover, participation in gatherings like this was not new. In fact, he had participated in gatherings organized by Ninagawa. A story passed down in the Ninagawa family is indicative: "I had heard this directly from my father [Ninagawa Teiichi]. [When gathering together,] each person would handle a piece of pottery one at a time and pass it on, examine it by hand, and make his own judgment. They used a blindfold, covering both eyes with a towel tied behind their head. [Each person] evaluated the piece in hand based on the surface texture of the pottery, and judged to which genealogy the piece belonged, what kind of pottery it was, who made it, and how old it was."[22] Further, in these situations, too, Morse was said to be successful in this speculative game as much as he "had the highest mark on odds."[23]

This gathering took place at Rakukōsha, whose name literally meant "a house of enjoying arts." The space functioned as a printing studio at Ninagawa's private residence in Tokyo.[24] Ninagawa administered his studio in cooperation with figures such as Ōyama Shūzō, an expert from the printing studio Gengendō noted for its lithographic innovation, and Hikita Keizō (1851–1914), a Western-style painter from Kyoto who studied at the Technical Fine Arts School (Kōbu Bijutsu Gakkō). There, they engaged in various types of printing, including lithography.[25] They also produced a list of rules which was signed by Hikita, Ōyama, and Ninagawa.[26] While Ninagawa's studio was equipped with the newest printing machines for its primary business of printing, it appears it was also used to host gatherings such as this. What is most striking about this anecdote is the fact that all participants carried out their evaluation and judgment of pottery through the sense of touch alone, as they were blindfolded. Comparing this to the description Morse left in *Japan Day by Day*, it remains doubtful that Ninagawa's gatherings always required their participants to be blindfolded.

There is a fundamental and critical overlap between these two gatherings. That is, by imposing specific rules on the participants, they both created an environment in which each one's judgment was less likely to be influenced by those of others at the gatherings. Morse's description of placing one's answer inside the lacquer cup and turning it over echoes the same underlying intention. At Ninagawa's gathering, the order of blindfolding made it impossible to see how other participants were acting. On the one hand, rules like these heightened the sense of playfulness—in short, the gathering took on the form of a game. Moreover, if the purpose of these rules was to guarantee equality among the players, this did not contradict the purpose of the gathering per se. The document setting out the purpose of the gathering of connoisseurs initiated by Watanabe Kazan encouraged participants to "dedicate ourselves together to learning." Both gatherings, the one organized by Kazan for the connoisseurship of calligraphy and painting, and the other by Noritane for examining pottery, shared a common principle that valued learning from each other to refine one's skills and to expand one's knowledge. Winning, then, was not the only goal of the gathering. Thus, we can understand that these rules emerged from the motivation to create a sense of equality among the participants by sitting in a circle. We can further suggest that the formats resembling games were selected to buttress the principle of learning from each other and mutually refining their skill.

The line of thinking that supported the activities of associations was not limited to such occasions of collective gathering. Indeed, the same logic was applied, more or less, to exhibitions, such as exhibitions of local products or those of calligraphy and painting. In other words, perhaps unexpectedly to us, the act of blindfolding and offering explanations without hesitation emerged out of similar inspiration. Those scholars of *materia medica* and antiquarians, it seems to me, had been closely intertwined through the shared axis of these various forms of associations and their activities. According to Morse, these gatherings of connoisseurship took place monthly. The Society of Old Things mentioned in the article that appeared in *Nature* also met monthly. Ninagawa's gathering his printing studio also seems to have been held regularly. In other words, these occasions were firmly embedded within their routine of everyday life.

SECTION 2: DEPICTING THINGS

CHANGING ILLUSTRATED CATALOGS: LITHOGRAPHIC AND WOODBLOCK PRINTS

Since the associations we have examined in this chapter dealt with questions of tradition, they too must have directly faced issues emerging out of the paradigm shift of the new and the old. Before we move on to examine how they faced this, let us examine their actual practices. As Morse noted, the act of editing illustrated catalogs stood at the intersection of the thought and practice of *materia medica* scholars and antiquarians. As we have seen in chapter 4, Aoki Masaru highlighted "the development of publications that included illustrations of things" in expanding his understanding of the study of names and things. Here, the issues that occupied the minds of scholars of *materia medica* and antiquarians begin to emerge.

First, I want to focus on the technological aspect of illustrated catalogs. One of the new challenges in this regard was the introduction of lithographic printing. Lithography was invented by Alois Senefelder (1771–1834) in Munich in 1798, and spread to other European cities and North America in the early nineteenth century. This technology and photography would become exemplary technologies of reproduction in the nineteenth century. Walter Benjamin (1892–1940) articulated the fundamental impact of lithography in "The Work of Art in the Age of Its Technological Reproducibility" when he stated:

> Lithography marked a fundamentally new stage in the technology of reproduction. This much more direct process—distinguished by the fact that the drawing is traced on a stone, rather than incised on a block of wood or etched on a copper plate—first made it possible for graphic art to market its products not only in large numbers, as previously, but in daily changing variations. Lithography enabled graphic art to provide an illustrated accompaniment to everyday life. It began to keep pace with movable-type printing. But only a few decades after the invention of lithography, graphic art was surpassed by photography.[27]

Lithographic technology was suited to mass reproduction, and could respond to printing demand immediately. Thus, it served as a standard means of reproduction in the nineteenth century, when industry developed rapidly and the market expanded significantly.

During the Ansei era (1855–60), demonstrations of lithographic technology took place at the trading house of the Dutch East India Company in Dejima, Nagasaki.[28] In 1860, Prussian delegates gifted a lithographic printer to the Tokugawa shogunate. Foreign delegations sent by the shogunate also witnessed lithographic printing in various foreign locations. Knowledge of lithographic technology, and this technology itself, thus permeated through Japan from the mid-nineteenth century onward. After the 1868 Meiji Restoration, lithography came to be seen as an important technology for practical purposes that required technological refinements, such as printing bills, postage stamps, certificates of bonds, and maps.[29] However, it was only in the later Meiji period that the fundamental advantages of lithography as a simple technology for mass reproduction would become widely accepted and implemented.

Compared to this later condition, the situation in the early Meiji was more complicated. The rise of lithographic prints over woodblock prints is clear among the illustrated catalogs I examine in this chapter. While the use of lithography in the early Meiji period represents a significant shift, its use is marked by recognizing an advance toward the technology itself, rather than as a tool of mass reproduction.

> During the era of Kaei (1848–55), I borrowed a Western lithographic print from a friend. I discovered that [this print] has qualities of representing the real in totality, and also a certain type of charm to it. I immediately had a desire to learn this technique, but it was difficult to find a way to acquire this knowledge. Day and night, I was frustrated with this situation. During this time, I thought that the only way to learn this was to inquire with officials so that I could become the apprentice of a foreigner. However, it was not possible for me to find procedures that would allow me to do so. I spent days feeling empty. Just prior to this time, the Institute for the Study of Barbarian Books was established, and I thought that perhaps I would be able to see an aspect of the Western method of making representations there.[30]

This is a well-known excerpt from the memoir *The Career of Takahashi Yuichi* (*Takahashi Yuichi rireki*, 1892), in which Takahashi narrated the initial impetus for him to study Western pictorial methods—the surprise he experienced when he first saw a lithographic print. One of the reasons why lithography gained attention in this period is echoed in Takahashi's experience during the Bakumatsu period. The focus of this attention was its ability to reproduce an image with a high level of fidelity. On this point, woodblock prints could not be compared to lithography.

Naturally, photographic technology possessed the same qualities of lithographic prints that had so attracted Takahashi, who went on to become a pioneer of Western-style painting. Perhaps photography was unrivaled in its fidelity to recreating the shape of an object seen through the lens. We cannot ignore the influence of photography, beginning with the Bakumatsu period. The introduction of lithography, then, must be considered in tandem with the availability of its rival, photography. However, in the early Meiji period, photography was not decisively connected with printing technology; this is why it did not supersede lithography in the realm of reproduced illustrations.

To summarize the argument ahead, the relationship between lithographic and photographic technologies became reversed in the Meiji twenties (1887–97). This was largely due to the emergence of the collotype, which enabled the use of photographic negative plates for printing. Even though the number of reproducible prints was limited, collotype prints better captured tonal expressions without the cross-hatching that characterized the halftone process of lithography. Thus, the collotype was understood as a better option for reproducing the illustrations of art objects. In fact, the introduction of the collotype instigated publications of a series of luxuriously illustrated books of art objects.[31] On the other hand, in the world of woodblock printing, the technology of wood engraving came onto the scene. Already in 1863 (Bunkyū 3), attempts were made to use this new technology.[32] Invented by the British woodblock printer Thomas Bevick (1755–1828), wood engraving enabled expressions of detail while also allowing multiple people to quickly create the master block. Because wood engraving could incorporate script fairly easily, its use was expanded for illustrations in newspapers and magazines. Traditional polychrome woodblock technology was also transformed through the development of multicolor and expensive printing technology; it, too, came to be incorporated into luxuriously illustrated books of art objects. Although lithography was at first deemed superior in its reproducibility to woodblock technology, it was surpassed by collotype photography. In the meantime, woodblock technology also surpassed lithography, through its multicolor applications and costly prints. In this situation, lithography developed in the direction of simplified mass reproduction, and it came to occupy a place quite removed from illustrated art books.

In chapter 2 I discussed the fact that Ninagawa Noritane used lithographic printing in his *Illustrated Book of Past Things: Ceramics Section*, and that Edward S. Morse praised this series of catalogs. Perhaps this is an opportune moment to review the illustrated catalogs that used woodblock prints, as a way to situate Ninagawa's lithography work. Among the catalogs contemporaneous to Ninagawa's are *Illustrated Catalog of Appreciating the Past* (*Shōko zuroku*, 1871 and 1876) by Yokoyama Yoshikiyo and *The Pleasures of Scattering Clouds* (*Hatsuun yokyō*, 1877) by Matsuura Takeshirō. Particularly noteworthy here is *Collecting the Past, Ten Kinds* (*Shūko jisshu*), compiled by Matsudaira Sadanobu (1758–1829), a grandson of the eighth shogun Tokugawa Yoshimune and the lord of the Shirakawa domain (present-day south part of Fukushima prefecture). Regarded as the central figure in the Kansei Reforms, which took place between 1787 and 1893, Matsudaira Sadanobu was also a well-informed antiquarian.[33] Although the exact date of publication is uncertain, the year noted in its preface, Kansei 12 (1800), provides some indication. The term "ten kinds" (*jisshu*) here refers to the following ten categories: epitaph inscriptions, bell inscriptions, armory (helmets and armor, banners, bows and arrows, swords, and harnesses), copper vessels, musical instruments, stationery, seals, *hengaku* tablets (framed tablets bearing inscriptions), portraiture, and calligraphy and paintings. In total, the work consisted of eighty-five volumes, an unprecedented scale. *Collecting the Past, Ten Kinds* would be republished in woodblock and letterpress printing several times toward the end of the Meiji period, thus extending its influence, although the republished versions were reduced in size. The original set, moreover, was almost 42 by 30 centimeters. Not only its scale, then, but its format was surprisingly large.[34] Needless to say, the publication size made it easy to depict objects in their actual sizes. It also included numerous ink rubbings, along with the illustrations of things from the past Matsudaira that had either collected or borrowed from others, including some things from temples and shrines. Moreover, the reason for selecting this size for publication was not limited to the availability of ink rubbings. We should also consider the fundamental tenet of antiquarian thinking in this context, that is, a proactive approach to render an object at actual size. This emerged out of the practice of making ink-rubbing prints. There are examples in these catalogs that tried to depict the three-dimensionality of an object through the deployment of a bird's-eye view. The same proactive approach often gave rise to include the phrase "size as large as the illustration" written next to such prints. Following this, we can ascertain that the detailed measurements of objects provided in illustrations of objects reduced in size also helped viewers to imagine the actual size of the depicted objects. This line of thinking that privileged the actual size, as demonstrated in their uses of ink rubbings, was carried over in the process of producing illustrations during the Meiji period.

In addition to *Collecting the Past, Ten Kinds,* Matsudaira Sadanobu also edited a set of hand-scroll paintings titled *A Collection of Past Pictures* (*Koga ruijū*), which consisted of thirty-six volumes. Although this large set never saw the light of day, Matsudaira selected the scenes from hand-scroll paintings and portraits kept in various collections that illustrated everyday tools, suits of armor, and palace interiors, as well as rare textiles; he cataloged the copied images of the scenes into a set of hand scrolls. In its preface dated 1795 (Kansei 7), he mentioned the significant effects of using illustrations. For instance, he noted that however one tried to convey color through a cunning choice of words, or through calligraphy with ink brushes, both methods imposed clear limitations. Following this, he said, "therefore, these limitations can be accommodated by illustrations, and it should be said that [words and images] together become traces of the past in the future."[35] It might appear a modest expression to suggest that illustrations supplement the texts. What can be discerned here in Matsudaira's note is a departure from a logocentric method of historical survey. Indeed, he promoted the idea of letting things speak for themselves, as it were, with the aid of illustrations. This logic itself is a strong piece of evidence for a shift in focus toward things. Although the objects of analysis in *A Collection of Past Pictures* differ from those of *Collecting the Past, Ten Kinds,* a similar logic is evinced in each. Both works consistently mobilize the type of thinking that characterizes the study of names and things.

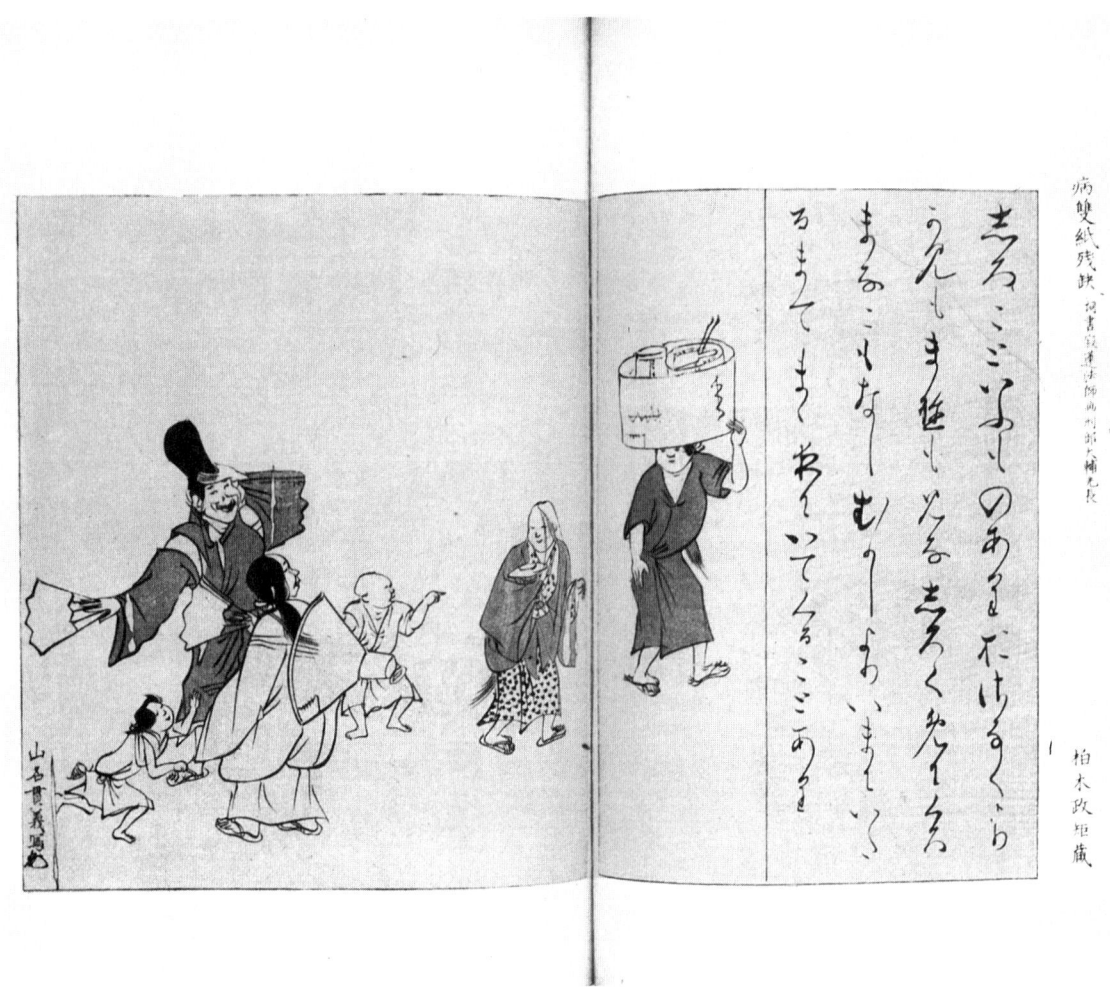

FIG. 15.

Yokoyama Yoshikiyo (Japanese, 1826–79). Tales of Diseases and Deformities, from *Illustrated Catalog of Appreciating the Past* (*Shōko zuroku*), 1871. Woodblock print, 25.2 × 36.4 cm. Tokyo Daigaku Sōgō Toshokan, 0003155272.

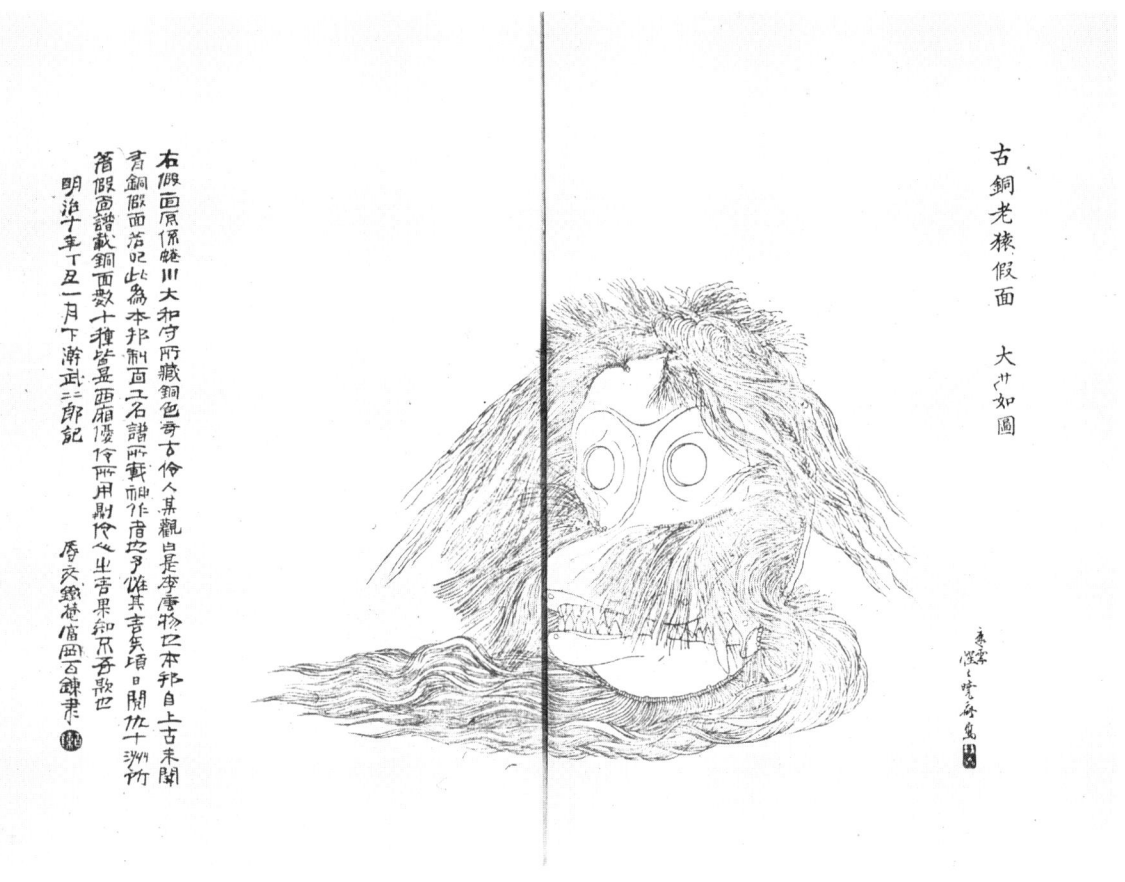

FIG. 16.

Matsuura Takeshirō (Japanese, 1818–88). Old Copper Mask of Aged Monkey, from *The Pleasures of Scattering Clouds* (*Hatsuun yokyō*), 1877. Woodblock print, 25.2 × 36.4 cm. Tokyo Daigaku Sōgō Toshokan, 0003155934.

Let us compare Matsudaira's catalogs to those from the early Meiji. Yokoyama Yoshikiyo's *Illustrated Catalog of Appreciating the Past* was published in 1871, in two volumes, and republished in 1876 (fig. 15). The first volume of Matsuura Takeshirō's *The Pleasures of Scattering Clouds* was published in 1877 (fig. 16), and the second in 1882. Although these catalogs did not reach the scale of *Collecting the Past, Ten Kinds*, they stand on an equal footing both in terms of the refinement of their illustrations in woodblock and in terms of size. Both of these books measured about 36 by 26 centimeters, and thus had the advantage of including large illustrations. In addition to illustrations of stone implements that Yokoyama himself collected,

Illustrated Catalog of Appreciating the Past includes illustrations taken from paintings belonging to the collection of Kashiwagi Kaichirō: the mythological demon *Shōki* (Ch. *zhōng kui*), a fragment of the *Tales of Buddhist Hells* (*Jigoku zōshi*) from the twelfth century, and *Shiroko*, depicting an albino from a fragment of the twelfth-century scroll *Tales of Diseases and Deformities* (*Yamai zōshi*). This set of catalogs, similarly to *Collecting the Past, Ten Kinds*, used the bookbinding method of "pouch-binding."[36] Therefore, each full spread illustration would have used two halves of woodblocks to compose the single image on the opened pages. For this reason, in *Illustrated Catalog of Appreciating the Past*, each full spread has the misfortune of being separated along the gutter of the book. On the other hand, in Matsuura's *The Pleasures of Scattering Clouds*, a laborious method of binding known as *gajō shitate* was used. Here, once the illustration sheet was produced from a single woodblock and folded at center inward, the folded sheets were gathered, and then each sheet was glued along the edge with each next sheet and bound together to construct the whole. In this form of bookbinding, it is easier to see the full-spread illustration as one continuous image. While this set of catalogs contains objects from his collection—including stone implements, old coins, bronze ware, and earthenware—the advantage of using life-size illustrations and the *gajō shitate* binding method are highlighted by the large size of the book.

Another characteristic of *The Pleasures of Scattering Clouds* is the fact that illustrations were signed by their printers. In addition to Kashiwagi Kaichirō, who was himself a collector, we can identify the signatures of painters such as Kawanabe Kyōsai (1831–89); Watanabe Shōka (1835–87), the second son of Watanabe Kazan; and Tazaki Sōun (1815–98).[37] While the inclusions of these individuals indicate Matsuura's expansive social circle, each painter's skill in producing representations was successfully brought to the fore, thanks to the use of *gajō shitate* bookbinding. The use of polychrome printing is another characteristic of this set of catalogs. While *Illustrated Catalog of Appreciating the Past* also incorporated polychrome, *The Pleasures of Scattering Clouds* used it more frequently. If we recalibrate our observation by removing ourselves from these differences, though, we come to see that at the foundational level, both publications embraced the logic of ink-rubbing prints witnessed in *Collecting the Past, Ten Kinds*. In each publication, the dimensions of the actual objects depicted in woodblock illustrations were noted in detail. Not only that, in some cases the weights of the objects were also included. When perspective images were reproduced, both publications added the phrase "size as large as the illustration" next to the illustrations. We can reason from these examples that until around 1877 (Meiji 10), the practices of illustration supported by woodblock technology in the study of names and things continued to be critical.

CHANGING ILLUSTRATED CATALOGS: POTENTIALS OF LITHOGRAPHIC TECHNOLOGY

The first attempt to incorporate lithographic printing into illustrated catalogs was found in *Illustrated Book of Past Things: Ceramics Section* by Ninagawa Noritane, a series of catalogs that I have mentioned in previous chapters. The colophon of the first volume noted that publication permission was sought on 8 March 1876 (Meiji 9). It listed Ninagawa as the author and publisher, and noted a price of one yen.[38] Kamei Shiichi was named as the lithographic artisan, and Gengendō was listed under "printing shop of copper-, lead-, wood-, and stone-based printing technologies." What was known as Gengendō at that time referred to the second master of the copper-etching printer in Kyoto, Matsuda Atsutomo (1837–1903), the first son of Matsumoto Yasuoki (1786–1867), who went by the name of Gengendō the First. Atsutomo took the name of Gengendō the Second, and opened a shop in Tokyo in 1869, in the town Gofukuchō in Nihonbashi district (present-day Chūō ward). He collaborated on the production of bank notes issued by the new Meiji government. For his part, Kamei Shiichi (1843–1905) studied Western-style painting with Yokoyama Matsusaburō, and is said to have secured employment at Gengendō through the recommendation of Yokoyama.[39] The fifth volume of Ninagawa's catalog, published in 1877, lists Shimokuni Kumanosuke as lithographic artisan, while the sixth volume, published in 1879, lists Kamei and Hiraki Masatsugu (1859–1943).

Indeed, Ninagawa had played a decisive role in Gengendō's involvement with lithographic printing technology. In the third volume of *Illustrated Book of Past Things: Ceramics Section*, which was submitted for a publication permit on May 24, 1877, Ninagawa inserted an additional remark in which he chronicled the history of the transmission of knowledge around lithographic technology.[40] Ninagawa noted, "The beginning of lithographic printing in our country dates back twenty-three years, between the second and third years of Ansei [1855–56]." He traced this history to events at Dejima, in Nagasaki. The Bureau of Printing and Printed Books, which was later renamed the Printing Bureau of the Finance Ministry, made a consorted effort to introduce and use the technology. In Ninagawa's words: "In the fifth months of the sixth year of Meiji [the Bureau of Printing and Printed Books] established a new section on lithography and, hired an American named Mr. [C. S.] Boynton, who introduced lithographic methods. It was only then that the resultant prints began to achieve more refinements."

Further, he noted, "I also learned the processes of lithographic printing from this American in the winter of the same year. We purchased a printing press from England, a stone from Germany, ink from Austria, and made several attempts." He added, "Matsuda Atsutomo had tried to master lithography for many years, but had not been able to acquire the skills and knowledge. Thus, I taught him the methods in January of the seventh year of Meiji (1874) and gave him all the necessary machines and supplies." Despite this, however, Matsuda could not produce a successful print. Ninagawa noted that he then "acquired an instructive book of lithography in French, and asked Mr. Mitsukuri to translate the content. By using this translation, lithography finally achieved more refinement."

The person whom Ninagawa asked to translate the instructive book, "Mr. Mitsukuri" is most likely Mitsukuri Rinshō, who began the project of translating *Encyclopedia* at the Ministry of Education (see chapter 2). As noted earlier, Mitsukuri and Ninagawa had known each other from their time at the Bureau of Institutional Investigation. According to Ninagawa, then, Gengendō the Second, Matsuda Atsutomo, was able to identify the goals and methods of lithographic printing with Ninagawa's help. In April 1874 (Meiji 7), Gengendō published a rather simple broadsheet titled "Experiments in Lithography" produced by Ishii Teiko (1848–97). Two years later, the first volume of *Illustrated Book of Past Things: Ceramics Section* was published. In these two years, Gengendō studio must have absorbed the knowledge expeditiously and expanded their experiments with lithographic printing. The resulting illustrations in Ninagawa's publication attest to this. Also, this echoes with the positive evaluations by Morse on lithographic prints in Ninagawa's catalogs.

Let us examine the characteristics of Ninagawa's catalogs, mainly the lithographic illustrations. After the publication of the first volume in 1876, *Illustrated Book of Past Things: Ceramics Section* was published in a total of seven volumes, the last of which was released in 1880. Each volume contains about ten pages of text by Ninagawa, and approximately eighteen illustrations. As such, the volumes are not bulky and thick. Moreover, Ninagawa used Western paper of a size measuring somewhere between 42 by 30 centimeters and 36 by 26 centimeters.[41] Laying them horizontally, he used a Japanese-style binding with four binding points. The printing is on one side only. While the common practice might have been to fold the paper in half, as for "pouch-binding," Ninagawa did not use this method. Rather, the book gives the impression that Ninagawa layered the prints and bound them at one end. For those who are used to books bound Western style, Ninagawa's book might appear rather simple, as it was a temporarily bound set of drafts. The printing did not deploy movable type. Instead, all texts, as well as illustrations, were produced by lithography. The section of Ninagawa's preface, in which the lithographic plate was made directly from Ninagawa's calligraphic writing, is reminiscent of the traditional practice in printing books without using movable type, where the calligraphic writing by an author was used to carve out the preface and postscript on wooden plates. On the cover of Ninagawa's book, the title of the book, taken directly from his own writing, is printed in lithography on a piece of paper and pasted in. From the perspective of those familiar with the traditional bookmaking format, Ninagawa's book must have appeared familiar. At the same time, it must be noted that a larger piece of paper was also pasted on the cover. This slip includes the book's title and the name of the author in Roman characters. The titles were given in French for volumes one to five, *Kwan ko dzu setsu, Notice historique et descriptive,*

Sur les arts et industries japonais, par Ninagawa Noritane, art céramique, and in English for volumes six and seven, *Kwan ko dzu setsu, A History of Japanese Antiquities, by Ninagawa Noritane, The Ceramic Art.* For readers of the time, this book must have given a fresh impression through its faint blue cover, and with the smooth surface of its Western paper.

The most overwhelming aspect of this publication, however, is the lithographic illustrations themselves (see plates 2 and 3). These convey a sense of fidelity to actuality to such an extent that one could feel as if the objects are situated in front of one's own eyes. These illustrations convey a subtle tonality through the sandlike fine-grained touch that characterized lithography of that time, which in turn represents objects with rich shadows, giving the images a three-dimensional appearance. In addition, the quality of transparency found in much of the glaze on ceramic pieces is superbly rendered in these illustrations. Such quality is conveyed by a strange sheen on the surface of areas colored by brush. The art historian Aoki Shigeru speculates that this particular quality was achieved by layering transparent lacquer or egg white over the color ink painted by hand.[42]

To put it in more abstract terms, here we witness a tense negotiation between the remarkable ability to represent objects in high fidelity and their eminent reproducibility, both features of lithographic technology. If a decrease in manual labor is an indicator of progress in printing technology, then the careful and attentive process of coloring that was incorporated into Ninagawa's catalogs counteracts this narrative of progression. It is worth noting here that the combination of woodblock prints with hand coloring could be found in early *ukiyo-e* productions from the late seventeenth century through the early eighteenth century. When lithographic printing became prevalent during the Meiji twenties (1887–97), prints called "framed pictures" (*gakue*), or broadsheet lithographic prints, became highly sought after; these, too, combined hand coloring and printing. In the period of anticipation for the popularization of chromolithography in Europe, there were examples of hand colorings as well. Such desire for color became further sublimated by the emergence of polychrome woodblock prints, *nishiki-e,* in the case of the former, and that of chromolithograph in the case of the latter.

However, it does not suffice to interpret Ninagawa's intention in using handcoloring in *Illustrated Book of Past Things: Ceramics Section* merely as an eclectic method peculiar to a transitional period before the introduction of the chromolithograph. We know that Ninagawa owned an album of chromolithographic prints from Germany. His set included lithographic reproductions of scenic views of the Near East, including the Pyramids painted by Karl Werner (1808–94). We can discern when and from whom Ninagawa acquired this album through an inscription written on the wrapping paper that reads: "Meiji six (1873) from the consul of Spain, Mr. Helen."[43] It was deemed technically difficult for Ninagawa to deploy chromolithography at that time. In addition to this reason, could Ninagawa have known that the resultant images appeared surprisingly flat? If we follow this thinking that

Ninagawa saw the flattening of images as a disadvantage of chromolithograph, then his use of hand-coloring can be interpreted as a decision based on prioritizing representational fidelity. At a foundational level, the two pursuits—one maintaining the representational fidelity of illustrations and the other weighing the efficient productivity of printing—were difficult to achieve at once. Here, then, Ninagawa intended to pursue both without easily compromising one over the other.

In addition, there were aspects in his illustrations that deliberately disregarded the advantages of lithographic printing, that is to say its facility as a technology of reproduction. By introducing hand coloring, a process that did not sit squarely with lithography, Ninagawa limited its suitability for mass reproduction. The representation of the unique quality achieved by hand coloring is difficult even for today's reproducible technologies. Indeed, Ninagawa's illustrations seem to refuse reproduction. In other words, illustrations themselves insist on being examined as a singular original, rather than a reproduced image of the original.

Ninagawa's illustrated book competed with the technology made for reproduction. This fact, then, turns the direction of our analysis to a more traditional character situated opposite from the new technology, lithography. The conversation that this *Illustrated Book of Past Things: Ceramics Section* created with the traditional cannot be grasped by merely imposing the perspective of technological history, that is, an interpretation that regards the illustrations in the catalogs as an example done through lithography *instead of* through woodblock printing. Specifically, it is noteworthy that each object is accompanied by its detailed dimensions, or by the phrase "size as large as the illustration." In other words, the logic emerging from rubbing as evinced in *Collecting the Past, Ten Kinds* is dutifully followed. The large bookmaking format with binding on the side presents a remarkable advantage for representing the objects in their actual size. Not only did the size of paper highlight the fidelity to the actual objects, but it also took full advantage of lithography, a technology that belonged to "the new." This new technology of reproduction did not overwhelmingly change the content of the illustrated catalogs. The deployment of lithography was based on attempts to overcome the limitations of woodblock printing, an already existing and refined technology of reproduction.

In his introduction in the first volume, Ninagawa suggested the advantage of illustrations of actual objects over their textual description when comparing historical books and actual objects. As we have already seen, this logic emerged out of the study of names and things. In other words, the new technology of reproduction allowed for the expansion and extension of thinking based on demonstrating and explaining things through pictorialization. We can discern here that when the new technology of reproduction surpassed the limitation of the representational capability of traditional printing methods, the invisible potential of woodblock illustrations in publications like *Collecting the Past, Ten Kinds; Illustrated Catalog of Appreciating the Past;* and *The Pleasures of Scattering Clouds* came to be liberated in the new form of Ninagawa's catalogs.

Moreover, we can identify another characteristic of *Illustrated Book of Past Things: Ceramics Section* by shifting our focus to the content of the publication and its supporting framework. Morse left the remark that in evaluating ceramics, Ninagawa had a proclivity to insist on examining the age of the objects. As I noted in chapter 1, Morse met Ninagawa in the spring of 1879 and began accumulating stories about collectors and collections in Japan from Ninagawa, which he then published in *Japan Day by Day*. Morse was himself an avid collector, and in his writing he left a compelling critique of collectors in Japan, noting, "He [Ninagawa] said that the Japanese have never specialized so much in their collecting as foreigners, and, I judge from what I have learned, were never so systematic or scientific and generally not so curious nor so exact as to the age and locality of the objects."[44]

At the same time, he seems to have had a different opinion on Ninagawa as a collector. In his writing on the visit to Kashiwagi Kaichirō in the winter of 1882, which we have examined earlier, he added, "Mr. Kashiwagi is one of the pleasantest men I have met in Japan. He is not afraid to say he doesn't know when some questions are asked of him, and does not approve of Ninagawa's method of trying to tell the exact age of an object."[45] That Ninagawa's attitude toward dating an object was exceptional among his peers is highlighted by comparison to Morse's general evaluation of other collectors he met.

Still, this is not to say that other publications of Ninagawa's time, such as *Illustrated Catalog of Appreciating the Past* and *The Pleasures of Scattering Clouds*, did not take dating seriously; they did include notable dates. What was different about *Illustrated Book of Past Things: Ceramics Section* was the manner in which the date of an object was reflected in its presentation. The first volume began with various works of ancient earthenware. Ordering the object chronologically, in general, to survey the passing of time from a bird's-eye view is a method that is invented and shaped by modern historical understanding. However, this method also visualized the ways in which the past and the present overlapped. This is my speculation, but it seems that Ninagawa thought of chronological ordering as a way to lead things out of the discursive condition shaped by the competing paradigm of the new and the old.

As we consider Ninagawa's *Illustrated Book of Past Things: Ceramics Section*, it becomes clear that he was putting into practice the challenges he had outlined in the introduction—that is to say, to bring the prevailing contrast of the new and the old to a more balanced state, and to find ways to put sufficient value upon things past, which of course belonged to the category of the old. Seen this way, his use of lithography and chronological ordering were indispensable to balancing the contrast between the new and the old. Here we witness the foresighted approach of this publication toward the paradigm of the new and the old, and see Ninagawa's own answers to the issues that this paradigm shift presented.

180 CHANGING ILLUSTRATED CATALOGS: TECHNIQUES OF SCALING

The seventh and last volume of Ninagawa Noritane's *Illustrated Book of Past Things: Ceramics Section* was published in 1880 (Meiji 13). It is helpful here to consider other examples of illustrated catalogs published around the same time. Although the reason and process differed from one to another, a characteristic of this period was work by Westerners, as in the case of Morse. Earlier examples of such books include two volumes of *Les produits de la nature japonaise et chinoise: Partie inorganique et minéralogique* by the Dutch pharmacologist A. J. C. Geerts (1843–83).[46] This book was published in two volumes in Yokohama by C. Levy, the first in 1878 and the second in 1883. The text in the body of the book was in French, but it also had a cover page in Japanese.[47] In its first volume, lithographic prints were included in an appendix. The prints depicted stone implements, and they did not use crosshatching methods, thereby having a simple, sketchlike quality. In the body of text, Geerts referred to *Records of Stones* (*Unkonshi*) by Kiuchi Sekitei and included a footnote on Morse's discovery of the Ōmori shell mounds.

A pair of contrasting publications appeared in 1879, a year after the release of the first volume of Geerts's catalog, and another pair in 1880. In 1879, C. Levy published *Notes on Japanese Archaeology with Especial Reference to the Stone Age* by Heinrich von Siebold. In the same year, the University of Tokyo published Morse's report on a prehistoric site, *Shell Mounds of Omori,* along with its Japanese translation, *Ōmori kaikyo kobutsu hen.* Heinrich von Siebold (1852–1908) was the second son of Philipp Franz von Siebold. Heinrich arrived in Japan in 1869 (Meiji 2), following his elder brother Alexander (the father and brother were discussed in chapter 3). Using his fluency in Japanese, Heinrich von Siebold worked for the Embassy of the Dual Monarchy of Austria-Hungary, particularly in amending trade treaties. At the Vienna World Exposition he, along with his brother, supported the participation of Japan.[48] In addition, he ardently collected things of the past. For example, in March 1878, along with the Western-style painter Goseda Yoshimatsu (1855–1915), he led a group to conduct research on the prehistoric sites of the Kabutoyama burial mound and Yoshimi *hyakketsu* (one hundred pit graves), both located in Musashi province (present-day Saitama prefecture). In August of the same year, he studied the Ainu in the Hidaka district of Hokkaido, and wrote an ethnographic report.[49] It appears that there was a rivalry between him and Morse regarding the excavation of Ōmori shell mounds. Their relationship seems to have been ambivalent, as they also had different opinions on various matters.[50] Indeed, Morse published a critique of Siebold's book in an article for a periodical.[51]

Just as their personalities differed, so too did the illustrations that they published in their catalogs. Let us examine illustrations in Siebold's book first (fig. 17). The size of the book is slightly smaller than 35 by 25 centimeters. The book included twelve plates of illustrations, including representations of stone implements, comma-shaped beads, earthenware, and terracotta burial figurines (*haniwa*). The illustrations were produced by gluing albumen prints of photographic images onto

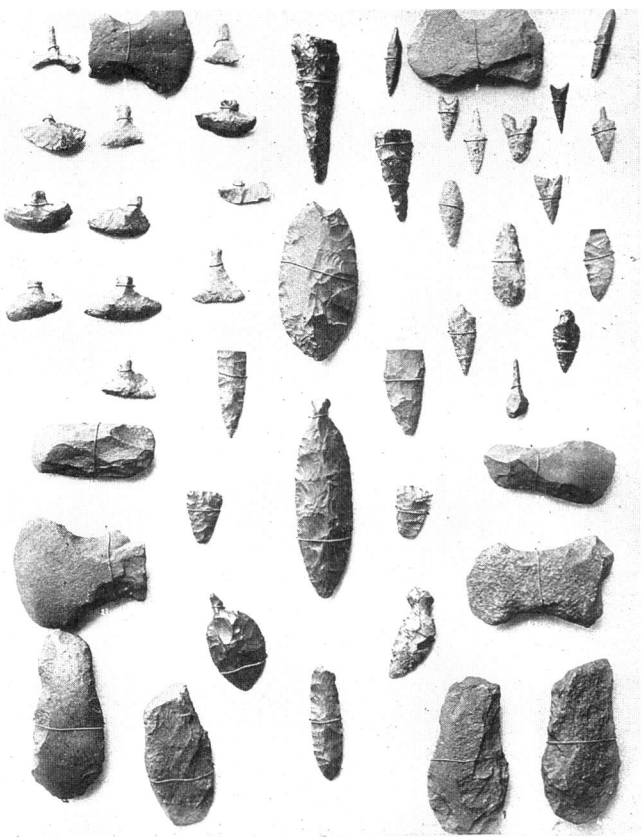

FIG. 17.

Heinrich von Siebold (German, 1852–1908). Early tool heads and implements, from *Notes on Japanese Archaeology with Especial Reference to the Stone Age*, table V, 1879. Albumen print, 21.5 × 27.98 cm.

---

the supporting paper, which were then bundled with the text into the book format. The photographs were approximately 25 by 18 centimeters. On the other hand, Morse used lithographic prints in his report (fig. 18). The report itself is about 30 by 21 centimeters and includes a frontispiece plate and eighteen plates of illustrations depicting relics unearthed from the Ōmori shell mounds, such as fragments of earthenware, stone implements, and seashells. In both his original publication in English and its translation in Japanese, the same lithographic illustrations were used. The illustrations were printed in a foldout whose size was about double that of the book. We can discern that Gengendō the Second, Matsuda Atsumoto worked on these printed illustrations, as at the end of his preface Morse wrote: "Acknowledgments are also due to Mr. Kimura the artist, Mr. Matsuda the lithographer, and the Nisshusha Printing Office, for the efforts they have made in securing accuracy in their respective lines of work."[52]

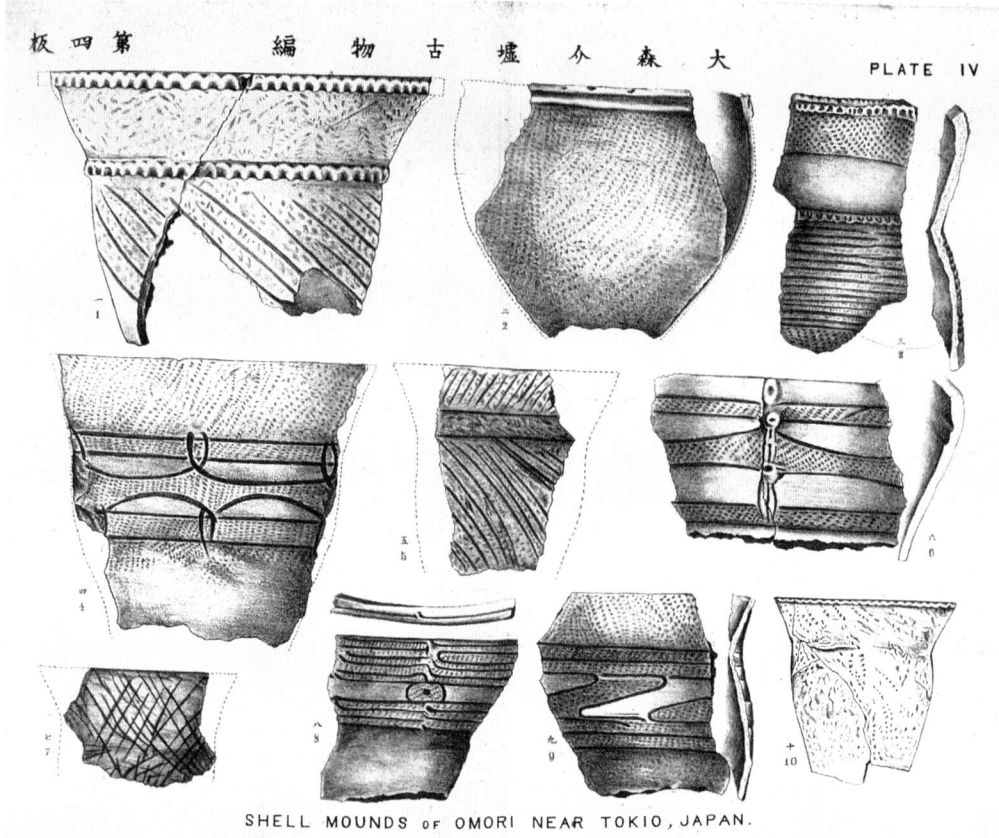

FIG. 18.

Edward S. Morse (American, 1838–1925).

Pottery shards, from *Shell Mounds of Omori,* plate IV, 1879. Lithographic print, approximately 28 × 37 cm.

In June 1879 Heinrich von Siebold published *The Outline of Archaeology* (*Kōko setsuryaku*), a catalog that is roughly a Japanese translation of his 1879 *Notes on Japanese Archaeology*. This book, printed in woodblock with six inserted foldout plates of illustrations in lithography (fig. 19), was bound in traditional pouch binding.[53] Interestingly, the illustrations here were lithographic prints, and different from those in *Notes on Japanese Archaeology*. In addition, he published an article on terracotta figurines, "Etwas über die Tsutschi Ningio," in the transactions of the German society of East Asia, *Mittheilungen der Deutschen Gesellschaft für Natur-unde Völkerkunde Ostasiens,* in which he included two bound-in plates of illustrations produced in tricolor woodblock printing.

In 1880 we witness publications of two pertinent articles: John Milne's "Notes on Stone Implements from Otaru and Hakodate, with a Few General Remarks on

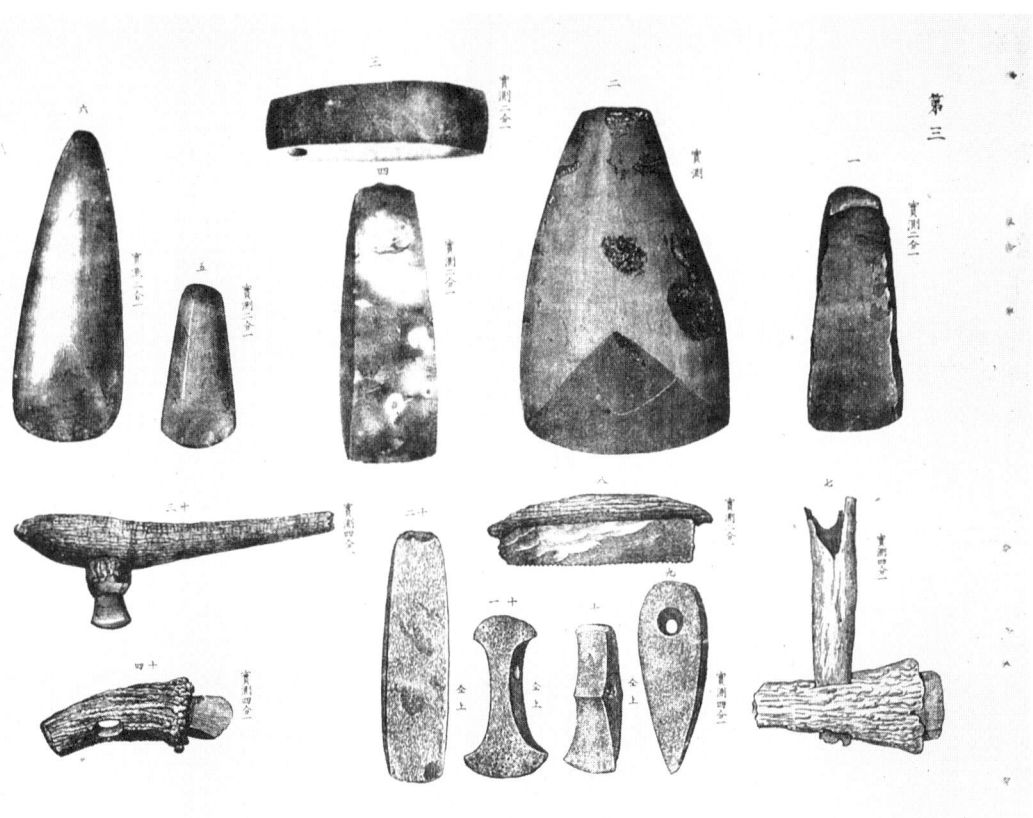

FIG. 19.

Heinrich von Siebold (German, 1852–1908). Early tool heads and implements, from *Kōko setsuryaku*, fig. 3, 1879. Lithographic print, 23.4 × 30.9 cm.

the Prehistoric Remains of Japan" and Ernest Satow's "Ancient Sepulchral Mounds in Kaudzuke," both of which were published in *Transactions of the Asiatic Society of Japan,* published in Tokyo (figs. 20, 21). This association had originally been a branch association of the Royal Asiatic Society, based in Shanghai, which consisted of mostly British members. Because in Japan the numbers of American-born members increased, "Royal" was dropped from the journal's name before the first annual meeting as Asiatic Society in October 1872 in Yokohama.[54] The Asiatic Society published a number of articles, and from the Bakumatsu period these associations that grew from British and German sources became places to present research in the field of Japanese studies.[55]

Ernest Mason Satow (1843–1929) was a well-known British diplomat who resided in Japan from the Bakumatsu to the early Meiji period. According to his

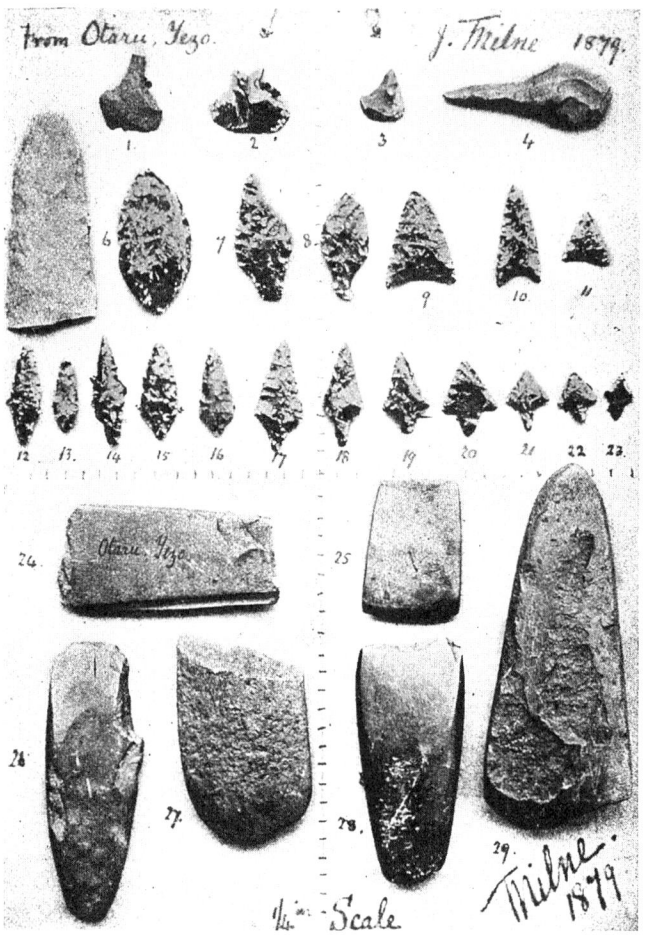

FIG. 20.

John Milne (British, 1850–1913).

Early tool heads and implements, from "Notes on the Stone Implements from Otaru and Hakodate, with a Few General Remarks on the Prehistoric Remains of Japan," in *Transactions of the Asiatic Society of Japan* 8, no. 1 (1880): fig. I. Pasted albumen print, 13.5 × 9.5 cm.

---

colleague Algerton B. Mitford, Satow was not only fluent in Japanese but also conducted "an accurate study of Japanese history and of Japanese customs and traditions."[56] Satow's biography included a list of articles that had resulted from his research and study.[57] One such study was based on his field work in March 1880 at the Maefutago burial mound in the Nishi Ōmuro town of Gunma prefecture (present-day Maebashi city). The details of this trip were recorded in his diary.[58] A painter accompanied Satow on this trip, and according to the documentation of Gunma prefecture, this would have been a man named Oda Kenkichi.[59] It is possible that this man was one of the painters working at Gengendō studio, Shida Kenkichi (pseudonym Shō'ūn). The journal *Transactions of the Asiatic Society of*

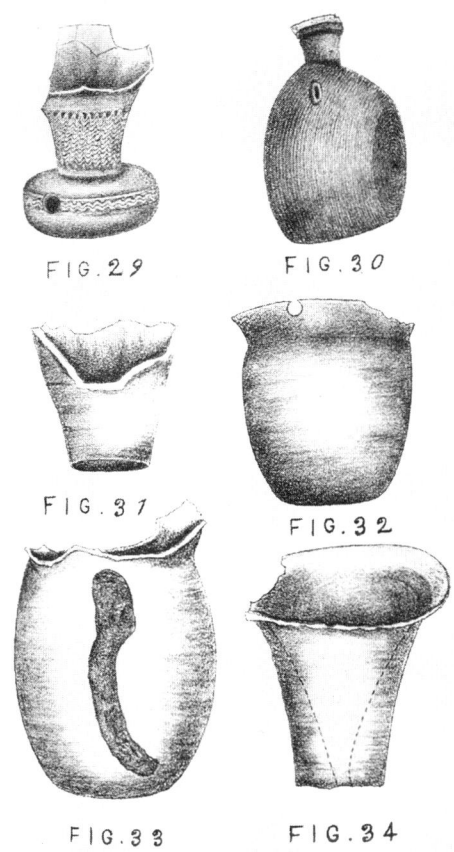

FIG. 21.

Ernest Satow (British, 1843–1929). Examples of ceramics, from "Ancient Sepulchral Mounds in Kaudzuke," from *Transactions of the Asiatic Society of Japan* 8, no. 3 (1880): 325. Lithographic print, 21.4 × 13.7 cm.

Japan is approximately 21 by 15 centimeters and the volume in which Satow's paper was published included seventeen bound-in lithographic plates that depicted relics such as stone implements, earthenware, and terracotta burial figurines. Although the size of the prints is the same size as the publication, their resulting images were more refined.

The British geologist and mining engineer John Milne (1850–1913) came from England to Japan in 1876 as a hired foreign expert at the School of Technology in Tokyo (*Kōgakuryō*) under the Public Works Ministry, where he taught geology and mining. He returned to England in 1896 after resigning from the Imperial College of Engineering. Milne's research in seismology is considered pioneering and significant.⁶⁰ His paper was based on stone implements he gathered during two spells of fieldwork: in Hakodate in 1878, and in Otaru in 1879, both in Hokkaido. The article included a map and five bound-in plates of illustrations. The illustrations were 10.2-by-12.7-centimeter photographic prints of stone implements on albumen paper, each of which was directly pasted onto the page.

Among these examples of publications from 1879 and 1880 that included plates of illustrations of stone implements and earthenware, we come to see a stark contrast between Siebold and Milne, who used photographic prints, and Morse and Satow, who mobilized lithographic printing. It is also noteworthy that Siebold used lithographic prints in *The Outline of Archaeology* (*Kōko setsuryaku*). At this historical juncture, in terms of technology and economy, prints in photography and lithography were seen to be on equal footing as options for plates of articles and books. While photographic prints on albumen paper were not suitable for mass reproduction, they yielded the highest-quality representation. However, we should note that lithographic printing was threatening photography in its quality to reproduce the image of an object. Indeed, the illustrations produced through lithographic prints from these publications represented the shapes and forms of the depicted objects with three-dimensionality, and in this sense, were not a far cry from photographic representations. In particular, the illustrations in Morse's publication are impressive for their tonal expression through cross-hatching.

What these four different examples of illustrations had in common, moreover, was their lack of visual logic based on the ink-rubbing technique. The sizes of these illustrations did not come close to *Collecting the Past, Ten Kinds*. They were much smaller than illustrations in other publications of the day, such as those in *The Pleasures of Scattering Clouds* by Matsuura Takeshirō and *Illustrated Book of Past Things: Ceramics Section* by Ninagawa Noritane. The largest were the foldout illustrations in Morse's *Shell Mounds of Omori* and its Japanese translation *Ōmori kaikyo kobutsu hen*, which came close to the size of Ninagawa's illustrated catalog. Compared to Matsuura's full spread illustrations, though, Morse's illustrations were about half the size. The illustrations inserted in Satow's publication were based on the size of the *Transactions of the Asiatic Society of Japan*, measuring slightly larger than 21 × 14 centimeters. In addition, photographic prints at this time had another disadvantage in that they could not be enlarged from negatives. Rather, they were direct contact prints from glass negative plates. If we convert their sizes to a contemporary standard, the illustrations of Siebold's article are about 26 by 18 centimeters, while Milne's illustrations are about 15 by 11 centimeters. Moreover, these small prints added an innovative tool to their representations. In the case of lithographic prints, they either included a representation of scale and dimension within the image or noted the scale in a caption. In the case of photographic prints, they captured an image of a real scale laid next to the objects. When the scale of the actual object could be communicated this way, then it was no longer necessary to produce large plates of illustrations to convey the actual size of the objects. Once the technique of scale reduction became adjustable, multiple images could be put together into one illustration plate. In each of the illustrations considered here, collected stone implements and earthenware were classified according to their shape and patterns, and were ordered and represented in one illustration. That is, comparisons among similar objects in one print became possible. The operative logic in constructing these illustrations was a technique of scale reduction, a logic quite opposed to that of the technique of ink rubbing.

After this period, the method of gluing photographic prints onto paper to produce plates would fall out of favor, probably because of the improvement in the quality and economy of lithographic printing. Morse's *Shell Mounds of Omori* bore the subtitle *Memoirs of the Science Department, Volume I, Part I,* and was published by the three faculties—Law, Science, and Letters—of the University of Tokyo.[61] After the publication of Morse's book, they continued their publication series using the subtitle "Memoires of the Science Department," including a frontispiece and illustrations in lithographic printing. The frontispieces of this series were particularly impressive, and could serve as a standard for the technical quality of that time. After Morse's title, the following books appeared in the series: volume 2, *On Mining and Mines in Japan* (1880) by Curt A. Netto; volume 3, *Report on the Meteorology of Tokio for the Year 2539* (1880) by Thomas C. Mendenhall; volume 4, *Geology of the Environs of Tokio* (1882) by David Brauns; appendix to volume 4, *Geology of Jōhoku Area* (1883) by Kochibe Tadayoshi; volume 5, *Measurements of the Force of Gravity at Tokio and on the Summit of Fujinoyama* by Mendenhall; and volume 6, *The Chemistry of Sake-Brewing* (1882) by Robert William Atkinson. Gengendō the Second (Matsuda Atsutomo) produced all the lithographic illustrations included in the series. The frontispiece of the second volume, which included lithographic prints with two-tone hand-coloring, is particularly impressive in both visual and technical terms. Its preface notes that "charts, illustrations, lithographic prints, paper, and others here are all produced by the hands of the Japanese, that is, drawing by Mr. Yamaoka and Mr. Oda, lithographic studio of the three faculties (where Mr. Kobayashi is the manager) and Gengendō, along with the printing press Nisshōsha." "Mr. Yamaoka" here might have referred to Yamaoka Shigeaki, who was a tutor of drawing at the University of Tokyo. In the volume 4 and its appendix, the preface mentioned "the painter Hirauchi Heizaburō." In particular, highly sophisticated illustrations of the landscape by this painter in Kochibe's *Geology of Jōhoku Area* are worth examining.

There are two other examples that require similar attention to the series *Memoirs of the Science Department* after its publication of Morse's volume: *Okadaira Shell Mound at Hitachi* (1882) co-authored by Iijima Isao (1861–1921) and Sasaki Chūjirō (1857–1938), and *Notes on Ancient Stone Implements, &c., of Japan* (1884) by Kanda Takahira. Both Iijima and Sasaki pursued zoological studies under Morse at the Faculty of Science at the University of Tokyo. *Okadaira Shell Mound at Hitachi* was also published by the University of Tokyo. Although it did not have a Japanese version, the report was published as "an appendix to memoir vol. I, part 1 of the Science Department," conceptually positioned as a supplemental publication to their teacher's report on shell mounds. We have come across Kanda Takahira before as a participant in the 1871 Exhibition of Local Products. Kanda's illustrated catalog was translated into English by his adopted son, Kanda Naibu (1857–1923).[62] Both illustrated books adhered fundamentally to the foldout format and to the size of illustrations in Morse's book, although their finishing results in lithography, especially its cross hatching, demonstrated a skill as refined as those in Morse's. In the acknowledgment lines of Iijima and Sasaki's book, they noted the names of the painters as "J. Nomura, M. Indō, K. Watanabe," most likely referring to Nonomura Jūjirō (Shigeyoshi), Indō Mataku (1861–1914), and Watanabe Kyū (Hisashi).[63] Nomura and Watanabe were Western-style painters who worked closely with the Gengendō studio, while Indō was known as a Western-style painter who had studied art at the Technical Fine Arts School.

INK RUBBINGS AND SPECIMENS

Okadaira Shell Mound at Hitachi, co-authored by Iijima and Sasaki, included plates of illustrations of relics found at the Okadaira shell mound, such as stone implements, earthenware, and seashells. It also followed the similar format of reporting deployed in *Shell Mounds of Omori.*[64] On the other hand, *Notes on Ancient Stone Implements, &c., of Japan* by Kanda mostly consisted of illustrations of stone implements belonging to collectors.[65] As we have discussed in chapter 4, Kanda himself was a collector. In addition to objects from his collection, moreover, Kanda's catalog recorded objects belonging to notable collectors such as Matsuura Takeshirō, Yokoyama Yoshikiyo, Ninagawa Noritane, and Kashiwagi Kaichirō. It cleverly used lithographic printing, and reduced the scale of objects rather freely. There was also a fresh perspective in their approach of vetting only the stone implements from their collections of antiquities.

However, there was a critical difference between the illustrations in these two publications that ought not to be overlooked. First, in the report by Iijima and Sasaki, what is striking is that each one of the relics depicted in illustrations was treated as a specimen with visibly distinguishable characteristics (fig. 22). By *specimen,* I mean a family of objects with shared characteristics that cohere within a group, such as the family of objects found in the Ōmori shell mounds. I refer here to a set of characteristics that allow the relics gathered at the shell mound of Okadaira, for example, to be visibly distinguished from those accumulated at other shell mounds. If one finds an object that belongs to a family of objects that demonstrates more acutely visible characteristics of that family, it can be swapped in seamlessly. What guarantees the status of any specimen in the same family is a set of the shared characteristics within the family group, rather than the individuality of the specimen itself. In other words, Iijima and Sasaki sifted through individual relics and their fragments to arrange illustrations for their report so as to arrive at an identification of the visibly distinguishable characteristics shared among them.

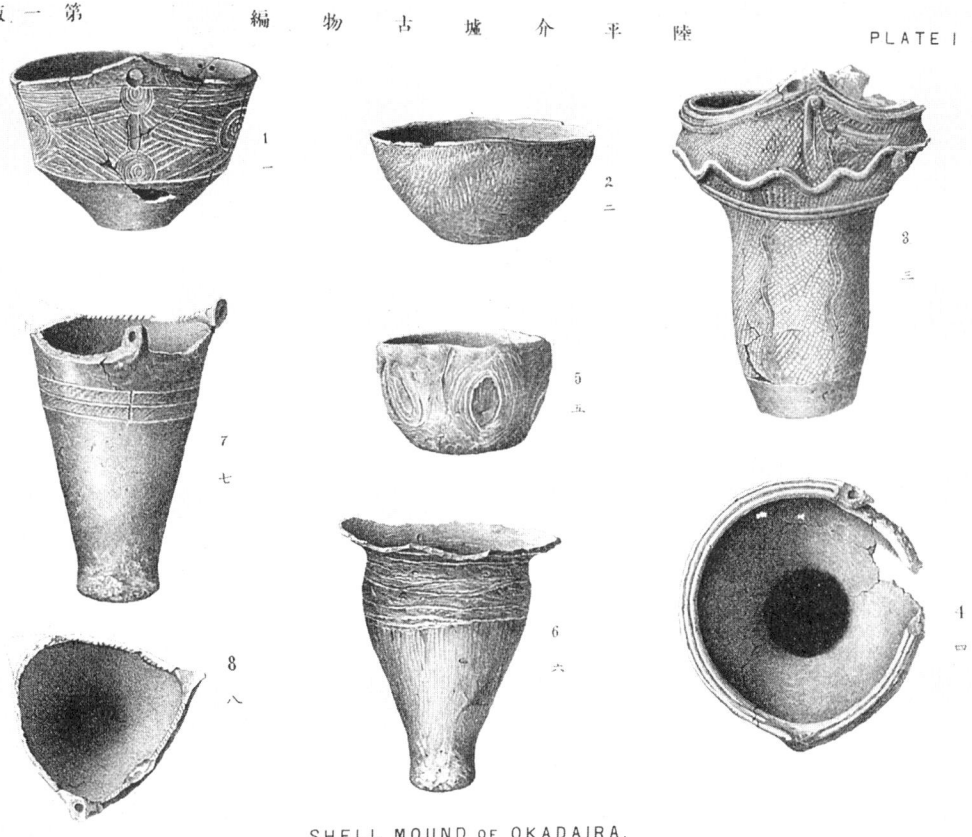

FIG. 22.

Iijima Isao (Japanese, 1861–1921) and Sasaki Chūjirō (Japanese, 1857–1938).

Examples of ceramics, from *Okadaira Shell Mound at Hitachi,* plate I, 1882. Lithographic print, approximately 27 × 38 cm.

Following this, we begin to see the fitting relationship between their approach to treating objects as specimens on the one hand, and their use of a scaling technique on the other. By scaling the objects smaller, they were able to place multiple artifacts on a single page, depicting their formal similarities, thus making it possible to compare them visually. To compare and contrast visually, it was necessary to isolate the shared denominator. Through this technique, rather than focusing on a singular object, one had to close one's eyes to its unique singularity, and instead prioritize the sameness shared within the family to which it belonged. In other words, objects came to function as a specimen by going through a process of abstraction that took away their individuality. The technique of scaling encouraged this process of abstracting objects.

A similar argument can be made with respect to color. In this historical context, one could not resort to color photography yet, and chromolithography was just beginning to be introduced. But there was another side to these seeming limitations of available technologies. The absence of color allowed for more straightforward comparisons among individual objects. In fact, polychrome can be regarded as an obstruction to the comparisons based on visual aspects of objects such as their forms and surface patterns. In this sense, the monochromatic printing of both photography and lithography was convenient for illustrations in this kind of publication. Once again, compared to the representation of a singular object, the elimination of color constituted a part of the process of abstracting things.

The illustrations in Kanda Takahira's catalog stand in stark contrast here (fig. 23). The stone implements collected in this publication were classified according to their names, and reduced in scale for a single-sheet illustration assigned to each name of the implements. At a glance, the illustrations in Kanda's catalog and those in Iijima and Sasaki's report might appear similar. However, they were entirely different. This difference does not lie in the final result or composition, but instead in their approaches to things. In Kanda's illustrations, stone implements were not treated as specimens. Their status was not recognized as members of a group sharing distinct characteristics. Instead, Kanda approached the stone implements in his catalog as individual and precious objects collected by respective collectors, and accordingly the status of each object was guaranteed by the individuality of the object differentiated from the rest of other objects. In other words, in Kanda's illustrations, the things depicted were not framed to highlight the differences among them against a background of presumed sameness. On the contrary, the meaning of the comparisons was brought out precisely *through* the varying degrees of difference among objects of the same taxonomic category. For this reason, and in this way, Kanda's illustrations served as illustrations of comprehensive knowledge of stone implements accumulated through a dedicated act of collecting.

This relationship toward things stood in stark contrast to the approach to things as a specimen. It was an approach at the core of the logic of ink rubbing that had underlined various types of catalogs such as Matsudaira Sadahide's *Collecting the Past, Ten Kinds,* Yokoyama Yoshikiyo's *Illustrated Catalog of Appreciating the Past,* Matsuura Takeshirō's *The Pleasures of Scattering Clouds*, and Ninagawa Noritane's *Illustrated Book of Past Things: Ceramics Section*. In this sense, Kanda, who illustrated the stone implements by reducing their sizes, compromised himself for this publication. At the same time, one could also posit this publication as Kanda's renewed experiment with the study of names and things. In composing the illustrations, Kanda would have paid attention to the order and relations among the collected objects, contrary to the case of Iijima and Sasaki.

In terms of color, the visual logic of ink rubbing stood in opposition to that of the specimen. In *Illustrated Book of Past Things: Ceramics Section,* Ninagawa Noritane insisted on coloring the illustration when he hand-colored lithographic prints. In

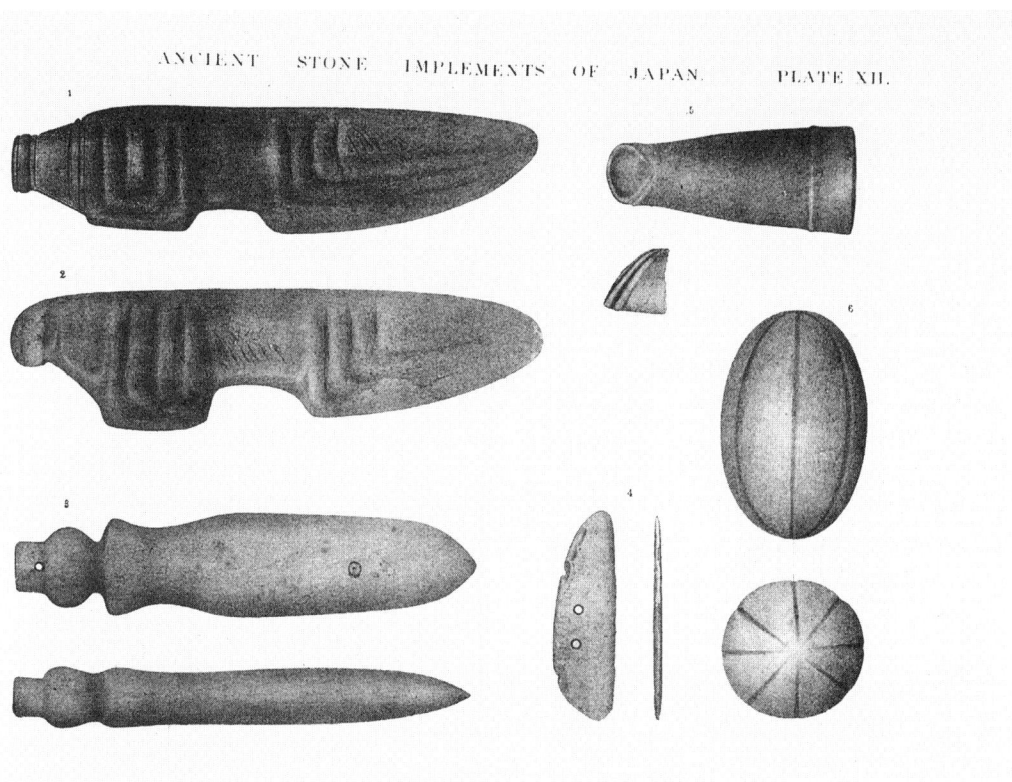

FIG. 23.

Kanda Takahira (Japanese, 1830–98). "Ancient Stone Implements of Japan," from *Notes on Ancient Stone Implements &c. of Japan,* plate XII, 1884. Lithographic print, approximately 27 × 38 cm.

1872, he compiled a photograph album of Edo Castle taken from various angles at that time.[66] The album, titled "Photographic Album of the Former Edo Castle," (Kyū Edojō shashin chō) consisted of sixty-three prints on albumen paper, all of which were hand colored by Takahashi Yuichi.[67] Recall here that publications such as *Collecting the Past, Ten Kinds; Illustrated Catalog of Appreciating the Past;* and *The Pleasures of Scattering Clouds* all used polychrome woodblock prints. Situating the logic of ink rubbing within the study of names and things, we come to see that colors, too, served as indispensable criteria to decipher the attributes of the singular uniqueness of things. This logic echoes remarks made by Matsudaira Sadahide in the preface to *A Collection of Past Pictures,* in which he pointed to the limits of expressing the quality of color in words.

In examining these contrasting illustrated books, we come to see that the ways in which the authors approached things and the manner in which they treated things directly shaped their illustrations. On the one hand, there was a line of thinking that held the study of names and things constituted by the logic of ink rubbing took the issue of actual size and color seriously. This line of thinking emphasized the singularity of an object. On the other hand, the logic of the specimen required letting go of that singularity. This manner of thinking presumed the visible and distinct characteristic of the family to which each of thing was assigned. To vet and identify the commonly held characteristics among individual things, this thinking necessarily engaged with processes of simplification and abstraction. The technique of scaling and the elimination of color in their illustrations buttressed this process of dealing with things.

It is easy to imagine how the balance between these opposing attitudes and approaches to things shifted from one to another. In this regard, the analysis above vividly demonstrates one instance, perhaps a cross section, of this change. Although on the surface the illustrations of *Okadaira Shell Mound at Hitachi* and *Notes on Ancient Stone Implements, &c of Japan* resemble each other, their crucial and decisive differences should now be clear. Needless to say, this shift was part and parcel of changes in the world of things. How did the changes in the world of things emerge, and what promoted them? Considering the fact that the technique of scale reduction was naturalized in illustrations of the books and articles by Morse, Siebold, Satow, and Miln published between 1879 and 1880, these changes must have originated in their field of study and in the discursive thinking deployed within their respective fields.

SECTION 3: THINGS AND LEARNING

THE "GREAT PUBLIC BENEFIT" OF LEARNING

In 1882 (Meiji 15), the English report co-authored by Iijima Isao and Sasaki Chūjirō was published. Two years earlier, in February 1879, the pair had published the outline of their research findings in Japanese, "Report on the Okadaira shell mound at Hitachi" (Jōshū Okadaira kaikyo hōkoku) in *Gakugei shirin,* a journal published by the three faculties of the University of Tokyo. In this article, Iijima and Sasaki explained their commitment to learning, one that indicated their intellectual debt to their teacher Morse. At the time, Sasaki was a fourth-year student in the Faculty of Science, and Iijima was a third-year student in the same department. The excerpt below arrives at the beginning of their article; although it is lengthy, let us examine their position.

> As the study of science becomes more rigorous even as additional subjects are added to it, scholars have come to hold a position of knowledge heretofore unseen. By directing their efforts higher rather than lower, deeper rather than

shallower, scholars can shed light on difficult issues—and they are moving in the direction of light rather than darkness. Despite this, archaeology [*kōkogaku*] alone has not progressed in recent years, save for efforts by a few scholars, so much so that it could be called a diminished field. There have not been new scholars in the field, and those who have been called "antiquarians" [*kobutsuka*] have merely been collecting things past and treating them as their playthings. Therefore, they fundamentally do not know the great public benefit of archaeology. The essence of archaeology lies in the study of geological science, which entails measuring the distance between the land and a nearby water source, or in finding a shell mound or a cave, which then is followed by excavation of the buried earthenware, stone implements, various bones and seashells, and then carefully studying their skillful or unskillful execution, appearance and substance, shape and condition, and type. From these inquiries, one would be able to understand what kind of people created the cave, how far back in time these people lived in the cave, what they did, and their differences from contemporary people.[68]

The lofty beginning of this quote illustrates the pair's intellectual vigor. What is particularly striking, moreover, is their scathing criticism of "antiquarians" (*kobutsuka*). Here, the phrase "great public benefit" stands out. In Sasaki and Iijima's understanding, the necessary role of archaeology included various activities, from the observation of geographical conditions to the consideration of ancient remains. The content of their inquiry appears closer to the field of anthropology, and for Iijima and Sasaki, the "great public benefit" of archaeology was to be found in precisely this mode of thought. Immediately following this quote, they listed the shell mounds of Ōmori as a concrete example of such intellectual work, and celebrated the contributions of their teacher Morse.

The "great public benefit" of archaeology identified by Iijima and Sasaki was more generally applicable to other subjects within the field of science, although their objects of analysis might have differed. In other words, their insistence on "great public benefit" emerged out of an evaluative standard grounded in benefit for the world, people, and progress. Consequently, they insisted that the purpose of a field of intellectual inquiry was to generate these kinds of benefits.

The intention of Iijima and Sasaki, therefore, was to evaluate the presence or lack of "great public benefit" as a standard to emphasize the difference between the new and the old fields of study. Still, it was quite harsh to take the antiquarians as the cause for the slow establishment of archaeology as a useful field; this accusation appears unfounded. They had not been criticized in this way in the past, but in the eyes of Iijima and Sasaki, the antiquarians only appeared to be entertaining themselves with the things from the past that they collected. The attitude implied here was a discriminating gaze of professionals looking down on amateurs. Here, we witness a birth of a new structure of the field that differentiated between amateurism (a form of hobby and entertainment) and professionalism (based on intellectual specialization).

This situation would have been unthinkable at the time when Matsudaira Sadanobu published *Collecting the Past, Ten Kinds.* In his preface to this book, Hirose Ten used the phrase "the past ritual utensils, armory, and scripts" to group together the "ten kinds" of objects, noting: "When we compare these [ancient] things to things of contemporary origin, we notice their beauty. Even as sketched objects, one is able to reach and enjoy a state of quiet and contemplative appreciation."[69] In other words, ancient things possess their own dignity and patina, incomparable with contemporary things. So much so that even when the encounter with them is mediated through an illustration, one is still able to enjoy them with "quiet and contemplative appreciation." Moreover, this tranquil and leisurely pleasure did not designate a mere hobby or amusement, but rather referred to the realm of a distinguished person like Matsudaira. One of the motivations to publish *Collecting the Past, Ten Kinds* was a universal aspiration to pass down illustrations of past things to later generations. In *Catalog of Writings by the Lord Rakuō* (*Rakuōkō chosho mokuroku*), which lists writings by Matsudaira, it was noted that when the catalogs were printed, they "were given to whoever wishes to have a copy, and were enjoyed among the antiquarians."[70] The antiquarians, then, proactively sought out things past, accumulated them, considered them, and displayed them in order to pass this knowledge on. Here, the term *antiquarians* included not only Matsudaira but also scholars of *materia medica*. Surveying the activities of antiquarians, the oppositional binary of amateur against professional—that is to say, the crucial dichotomy drawn by Iijima and Sasaki—cannot be found.

"Their" activities continued. As usual, they continued to edit illustrated catalogs, and proceeded to organize exhibitions, both of calligraphy and paintings and of local products. But the trend of the time was about to shake "their" world to the foundations. The cause of the change lies in the emergence of academic professionals, to which a conception of "the amateur" was opposed. The establishment of the University of Tokyo in 1877 marked the beginning of this change. As professionals began to occupy and monopolize the world of academia and to behave accordingly as authorities, this new framing gained momentum and clarity. Many antiquarians and scholars of *materia medica* were cornered into the amateur realms of hobbyism, or simple leisure. As a result, it became impossible to overcome the incongruence between these two values and return them to a balanced state. This was the biggest crisis facing "them."

The problem I want to address, however, lies further ahead. On the one hand, we can understand the ways in which, as students of Morse, Iijima and Sasaki might have come to naturally acquire their attitude—one in which they rigorously defended professional academic ranks, took pride in bringing about "great public benefit" through their research, took a distinctively cool stance toward amateurs. One can further postulate that their attitude inevitably followed the introduction of modern Western science, which treated things as specimens. But the historical reality was not quite this simple. Here, Morse's words and activities are helpful to guide us. Not only did Morse demonstrate an affinity toward antiquarians; he also saw their activities in a positive light. He proactively engaged with them, even at a purely social level. In other words, Morse's attitude toward "them" was completely opposite to that of Iijima and Sasaki.

Let us listen to Morse's words. One of his students in zoology was Matsura Sayohiko, who died of typhus at the young age of twenty-two in July 1878. Morse described his funeral service in *Japan Day by Day*.[71] When his cohorts gathered to place a tombstone for Matsura at the graveyard of Tennōji Temple in Yanaka (present-day Yanaka cemetery in Taitō ward), Morse provided the following epitaph to inscribe on the stone:

> A faithful student, a sincere
> Friend, a lover of nature.
> Holding the belief that in
> Moral as well as in physical
> Questions "the ultimate court
> Of appeal is observation and
> Experiment, and not authority"
> Such was Matsura.
>   — Edward S. Morse

Morse's words succinctly captured the earnest personality of Matsura in a simple verse. At the same time, in this text we can also detect Morse's principles and beliefs. It's not surprising for a student to hold the same principles as a teacher. Just after Morse himself passed away, one of his students published an article reminiscing about him in which he said that the basic principle by which Morse instructed his students was: "Study nature, not books." This phrase, moreover, was a phrase used by Morse's own mentor, the Swiss-born zoologist Jean Louis Rodolphe Agassiz (1807–73).[72] Although Agassiz and Morse grew apart from each other due to a disagreement about the theory of natural selection, Agassiz's motto was passed on to Morse, who then passed it down to his own students. This phrase and Morse's epitaph for Matsura shared striking similarities. To study an element of nature, one must observe and experiment, as the epitaph noted. One should not, on the other hand, rely on authority, "books" in Agassiz's phrase. In short, an uncritical absorption of text can be dangerous. The fact that they extended this academic approach to the world of morality indicates the characteristics of Matsura's and Morse's principles.

As students of Morse, Iijima and Sasaki must have accepted this motto, as did Matsura. In this light, it is hard to imagine that Morse's apprentices would have deliberately made a show of their authority. Indeed, their belief in the "great public benefit" of academic pursuits and their pride in going through specialized intellectual training both came about through their experience studying with Morse. What, then, brought about such a difference between the teacher and the students when it came to antiquarians? Among the reasons hides an important key to understanding Morse's own interpersonal relationships with antiquarians.

THE SCHOLARLY ENVIRONMENT OF THE LATE NINETEENTH CENTURY

According to the historian of science Watanabe Masao, "although modern science was born in the seventeenth century in the West, the emergence of 'scientists' as a category of professional experts had to wait, even in the West, until the late nineteenth century. Until then, clergy, medical doctors, and legal specialists were the few specialized intellectual professions."[73] The period between the Bakumatsu and early Meiji corresponded to the time when academic professionals emerged in the West. As I have already mentioned, the establishment of the University of Tokyo by the Ministry of Education in 1877 (Meiji 10) marked an important shift. It was established through merging the Tokyo Medical School, which had been called the East School of Daigaku, with Tokyo Kaisei School, which had been the South School of Daigaku. Nine years later, when the government streamlined the system of higher education, the University of Tokyo was renamed Imperial University. Even leaving aside the example of Iijima Isao and Sasaki Chūjirō, the birth of academic professionals was inseparable from the establishment of the University of Tokyo.

Moreover, when we trace the birth of academic professionals, it was not as if the paradigm of "the new and the old" overturned the prior infrastructure of the scholarly world as we have examined it so far. Rather, as I have stressed in this book, an enormous effort was made to update the wardrobe for a new season, as it were—that is, to adjust to and accommodate these new changes. For example, in the field of the study of local products during the Bakumatsu, new responses were expected in light of "the new." In response to this situation, Itō Keisuke was assigned as the official for the study of local products at the Institute for the Study of Barbarian Books in 1861. At this time, the chiefs of the office, Koga Kin'ichirō and Katsu Rintarō (later known as Katsu Kaishū) wrote a proposal for the study of local products that advocated the significance of this field.[74] It noted, "With respect to the study of local products [*bussangaku*], it is a necessary subject and provides a foundation for governing the nation and assisting the people." In other words, they acknowledged not only the practical value of the study of local products, but also its scholarly value as a foundational resource for the administration of the state. Here we witness a proactive approach to face "the new" directly through the expansion of the study of names and things.

However, when we examine whether the study of local products in the Bakumatsu period bore fruit with the industrializing policies promoted by the Meiji government, the story is quite different. Here Tanaka Yoshio's "Narrative of My

Career," which we examined in chapter 4, provides us with concrete evidence. According to this transcript of a lecture, the following exchange took place when the Institute for the Study of Barbarian Books was renamed the Institute for the Investigation of Western Books in the fifth month of 1862.

> There was an argument put forward that asserted that the establishment of the office of the study of local products was critical to expanding the paths to encourage industries, thereby enriching the nation. They established the Bureau of Local Products with the understanding that their primary purpose was to study the path to encourage industries, and therefore education was secondary. However, although Professor Itō Keisuke was a forerunner in the study of natural history, he was not as well suited to promote and encourage industry. Indeed, this was not a unique case of my teacher Itō. Many of our teachers at that time were quite knowledgeable about farming plants and potted plants, but they as engaged with what might be called research. They were quite distant from matters related to, for example, radishes, carrots, and burdock, and when it came to exploring everyday produce farmed by farmers, they were thoughtless to a rather surprising degree. In terms of encouraging industry, they were extremely inept. Other teachers came to join the institution, but they were trained either as scholars of Western learning or of what was called in the past the study of *materia medica*. Therefore, they too could not help but remain unskilled in the encouragement of industry.[75]

This excerpt is taken from a written record of a speech given by Tanaka at an exhibition commemorating his seventy-sixth birthday in 1913.[76] In other words, this was a recollection by Tanaka over fifty years after the event. We should also bear in mind that Tanaka was examining the historical situation of the study of local products during the Bakumatsu period from the point of view of the "encouragement of industry," the policy promoted by the Meiji government. Still, Tanaka's critical evaluation of his mentor Itō Keisuke as a scholar ill-suited to promote and encourage industrialization suggests that the study of local products in the Bakumatsu period did not directly lead to the industrializing policies of the Meiji period. At the very least, the connection between the study of *materia medica* and industry in Tanaka's assessment emerged out of a completely different line of thought than that of Sano Tsunetami, whose thoughts on the future of expositions and museums in the wake of the Vienna World Exposition we explored in chapter 3. It could be said that from the perspective of the Tokugawa shogunate, the potential of the study of local products in the Bakumatsu period was co-opted by the industrializing policies of the Meiji government. Similar interpretations can be made with respect to the role of Tanaka himself. It was certain that Tanaka, who proactively engaged with the Society of Agriculture of Greater Japan and the Society of Fisheries of Greater Japan, explored the study of local products that could have been used in an industrial context. However, it is questionable whether the very same Tanaka, who would virtually retire from museum management in 1883, actually cut all of his ties with the study of *materia medica* that he had learned from Itō Keisuke.

Ninagawa Noritane also shared a similar pattern of life decisions. Ninagawa retired from the front lines earlier than Tanaka, in January 1877. The publication of *Illustrated Book of Past Things: Ceramics Section* began around the time of his retirement. It appears that Ninagawa continued to engage with illustrations of antiquities, as expressed in the 1871 proposition by Daigaku, which we have examined in chapter 2. Perhaps he felt a sense of discomfort toward the industrializing policies promoted by the government. The method of study based on the logic fostered by the study of names and things exemplified in Ninagawa's activities does not seem to have been adapted into the academic world that was given physical and concrete shape after the establishment of the University of Tokyo in 1877. Rather, it is more accurate to note that the thinking based on the study of names and things and the academic world never intersected. Here, it might be easy to identify the limits of thought based on the study of names and things. However, disregarding their activities because of such restrictions would amount to taking the side of Iijima and Sasaki, who specialized in knowledge production as a profession—a position best characterized as high-handed and arbitrary.

Based on this analysis, it is impossible to ignore the outstanding personality of Edward S. Morse, who fostered a friendship with Ninagawa and learned from him how to evaluate pottery. It seems necessary, then, to follow the path of Morse's own learning.

Although Morse became the first professor of zoology at the University of Tokyo, his purpose in coming to Japan was to collect and research brachiopods.[77] In June 1877, Morse arrived in Yokohama and visited David Murray at the newly established University of Tokyo with a letter of introduction. Murray was a superintendent of educational affairs at the Ministry of Education. With Murray's help, Morse rented a house on Enoshima Island (present-day Kanagawa prefecture). Morse treated his rented house as "the world's first" marine laboratory facing the Pacific, and he spent a great deal of effort collecting and preserving brachiopods, with the help of assistants. In exchange for such favorable conditions, Morse was then asked to take on the job of teaching zoology at the university that was about to be established.[78] When he first took a train from Yokohama to Tokyo, he astutely identified the existence of shell mounds, which led to his discovery of Ōmori shell mounds. Morse's activities, including the fact he taught the evolutionary theory of zoology in his university lectures as well as public lectures, are well known in Japan. His book *Japan Day by Day* also includes detailed descriptions of his activities in Japan.

Morse's wide-ranging activities were also reflected in his publications. In August 1879, his contract with the university ended, and he returned to the United States. He returned to Japan in June 1882 for the third time. Since 1880, he had been the director of the Peabody Museum (present-day Peabody Essex Museum), located in the port town of Salem, Massachusetts. The purpose of this third visit was to collect Japanese pottery. Later, his collection of pottery moved to the Museum of Fine Arts, Boston, where Morse was asked to classify and catalog the works in the collection. The result of his work was the volume *Catalogue of the Morse Collection of Japanese Pottery* (1901).[79] This thick, large-format catalog included detailed descriptions and plates of illustrations produced in collotype (fig. 24). Although I have referred to *Japan Day by Day* and *Japanese Homes and Their Surroundings*, Morse's specialization was zoological studies, and his *First Book of Zoölogy* (1875) was published before his first trip to Japan in 1877.[80]

Morse had another publication, on the topic of astronomy: *Mars and Its Mystery*, published in 1906. Ishikawa Chiyomatsu, one of Morse's zoology students, provided an anecdote about this book. This happened when Ishikawa visited Morse's home in Salem. According to Ishikawa, Morse said: "If you bring this book back to Japan and tell my friends that Morse has written a book about Mars, they

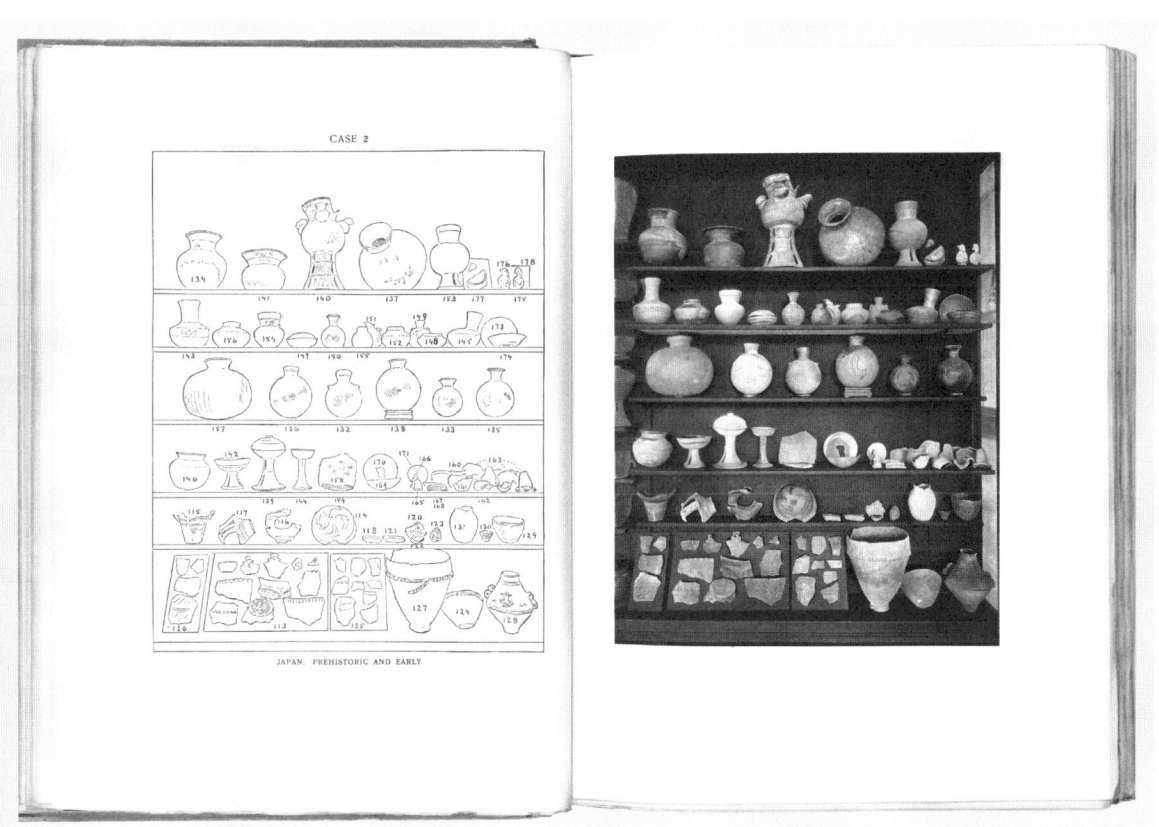

FIG. 24.

Edward S. Morse (American, 1838–1925). Case 2, Japan Prehistoric and Early. From Edward S. Morse, *Catalogue of the Morse Collection of Japanese Pottery* (Cambridge, MA: Riverside, 1901), after p. 36. Los Angeles, Getty Research Institute, 1570-244.

will think I have lost my mind." After saying this to a rather surprised Ishikawa, Morse proceeded to show him his membership card in the American Astronomical Society, in order to prove his sanity. Ishikawa also listed other specific examples of Morse's positive attitude, noting that "he was versatile and multi-talented, and there was no topic he did not show interest in."[81] As Ishikawa's astonishment indicated, the breadth of Morse's academic interests and his energy to engage with them demonstrated his vigor. His friendship and interactions with the antiquarians in Japan might be explained by these personal traits—but is the source for this aptitude confined to his personality alone?

THE CURRICULUM VITAE OF EDWARD S. MORSE

In the explanatory notes to *Japan Day by Day,* written for an edition of the Japanese translation, the scholar of American literature Fujikawa Haruto noted that because of the breadth of Morse's intellectual curiosity, he was able to achieve "results akin to those of specialists" in various fields.[82] There is, however, some disagreement on this assessment. The sociologist Sonoda Hidehiro has asserted that "one cannot presume Morse's research, which resulted from diverse intellectual curiosity, was meant to satisfy amateur standards only," thereby disputing Fujikawa's claim. Sonoda's central aim in his article was "to make things clear through Morse's individual experience, and the historical experiences of collectives who engaged with scientific research" among Morse's colleagues. According to Sonoda, this process would lead to a "more profound understanding of historical roles that Morse played for Japan."[83]

Sonoda continued to say that in our contemporary understanding, "specialized researcher" refers to "those who have attained proper intellectual training at universities and other institutions of higher education and who, using specialized knowledge, later immerse themselves in specialized research." In contrast, Sonoda argued that Morse, who spent over seven decades conducting research, "lacked the orientation of a specialized researcher in the modern sense of the word." Instead he suggested that Morse's life "as a scientist was characterized by an amateur tinge."[84]

Sonoda then focused on the generation of people born in the 1830s. He cites Burton J. Bledstein's *The Culture of Professionalism: The Middle Class and the Development of Higher Education in America,* which notes: "Historians are only beginning to realize the extent to which our modern notions of career and profession were first becoming a recognizable experience in mid-nineteenth-century America."[85] According to Bledstein, the birth of professionalism, a historical experience that North Americans underwent at that time, "corresponded in time to the coming of age and the vocational decisions of...a generation of men born in the 1830s."[86] Born in 1838, Morse certainly belongs to this generation. In this sense, according to Sonoda, Morse "belonged to the first generation of scientists who had acquired the basic understanding of specialized training centered on zoology in an intellectual context that benefited from historical serendipity."[87] If we are to project the schema of a transition from amateurism to professionalism onto this historical condition, Sonoda asserts, Morse can be posited as a figure who belonged "to the last generation of the amateurish study of natural history, and also to the first generation of the premature birth of the professionalized study of natural history."[88]

Sonoda further claims that the "amateurish characteristics" of Morse's research are best explained by "the characteristics of the time and the society in which he lived," rather than by his individual traits.[89] This is, he claims, best analyzed by focusing on the intellectual environment of North America at the time Morse began and built his career. In early nineteenth-century New England, collecting rare objects from foreign countries was a popular custom, and by the mid-nineteenth century, Sonoda notes, "collecting objects of natural history and accumulating knowledge about natural history was seen as part of the education of gentlemen, attracting many intellectuals and the public at that time" as an object that "satisfied their amateurish curiosity about scientific inquiries."[90] Various societies for those interested in natural history were established, one of which was the Portland Natural History Society in Portland, Maine—Morse's hometown. Morse, who started to make his living as a draftsman for a train company, joined the society in 1854, and was elected as secretary in 1858 when he published the article "The Development of Conchology as a Science" in the journal of the society.[91] Among such societies, the Boston Society of Natural History surpassed all others as "an academic association that included natural history scientists of the highest caliber in mid-nineteenth-century America."[92] Even in such a society, Sonoda claims, leading members were "amateur researchers who had other occupations in professions such as medicine and business." However, Sonoda warns that "it is an utter mistake to think that research into natural history practiced as a hobby and entertainment constitutes low-level research."[93]

Morse, who grew up in such an intellectual environment, experienced a turning point in 1859. Louis Agassiz, a zoologist and geological scientist from Switzerland, became a professor at Lawrence Scientific School, which was established within Harvard University through a donation of the family of a Boston entrepreneur. In 1859, Morse became a special student through Agassiz's approval, and acquired the qualification to audit Agassiz's lectures. Morse was also given several responsibilities to organize and catalog the collections of natural history and to conduct scientific research. He also became a full member of the Boston Society of Natural History, and came to be known as a young collector and researcher of shellfish throughout New England. Although Morse never graduated from Lawrence Scientific School, he received "proper academic training on zoology and geology" from Agassiz.[94] Those students of Agassiz born in the 1830s would later leave a significant impact in fields such as zoology, archaeology, and ethnology in the United States. Dorothy G. Wayman, who authored a biography of Edward S. Morse, characterized this group in the following way: "To call the roll of Agassiz's student-assistants for the year 1859–60 is to recite the names foremost in American natural history forty years later, authors of standard textbooks, curators of splendid collections, directors of great museums in every large city of the Eastern seaboard."[95] Indeed, before coming to Japan, Morse had worked as a professor of comparative anatomy and zoology from 1871 to 1874 at Bowdoin College in Maine, and served as a vice president of the American Association for the Advancement of Science, one of the central associations for the promotion of science in the United States. To borrow Sonoda's characterization, "the era of specialists began with the career of Morse."[96]

However, the beginning of a new era also clearly threw into relief the divide between the professional and the amateur. An entry from Morse's diary dated 25 May 1860 is particularly telling in this regard. He noted: "Walked home with Prof. [Agassiz]. He said that it would be better if there was no Natural History Society in Boston because we go in there and see at once that we know more than they do and it makes us rambling in our studies."[97] Sonoda takes this entry as an indication of "the waft of a new era where the supremacy of the specialist reigns."[98] "However, he notes, the era of specialists in scientific studies had to wait until the 1880s when those who were born in the 30s, like Morse, and returned from study abroad in Germany, like [Charles William] Eliot and [Daniel Coit] Gilman, became the central figures who reformed universities like Harvard and Yale as institutions that valued research as well as education."[99]

On the other hand, Sonoda argues that Japanese students "learned the authority of 'professionalism' detached from the background of amateurism" from these American scholars who were in the process of transforming their fields from amateur to professional pursuits.[100] This put Morse in an ambivalent position. One of Morse's beloved students, Ishikawa Chiyomatsu, remembered his teacher by saying: "If my teacher spent all his energy in only one direction, be it zoology or anthropology, it would have led him to a truly remarkable work."[101] Although Ishikawa always paid the greatest respect to his teacher, this does not change the fact that this critical characterization of Morse targeted the "amateurish characteristics" of Morse's studies. Ishikawa's attitude here was consistent with those professionals who had accumulated intellectual training and were immersed in specialized research. In this regard, Ishikawa's criticism of Morse was clearly connected to the criticisms of antiquarians by Iijima and Sasaki.

THE ANTIQUARIANS EXIT THE STAGE

If the emergence of professionalism is what brought about the dichotomy of professionalism versus amateurism, then what were the characteristics of such "amateurism" before this dichotomy emerged? Historically speaking, could we not hear some echoes of Enlightenment thinking in "amateurish" inquiries?

There was a period when Agassiz's students of the same generation, namely Morse, the entomologist and paleontologist Alpheus S. Packard (1839–1905), the zoologist and paleontologist Alpheus Hyatt (1838–1902), and the anthropologist

Frederick W. Putman (1839–1915), were estranged from their teacher and were all based at the Essex Institute in Salem, Massachusetts.[102] This institution was a predecessor to the Peabody Essex Museum, and in this sense, it had a long-established relationship with Morse. They began to publish *The American Naturalist,* a monthly journal with the subtitle "popular illustrated magazine," from the institute. This publication was highlighted with attractive illustrations in lithography and wood engraving. Publication began in 1867, the height of the Bakumatsu period.

The introduction to the inaugural issue offered an insight into the underlying principle of this journal. The editors imagined their readership to be "all lovers of nature." Recall that Morse used this same phrase in the epitaph for his student Matsura Sayohiko. Those who founded this journal, including Morse, understood themselves as such. The introduction continues: "The rapidly increasing interest in the study of the various departments of Natural History invites the establishment of a journal which shall popularize the best results of scientific study, and thus serve as a medium between the teacher and the student, or, more properly, between the older and the younger student of nature."[103] The purpose of publishing this journal, therefore, was to popularize natural science. In other words, this journal served as a device to connect the editors' interests in natural history, which stood at the origin of their academic pursuit, to the spirit of Enlightenment.

Scientists of Morse's generation—in Sonoda's phrase, "the first generation [of scientists] who had acquired the basic understanding of specialist training centered on zoology"—strived to bridge the professional and the amateur. The reasons for Morse's active and varied projects in Japan emerged from this fundamental approach to his scientific studies. When Morse came into contact with associations of antiquarians and scholars of *materia medica,* or when he witnessed the results of their activities, he must have recalled his own experiences with associations of natural history in Boston and Portland. What Sonoda describes as the consistently "amateurish characteristics" of Morse's works, in other words, is what allowed him to find shared academic interests among the antiquarians and scholars of *materia medica* who had been active since the Tokugawa period.

Similar arguments can be made from the point of view of the antiquarians and scholars of *materia medica.* For them, Morse must have appeared as a realized example of "the new." More importantly, however, many of those who interacted with Morse must have been sympathetic to the academic method through which Morse approached his subjects. Ninagawa Noritane was undoubtedly one of those who shared Morse's method.

This leads to another interesting similarity between Morse and the people he met in Japan, along the lines of what Sonoda describes as "historical serendipity." Here is a list of the birth dates of those who have played pivotal roles in my argument so far (the list takes advantage of both lunar and solar calendars): Ninagawa Noritane was born in 1835 or Tenpō 3; Tanaka Yoshio, Machida Hisanari, and Uchida Masao in 1838 or Tenpō 9; Kanda Takahira in 1830 or Tenpō 1; Takemoto

Yōsai in 1831 or Tenpō 2; and Narushima Ryūhoku in 1837 or Tenpō 8, all belonging to the same generation as Morse. Kashiwagi Kaichirō, born in 1841 or Tenpō 12, was slightly younger than these figures but belonged to the group through the era of Tenpō. Ito Keisuke was born in 1803 or Kyōhō 3, and Matsuura Takeshirō in 1818 or Bunsei 1. If we borrow the turn of phrase used by Sonoda when evaluating Morse, these Japanese figures belonged to "the last generation of amateurish study" of names and things. What differentiates the latter figures from those of Morse's generation is that although more than half of those in Japan did experience the West directly during the Bakumatsu period, they did not become "the first generation at the premature birth of professionalized study of natural history," to borrow Sonoda's phrase.

Compared to those born in the 1830s in Japan, those born in the 1850s mark a stark contrast. When Morse left Japan in August 1879, he left behind four students: Sasaki Chūjirō, who would become a third-year student in September, second-year students Iijima Isao and Iwakawa Tomotarō (1854–1933), and first-year student Ishikawa Chiyomatsu. In order of seniority, Iwakawa was born in the year Ansei 1, Sasaki in 1857 or Ansei 4, Ishikawa in 1860 or Man'en 1, and Iijima in 1861 or Bunkyū 1. Later, all four became essential figures in the academy. Sasaki became a professor of entomology at the College of Agriculture of the Imperial University and Ishikawa became a professor of zoology at the same college. After studying abroad in Leipzig, Iijima became a professor at the College of Science at the Imperial University, and the conchologist Iwakawa became a professor at Tokyo Women's Higher Normal School.[104] Their publications, such as Iijima's *Manual of Zoology* (*Dōbutsugaku teiyō*, 1918) and Sasaki's *Japanese Netsuke* (*Nihon no netsuke*, 1936), remind us of various publications by Morse.

Yatabe Ryōkichi, who translated Morse's *Shell Mounds of Omori* into Japanese, went to study at Cornell University and became a professor of botany at the University of Tokyo. He was born in 1851 or Kaei 4, which would place him in the same generation as those above. Although a few of them were born in the 1860s, the majority were born in the 1850s. Including those studied abroad, such as Yatabe, this group became literally "the first generation [of scientists] who had acquired the basic understanding of specialist training," to borrow Sonoda's terms again.

Although I have focused on the individual experience of Morse and his interpersonal relations in Japan, many hired foreign experts who came from Europe and the United States during this time had more or less similar experiences to Morse. In addition, the experiences of Iijima, Sasaki, and Yatabe must have been shared in other academic fields as well. When these new generations of scientists emerged, the antiquarians and the scholars of *materia medica* exited the stage. This shift happened between the late 1870s and the early 1880s. The central topic of this book, the shift in the world of things past, also took place around this period. Japan's participation in Vienna World Exposition of 1873 and the first National Industrial Exposition in 1877, played significant roles in these shifts. They took samples, and specimens were displayed inside glass boxes. Similar movements took place within academia. As objects of study, things came to be understood as abstractions or representations, rather than as materials with sensory qualities. These shifts also led to configuration of things in hierarchical order, individuated by an infinite number of differences. To echo Yamaguchi Masao, the world of things that had constituted a universe characterized by a "mandala-like arrangement" was shaken to its foundations, and rapidly compartmentalized into specialized areas. As such, the worldview that grounded the study of names and things receded into the distant past.

Let us briefly sketch some of the processes that took place later on. This is most evident through examining the academic world. After Morse's departure from the University of Tokyo, Charles O. Whitman (1842–1910) came to replace him. A young returnee from study abroad in Germany, he used microscopes extensively in his teaching. He promoted the research-oriented approach he had learned in Germany, and under his tutelage, Sasaki, Iijima, and Iwakawa graduated in July 1881 (Meiji 14).[105] Another example is Ernest F. Fenollosa, born in 1853. After graduating from Harvard University, he came to Japan through the introduction of Morse in 1878, and lectured on philosophy and political economy at the University of Tokyo. In chapter 1, we have explored his role in the research on treasures organized by the Ministry of Education in 1884 to investigate old temples and shrines in the Kinki region. Together with Okakura Kakuzō (Tenshin), ten years his junior, Fenollosa played a pivotal role in securing the concept of "*bijutsu*" (fine arts) in later Meiji Japan. On the other hand, in 1884 figures such as Tsuboi Shōgorō and Shirai Mitsutarō, whom we explored in chapter 4, founded the Tokyo Anthropology Society. Both Tsuboi and Shirai were born in 1863 or Bunkyū 3, the same year as Okakura. The study of archaeology branched off from the field of anthropology in 1895, which laid the foundation for the structure of this field today.[106]

In terms of the technology of mechanical reproduction, we also witness a process of specialization regarding the world of things. Under the guidance of Tokuno Ryōsuke (1825–83), the Printing Bureau under the Finance Ministry developed a refined printing technology of chromolithography from the late 1870s. Resulting publications attested to their success: illustrated catalogs including the series of *Everlasting Glories of the Nation* (*Kokka yohō*, 1880–81), *Brocade on the Waves* (*Namima no nishiki*, 1883), and *Appreciation at the Residence of Chōyōkaku: Part of Brocades* (*Chōyōkaku kanshō kinshū no bu*, 1883).[107] On the other hand, when Okakura Kakuzō and others founded the monthly art journal *The Glory of the Country* (*Kokka*) in 1889, they deployed collotype technology for their illustration plates, using a printing method the photographer Ogawa Kazumasa (1860–1929) had brought back from the United States.[108] For their color plates of illustrations, they revived the traditional technique of polychrome woodblock printing. By contrast, the journal of the Tokyo Anthropology Society established by Tsuboi and Shirai, *Reports on Anthropology* (*Jinruigakkai hōkoku*), used lithographic reproductions when it began publishing in 1886. In the field of archaeology, the technique of scale reduction was introduced to illustrations. Among them, the use of plates containing a collection of reduced illustrations (*shūseizu*) became part of the mainstream.[109] In other fields of study, *Rhopalocera Nihonica: A Description of the Butterflies of Japan* by Henry J. S. Pryer (1850–88), published in Yokohama in 1886, used chromolithography. The rough cross hatching used on the wings of the butterflies conveyed an impressive sense of presence. The technology of mechanical reproduction during the Meiji period, thus, ran parallel to the specialization of academic subjects (see appendixes, table 2).

What, then, happened to the antiquarians? There was a brief period of harmony between professionals and amateurs. An association founded by Tsuboi Shōgorō, the Tokyo Anthropology Society, is said to have taken advantage of the network of antiquarians in an effort to organize their society.[110] In 1896, Tsuboi and others founded an association called Shūkokai, literally meaning the "meeting of collecting the past." They aimed to "promote the knowledge of past things in between and through conversation and entertainment," reminding us of associations of scholars of *materia medica* that flourished in previous years.[111] One notable member of this society was Yamanaka Emu (1850–1928), also known as Yamanaka Kyōko, who was born into a vassal family of the shogun and became one of the first Methodist priests in Japan. While evangelizing, Yamanaka studied ethnography, collected things past, became friends with Matsuura Takeshirō, and established the Tokyo Numismatic Society (Tokyo kosenkai).[112] According to the Protestant priest and essayist Ōta Aito, Yamanaka was active in various fields, "for he was an example where within an individual two parallel directions grew: on the one hand, the stance of the Japanese spirit and Western learning, and the spirit of the East which characterize the Protestantism of Meiji, and on the other, the interest in arts and sciences of the West."[113]

But once drawn, a border cannot be erased. At the twenty-third general meeting of the Archaeological Society on 19 May 1918, which took place at the Tokyo School of Fine Arts, an exhibition titled *Materials of Twelve Archaeologists* (*Jūni kōkoka shiryō tenarankai*) was held. The exhibition celebrated twelve pioneers of archaeology, beginning with the Confucianist of the Tokugawa period Arai Hakuseki. Included among these figures were Matsuura Takeshirō, Kanda Takahira, Ninagawa Noritane, and Machida Hisanari. It demonstrated that by the early twentieth century, all these pioneers had become historical figures to be remembered. Yamanaka's article "A Historical Outline of Numismatic Studies in Japan," published in the *Journal of the Archaeological Society of Nippon* in 1917, is quite telling in this regard. He used a botanical image to describe the numismatic research of the past and asserted: "In the past, there were many horticulturists of numismatics, but only a handful of botanists." That is, Yamanaka saw "amateurish characteristics" among prior studies that did not reach a specialist level that would be informed by numismatics.[114] Born in 1850 or Kaei 3, Yamanaka's interpretation of the past recalls an interpretation of Morse's studies that had been made by his contemporary, Ishikawa Chiyomatsu. On the other hand, there was an insurmountable divide between Yamanaka and Ishiwaka, between amateurism and professionalism. As this border became more clearly articulated, someone like Yamanaka who came from an antiquarian background came to be regarded as a non-academic researcher, while Ishikawa, who continued to occupy his position within the academy, was regarded as an authority. Consequently, the field of study that directly engaged with things, such as numismatics and epigraphy, in which Yamanaka was involved, came to be positioned as merely supplementary areas to academic fields of study like anthropology, archaeology, history, and art history. Like the world of things, the world of academia, too, came to be ordered by a hierarchical structure.

The antiquarians exited the stage. In their attempt to grapple with the shifting world around them, there were setbacks and successes. Later generations would piece together the remains left behind by their setbacks and tell the stories of their success as evidence of a mythologized past. Their activities and inquiries, as well as the world of things that served as their central stage, became sealed into the strata of their own age.

NOTES

1   The entry in Chambers's *Information for the People* reads: "it has now been universally adopted in its largest sense to give name to the science which deduces history from the relics of the past." William and Robert Chambers eds., *Chambers's Information for the People* (London and Edinburgh: W. & R. Chambers, 1833–35), 721.

2   The entry in Chambers reads: "The word, however, literally signifies the description of ancient things." Chambers, *Chambers's Information,* 721.

3   Edward S. Morse, *Shell Mounds of Omori* (Tokyo: University of Tokio, 1879), iv.

4   Morse, *Shell Mounds of Omori,* iv. Some scholars identify this "native Archaeological Society" as the "Archaeology Club" organized by scholars associated with the University of Tokyo. See Yoshirō and Sahara Makoto, "Kaisetsu," in Edward S. Morse, *Ōmori kaizuka,* trans. Kondō and Sahara (Tokyo: Iwanami Shoten, 1983), 195. However, their interpretation is misled by Yatabe's translation of this phrase, in which he used the Japanese word *gakushi*, meaning "university graduates."

5   Morse, *Shell Mounds of Omori,* 22.

6   "Notes," *Nature* 17 (31 January 1878): 271. See also Sahara Makoto, "Nihon kindai kōkogaku no hajimaru koro: Mōsu, Shiiboruto, Sasaki Chūjirō shiryō ni yosete," in Moriya Takeshi, ed., *Mōsu to Nihon: Kyōdō kenkyū* (Tokyo: Shōgakukan, 1988), 262–63, 266.

7   Sahara, "Nihon kindai kōkogaku no hajimaru koro," 271–72.

8. Josef Kreiner, "Hainrihhi fon Shiiboruto: Nihon kōkogaku minzoku bunka kigenron no gakushi kara," in Heinrich von Siebold, *Shō Shiiboruto Ezo kenbunki*, trans. Harada Nobuo, Harald Suppanschitsch and J. Keiner (Tokyo: Heibonsha, 1996), 251.

9. Kiyono Kenji, *Nihon kōkogaku jinruigaku shi* (Tokyo: Iwanami Shoten, 1954), 1:408–58.

10. Ueno Masuzō, *Nihon hakubutsugaku shi* (Tokyo: Heibonsha, 1986), 126–29.

11. Kiyono, *Nihon kōkogaku jinruigaku shi*, 400–402.

12. Saitō Gesshin, *Zōho bukō nenpyō* (Tokyo: Heibonsha, 1968), 19.

13. Kitajima Yutaka, "Owari Nagoya ni okeru shogakai ni tsuite," *Bijutsushi kenkyū* 36 (1998): 59–62.

14. Robert Campbell, "Kanshō no nagare: shogakai shi seki sono ichi, Ginkakuji Higashiyama dono sanbyaku kaiki," *Bungaku* 8, no. 2 (April 1997): 140–41.

15. Kiyono, *Nihon kōkogaku jinruigaku shi*, 406.

16. Ōhashi Bishō (Yoshizō, Bishōshōshi), "Kazan no shūkai kiyaku," *Shūkokaishi* 4 (1908): 5.

17. Ōhashi, "Kazan no shūkai kiyaku," 5–6.

18. Ōhashi, "Kazan no shūkai kiyaku," 5–6.

19. Edward S. Morse, *Japan Day by Day* (Boston and New York: Houghton Mifflin, 1917), 2:399–400.

20. For this stay, Morse arrived at Yokohama in June 1882.

21. Morse, *Japan Day by Day*, vol. 2, 190.

22. Ninagawa Chikamasa, "Mōsu no Nihon tōki korekushon to Ninagawa Noritane," *Jinruigaku zasshi* 87, no. 3 (1979): 315.

23. Ninagawa, "Mōsu no Nihon tōki korekushon to Ninagawa Noritane," 315. After the death of Noritane, his elder sister arranged to have Teiichi, the grandson of Noritane's younger sister, adopt Noritane's son. This story had been quite well known among the family members, and Teiichi heard it directly from Tokiko, Noritane's elder sister. Sakai Seiichi, *Henreki no buke: Ninagawa shi no rekishiteki kenkyū* (Tokyo: Yoshikawa Kōbunkan, 1963), 88; Ninagawa Chikamasa, "Mōsu no tōki shūshū to Ninagawa Noritane," in Moriya Takeshi ed., *Mōsu to Nihon: Kyōdō kenkyū* (Tokyo: Shōgakukan, 1988), 393.

24. Ninagawa Chikamasa, "Mōsu no Nihon tōki korekushon to Ninagawa Noritane," 315.

25. Tsukahara Akira, "Sekihanga kanren jinmei gyōsha roku," in Kobe Shiritsu Hakubutsukan, ed., *Egakareta Meiji Nippon: Sekihanga (ritogurafu) no jidai, kaisetsu zuroku kenkyū hen* (Kobe: Egakareta Meiji Nippon Ten Jikkōiinkai, 2002), 325.

26. Kyoto Bunka Hakubutsukan, *Kyoto yōga no akebono* (Kyoto: Kyoto Bunka Hakubutsukan 1999), 130.

27 Walter Benjamin, "The Work of Art in the Age of Its Technological Reproducibility, Second Version," in *Walter Benjamin Selected Writings,* vol. 3: 1935–38, trans. Edmund Jephcott and Howard Eiland (Cambridge, Mass.: Harvard University Press, 2002), 102.

28 Mashino Keiko, "Nihon ni okeru sekihanjutsu juyō no shomondai: Ninagawa Noritane *Kanko zusetsu tōki no bu* 3 'Fugen' o megutte," in Machida Shiritsu Kokusai Hangabijutukan, ed., *Kindai Nihon hanga no shosō* (Tokyo: Chūō Kōron Bijutsu Shuppan, 1998), 166–77.

29 Ono Tadashige, *Nihon no sekihanga* (Tokyo: Bijutsu Shuppan, 1967), 9–38.

30 Aoki Shigeru and Sakai Tadayasu, eds., *Bijutsu* (Tokyo: Iwanami Shoten, 1989), 170.

31 Murakado Noriko, "Shinbi Shoin no bijutsu zenshū ni miru 'Nihon bijutsushi' no keisei" *Kindai gasetsu* 8 (December 1999): 36.

32 Mori Noboru, "Umemura Suizan no seiyōryū koguchi mokuhan: Dō sekihanga ibun kyū," *Issun* 11 (August 2002): 24–25.

33 Numata Raisuke, "Kōkogaku jō yori mitaru Rakuō kō," *Kōkogaku zasshi* 11, no. 7 (March 1921): 5–30.

34 Fukushima Kenritsu Hakubutsukan, ed., *Shūko jisshu: Aruku utsusu atsumeru, Matsudaira Sadanobu no kobunkazai chōsa* (Aizu Wakamatsu: Fukushima Kenritsu Hakubutsukan, 2000). For later reprinting, see especially in this volume Satō Yōichi, "Tenji shiryō *Shūko jisshu* no shohon ni tsuite," 92–99.

35 Tokyo Kokuritsu Hakubutsukan, ed., *Chōsa kenkyū hōkoku: Koga ruijū honmon hen* (Tokyo: Tokyo Kokuritsu Hakubutsukan, 1990), 70.

36 Pouch-binding is a traditional East Asian method of bookbinding in which the sheets of paper printed on one side only are folded into two at the center on the outside, stacked, and stitched with strings along the unfolded edge.

37 Yoshida Takezō, *Shūi Matsuura Takeshirō* (Tokyo: Matsuura Takeshirōden Kankōkai, 1964), 5–57.

38 To identify Ninagawa, it referred to his origin and present address, "commoner in the city of Kyoto, temporally residing at house number 2, Dōsanchō town, Tatsunokuchi, Tokyo."

39 Kanagawa Kenritsu Kindai Bijutsukan, ed., *Bakumatsu ishin no dōhanga: Gengendō to sono ippa ten zuroku, e ni miru mikuro no shakaigaku* (Kamakura: Kanagawa Kenritsu Kindai Bijutsukan, 1998), 7–11; 88.

40 Mashino, "Nihon ni okeru sekihanjutsu juyō no shomondai," 167, 187–88.

41 Or approximately 17 by 11 and 15 by 10 inches.

42 Aoki Shigeru, "Ninagawa Noritane ni tsuite," in Ninagawa Chikamasa ed., *Shintei kanko zusetsu* (Tokyo: Chūō Kōron Bijutsu Shuppan, 1990), 59.

43 Kinoshita Naoyuki, *Bijutsu toiu misemono* (Tokyo: Heibonsha, 1993), 112.

44 Morse, *Japan Day by Day,* 2:106–7.

45 Morse, *Japan Day by Day,* 2:371.

46 Shōji Mitsuo, "Kaisetsu" in A. J. C. Geerts, *Heerutsu Nihon nenpō*, trans. Shōji Mitsuo (Tokyo: Yūshōdō, 1983), vol. 2, no. 5 of the series Shin ikoku sōsho, 471–74.

47 Japanese title page of the first volume reads, "Oranda kyōshi awase Geerutsu cho, *Shinsen honzō kōmoku kōbutsu no bu*, dai ippen, Meiji jūichi nen, Dai Nihon Yokohama, Ōkyō-sha, Reuhi jōshi" [by the Dutch teacher A. J. C. Geerts, *Compendium of Materia Medica, New Edition: Minerals*, vol. 1, published by Ōkyō-sha "Levy" in Yokohama, Great Japan].

48 Kreiner, "Hainrihhi fon Shiiboruto," 228–33.

49 "Hainrihhi fon Shiiboruto ryaku nenpu," in Siebold, *Shō Shiiboruto Ezo kenbunki,* 297–98.

50 Harada Nobuo, "Hainrihhi fon Shiiboruto to Hokkaidō," in Siebold, *Shō Shiiboruto Ezo kenbunki,* 289.

51 Edward S. Morse, *Ōmori kaizuka,* ed. and trans. Kondō Yoshirō and Sahara Makoto (Tokyo: Iwanami Shoten, 1983), 178–83.

52 Morse, *Shell Mounds of Omori*, iv.

53 Saitō Tadashi, ed., *Nihon kōkogakushi shiryō shūsei*, vol. 2: *Meiji, Part I* (Tokyo: Yoshikawa Kōbunkan, 1979), 35–64.

54 Kusuya Shigetoshi, "Nihon Ajia kyōkai no seiritsu to Japanorojisuto," in Yokohama Kaikōshiryōkan, ed., *Yokohama kyoryūchi to ibunka kōryū: Jūkyū seiki kōhan no kokusai toshi o yomu* (Tokyo: Yamakawa Shuppansha, 1996), 292–957.

55 Yamada Keiji, "Ishin zengo ni okeru ajia kyōkai no Nihon kenkyū," *Rangaku shiryō kenkyū* 7, no. 111 (June 1962): 183–87.

56 Hugh Cortazzi, ed., *Mitford's Japan: Memories and Recollections, 1866–1906* (London: Athlone Press, 1985), 22.

57 "Appendix: List of Writings of Sir Ernest Satow," in Bernard M. Allen, *The Rt. Hon. Sir Ernest Satow G.C.M.G., a Memoir* (London: Kegan Paul, Trench, Truebner, 1933), 145–49.

58 Ernest Mason Satow, *The Diaries of Sir Ernest Mason Satow: 1870–1883*, ed. Ian Ruxton (Tokyo: Eureka, 2015), 355–56.

59 Kabe Nitaka, "Aanesuto Satō cho 'Kōzuke chihō no kofun gun' no gakushiteki ichi: Eikoku gaikōkan no kōkogaku tankyū," *Kokuritsu rekishi minzoku hakubutsukan kenkyū hōkoku* 76 (March 1998): 103 n. 38.

60 Ueno Masuzō, *Oyatoi gaikokujin* (Tokyo: Kajima Shuppankai, 1968), 161–84.

61 Isono Naohide, "*Memoa* to rika kaisui," in *Gakumon no arukeorojii* (Tokyo: Tokyo Daigaku Shuppankai, 1997), 323–26.

62 In 1886 (Meiji 19), two years later, the original Japanese text by Kanda Takahira was published under the title *Nihon taiko sekki kō,* but the illustrations were excluded from this edition.

63 To identify these lithographic painters, see, Tsukahara, "Sekihanga kanren jinmei gyōsha roku," 302–26; and Kanagawa Kenritsu Kindai Bijutsukan, *Bakumatsu ishin no dōhanga,* 87–88.

64 Saitō Tadashi, Iijima Isao, and Sasaki Chūjirō, *Okadaira Shell Mound at Hitachi* (Tokyo: Daiichi Shobō, 1983).

65 Kanda Takahira and Saitō Tadashi, *Notes on Ancient Stone Implements, &c., of Japan* (Tokyo: Daiichi Shobō, 1983).

66 The castle of the Tokugawa shogunate in the capital Edo. After the Restoration of 1868, the castle was transferred to the new Meiji government. The emperor Meiji moved to the castle from Kyoto in the ninth month of the year, and the castle was designated as the imperial palace and renamed Tokyo Castle in the tenth month.

67 This photograph album is in the collection of the Tokyo National Museum. The images were selected from the hundreds of photographs of the castle that Ninagawa had asked Yokoyama Matsusaburō to take in 1871 (Meiji 4). In 1878 Ninagawa published *Kanko zusetsu jōkaku no bu ichi* (*Illustrated Book of Past Things: Castle Section, Part I*), containing seventy-three photographs of Edo castle, selected from Yokoyama's photographs, but none of the images in the catalog were hand-colored: Ninagawa Noritane, *Kanko zusetsu jōkaku no bu ichi* (Tokyo: H. Arhens, 1880); and Ninagawa Chikamasa, *Shintei kanko zusetsu: Jōkaku no bu,* 55–56.

68 Sasaki Chūzaburō and Iijima Isao, "Jōshū Okadaira kaikyo hōkoku," *Gakugei shirin* 6, no. 31 (February 1880): 91–92.

69 Quotations are from Hirose Ten, preface, *Collecting the Old, Ten Kinds,* dated the first month of 1800 (Kansei 12).

70 Tōno Haruyuki, "*Koga ruijū no seiritsu,*" in Tokyo Kokuritsu Hakubutsukan, ed., *Chōsa kenkyū hōkoku,* 83.

71 Morse, *Japan Day by Day,* 1:408–10.

72 Ueno Masuzō, "Nihon saisho no dōbutsugaku kyōju Mōsu," *Jinruigaku zasshi* 87, no. 3 (March 1979): 288.

73 Watanabe Masao, *Nihonjin to kindai kagaku: Seiyō eno taiō to kadai* (Tokyo: Iwanami Shoten, 1976), 9.

74 Tokyo Kokuritsu Hakubutsukan, *Tokyo Kokuritsu Hakubutsukan hyakunenshi: Shiryōhen* (Tokyo: Tokyo Kokuritsu Hakubutsukan, 1973), 563.

75 Tokyo Kokuritsu Hakubutsukan, *Tokyo Kokuritsu Hakubutsukan hyakunenshi: Shiryōhen,* 564.

76 The exhibition was titled *Commemorating the Seventy-Sixth Birthday of Mr. Yoshio Tanaka* (*Tanaka Yoshio kun shichi roku tenrankai*). Dai Nihon sanrinkai, ed., *Tanaka Yoshio kun*

shichi roku tenrankai kinenshi (Tokyo: Dai Nihon Sanrinkai, 1913). The exhibition has been referred to in chapter 4.

77 Brachiopods are ocean creatures that appear to have been left behind in evolution. There are many such species, including lampshells and Lingulata Brachiopods, on the Pacific coast of Japan. Morse, *Japan Day by Day*, 1:138.

78 Ueno, "Nihon saisho no dōbutsugaku kyōju Mōsu," 280–82.

79 Ninagawa, "Mōsu no Nihon tōki korekushon to Ninagawa Noritane," 326.

80 Ueno, "Nihon saisho no dōbutsugaku kyōju Mōsu," 288.

81 Ishikawa Chiyomatsu, "Jo: Mōsu sensei," in Edward S. Morse, *Nihon sono hi sono hi*, trans. of *Japan Day by Day* by Ishikawa Kin'ichi (Tokyo: Heibonsha, 1970), 3–5.

82 Fujikawa Haruto, "Kaisetsu," in Morse, *Nihon sono hi sono hi,* 257.

83 Sonoda Hidehiro, "Nyū Ingurando ni okeru Mōsu no chiteki kankyō," in Moriya, *Mōsu to Nihon,* 439.

84 Sonoda, "Nyū Ingurando," 439–43.

85 Burton J. Bledstein, *The Culture of Professionalism: The Middle Class and the Development of Higher Education in America* (New York: Norton, 1976), 178.

86 Bledstein, *The Culture of Professionalism,* 178.

87 Sonoda, "Nyū Ingurando," 460.

88 Sonoda, "Nyū Ingurando," 462.

89 Sonoda, "Nyū Ingurando," 444.

90 Sonoda, "Nyū Ingurando," 446.

91 Dorothy Godfrey Wayman, *Edward Sylvester Morse: A Biography* (Cambridge, Mass.: Harvard University Press, 1942), 15.

92 Sonoda, "Nyū Ingurando," 448.

93 Sonoda, "Nyū Ingurando," 448.

94 Sonoda, "Nyū Ingurando," 457.

95 Wayman, *Edward Sylvester Morse,* 69.

96 Sonoda, "Nyū Ingurando," 461.

97 Wayman, *Edward Sylvester Morse,* 123.

98 Sonoda, "Nyū Ingurando," 462.

99 Sonoda, "Nyū Ingurando," 462.

100 Sonoda, "Nyū Ingurando," 462.

101 Ishikawa Chiyomatsu, "Onshi Mōrusu sensei," *Tōyō gakugei zasshi* 42, no. 514 (1926): 124.

102 Ueno, "Nihon saisho no dōbutsugaku kyōju Mōsu," 283–84.

103 "Introductory," *American Naturalist* 1, no. 1 (March 1867): 1.

104 Ueno, "Nihon saisho no dōbutsugaku kyōju Mōsu," 289.

105 Ueno, *Oyatoi gaikokujin,* 46–49.

106 Yagi Sōzaburō, "Meiji kōkogakushi," *Dorumen* 39 (June 1935): 9–24.

107 Kōno Minoru, "Nihon no sekihanga," in Kobe Shiritsu Hakubutsukan, ed., *Egakareta Meiji Nippon,* 9–10.

108 Okatsuka Akiko, "Ogawa Kazumasa no 'Kinki hōmotsu chōsa shashin' ni tsuite," *Tokyoto shashin bijutsukan kiyō* 2 (2000): 41–42.

109 Uchida Yoshiaki, "Nihon no shūseizu," *Kōkogakushi kenkyū* 5 (November 1995): 25–26.

110 Sakano Tōru, "Nihon jinrui gakkai no tanjō: Kobutsu shumi to kindai kagaku no aida," *Kagakushi kenkyū* 209 (March 1999): 12–15.

111 Kiyono, *Nihon kōkogaku jinruigaku shi*, 6–7.

112 Iijima Yoshiharu, "Kaisetsu: Yamanaka Kyōko no hito to gakumon," in Yamanaka Kyōko, *Kyōko zuihitsu* (Tokyo: Heibonsha, 1995), 343–46, 350–52.

113 Ōta Aito, *Meiji kirisutokyō no ryūiki: Shizuoka bando to bakushin tachi* (Tokyo: Chūō Kōronsha, 1992), 120.

114 Yamanaka Emu (Kyōko), "Nihon ni okeru kosen kenkyū no enkaku," *Kōkogaku zasshi* 7, no. 12 (August 1917): 760.

Epilogue

In the end, does this book belong to art history? I have written it with the current state of art-historical studies in mind, but at the same time, I have deliberately forgone the commonly accepted distinction between art and non-art. In this sense, one could argue for or against the idea that this book belongs to art history. Perhaps I should explain the reasons for taking such a position; this would, I hope, help readers to better understand the contents of this book.

Looking back on it now, art-historical research in Japan produced immense results during the 1990s. The study of modern art blazed a trail, and always stood at the front of the field. The most significant of these results was the clarification that the concept of *bijutsu,* the contemporary word for "fine art," was not a universal, eternal category, but merely one of many historically constructed concepts that were coined to translate Western words during the Bakumatsu period and the early Meiji era.

As mentioned in chapter 1, the term *bijutsu* was a neologism that first appeared when terms and conditions for the Vienna World Exposition of 1873 were translated into Japanese. Basil Hall Chamberlain, an early Japanologist, arrived in Japan the same year and lived there for more than four decades. His *Things Japanese: Being Notes on the Various Subjects Connected with Japan* (1890) included a section on art. In a footnote, he offered a telling insight: "A curious fact, to which we have never seen attention drawn, is that the Japanese language has no genuinely native word for 'art.' To translate the European term 'fine art,' there has recently been invented the compound of *bi-jutsu,* by putting together the two Chinese characters *bi,* 'beautiful,' and '*jutsu,*' meaning 'craft,' 'device,' 'legerdemain.'"[1]

Until the 1990s I had been an art historian engaged with researching objects from before the Tokugawa period. These discussions in the 1990s had, in effect, cornered an art historian like myself. For, before that point, we art historians called objects from before the Meiji period "art" without any doubts. The new research claimed that, in fact, such objects had acquired this status only after the Meiji period, and that there was no concept of *bijutsu* before then. We had never questioned the status of these objects as art. Taking this point seriously, then, how were we art historians to interact with these objects anew? We were left with this urgent but intractable problem.

It was not easy to find a clue to solve this issue. The reason was clear: the field of art history had presumed a certain concept of *bijutsu,* and had been constituted on this basis from the very start. If an art historian was to deal with objects that were not considered *bijutsu,* then this would be a contradiction in terms from the beginning.

Some scholars might disagree here. For instance, in East Asia, there had been a traditional genre of arts, the grouping called calligraphy and painting (Ch. *shuhua,* J. *shoga*). Why not deal with this category? Unfortunately, this category with its regional past cannot be unconditionally guaranteed to be an object of art-historical study. Historically speaking, we will not be able to find any evidence that the genre of calligraphy and painting was grafted onto that of *bijutsu,* Quite the contrary, in the edict regarding the preservation of *kokikyūbutsu* (old and ancient objects) issued by the Grand Council of State in the fifth month of 1871, the category of calligraphy and painting constituted only one of the thirty-one sections of *kokikyūbutsu.*

Might the root of the problem lie in the fact that each one of us art historians has for too long been sitting in the overly comfortable, overly complicit seat given to us within the academy and society at large? To get out of such a situation, in my opinion, one should make an effort to find a way to resolve the problem within one's own past, rather than relying on others to take action. Once we come to frame the problem like this, I believe, we may be able to find multiple measures to tackle the issue.

For instance, what kind of world was evolving between the time when the neologism *bijutsu* came into being and when the term came to be accepted by the general public? We must explore how the world was ordered when objects had not yet been separated into *bijutsu* and non-*bijutsu*. If we could take on this inquiry, we could extend the discussions that emerged in the 1990s. Perhaps we might find a clue for the conundrum somewhere near this line of inquiry. Such thoughts were the seed for writing this book.

As a result, this book may have diverted from and moved beyond the world of art history that is constituted by sorting objects into the categories of *bijutsu* and non-*bijutsu*. Perhaps such a move is constructive. Once outside the field, we would be able to clearly see the contours of a question: What has art history been and done? In addition, we might be able to gain an unexpected insight into our field of study. It would be important to continue to trace the process in which art history today has come to be, more tenaciously and more thoroughly. In my next project, I hope to trace the process by which distinctions were made between *bijutsu* and non-*bijutsu* as a result of sifting through things past. I only hope the small attempt made in this book serves as an adequate preparation for this new investigation.

Lastly, I would like to express my sincere gratitude to Professor Satō Dōshin at Tokyo University of the Arts, who encouraged me to write this book, and to Mr. Nagataki Minoru and Ms. Okada Hisayo, who assisted in editing this book.

Suzuki Hiroyuki
August 2003

NOTES

1. Basil Hall Chamberlain, *Things Japanese: Being Notes on the Various Subjects Connected with Japan* (London and Tokyo: K. Paul, Trench, Trübner, Hakubunsha, 1890), 55.

Appendixes

Table 1.
Exhibition Practices and Policy Changes from the Late Tokugawa to the Early Meiji Periods

MONTH AND YEAR IN GREGORIAN CALENDAR	MONTH AND YEAR IN JAPANESE CALENDAR	DESCRIPTION OF EVENTS
1856	Ansei 3	The Institute for the Study of Barbarian Books is established
1861	Bunkyū 1	Study of Local Products is established within the Institute for the Study of Barbarian Books
1 May–1 Nov. 1862	Third day of fourth month—tenth day of ninth month, Bunkyū 2	Great London Exposition
June 1862	Fifth month, Bunkyū 3	The Institute for the Study of Barbarian Books is renamed the Institute for the Investigation of Western Books
Sept. 1863	Eighth month, Bunkyū 3	The Institute for the Investigation of Western Books is renamed the Institute for Studying the West
1 April–3 Nov. 1867	Twenty-seventh day of second month—eighth day of tenth Month, Keiō 3	Exposition Universelle, Paris
1868	Keiō 4	Edict on the Separation of Shintoism and Buddhism is issued by the Grand Council of State
Jan. 1870	Twelfth month, Meiji 2	The Institute for Studying the West becomes part of the South School of Daigaku
Sept. 1870	Ninth month, Meiji 3	Bureau of Local Products is established within the South School of Daigaku

MONTH AND YEAR IN GREGORIAN CALENDAR	MONTH AND YEAR IN JAPANESE CALENDAR	DESCRIPTION OF EVENTS
Jun. 1871	Fourth month, Meiji 4	Daigaku submits proposals for the preservation of *kokikyūbutsu* (old and ancient objects), including building of *shūkokan* to the Grand Council of State
1–7 July 1871	Fourteenth day of fifth month—twentieth day of fifth month, Meiji 4	Exhibition of Local Products organized by the South School of Daigaku takes place at Shōkonsha Shrine in Kudan area of Tokyo
June 1871	Fifth month, Meiji 4	Edict regarding the preservation of *kokikyūbutsu* is issued by the Grand Council of State
Aug. 1871	Seventh month, Meiji 4	Daigaku is abolished, Ministry of Education is established in its place
Oct. 1871	Ninth month, Meiji 4	Museum Bureau is established in the Ministry of Education
22 Nov.–22 Dec. 1871	Tenth day of tenth month—eleventh day of eleventh month, Meiji 4	Kyoto Exposition takes place at Ōshoin, Nishi Honganji Temple, in Kyoto
Dec. 1871	Eleventh month, Meiji 4	Nagoya Exposition takes place at Sōkenji Temple, Nagoya, for five days
March 1872	Second month, Meiji 5	Exposition Bureau is established in the Central Council of the Grand Council of State to prepare for 1873 Vienna World Exposition (Weltausstellung Wien)
17 April–5 June 1872	Tenth day of third month—the last day of fourth month, Meiji 5	Exhibition organized by the Ministry of Education takes place at Confucian shrine (Seidō) in Yushima, Tokyo
1872	Meiji 5	Exhibitions take place in cities of Kyoto, Okazaki, Wakayama, Itsukushima, Kanazawa, Tsuchiura, and Kōchi
1872	Third day of twelfth month, Meiji 5	Meiji government adopts the Gregorian calendar, rendering the third day of the twelfth month of Meiji 5 as 1 January 1873 (Meiji 6)
Sept 1872	Eighth month, Meiji 5	The Ministry of Education conducts research on treasures in Western regions (Kinki and Tōkai areas); the Shōsōin Repository in Tōdaiji Temple in Nara is opened for the first time since the Tenpō era (1831–45); Machida Hisanari, Uchida Masao, Ninagawa Noritane and others participate

MONTH AND YEAR IN GREGORIAN CALENDAR	MONTH AND YEAR IN JAPANESE CALENDAR	DESCRIPTION OF EVENTS
March 1873	March Meiji 6	Exposition Bureau absorbs Museum Bureau in the Ministry of Education
15 April–31 July 1873	15 April–July 31 Meiji 6	Exhibition by the Ministry of Education takes place at the museum in Uchiyamashitachō
1 May–2 Nov. 1873	1 May–2 Nov. Meiji 6	Vienna World Exposition (Weltausstellung Wien)
1873	Meiji 6	Exhibitions take place in the following administrative regions: Kyoto, Ise Yamada, Ibaragi, Fukuoka, Konpira, Kōchi, Chikuma, Nara, Miyagi, Shimane, Okayama
16 March–10 June 1874	16 March–10 June Meiji 7	Exhibition by the Ministry of Education takes place at the museum in Uchiyamashitachō
1–31 May 1874	1–31 May Meiji 7	A calligraphy and painting exhibition known as Shōheizaka shogakiai takes place at the Taiseiden Hall of the Confucian shrine (Seidō) in Yushima, Tokyo, named as the second site for the exhibition
1874	Meiji 7	Exhibitions take place in the following regions: Kyoto, Nagoya, Niigata, Kanazawa, Nara
March 1875	March Meiji 8	Exposition Bureau is transferred to Home Ministry, renamed as Museum
March 1875	March Meiji 8	The Shōsōin Repository in Tōdaiji Temple in Nara is once again explored; administrative control of Shōsōin is transferred to Museum, Home Ministry
1875	Meiji 8	Exhibitions take place in the following administrative regions: Kyoto, Shin Yoshiwara, Nara, Kumamoto, Niigata
April 1876	April Meiji 9	Museum (within Home Ministry) renamed Museum Bureau
10 May–10 Nov. 1876	10 May –10 Nov. Meiji 9	Philadelphia World Exposition
1876	Meiji 9	Exhibitions take place in the following administrative regions: Kyoto, Sakai, Nara, Miyagi, Hakone, Toyama, and Matsumoto
Jan. 1877	Jan. Meiji 10	Bureau of Temples and Shrines is established within Home Ministry

MONTH AND YEAR IN GREGORIAN CALENDAR	MONTH AND YEAR IN JAPANESE CALENDAR	DESCRIPTION OF EVENTS
21 Aug.– 30 Nov. 1877	21 Aug.– 30 Nov. Meiji 10	Home Ministry holds the First Domestic Exposition for the Promotion of Industry at Ueno Park, Tokyo
1 May –10 Nov. 1878	1 May – 10 Nov. Meiji 11	Exposition Universelle, Paris
1879	Meiji 12	Dragon Pond Society (Ryūchi-kai) is established, naming Sano Tsunetami as president and Kawase Hideji as vice president
April 1880	April Meiji 13	Home Ministry holds the first meeting of Appreciation of Ancient Art (Kanko bijutsu kai); this gathering would be organized by the Dragon Pond Society from the following year
Jan. 1881	Jan. Meiji 14	Museum designed by Josiah Condor completed in Ueno Park; it is then used as an art museum for the Second Domestic Exposition for the Promotion of Industry
1 March –30 June 1881	1 March –30 June Meiji 14	Home Ministry and Finance Ministry jointly hold the Second Domestic Exposition for the Promotion of Industry at Ueno Park
April 1881	April Meiji 14	The Section for the Promotion of Industry and Agriculture within the Home Ministry and the Commerce Bureau within the Finance Ministry merge to form the Ministry of Agriculture and Commerce; transfer of administrative control of Museum Bureau to Ministry of Agriculture and Commerce.
March 1882	March Meiji 15	Ministry of Agriculture and Commerce opens Museum in Ueno
Oct. 1882	Oct. Meiji 15	Ministry of Agriculture and Commerce holds first exhibition of National Painting Fair (Naikoku kaiga kyōshinkai)
1882	Meiji 15	*True Meaning of Art* (*Bijutsu shinsetsu*), a collection of Ernest Fenollosa's speeches translated into Japanese, is published by Dragon Pond Society
Feb. 1884	Feb. Meiji 17	Painting Appreciation Society (Kangakai) is founded by Fenollosa and Okakura Kakuzō
April 1884	April Meiji 17	Ministry of Agriculture and Commerce holds the Second National Painting Fair at Ueno Park

MONTH AND YEAR IN GREGORIAN CALENDAR	MONTH AND YEAR IN JAPANESE CALENDAR	DESCRIPTION OF EVENTS
May 1884	May Meiji 17	Administrative control of the Shōsōin Repository in Tōdaiji Temple in Nara is transferred from Museum Bureau under Ministry of Agriculture and Commerce to the Imperial Household Ministry
June 1884	June Meiji 17	The Ministry of Education asks Okakura Kakuzō to research old temples and shrines in Kyoto and Osaka areas; he is joined by Fenollosa and Kanō Tessai as consultants; they "discover" Guze Kannon at the octagonal hall of dreams within Hōryūji Temple
July 1885	July Meiji 18	Administrative control of the Shōsōin Repository in Tōdaiji Temple in Nara is transferred to the Library Office of the Imperial Household Ministry
March 1886	March Meiji 19	Administrative control of Museum under Museum Bureau at Ministry of Agriculture and Commerce is transferred to Imperial Household Ministry
Dec. 1887	Dec. Meiji 20	Dragon Pond Society is renamed to Japan Art Association (Nihon bijutsu kyōkai) with Sano Tsunetami as its president
Jan. 1888	Jan. Meiji 21	Administrative control of the Museum Bureau is transferred to the Library Office, Imperial Household Ministry, renamed as Museum Attached to the Library Office
May–Sept. 1888	May–Sept. Meiji 21	Kuki Ryūichi of the Imperial Household Ministry conducts research on treasury in Osaka, Kyoto, Nara, Wakayama, and Shiga prefectures; he is joined by Maruoka Kanji (Home Ministry), Hamao Arata (Ministry of Education, Tokyo Fine Art University), Fenollosa, Okakura Kakuzō, Imaizumi Kōsaku (Tokyo Fine Art University), William Sturgis Bigelow, Yamagata Tokuzō, Inō Shinri (Imperial Household Ministry), Yagi Tsuyoshi, Ito Kagehiro (Bureau of Temples and Shrines, Home Ministry), Kawada Tsuyoshi (Bureau of Historiography, Cabinet), and Ogawa Kazumasa (photographer)
Sept. 1888	Sept. Meiji 21	The Provisional Bureau for the Inspection of National Treasures is established within the Imperial Household Ministry, with Kuki Ryūichi as chairman
May 1889	May Meiji 22	Establishment of Imperial Museum in Tokyo, Imperial Museum of Nara, and Imperial Museum of Kyoto; Kuki Ryūichi becomes first director of the Imperial Museums

MONTH AND YEAR IN GREGORIAN CALENDAR	MONTH AND YEAR IN JAPANESE CALENDAR	DESCRIPTION OF EVENTS
1 April –31 July 1890	1 April –31 July Meiji 23	Ministry of Agriculture and Commerce holds the Third Domestic Exposition for the Promotion of Industry
Oct. 1890	Oct. Meiji 23	The academy system for imperial artists is established
1 May –30 Oct. 1893	1 May –30 Oct. Meiji 26	World Columbian Exposition, Chicago
Dec. 1894	Dec. Meiji 27	Imperial Museum of Nara, designed by Katayama Tōkuma, is completed; it opens in 1895 (Meiji 28)
1 April –31 July 1895	1 Apr –31 July Meiji 28	Ministry of Agriculture and Commerce holds the Fourth Domestic Exposition for the Promotion of Industry at Kyoto's Okazaki Park
April 1895	April Meiji 28	Association for the Preservation of Old Temples and Shrines established
Oct. 1895	Oct. Meiji 28	Imperial Museum of Kyoto, designed by Katayama Tōkuma, is completed; it opens in 1897 (Meiji 30)
April 1896	April Meiji 29	The rules for the Association for the Preservation of Old Temples and Shrines are established under the Ministry of Home Affairs, and its committee is selected from learned and experienced members; its chairman is Kuki Ryūichi, and its members include Okakura Kakuzō and Itō Chūta.
June 1897	June Meiji 30	The Law for the Preservation of Old Shrines and Temples is enacted; systems for Buildings and Structures under Special Protection and National Treasure are established
Sept. 1897	Sept. Meiji 30	The Provisional Bureau for the Inspection of National Treasures is abolished; its administration is transferred to the Office for Research on Treasures inside the Imperial Museums
1899	Meiji 32	Imperial Museum edits "Manuscript of the Abridged History of Imperial Japanese Art History"
1 April–12 Nov. 1900	1 April–12 Nov. Meiji 33	The Paris Exposition of 1900 (Exposition Universelle); *Historie de l'art du Japon* published
June 1900	June Meiji 33	Imperial Museums are renamed to Imperial Household Museums

MONTH AND YEAR IN GREGORIAN CALENDAR	MONTH AND YEAR IN JAPANESE CALENDAR	DESCRIPTION OF EVENTS
1 March –31 July 1903	1 March –31 July Meiji 36	Ministry of Agriculture and Commerce holds the Fifth Domestic Exposition for the Promotion of Industry at Tennōji, Osaka and Sakai Ohama Park
14 May –31 Oct. 1910	14 May –31 Oct. Meiji 43	Japan-British Exhibition held in London; Home Ministry publishes *A Book of National Treasures and Buildings under Special Protection* (*Tokubetsu hogo kenzōbutsu oyobi kokuhōchō*).
June 1913	June Taishō 2	Bureau of Religion from Home Ministry is moved to Ministry of Education
March 1929	March Showa 3	The Law for the Preservation of National Treasures is enacted
April 1933	April Showa 8	The Law Relating to the Preservation of Important Fine Arts is enacted
May 1950	May Showa 25	The Law for the Preservation of National Treasures is enacted

This list is based on the following three publications: Takagi Hiroshi, *Kindai tennōsei no bunkashiteki kenkyū—tennō shūningirei/nenjū gyōji/bunkazai* (Tokyo: Azekura Shobō, 1997); Dōshin Satō, *Modern Japanese Art and the Meiji State* (Los Angeles: Getty Research Institute, 2011); and Tokyo Kokuritsu Hakubutsukan, *Tokyo Kokuritsu Hakubutsukan hyakunenshi* (Tokyo: Tokyo Kokuritsu Hakubutsukan, 1973).

Table 2.
Significant Meiji Publications with Reproduced Illustrations

YEAR OF PUBLICATION	TYPES OF REPRODUCTIVE TECHNOLOGY USED	NUMBER OF ILLUSTRATIONS	BIBLIOGRAPHICAL INFORMATION
1871, 1876	monochrome and multi-color woodblock		Yokoyama Yoshikiyo, *Illustrated Catalog of Appreciating the Past* (*Shōko zuroku*), 2 vols.
1875	tri-color woodblock	2	Henrich von Siebold, "On Terracotta Figurines" (Etwas über die Tsutschi Ningio), in *Mittheilungen der Deutschen Gesellschaft für Natur- und Völkerkunde Ostasiens*, Yokohama: Echo du Japon, vol. 1, no. 8.
1876–80	hand-colored lithography		Ninagawa Noritane, *Kwan ko dzu setsu: Notice historique et descriptive sur les arts et industries japonais*, 7 vols.
1877, 1882	monochrome and multi-color woodblock		Matsuura Takeshirō, *The Pleasures of Scattering Clouds* (*Hatsuun yokyō*), 2 vols.
1877	multicolor lithography		Paper Bill Bureau, Finance Ministry, *Illustrated Catalogue of Coinage in Greater Japan* (*Dainihon shihei seizu*).
1878	hand-colored albumen prints		Ninagawa Noritane, photography by Yokoyama Matsusaburō, *Illustrated Book of Past Things: Section on Castles*.
1878	lithography	17	A.J.C. Geerts, "Pierres taillées préhistoriques," in *Les produits de la nature japonaise et chinoise: Partie inorganique et minéralogique*, vol. 1, Yokohama: C. Levy.
1879	albumen prints	12	Heinrich von Siebold, *Notes on Japanese Archaeology with Especial Reference to the Stone Age*, Yokohama: C. Levy.
1879	lithography	6	Heinrich von Siebold, *The Outline of Archaeology* (*Kōko setsuryaku*).
1879	lithography	18	Edward S. Morse, *Shell Mounds of Omori*. Published as vol. 1, part 1, of Memoirs of the Science Department, University of Tokio

YEAR OF PUBLICATION	TYPES OF REPRODUCTIVE TECHNOLOGY USED	NUMBER OF ILLUSTRATIONS	BIBLIOGRAPHICAL INFORMATION
1879	lithography	18	Edward S. Morse, *Ōmori kaikyo kobutsu hen*, trans. Yatabe Ryōkichi, Terauchi Shōmei transcriber.
1880	albumen prints	5	John Milne, "Notes on Stone Implements from Otaru and Hakodate, with a Few General Remarks on the Prehistoric Remains of Japan," in *Transactions of the Asiatic Society of Japan* 8, part 1.
1880	lithography	17	Ernest Satow, "Ancient Sepulchral Mounds in Kaudzuke," in *Transactions of the Asiatic Society of Japan* 8, part 3.
1880	albumen prints and lithography		Museum Bureau, *Fine Works of Ancient Art* (*Kanko bijutsukai shuei*) (Paintings Part, Lacquerware Part, Textile Part, Carvings Part, Ceramics Part).
1880	albumen prints	24	Printing Bureau, Finance Ministry, *Proud Heritage of Our Nation* (*Kokka yohō*), vol. 1 (photographs of temples and shrines, including Ise Shrine, and buildings of the Finance Ministry, including the factory of the Printing Bureau).
1880–81	chromolithography		Printing Bureau, Finance Ministry, *Proud Heritage of Our Nation* (*Kokka yohō*) (*Imperial properties*, 2 vols.; *Sacred Treasures of the Inner and Outer Shrines of Ise*, 1 vol.; and *Antiquarian Books*, 1 vol.).
1882	lithography	8	David Brauns, *Geology of the Environs of Tokio*, trans. Nishimatsu Jirō, Memoirs of the Science Department, University of Tokio, no. 4.
1882	lithography	11	I. Iijima and C. Sasaki, *Okadaira Shell Mound at Hitachi*, appendix to vol. 1, part 1, of Memoirs of Science Department, University of Tokio.
1883	chromolithography	10	Printing Bureau, Finance Ministry, *Appreciation at the Residence of Chōyō-kaku: Brocades* (*Chōyōkaku kanshō kiinshū no bu*).

YEAR OF PUBLICATION	TYPES OF REPRODUCTIVE TECHNOLOGY USED	NUMBER OF ILLUSTRATIONS	BIBLIOGRAPHICAL INFORMATION
1883	chromolithography		Printing Bureau, Finance Ministry, *Brocade on the Waves* (*Namima no nishiki*).
1884	lithography	8	Kochibe Tadatsune, "General Geography of Jōhoku Area" (*Gaisoku Jōhoku chishitsu hen*), appendix to vol. 4 of *Rikakaisui*, University of Tokio
1884	lithography	24	T. Kanda, trans., N. Kanda, *Notes on Ancient Stone Implements &c., of Japan*, Tokyo: Kokubunsha.
1886.2–	lithography and hand-colored lithography		Tokyo Anthropological Society, *Reports of Anthropological Society* (*Jinruigakkai hōkoku*), vols. 1–4.
1886–89	chromolithography	10	Henry J.S. Pryer, *Rhopalocera Nihonica: A Description of the Butterflies of Japan*, Yokohama: H. Pryer.
1889	collotype and multicolor woodblock prints		Art journal *Kokka*.
1889	chromolithography	37	Numata Yorisuke, Ōno Ungai/ revised by Tsuboi Shōgōrō, *Illustrated Japanese Archaeology* (*Nihon kōko zufu*), Tokyo: Sūzanbō

Table 3. Glossary

INDIVIDUALS

Ninagawa Noritane (1825–82)	蜷川式胤
Ishikawa Kiyomatsu (1860–1935)	石川千代松
Tamamushi Sadayū Yasushige (1823–1869)	玉蟲左太夫誼茂
Okakura Kakuzō (1863–1913)	岡倉覚三
Takamura Kōun (1852–1934)	高村光雲
Yatabe Ryōkichi (1851–99)	矢田部良吉
Fukuzawa Yukichi (1834–1901)	福沢諭吉
Tanaka Yoshio (1838–1916)	田中芳男
Shimizu Usaburō (1829–1910)	清水卯三郎
Itō Keisuke (1803–1901)	伊藤圭介
Takemoto Yōsai (1831–99)	竹本要斎
Uchida Masao (1838–76)	内田正雄
Matsuura Takeshirō (1818–88)	松浦武四郎
Kashiwagi Kaichirō (1841–98)	柏木貨一郎
Gengendō	玄々堂
Matsudaira Sadanobu (1758–1829)	松平定信
Machida Hisanari (1838–97)	町田久成
Yokoyama Yoshikiyo (1826–79)	横山由清
Kanda Takahira (1830–98)	神田孝平
Iijima Isao (1861–1921)	飯島魁
Sasaki Chūjirō (1857–1938)	佐々木忠次郎

DISCIPLINARY CATEGORIES

Bussangaku	物産学	Study of local products
Hakubutsugaku	博物学	Encyclopedic study
Kobutsugaku	古物学	Study of things past
Honzōgaku	本草学	Study of *materia medica*
Meibutsugaku	名物学	Study of names and things

BOOKS

Bakumatsu ishin kaikodan	『幕末維新懐古談』	Recollecting the Bakumatsu and the Restoration
Kanko zusetsu tōkinobu	『観古図説陶器之部』	Illustrated Book of Past Things: Ceramics Section and Kwan-ko-dzu-setsu: Notice historique et descriptive sur les arts et industries japonais: Art céramique, Poterie
Hyakka zensho	『百科全書』	Encyclopedia
Seiyō jijō	『西洋事情』	Conditions in the West
Edo hanjōki	『江戸繁昌記』	An Account of the Prosperity of Edo
Tokyo kaika hanjōshi	『東京開花繁昌誌』	An Account of Prosperity by Enlightenment in Tokyo
Hatsuun yokyō	『撥雲餘興』	The Pleasures of Scattering Clouds
Shōko zuroku	『尚古図録』	Illustrated Catalog of Appreciating the Past
Shūko jisshu	『集古十種』	Collecting the Past, Ten Kinds

TYPES OF EVENTS

hakurankai	博覧会	exposition, exhibition (see translator's note)
kaichō	開帳	temporary exhibitions popular during the Tokugawa period in metropolitan areas. They often included *misemono*.
misemono	見世物	spectacle, sideshow
shogakai	書画会	gathering of painting and calligraphy
honzōkai	本草会	gathering of *materia medica*
bussankai	物産会	gathering of local products

CONCEPTS

kokikyūbutsu	古器旧物	old and ancient objects
shūkokan	集古館	literally, building for assemblages of things past
kōkoka	好古家	antiquarian
atarashi or *shin*	新	the new
furui or *kyū*	旧	the old
mezurashi or *ki*	奇	the novel
hinekuru or *chin*	陳	the ordinary
furui or *ko*	古	the past
ima or *kon*	今	the present

Works Cited

Aararenoya Shujin. "Uchida Tsunejirō shōden." *Kyū bakufu* 3, no. 1 (January 1899): 53–59.

Allen, Bernard M. *The Rt. Hon. Sir Ernest Satow G.C.M.G., a Memoir.* London: Kegan Paul, Trench, Truebner, 1933.

Anonymous. "Machida Hisanari ryakuden." The Historiographical Institute, the University of Tokyo.

Anonymous. "Meiji ju nen naikoku kangyō hakurankai kisoku chō."

Anonymous. *Meiji jū nen naikoku kangyō hakurankai shuppinsha kokoroe.* 1877.

Aoki Masaru. *Chūka meibutu kō.* Tokyo: Heibonsha, 1988.

Aoki Shigeru and Sakai Tadayasu, eds. *Bijutsu.* Tokyo: Iwanami Shoten, 1989.

Asakura Musei. *Misemono kenkyū.* Kyoto: Shibunkaku Shuppan. 1977.

Benjamin, Walter. "The Work of Art in the Age of Its Technological Reproducibility, Second Version," in *Walter Benjamin Selected Writings,* volume 3 (1935–1938), 101–133. Translated by Jephcott, Howard Eiland, et al. Cambridge Mass.: Harvard University Press, 2002.

Bledstein, Burton J. *The Culture of Professionalism: The Middle Class and the Development of Higher Education in America.* New York: Norton, 1976.

Campbell, Robert. "Kanshō no nagare: Shogakai shi seki sono ichi, Ginkakuji Higashiyama dono sanbyaku kaiki." *Bungaku* 8, no. 2 (April 1997): 140–41.

———. "Kanshō no nagare: Shogakai shi seki sono ni, Edo Kan'ōji seien gashū." *Bungaku* 8, no. 3 (1997): 2–3.

Chamberlain, Basil Hall. *Things Japanese: Being Notes on the Various Subjects Connected with Japan.* London and Tokyo: K. Paul, Trench, Trübner, Hakubunsha, 1890.

Chambers, William, and Robert Chambers. *Chambers's Information for the People.* London and Edinburgh: W. & R. Chambers, 1833–35.

———. *Hyakka zensho.* Tokyo: Maruya Zenshichi, 1883.

Chikuma hakuran kaisha, ed. *Chikuma kenka Matsumoto hakurankai kisoku.* Matsumoto: Matsumoto Hakuran Kaisha, 1873.

Clark, John. "The Worlding of the Asian Modern." In *Contemporary Asian Art and Exhibitions,* edited by Michelle Antoinette and Caroline Turner, 67–88. Canberra, Australia: ANU Press, 2014.

Cortazzi, Hugh, ed., *Mitford's Japan: Memories and Recollections, 1866–1906.* London: Athlone, 1985.

Dainihon meisho zue. Tokyo: Tōyōdō, 1908.

Dai Nihon Sanrinkai, ed. *Tanaka Yoshio kun shichi roku tenrankai kinenshi.* Tokyo: Dai Nihon Sanrinkai, 1913.

Dave-Mukherji, Parul. "Art History and Its Discontents in Global Times." In *Art History in the Wake of the Global Turn,* edited by Jill H. Casid and Aruna D'Souza, 91–95. Williamstown, MA: Sterling and Francine Clark Art Institute, 2014.

———. "Whither Art History in the Globalizing World." *Art Bulletin* 96, no. 2 (2014): 151–55.

Davis, Whitney. "Comment: World without Art." *Art History* 33, no. 4 (2010): 711–16.

Derrida, Jacques. *The Truth in Painting*. Translated by Geoff Bennington and Ian McLeod. Chicago: University of Chicago Press, 1987.

Dower, John W. "Throwing Off Asia I." Accessed 30 June 2020. https://visualizingcultures.mit.edu/throwing_off_asia_01/pdf/toa1_essay.pdf.

Fenollosa, Ernest F. *Epochs of Chinese and Japanese Art: An Outline History of East Asiatic Design*. London: William Heinemann, 1912.

Foucault, Michel. *The Order of Things: An Archaeology of the Human Sciences*. New York: Vintage Books, 1994.

Fujiwara Masato, ed. *Meiji zenki sangyō hattatsushi shiryō*. Tokyo: Meiji Bunken Shiryō Kankōkai, 1964.

Fukukama Tatsuo. *Meiji shoki hyakka zensho no kenkyū*. Tokyo: Kazama Shobō, 1968.

Fukuoka, Maki. *The Premise of Fidelity: Science, Visuality, and Representing the Real in Nineteenth-Century Japan*. Stanford, CA: Stanford University Press, 2012.

Fukushima Kenritsu Hakubutsukan. *Shūko jisshu: Aruku utsusu atumeru, Matsudaira Sadanobu no ko-bunka-zai chōsa*. Aizu Wakamatsu: Fukushima Kenritsu Hakubutsukan, 2000.

Fukuzawa Yukichi. 1866. *Seiyō jijō*. Edo: Okadaya Kashichi, Shōkodō, 1866.

———. *Fukuzawa zenshū*. Tokyo: Jiji Shinpōsha, 1898.

———. *Fukuzawa Yukichi zenshū*. Tokyo: Iwanami Shoten, 1969.

Goto Bijutsukan. *Donnō no me: Masuda Donnō no bi no sekai*. Tokyo: Goto Bijutsukan, 1998.

Hasebe Kotondo. "Jindai ishi." *Kōkogaku zasshi* 30, no. 10 (October 1940): 1–15.

Higuchi Hideo. "Tanaka Yoshio to 'Kunshūjō': Tokyo Kokuritsu Hakubutsukan no hyakunen." *Hakubutsukan nyūsu* 296 (1972): 4.

Hirose Chika. *Yamanaka Kyōko nōto*. Tokyo: Seitōsha, 1973.

Hiruma Hisashi. "Edo no kaichō." In *Edo chōnin no kenkyū*, edited by Nishiyama Matsunosuke, 273–472. Tokyo: Yoshikawa Kōbunkan, 1973.

Ichikawa Seiryū. *Bakumatsu ōshū kenbunroku: Oba'e ōkō manroku*. Edited by Kusuya Shigetoshi. Tokyo: Shinjinbutsu Oraisha, 1992.

Iidashi Bijutsuhakubutsukan. *Nihon no hakubutsukan no chichi Tanaka Yoshio ten*. Iida: Iidashi Bijutsuhakubutsukan, 1999.

Iijima Yoshiharu. "Kaisetsu: Yamanaka Kyōko no hito to gakumon." In Yamanaka Kyōko, *Kyōko zuihitsu*, 343–62. Tokyo: Heibonsha, 1995.

Ikeda Atsufumi. "*Yochi Shiryaku* to *Bankoku shashinchō*." *Museum* 501 (December 1992): 26–38.

Ishii Kendō. *Meiji jibutsu kigen*. Tokyo: Chikuma Shobō. 1997.

Ishikawa Chiyomatsu. "Onshi Mōrusu sensei." *Tōyō gakugei zasshi* 42, no. 514 (1955): 121–25.

Ishikawa Gen. "Kaidai." In *Toyō gakugei zasshi,* edited by Meiji Bunka Kenkyū Kai, 10–11. Tokyo: Nihon Hyōronshinsha, 1955.

Isono Naohide. "Tanaka Yoshio no harimazechō to zatsurokushū." *Keiō daigaku Hiyoshi kiyō: Shizen kagaku* 18 (September 1995): 27–42.

———. "*Memoa* to *Rika kaisui*." In *Gakumon no arukeorojii,* edited by Tokyo Daigaku, 323–32. Tokyo Daigaku Shuppankai, 1997.

Itō Keisuke. *Taisei honzō meiso*. Reprint. In *Nagoya sōsho sanpen,* edited by Nagayoshi Hōsabunko. Nagoya; Nagoya Kyōiku Iinkai, 1982.

Jippōan Keijun. *Yūreki zakki*. Edo sōsho 6. Tokyo: Hōbun Shokan, 1992.

Kabe Nitaka. "Aanest Satou cho 'Kōzuke chihō no kofun gun' no gakushi teki ichi: Eikoku gaikō-kan no kōko-gaku tankyū." *Kokuritsu rekishi minzoku hakubutsukan kenkyū hōkoku* 76 (1998): 83–119.

Kaibara Ekken. *Kōchū Yamato honzō*. Edited by Shirai Mitsutarō. Tokyo: Shun'yōdo, 1932.

Kanagawa Kenritsu Kindai Bijutsukan, ed., *Bakumatsu ishin no dōhanga: Gengendō to sono ippa ten zuroku, e ni miru mikuro no shakaigaku*. Kamakura: Kanagawa Kenritsu Kindai Bijutsukan, 1998.

Kanda Takahira and Saitō Tadashi. *Notes on Ancient Stone Implements, &c., of Japan*. Tokyo: Daiichi Shobō, 1983.

Kaneyuki Shinsuke, Aoki Yūsuke, and Tsunoda Mayumi. "Edo no kenchiku, toshikeikan to shashin shiryō." *Kenchiku shigaku* 35 (2000): 63–79.

Katori Hotsuma. "Dōkan sanbō zakki." *Gasetsu* 8 (1937): 183–88.

Kinoshita Naoyuki. *Bijutsu to iu misemono: Aburae jaya no jidai*. Tokyo: Heibonsha, 1993.

———. "Daigaku Nankō bussankai ni tsuite." In *Gakumon no arukeorojii*, edited by Tokyo Daigaku, 86–104. Tokyo Daigaku Shuppankai, 1997.

Kitajima Yutaka. "Owari Nagoya ni okeru shoga kai ni tsuite." *Bijutsushi kenkyū* 36 (1998): 59–76.

Kiyono Kenji. *Nihon kōkogaku jinruigaku shi*. Tokyo: Iwanami Shoten, 1954.

Kobe Shiritsu Hakubutsukan, ed. *Egakareta Meiji Nippon: Sekihanga (ritogurafu) no jidai, kaisetsu zuroku kenkyū hen*. Kobe: Egakareta Meiji Nippon Ten Jikkōiinkai, 2002.

Kōda Shigetomo. "Yokoyama sensei ni tsuite." In *Nihon densei shi,* edited by Yokoyama Yoshikiyo, 365–69. Tokyo: Ōokayama Shoten, 1926.

Kōno Minoru. "Nihon no sekihanga." In *Egakareta Meiji Nippon: Sekihanga (ritogurafu) no jidai, kaisetsu zuroku kenkyū hen,* edited by Kobe Shiritsu Hakubutsukan, 7–15. Kobe: Egakareta Meiji Nippon Ten Jikkōiinkai, 2002.

Kreiner, Josef. "Hainrihhi fon Shiiboruto: Nihon kōkogaku minzoku bunka kigenron no gakushi kara." In Heinrich von Siebold, *Shō Shiiboruto Ezo kenbun-ki,* translated by Harada Nobuo, Harald Suppanschitsch, and J. Keiner, 227–65. Tokyo: Heibonsha, 1996.

Kurimoto Joun. *Hōan Jisshu*. Tokyo: Kyūsenkan, 1869.

———. *Narushima Ryūhoku, Hattori Bushō, Kurimoto Joun shū*. Edited by Shiota Ryōhei. Tokyo: Chikuma Shobō, 1969.

Kusuya Shigetoshi. "Nihon Ajia kyōkai no seiritsu to japanorojisuto." In *Yokohama kyoryūchi to ibunka kōryū: Jūkyū seiki kōhan no kokusai toshi o yomu,* edited by Yokoyama Kaikō Shiryōkan, 277–97. Tokyo: Yamakawa Shuppansha, 1996.

Kyoto Bunka Hakubutsukan, ed. *Kyoto yōga no akebonno*. Kyoto: Kyoto Bunka Hakubutsukan, 1991.

Kwan, Damien. *A Dictionary of Buddhism*. Oxford: Oxford University Press, 2004.

Maruyama Hiroshi. "Meiji shoki no Kyoto hakurankai." In *Bankoku hakuarankai no kenkyū,* edited by Yoshida Mutsukuni, 221–48. Kyoto: Shibunkaku Shuppan, 1986.

Maruyama Keizaburō. *Soshūru o yomu*. Tokyo: Iwanami Shoten, 1983.

Maruzen Kabushiki Gaisha. *Maruzen hyakunenshi: Nihon kindaika no ayumi to tomoni*. Tokyo: Maruzen, 1980.

Mashino Keiko. "Nihon ni okeru sekihanjutsu juyō no shomondai: Ninagawa Noritane *Kanko zusetsu tōki no bu* 3 'Fugen' o megutte." In *Kindai Nihon hanga no shosō,* edited by Machida Shiritsu Kokusai Hangabijutsukan, 165–211. Tokyo: Chūōkōron Bijutsu Shuppan, 1998.

Masuda Yoshinobu. "Kaden no 'Genji emaki': Watakushi no kokuhō." *Geijutsu shinchō* 4, no. 10 (October 1953): 129–31.

Masuo Fubō. "Kinsei kosen-ka retsuden dai san kai: Narushima Ryūhoku." *Hōsenka* 3 (August 1993): 80–93.

Meiji Bunka Kenkyū Kai, ed. *Meiji bunka zenshū*, rev. ed., volume 8. Tokyo: Nihon Hyōron Shinsha, 1955.

Meiji Gakuin University Library Digital Archives. Waeigorinshūsei. Accessed 19 January 2019. http://www.meijigakuin.ac.jp/mgda/waei/search/.

Mitchell, W. J. T. *Image Science: Iconology, Visual Culture, and Media Aesthetics.* Chicago: University of Chicago Press, 2015.

Mizutani Shinjō. "Kaisetsu." In *Zuien shokutan (Suiyuan shidan)*, translated by Aoki Masaru, 238–98. Tokyo: Iwanami Shoten, 1980.

Mori Noboru. "Umemura Suizan no seiyōryū koguchi mokuhan: Dō sekihanga ibun 9." *Issun* 11 (2002): 21–5.

Mori Senzō and Koide Masahiro, eds. *Shinpen Meiji jinbutsu yawa*. Tokyo: Iwanami Shoten, 2001.

Moriya Takeshi, ed. *Mōsu to Nihon: Kyōdō kenkyū.* Tokyo: Shōgakukan, 1988.

Morse, Edward S. *Shell Mounds of Omori.* Tokyo: University of Tokio, 1879.

———. *Japanese Homes and Their Surroundings.* Boston: Ticknor, 1886.

———. *Japan Day by Day: 1877, 1878–79, 1882–83.* Boston and New York: Houghton Mifflin, 1917.

———. *Nihon sono hi sono hi.* Translation by Ishikawa Kin'ichi of *Japan Day by Day.* Tokyo: Heibonsha, 1970.

———. *Ōmori Kaizuka.* Translation by Kondō Yoshirō and Sahara Makoto of *Shell Mounds of Omori.* Tokyo: Iwanami Shoten, 1983.

Mounsey, Augustus H. *The Satsuma Rebellion: An Episode of Modern Japanese History.* London: John Murray, 1879.

Murakado Noriko. "Shinbi shoin no bijutsu zenshū ni miru 'Nihon bijutsushi' no keisei." *Kindai gasetsu* 8 (1999): 33–51.

Murakami Senjō, Tsuji Zen'nosuke, and Washio Junkyō, eds. *Meiji ishin shinbutsu bunri shiryō.* Tokyo: Meicho Shuppan, 1970.

Murata Fumio. *Seiyō bunkenroku.* Hiroshima: Idzutsuya Shōjirō, 1869.

[Naikoku kangyō hakurankai jimukyoku, ed.] *Meiji jūnen naikoku kangyō hakuran kaijō annai.* Tokyo: Naikoku Kangyō Hakurankai Jimukyoku, 1877.

Nakayama Gen. *Fūkō nyūmon.* Tokyo: Chikuma Shobō, 1996.

Nakayama Shigeru. *Teikoku daigaku no tanjō: Kokusai hikaku no naka de no Tōdai.* Tokyo: Chūō Kōronsha, 1978.

Namiki Seishi. "Nihon bijutsushi kenkyū no genzai." In *Geijutsugaku o manabu hito no tame ni*, edited by Ōta Takao, 122–25. Kyoto: Sekaishisōsha, 1999.

Ninagawa Chikamasa. "Ninagawa Noritane to *Kanko zusetsu* ni tsuite." In Ninagawa Noritane, *Kanko zusetsu fukusei ban*, 11–22. Tokyo: Rekishitoshosha, 1973.

———. "Mōsu no Nihon tōki korekushon to Ninagawa Noritane." *Jinruigaku zasshi* 87, no. 3 (1979): 311–30.

———. "Mōsu no tōki shūshū to Ninagawa Noritane." In *Mōsu to Nihon: Kyōdō kenkyū*, edited by Moriya Takeshi, 381–424. Tokyo: Shōgakukan, 1988.

Ninagawa Chikamasa, ed. *Shintei kanko zusetsu: Jokaku no bu.* Tokyo: Chūō Kōron Bijutsu Shuppan, 1990.

Ninagawa Noritane. *Kanko zusetsu tōkinobu.* Tokyo: Ninagawa Noritane, 1876.

———. *Kwan-ko-dzu-setsu: Notice historique et descriptive sur les arts et industries japonais. Art céramique, poterie.* Tokyo: Ahrens, 1876–78.

———. *Kanko zusetsu.* Tokyo: Rekishitoshosha, 1973.

Ninagawa Teiichi, ed. *Ninagawa Noritane tsuibo roku.* Kyoto: Gotandaen, 1933.

Numata Jirō and Matsuzawa Hiroaki, eds. *Seiyō kenbunshū.* Tokyo: Iwanami Shoten, 1974.

Numata Raisuke. "Kōkogaku jō yori mitaru Rakuō kō," *Kōkogaku zasshi* 11, no. 7 (March 1921): 5–30.

Ōhashi Bishō (Yoshizō, Bishō-shōshi). "Kazan no shūkai kiyaku." *Shūkokai shi* 4 (1908): 4–6.

Okanoya Shigezane. "Nara Shōsōin no hōki, tsuketari Machida Hisanari kun itsuwa." *Shidankai sokkiroku* 275 (1916): 13–25.

Okatsuka Akiko. "Ogawa Kazuma no 'Kinki hōmotsu chōsa shashin' ni tsuite." *Tokyo-to shashin bijutsukan kiyō* 2 (2000): 37–55.

Ōkawa Mitsuo. "Kōshō Kashiwagi Kaichirō no keireki to sono shiteki hyōka ni tsuite." *Nihon kenchiku gakkai keikakukei ronbunshū* 459 (May 1994): 147–56.

Ōkoku Hakurankai Jimukoku. *Ōkoku hakurankai hōkokusho.* Tokyo: Ōkoku Hakurankai Jimukyoku, 1875.

Ono Tadashige. *Nihon no sekihanga.* Tokyo: Bijutsu Shuppan, 1967.

Ortega y Gasset, José. "Meditation on the Frame." Translated by Andrea L. Bell. *Percepta* 26 (1990): 185–90.

Osatake Takeki. *Bakumatsu kengai shisetsu monogatari: Iteki no kuni e.* Tokyo: Kōdansha, 1989.

Ōta Aito. *Meiji kirisutokyō no ryūiki: Shizuoka bando to bakushin tachi.* Tokyo: Chūō Kōronsha, 1992.

Ōtsuka Takematsu, ed. *Kengai shisetsu nikki sanshū.* Tokyo: Nihon Shiseki Kyōkai, 1928.

Sahara Makoto. "Nihon kindai kōko-gaku no hajimaru koro: Mōsu, Shiiboruto, Sasaki Chūjirō shiryō ni yosete." In *Mōsu to Nihon: Kyōdō kenkyū,* edited by Moriya Takeshi, 147–93. Tokyo: Shōgakukan, 1988.

Saitō Chōshū, Ichiko Natsuo, and Suzuki Ken'ichi. *Shintei Edo meisho zue.* Tokyo: Chikuma Shobō, 1997.

Saitō Gesshin. *Zōho bukō nenpyō.* Edited by Kaneko Mitsuharu. Tokyo: Heibonsha, 1968.

Saitō Tadashi. *Nihon kōkogakushi.* Tokyo: Yoshikawa Kōbunkan, 1974.

———. "Matsuura Takeshirō no kōkogaku kan." *Nihon rekishi* 378 (November 1979): 60–74.

Saitō Tadashi, ed. *Nihon kōkogakushi shiryō shūsei.* Tokyo: Yoshikawa Kōbunkan, 1979.

Saitō Tadashi, Iijima Isao, and Sasaki Chūjirō. *Okadaira Shell Mound at Hitachi.* Tokyo: Daiichishobō, 1983.

Sakai Seiichi. *Henreki no buke: Ninagawa shi no rekishiteki kenkyū.* Tokyo: Yoshikawa Kōbunkan, 1963.

Sakano Tōru. "Nihon jinrui gakkai no tanjō: Kobutsu shumi to kindai kagaku no aida." *Kagakushi kenkyū* 209 (March 1999): 11–20.

Sakurai Takehito. "Kaiseijo no yakugo to Tanaka Yoshio: Tenjiku nezumi (morumotto) no yakugo o tegakari ni." *Kokugo kokubun* 812 (2002): 1–16.

Sasaki Chūzaburō and Iijima Isao. "Jōshū Okadaira kaikyo hōkoku." *Gakugei shirin* 6, no. 31 (February 1880): 91–110.

Satō Dōshin. *"Nihon bijutsu" tanjō: Kindai Nihon no "kotoba" to senryaku*. Tokyo: Kōdansha, 1996.

———. *Bijutsu no aidentitī*. Tokyo: Yoshikawa Kōbunkan, 2007.

———. *Modern Japanese Art and the Meiji State: The Politics of Beauty*. Translated by Hiroshi Nara. Los Angeles: Getty Research Institute, 2011.

Satow, Ernest. *Nihon ryokō nikki*. Tokyo: Heibonsha, 1992.

———. *The Diaries of Sir Ernest Mason Satow: 1870–1883*. Edited by Ian Ruxton. Tokyo: Eureka Press, 2015.

Shimada Isao. "Kaisetsu." In Hitomi Hitsudai, *Honchō shokkan*, edited by Shimeda Isao. Tokyo: Heibonsha, 1976.

Shimizu Usaburō. "Sekihan oyobi insatsu kikai no ranshō ni tsuite." *Meika dansō* 18 (1897): 68–69.

Shiota Ryōhei, ed. *Narushima Ryūhoku, Hattori Bushō, Kurimoto Joun shū*. Tokyo: Chikuma Shobō, 1969.

Shirai Mitsutarō. *Shirai Mitsutarō chosakushū*. Edited by Kimura Yōtarō. Tokyo: Kagaku Shoin, 1985.

Siebold, Heinrich von. *Shō Shiiboruto Ezo kenbunki*. Volume includes translation of "Ethnologische Studien über die Aino auf der Insel Yesso," originally the full volume of *Zeitschrift für Ethnologie: Organ der Berliner Gesellschaft für Anthropologie, Ethnologie und Urgeschichte* 13, suppl. (1881), and other published and unpublished writings by Siebold. Translated by Harada Nobuo, Harald Suppanschitsch, and J. Keiner. Tokyo: Heibonsha, 1996.

Shōji Mitsuo. "Kaisetsu." In A. J. C. Geerts, *Heerutsu Nihon nenpō*, translation by Shōji Mitsuo of *Les produits de la nature japonaise et chinoise: Partie inorganique et minéralogique*, 471–74. Tokyo: Yūshōdō, 1983.

Smith, Henry D. *Taizansō and the One-Mat Room*. Mitaka: International Christian University, Hachirō Yuasa Memorial Museum, 1993.

Sonoda Hidehiro. "Nyū Ingurando ni okeru Mōsu no chiteki kankyō." In *Mōsu to Nihon: Kyōdō kenkyū*, edited by Moriya Takeshi, 439–62. Tokyo: Shōgakukan, 1988.

Sugimoto Isao. *Itō Keisuke*. Tokyo: Yoshikawa Kōbunkan, 1988.

Takagi Hiroshi. *Kindai tennōsei no bunkashiteki kenkyū*. Tokyo: Azekura Shobō, 1997.

Takahashi Tsutomu. *Yomigaeru rakan tachi: Tokyo no gohyaku rakan*. Tokyo: Toyō Bunkashuppan, 1981.

Takamizawa Shigeru. *Tokyo kaika hanjō shi*. Tokyo: Yamatoya Kehei, 1874.

Takamura Kōun. *Kōun kaikodan*. Tokyo: Banrikaku Shobō, 1929.

———. *Bakumatsu ishin kaikodan*. Tokyo: Iwanami Shoten, 1995.

Tamamuro Fumio. "Edo bakufu no bukkyō tōsei." In Tsuji Nobuo, ed., *Shomin bukkyō*. Tokyo: Shinchōsha, 1990.

Tanaka Yoshio and Hirayama Narinobu, eds. *Ōkoku hakurankai sandō kiyō*. Tokyo: Moriyama Sunyō, 1897.

Teeuwen, Mark. "*Kokugaku* vs. Nativism." *Monumenta Nipponica* 61, no. 2 (2006): 227–42.

Terakado Seiken, Ryūhoku Narushima, Tatsuo Hino, and Akihiro Satake. *Edo hanjō ki*. Tokyo: Iwanami Shoten. 1989.

Terashima Ryōan. *Wakan sansei zue*. Tokyo: Heibonsha, 1985.

Terashita Tsuyoshi. *Hakurankai kyōki*. Osaka: Ekisupuran, 1987.

Tezuka Yutaka. "Seidokyoku minpō kaigi to Ninagawa Noritane nikki: Meiji hōsei shiryō shūi (2)," *Hōgaku kenkyū* 42, no. 8 (1969): 67–84.

Tsukasa Tadashi, ed. *Maruzen shashi*. Tokyo: Maruzen, 1951.

Tokyo Bunkazai Kenkyūjo. *Meijiki fuken hakurankai shuppin mokuroku: Meiji 4–9*. Tokyo: Chūō Kōron Bijutsu Shuppan, 2004.

Tokyo Kokuritsu Hakubutsukan. *Tokyo Kokuritsu Hakubutsukan hyakunenshi*. Tokyo: Tokyo Kokuritsu Hakubutsukan, 1973.

———. *Tokyo Kokuritsu Hakubutsukan hyakunenshi: Shiryōhen*. Tokyo: Tokyo Kokuritsu Hakubutsukan, 1973.

———. *Chōsa kenkyū hōkoku: Koga ruijū honmon hen*. Tokyo: Tokyo Kokuritsu Hakubutsukan, 1990.

Tokyo Nichinichi shinbun, February 27, 1890.

Uchida Yoshiaki. "Nihon no shūseizu." *Kōkogakushi kenkyū* 5 (November 1995): 25–65.

Ueda Toyokichi, ed. *Waguneru den*. Kyoto: Hakurankai Shuppan Kyōkai, 1925.

Ueno Kenji. "Shoga kai annai shū." *Tochigi kenritsu bijutsukan kiyō* 6 (1979): 56–69.

Ueno Masuzō. *Oyatoi gaikokujin*. Tokyo: Kajima Shuppankai, 1968.

———. "Nihon saisho no dōbutsugaku kyōju Mōsu." *Jinruigaku zasshi* 87, no. 3 (March 1979): 279–95.

———. *Nihon hakubutsugaku shi*. Tokyo: Heibonsha, 1986.

van der Laan, Dirk. "Bakumatsu Meijiki no Doitsu shōsha." In *Yokohama kyoryūchi to ibunka kōryū: Jūkyū seiki kōhan no kokusai toshi o yomu*, edited by Yokohama Kaikō Shiryōkan and Yokohama Kyōryūchikai, 81–94. Tokyo: Yamakawa Shuppansha, 1996.

Watanabe Kanenobu. "Kobutsugaku no teihon." In *Kōkogaku zasshi* 63, no. 1 (1977): 1–21.

Watanabe Masao. *Nihonjin to kindai kagaku: Seiyō eno taiō to kadai*. Tokyo: Iwanami Shoten, 1976.

Wayman, Dorothy Godfrey. *Edward Sylvester Morse: A Biography*. Cambridge, Mass.: Harvard University Press, 1942.

Yagi Sōzaburō. "Meiji kōkogakushi." *Dorumen* 39 (June 1935): 9–24.

Yamada Keiji. "Ishin zengo ni okeru Ajia kyōkai no Nihon kenkyū." *Rangaku shiryō kenkyū* 7, no. 111 (June 1962): 183–87.

Yamaguchi Masao. *"Haisha" no seishinshi*. Tokyo: Iwanami Shoten, 1995.

Yamanaka Emu (Kyōko). "Nihon ni okeru kosen kenkyū no enkaku." *Kōkogaku zasshi* 7, no. 12 (1917): 753–60.

Yokoyama Megumi. "Takemoto Yōsai to 'Gansui-en' no sōgyō ni tsuite." *Toshimakuritsu kyōdo shiryōkan nenpō, fu kenkyū kiyō* 12 (1998): 7–14.

———. "Meiji shonen no bussankai to Takemoto Yōsai." *Toshimakuritsu kyōdo shiryōkan nenpō, fu kenkyū kiyō* 13 (1999): 17–19.

Yokoyama Yoshikiyo. *Nihon densei shi*. Tokyo: Ōokayama Shoten, 1926.

Yoshida Itaru. "Itō Keisuke shūshū no sekki." *Kōkogaku zasshi* 62, no. 3 (December 1976): 1–5.

Yoshida Takezō. *Shūi Matsuura Takeshirō*. Tokyo: Matsuura Takeshirōden Kankōkai, 1964.

———. *Matsuura Takeshirō*. Tokyo: Yoshikawa Kōbunkan, 1967.

Yoshimi Shun'ya. *Hakurankai no seijigaku: Manazashi no kindai*. Tokyo: Chūō Kōronsha, 1992.

Yuan Mei. Translated by Aoki Masaru. *Zuien shokutan (Suiyuan shidan)*. Tokyo: Iwanami Shoten, 1980.

Illustration Credits

Every effort has been made to identify and contact the copyright holders of images published in this book. Should you discover what you consider to be a photo by a known photographer, please contact the publisher. Photographs of items in the holdings of the Getty Research Institute are courtesy the Research Institute. The following sources have granted additional permission to reproduce illustrations in this volume.

Plate 1, figs. 7, 8, back cover. TNM Image Archives.
Plates 2, 3, figs. 1, 2, 24, front cover. Getty Research Institute.
Fig. 3. Tokyo, Kokuritsu Kokkai Toshokan.
Fig. 4. Nishio, Iwase Bunko Library.
Fig. 5. Edo-Tokyo Hakubutsukan.
Fig. 6. Tokyo Metropolitan Central Library Special Collection Room.
Fig. 9. Tachikawa, Kokuritsu Kokugo Kenkyūjo.
Figs. 10, 11. Edo-Tokyo Hakubutsukan.
Figs. 12, 14, 22. Archive.org
Fig. 13. Tokyo Bunkazai Kenkyūjo.
Fig. 15, 16. Tokyo Daigaku Sōgō Toshokan.
Figs. 17–21. Hathi Trust.

Biographical Notes on the Author and Translator

Hiroyuki Suzuki is professor emeritus at Tokyo Gakugei University, where he taught Japanese art history from 2005 to 2018. He is also the director of Toyama Memorial Museum and was formerly the head of Asian art at Tokyo National Institute for Cultural Properties. Suzuki has engaged in numerous transnational and transcultural activities, including publications and visiting professorships, to expand the discourse on Japanese art in the Anglophone world.

Maki Fukuoka is associate professor of the history of art in the School of Fine Art, History of Art and Cultural Studies at the University of Leeds. Her work focuses on histories of seeing and modes of knowing. She is the author of *The Premise of Fidelity: Science, Visuality, and Representing the Real in Nineteenth-Century Japan* and she has written on early photography in Japan.

Index

Note: page numbers in italics refer to figures. Those followed by *t* refer to tables. Those followed by n refer to notes, with note number.

academic system, and border between professional and amateur spheres, 68, 200–205
academy system of imperial artists, founding of, 29
Account of Prosperity by Enlightenment in Tokyo (Takamizawa), 103
An Account of the Prosperity of Edo (*Edo hanjō ki*) (Terakado), on *kaichō* shows, 83, 85, 106
actual objects
  life-size images of, as norm, 171, 174, 178
  observation of, *vs.* book study, 55, 61–62, 63, 67, 152, 178, 195
  Shirai on, 144
  and study of names and things, 143–44
  value of images of, 178
  See also scaling of images in illustrated catalogs
Agassiz, Jean Louis Rodolphe, 195, 201, 202–3
Akamatsu Noriyoshi, 125, 142
An Account of Prosperity by Enlightenment in Tokyo (*Tokyo kaika hanjōshi*) (Hagiwara), 101
An Account of Prosperity by Enlightenment in Tokyo (*Tokyo kaika hanjōshi*) (Takamizawa), 101–3, *102*, 106
"Ancient Sepulchral Mounds in Kaudzuke" (Satow), 183–84, *185*, 186
Anthropological Society of Tokyo, 139
anti-Buddhist movement
  and edict on *kokikyūbutsu*, 33–37, 48–49
  kaichō shows and, 88–89
antiquarians
  and archaeology, impact of introduction of, 67
  and Enlightenment thinking, 202–3
  fading of, with new scientific paradigm, 204, 206–7
  Iijima and Sasaki's disparagement of, 193
  and mandala-like arrangement of knowledge in Tokugawa period, 151–52, 205
  Morse on, 45–47, 195; friendships among, 47; publications for, 46, 62; types of objects collected by, 46, 47–48, 62; use of term, 143
  opportunities in early Meiji period, 31–32
  and roofing tiles, collection of, 48
  separation from professionals, in emergence of scientific paradigm, 193–94
  and shells and fossils, collection of, 48
  and structure of art historical categories, 4, 6
  terms for, 42n56, 47, 68n1
  types of objects collected by, and edict on preservation of *kokikyūbutsu*, 47–48

Aoki Masaru, 145–47, 152, 168
Archaeological Society of Japan (*kobutsukai*), 160–61, 163, 167, 206
archaeology
  absorption into academic system, 68
  early publications in Japan on, 64, 65–66
  in *Encyclopedia* article on *Study of Things Past* (*Kobutsugaku*), 66–67, 70nn29–30, 159–60
  introduction of term for, 65–66
  Japanese interest in, Morse on, 45, 46
  Morse's use of term, 45, 46
  as scientific field, 192–93; and border between professional and amateur, 68; impact on antiquarians, 63, 67; and understanding old in terms of new, 66
Art as Spectacle (*Bijutsu to iu misemono*) (Kinoshita), 81, 86, 98
art historical studies in Japan
  and *bijutsu*, problems of term, vi–vii, 2, 214–15
  decolonization in, 2, 3, 7n3
  epistemological structure of, as frame, 1–2
  and estrangement of premodern and modern art, vii
  future directions, as unclear, vii
  and globalization, 3–4
  ongoing issues in, vii
  periodization based on political events, 2
  revisionists' shakeup of discipline in 1990s, vi–vii, 214; effects of, 2; and Eurocentric structure, dismantling of, 2, 3, 7n3; influence of Western critical theory on, vii; negative responses to, vii
  separation from aesthetics, vii
  and subject of this book, 214, 215–16
Art History in the Wake of the Global Turn (2014), 3
Asiatic Society, 183
Assemblage of Rare Things of the Past and the Present (*Kokon chinbutsu shūran*) (Ichiyōsai), 12–13, 140
associations of collectors and antiquarians, 160–65
  discussions in, 163–64
  exhibitions by, 162–63, 167
  learning as goal of, 167
  Morse on, 160–61
  pottery connoisseur gatherings, 165–67, *166*
  rules for meetings, 163–65
  in Tokugawa period, 161–62
  See also Archaeological Society of Japan

bijutsu (fine art), as term
  vs. calligraphy and painting, 214
  Chamberlain on, vi
  coining by Meiji government, vi, 29, 214

effect on art historical studies, vi–vii, 2, 214–15
and estrangement of premodern and modern art, vi
Fenollosa and, 205
Boshin War, 58, 111n15, 117, 127, 137, 141
Boston Society of Natural History, 201, 202
British Museum, Murata on, 80, 103
buffoonery *kaichō* (*odoke kaichō*), 88
Bureau of Institutional Investigation, 134–35, 138, 139, 142, 176
Bureau of Local Products, 26, 117, 119, 123, 127, 197

The Career of Takahashi Yuichi (*Takahashi Yuichi rireki*) (Takahashi), 169
career/profession, history of concepts in U.S., 200–202
Catalog of Coins: Meiji New Edition (*Meiji shinsen senpu*) (Narushima), 141
The Catalog of Displayed Imported Objects (*Hakuraihin chinretsu mokuroku*) (1874), 104
"Catalog of the Gathering of Local Products in the Year of *Shinpi* of Meiji" (*Meiji shinpi bussankai mokuroku*) (1871), 117, 129
Catalog of the Kanazawa Exhibition (*Kanazawa tenrankai hinmoku*) (1872), 95–96
Catalog of Writings by the Lord Rakuō (*Rakuōkō chosho mokuroku*), 194
catalog(s). *See* illustrated catalogs; old and ancient objects, catalogs of
Catalogue of the Morse Collection of Japanese Pottery (Morse), 199, 199
Chamberlain, Basil Hall, vi, 214
Chambers, William and Robert, 64, 159
Chambers's Information for the People (Chambers and Chambers), 64–66, 159
Chronicles of Edo (*Bukō nenpyō*) (Saitō), 31, 85, 163
civilization
study of, archaeology and, 67
study of, old and ordinary and, 54, 55
Western, as source of new and novel, 55
"civilization and enlightenment"
association with Western culture, 59, 69n9
and disregarding old in pursuit of new, 56–57, 59
exhibitions as part of, 90, 116
glass display cases as symbol of, 103
and *kaichō* shows, 88–89
variety of expressions of, 90
Clark Studies in the Visual Arts, 3
classification systems. *See* taxonomy
Collected Illustrations of the Three Realms (Wang), 147
Collected Talks on Notable Men of Calligraphy and Paintings in Recent Times (*Kinsei meika shogadan*) (Anzai), 163
Collecting the Past, Ten Kinds (*Shūko jisshu*) (Matsudaira)
distribution of, 194
focus on unique beauty of objects, 194
presentation of objects as unique, 190
size of illustrations in, 186
use of woodblock prints in, 170, 171, 178, 191
A Collection of Past Pictures (*Koga ruijū*) (Matsudaira), 171, 191

comparison of objects, as point of expositions, 91, 93, 107–9
Compendium of Materia Medica (Shizhen), 148
Concise Typography of the World (*Yochi shiryaku*) (Uchida), 126
Conditions in the West (*Seiyō jijō*) (Fukuzawa), 71, 89, 118
A Confused Account of a Trip to Europe, Like a Fly on a Horse's Tail (*Oba'e ōkō manroku*) (Ichikawa), 137
Conglomerate of Garrisons (*Chindaifu*), 127
Consideration on Cave Habitation (*Kekkyokō*) (Kurokawa), 139
"Crowds of People at the Exposition" (*Hakurankai shojin gunshū no zu*) (Ikkei), 85
curio gathering (*kottōkai*) *vs.* exhibitions, 116–17

Daigaku
closing of, 26, 60, 66, 119
on confusion about sale of *kokikyūbutsu*, 42–43
and edict to protect *kokikyūbutsu*, 26, 58
Katō at, 131–32
Machida at, 131–32
Uchida at, 126
Daigaku proposal to build *shūkokan*, 26, 58
completion by Ministry of Education, 60
European nations' *shūkokan* as model for, 59, 60
and examination of both old and new things, 60
and framework of *kokikyūbutsu*, use of, 60
Machida and, 132
and "the new and the old" paradigm, 58–60
Ninagawa and, 198
vs. Ninagawa's call to value old and ordinary, 59–60
as part of new European-influenced episteme, 59, 60
stop-gap proposal for catalogs of *kokikyūbutsu*, 61
on trend toward disparaging old, 58–59
on understanding old in terms of new, 66
Diary of a Delegate to the United States (*Kenbeishi nikki*) (Muragaki), 75
Diary of a Journey to the West (*Kōsei nichijō*) (Narushima), 141
The Direction of Modern Art series, vi, 2
disciplinary field of early exhibitors, impossibility of defining, 142–43
disciplines for study of things before Bakumatsu period, 143–47
Aoki Masaru on, 144–47, 148–49
history of, 144–46
Shirai Mitsutarō on, 143–44, 147, 148
study of ancient texts and linguistics and, 145
study of names and things (*mingwuxue*) and, 145–47
study of "three rites" and, 145, 146
three disciplines in Tokugawa period, 143–44
Documents in Memory of Ninagawa Noritane (*Ninagawa Noritane tsuibo roku*) (1933), 133–34
Domestic Exposition for the Promotion of Industry (Ueno Park, Tokyo, 1877), 90
awards given at, 93
brochure for exhibitors, 107–8, 115n103

and scientific paradigm in Japan, 204–5
emphasis on comparison and evaluation, 107–9
functions of, 27, 28
government efforts to promote, 92
Guidebook and "Advice to Visitors" for, 90–91, 107
and necessary *vs.* unnecessary items, 108–10
and spectacle, rejection of, 107
Takamura on, 92–93
Domestic Exposition for the Promotion of Industry (Ueno Park, Tokyo, 1881), 28, 137
Domestic Exposition for the Promotion of Industry (Ueno Park, Tokyo, 1890), 101
"Draft of a Catalog of Exhibited Items at the Exhibition in the year Meiji 5" (Meiji gonen hakurankai shuppin mokuroku sōkō), 139–40

East School of Daigaku, 29, 68, 196
Edict on the Separation of Shintoism and Buddhism (1868), cultural disruption from
and need for edict on preserving *kokikyūbutsu*, 33–37
and old and ancient things entering art market, 33, 41
Encyclopedia (*Hyakka zensho*), 63–66
Maruzen's publication of, 64–65, 70n24
Ministry of Education publication of, 63–64, 66, 70n24
and new terms, introduction of, 65–66, 70n27
sales of, 64
Study of Things Past volume, on archaeology, 65–67, 70nn29–30, 159–60
Study of Things Past volume in, 64
topics covered in, 65
translation of, 64, 65–66, 69nn21–22, 176
as translation of *Chambers's Information for the People*, 64
volume on psychology, translation issues in, 65
encyclopedic study
antiquarians and, 95, 143
as discipline before Bakumatsu period, 80, 145, 147, 148
in West, Murata on, 80
Enkōan Kōriki Takanobu, *82, 83–84, 84*, 106
entertainment at exhibitions, 94–95, 96
prohibition on, 90–91
separate entertainment areas at *kaichō* shows, 88
See also spectacles (*misemono*)
Essay of Ten Kinds by Hōan (*Hōan jusshu*) (Kurimoto), 79
Europe
contact with, and disparagement of old, 59
museums of, as model for Japanese *shūkokan*, 59
See also museums, Western; overseas delegations
Everlasting Glories of the Nation (*Kokka yohō*) (1880–81), 205
exhibition at Yushima Seidō, Tokyo (1872), 90, 139–42
Buddhist temples contributing items to, 139
catalog for, 139

vs. Exhibition at Shōkonsha Shrine (1871), 140
as first use by government of "exhibition," 26
glass cases used at, 103, *104, 105*
institutions contributing items to, 139
number and types of items submitted, 139–40
number of individuals contributing items to, 139, 140
as origin of exhibition practice, 116–17
owners of objects, 140–42
popularity of, 139–42
as preparation for Vienna Exhibition, 27
prints of, *12–13*, 140
and study of names and things, 152–53
Exhibition Bureau of Grand Council of State (*Hakurankai Jimukyoku*), 26–27, 44
Exhibition of Local Products (*bussankai*) at Shōkonsha Shrine, Tokyo (1871), 116–18
catalog of items in, 117
central figures in, 122–23
continuity with early exhibition practices, 117–18, 123
continuity with studies of Western learning, 128
vs. exhibition at Yushima Seidō, Tokyo (1872), 140
existing types of exhibitions and, 143
as first exhibition, 26, 90
as first museum-like event, 60
as government-organized, 60
as "old" type of exhibition, 118
owners of objects exhibited, 118–39, 142
and preservation policies, 44, 60
and study of names and things, 152–53
types and number of items displayed in, 117–18, 119, 120, 121–24, 125, 128–29, 131, 132, 137, 138
Exhibition of Local Products (*bussankai*) in Osaka (1760), 163–64
exhibitions
of calligraphy and painting at Shōheizaka (1874), 131
Centennial International Exhibition (Philadelphia, 1876), 27, 90, 99
and "civilization and enlightenment" movement, 90
by collectors in Tokugawa period, 122, 162–63, 167
Commemorating the Seventy-Sixth Birthday of Mr. Yoshio Tanaka (1912), 127
as critical mechanism in public display of objects, 26
display of artworks and *kokikyūbutsu* at, 95–96
early: by associations, 162–63; continuity with antiquarians' practices, 116–18, 123; overseas delegations and, 74
early confusion about, 92–93
elimination of *kaichō*-style orators, 106
vs. exposition, 9–10
first uses of term by Meiji government, 26–27
global, 97–101
government-organized: and antiquarians' choice to join public or government side, 60; Shōkonsha Shrine exhibition (1871) as first of, 60
vs. international exhibition, 10

at Itsukushima Shrine (1862), 114n72
and *kaichō* shows, similarities between, 80–81, 89, 96, 97, 98, 100–101
in Kanazawa City (1872), 95–96
in Khoto (1871), 94
and *kokikyūbutsu*, revised conceptualization of, 110
kokikyūbutsu catalogs in development of, 44, 49
of local products as common, 122
in Matsumoto (Chikuma Prefecture, 1873), 94–95
at Ministry of Education museum, Tokyo, 27, 90
and museums, complementary functions of, 72–73
in Nagoya (1871), 94
number of, 94
origin in spectacles (*misemono*), 81
practices and policy changes, 1856–1950, 217t–23t
in prefectures, 94–96
by private companies, 94
prohibition on entertainment and frivolity at, 90–91
promotion of industry as goal of, 90
purpose of, government brochure on, 91, 93
rise of, in mid-nineteenth century, 89–90
sale of items from, 96
spectacles and entertainments at, 94–95, 96
spectacles as link from *kaichō* to, 101, 116
and study of names and things, 152–53
and symbolization of things, 107–10
Taiseiden Hall, Yushima Seidō (1874), 27, 90
three types of (local products (*bussankai*), *materia medica* (*honzōkai*), calligraphy and painting (*shogakai*), 142–43
and tickets, introduction of, 107
in Tokyo, 89–92
Wagener report on, 99
See also glass cases in exhibitions; Paris World Exhibition
"Experiments in Lithography" (Matsuda), 176
expositions
absorption into industrializing policies, 137
vs. exhibition, 9–10
First National Industrial Exposition (1887), 137
Great (Crystal Palace) Exhibition of 1851, 73
in Kyoto (1871), Ninagawa and, 135
and museums, shared purpose of, Sano on, 106
See also Vienna World Exposition (1873)

The Far East (newspaper), 37, 38, *38*, 39
Fenollosa, Ernest F., 28, 205
Flying Sacred Treasure (*tonda reihō*), 86, 87, *87*–88
Foucault, Michel, 4, 16–19, 57, 150, 151
frames
Derrida on, 7n2
Ortega y Gasset on, 1, 6
Fukuba Bisei, 140, 142
Fukuzawa Yukichi, 89, 118, 126
The Complete Works of Fukuzawa Yukichi, 71
Conditions in the West (*Seiyō jijō*), 71, 72, 79

great knowledge of West, 73, 79
travel overseas, 73, 74
on Western museums and exhibitions, 72
on Western politics and customs, 71

glass cases in exhibitions, 101–6, *102*
and focus on visual perception, 104–6, 107, 116
and shifting meaning of displayed objects, 116
use of French glass, 103, 104
government duty to study old and ordinary in pursuit of improvement, 54, 55, 56, 59
Grand Council of State (*Dajōkan*)
on confusion about sale of *kokikyūbutsu*, 42–43
edict on preservation of old and ancient objects, 21–25, 29, 58, 61, 140, 215
personnel at, 135, 138
use of exhibition (*hakurankai*) as term, 26–27, 58
See also Exhibition Bureau of Grand Council of State
Great Buddha of Raincoats (*kappa daibutsu*), 86, 88
Great London Exhibition (1862), Japanese at, 77
Guidelines for Exhibitors to the Domestic Exposition for the Promotion of Industry in 1877 (*Meiji jū nen naikoku kangyō hakurankai shuppinsha kokoroe*) (1877), 107–8, 115n103
Guide to the Site of the Domestic Exposition for the Promotion of Industry in 1877 (*Meiji jūnen naikoku kangyō hakuran kaijō annai*), 90–93, 103
Guze Kannon statue, discovery of, 28

Hiraga Gennai, 162–63
Hiruma Hisashi, 81, 85, 86, 87, 88, 89
historical books
as link between past and present, 54–55, 61–62, 67
study of, *vs.* actual objects, 55, 61–63, 67, 152, 178
"A Historical Outline of Numismatic Studies in Japan" (Yamanaka), 206–7
historical research, teleological approach to, 32–33
Histories of Material Crafts (*Kōgei shiryō*) (Kurokawa), 129
honzō gathering (*honzōkai*), *vs.* exhibition, 116–17
horticulture, as discipline before Bakumatsu period, 146
Hōryūji Temple, Nara, Guze Kannon statue in, 28

Ibunkai, 161–62
Ichida Shōshichirō, 86–87
Ichiyōsai Kuniteru, *12–13*, 140
Iijima Isao, 187–88, 192–96, 204, 205
See also Okadaira Shell Mound at Hitachi (Iijima and Sasaki)
Illustrated Book of Past Things: Ceramics Section (*Kankozusetsu tōkinobu*) (Ninagawa)
artists and printers for, 175
on connection of past and present, books *vs.* images in, 54–55, 61–62, 67
on Daigaku proposal to build *shūkokan*, 59–60
expected sales in Europe and United States, 54

as first lithograph-printed illustrated catalog, 175
French translation of texts included in, 53
on illustrations in study of names and things, 152
lithographs in, hand-painted, 53, 170; as both new and old, 63; high quality of, 177–78; and lithograph technology, 63; Morse on, 53, 63, 170; and presentation of objects as unique, 190–91; size of, 186; *vs.* woodblock printing, 178
modern chronological presentation of objects in, 179
and Ninagawa as antiquarian, 133
Ninogawa's collection of images for, 62
paper and binding used in, 176
and paradigm of the new and the old, 179
printing of, 176
publication history of, 136, 175, 176, 180
and rebalancing of "old" and "new," 53
on trend toward disregarding old and ordinary and pursuing new and novel, 54, 55, 56–57
on value of examining new and novel, 54, 55–56, 59–60
on value of preserving the old and ordinary, 54–56
volumes, described, 176–77
Illustrated Catalog of Appreciating the Past (*Shōko zuroku*) (Yokoyama), 138, 170, 172, 173–74, 178, 190, 191
illustrated catalogs, 180–88
analytic grouping of objects in, 188–92
chromolithography and, 205
collotype and, 169–70, 205
life-size images in, as norm, 171, 174, 178
in Ministry of Education *Jinshin* survey, 61–62
and multiple images per plate, 187
publication of, in Tokugawa period, 62
and scaling of images, 186–87, 188–89, 192, 205–6
size of images in, 186–87, 188
using lithographs, 168–70, 180, 182, *183*, 186–88
using photographs, 168–70, 180–81, *181*, 186–87
using woodblock printing, 170–74, 182
by Westerners, 180–88, *181*–*85*
Illustrated Famous Places of Edo (*Edo meisho zue*, 1834–36) (Saitō), 37, *82*, 82–83
Illustrated Famous Places of the Great Japan (*Dainihon meisho zue*, 1908), 37
Illustrated Notable Places of Tokyo (*Tokyo meisho zue*, 1877) (Okabe), on Rajanji Temple, damage to, 37, 38
illustrated publications, 1871–89, 224t–26t
illustrated works by scholars and antiquarians, 168–74
Aoki Masaru on, 152, 168
collotype and, 170
lithograph printing, impact of, 168, 169
photography and, 169–70
woodblock printing and, 169–70
imperial constitution, establishment of, 29
Imperial Household Ministry, 26, 28, 29, 30, 134, 139
Imperial University, founding of, 29–30, 68, 196

ink rubbings
in illustrated catalogs, 171, 174
introduction of scaled illustrations and, 186–87
presentation of objects as unique, 190, 191–92
Inokuma Nobuo, 133–34
Institute for Confucian Learning, 126–27
Institute for Medical Studies, 126–27
Institute for Studying the West, 26, 119, 126–28, 132, 139, 142
Institute for the Investigation of Western Books, 127, 197
Institute for the Study of Barbarian Books, 100, 119–20, 127, 129, 139, 169, 196, 197
Ishii Kendō, 73, 90, 93, 94, 97–98, 116
See also Origins of Things Meiji (*Meiji jibutsu kigen*) (Ishii)
Ishikawa Chiyomatsu, 46, 199–200, 202, 204, 206–7
Ishikawa Kin'ichi, 46–47, 68n1
Itō Keisuke
background and career, 120–22, 126, 127, 153n11, 196
as biologist, Morse on, 143
breadth of collection of, 143, 149
and exhibition at Yushima Seidō, Tokyo (1872), 140
items shown in Exhibition at Shōkonsha Shrine (1871), 118–20, 121–23, 126
and last generation of amateurish study, 204
Matsurra and, 129
and Meiji industrializing policies, 197
Morse and, 121
and study of names and things, 151–52
Tanaka and, 120, 136
Iwakawa Tomotarō, 204, 205
Iwase Tadanari, 74–75

Japan Day by Day (Morse)
on antiquarians, 46, 47–48, 62, 179
on epitaph for Matsura, 195
on gathering of pottery connoisseurs, 165–66, *166*, 167
Japanese translation of, 46–47, 68n1
on museum at Yushima Seidō, 103
on Ninagawa as antiquarian, 53
on Ninagawa's *Illustrated Book of Past Things*, 53, 54, 63
Jinshin survey. *See* Ministry of Education, survey of treasures in shrines and temples
Jippōan Keijun, 86, 88
Journal of a Voyage to the United States (*Kōbei nichiroku*) (Tamamushi), 75–76, 77–78, 79

kaichō shows
descriptions of, *82*, 82–84, *84*, *85*, 85–89
displays of sacred and magical objects at, 83
and exhibitions, similarities, 80–81, 89, 96–98, 100–101
as fundraisers for temples, 81–82, 83
giant sculptures at, 86–87, 98
in-house (*igaichō*) *vs.* traveling (*degaichō*), 81
and lodging temples (*shukuji*), 81
loss of religious significance over time, 88
novelty sculptures at, *87*, 87–88
number of, in Edo, 81, 82

performances, spectacles and food at, 81, 85–88, 87
period of popularity, 80, 81, 88–89
permits for, 81–82
popular attractions at, 112n35
separate entertainment areas at, 88
unexpected juxtapositions at, 88
"Kaichō Shows in the City of Edo" (Edo no kaichō) (Hiruma), 81, 85, 86, 87, 88, 89
Kaisei School (*Kaisei Gakko*), 26, 127
Kanda Takahira
   background and career of, 139, 142
   exhibition on, at Archaeological Society, 206
   items shown in Exhibition at Shōkonsha Shrine (1871), 139
   and last generation of amateurish study, 203–4
   See also Notes on Ancient Stone Implements, etc., of Japan (*Nihon taiko sekkikō*) (Kanda)
Kashiwagi Kaichirō
   background and career of, 129–30, 131, 155n40
   as collector, 130, 131
   and exhibition at Yushima Seidō, Tokyo (1872), 140
   as illustrator, 131, 174
   items shown in Exhibition at Shōkonsha Shrine (1871), 129, 131
   and Kanda's *Notes*, 188
   and last generation of amateurish study, 204
   Masuda and, 131
   Matsuura and, 129
   Morse and, 130, 143, 179
   painting collection of, 174
   retirement of, 136
Katō Hiroyuki, 131–32, 137–38, 142
Katsu Kaishū (Katsu Rintarō), 74, 196
Kimura Masakoto, 138, 140
Kinoshita Naoyuki, 2, 81, 86, 98
Kiuchi Sekitei, 162, 180
knowledge, structure of
   in modern epistemology, as hierarchical, 150, 205
   in Tokugawa period, as mandala-like, 150–51, 205
Kotohira Shrine, exhibition at (1862), 114n72
Kurokawa Mayori, 129, 138–39
Kwan-ko-dzu-setsu, notice historique et descriptive sur les arts et industries japaonais par Ninagawa Noritané, art céramique (Ninagawa), 53

Law for the Preservation of Old Shrines and Teimples (1897), 29, 36–37, 44
list(s)
   of items in edict on protection of *kokikyūbutsu*, 22–24, 44–45, 47, 48, 151
   of *kokikyūbutsu*, edict for creation of, 43–44, 49
   and mandala-like arrangement of knowledge in Tokugawa period, 151–52, 205
   in Ministry of Education survey of treasures in shrines and temples (*Jinshin* survey), 61–62
lithograph printing
   and hand coloring, 177, 190–91
   impact on illustrated works, 168, 169, 175
   vs. ink-rubbing techniques, 186–87
   invention and spread of, 168–69, 175
   quality *vs.* photographs, 186
   and scale, conveying of, 186
local products, study of
   associations for, 162
   as discipline before Bakumatsu period, 143, 146–47
   and early exhibitions of, 162–63
   efforts to accommodate new scientific paradigm, 196–97
   and Meiji industrializing policies, 196–98
   objects of study, 144
   as study of names and things, 146–47

Machida Hisanari
   as advisor for Vienna Exposition of 1873, 132
   background and career of, 131–32, 136, 156n52
   and early exhibitions and museums, support for, 136
   and exhibition at Yushima Seidō, Tokyo (1872), 140
   exhibition on, at Archaeological Society, 206
   items shown in Exhibition at Shōkonsha Shrine (1871), 132
   and *Jinshin* survey, 132, 136
   and Katō, 137–38
   and Kuroda, 140
   and last generation of amateurish study, 203–4
   at Paris Exposition of 1867, 131
   as passionate antiquarian, 132–33
   and Sawa Nobuyoshi, 141
Materials of Twelve Archaeologists (*Jūni kōkoka shiryō tenarankai*) (1918 exhibition), 206
materia medica (*honzōgaku*)
   as discipline before Bakumatsu period, 146, 148; continuity with early exhibition practices, 117–18; early texts, 146; illustrations and, 62; and mandala-like arrangement of knowledge, 150; objects of study, 143, 144; Shōhyakusha and, 121; as study of names and things, 146, 148, 151–52
   Itō's study of, 120, 121
   scholars of: and antiquarians, ties between, 167; fading of, with new scientific paradigm, 204; and Morse as example of "the new," 203
   Tanaka's study of, 120
Matsuda Atsutomo (Gengendō the Second), 175–76, 181, 187
Matsudaira Sadanobu, 170–71, 194
Matsura Sayohiko, Morse's epitaph for, 195
Matsuura Hiroshi (Matsuura Takeshirō)
   as antiquarian, Morse on, 143
   background and career of, 128
   collections of, 128
   and exhibition at Yushima Seidō, Tokyo (1872), 140
   exhibition on, at Archaeological Society, 206
   items shown in Exhibition at Shōkonsha Shrine (1871), 128–29
   and Kanda's *Notes*, 188
   Kashiwagi and, 129
   and last generation of amateurish study, 204
   study built from historic wood, 128, 150–51
   Yamanaka and, 206
   See also *The Pleasures of Scattering Clouds* (*Hatsuun yokyō*) (Matsuura)
Meiji government
   continuation of shogunate educational institutions under, 126–27

institutionalization of art by, 3
political changes, late 1880s–early 1890s, 29
switch to Gregorian calendar, 21
Memories Recalled by the Window at Dawn (*Gyōsō tsuiroku*) (Kurimoto), 79
Milne, John, 182–83, *184*, 185–86
Ministry of Agriculture and Commerce, 28, 29, 119, 129, 132, 137
Ministry of Education
    and *Encyclopedia* (*Hyakka zensho*), 63–64, 66, 70n24
    enlightenment campaign of, 66
    establishment of, 26, 66
    exhibitions organized by, 90
    and Imperial University, establishment of, 68
    research initiatives by, 27
    and *shūkokan*, building of, 60
    survey of treasures in shrines and temples (*Jinshin* survey), 27, 28, 61–62, 126, 129, 132, 136
    and University of Tokyo, founding of, 68
Mitsukuri Rinshō, 64, 119, 126, 142, 176
Modern Japanese Art and the Meiji State (Satō), 3
Morata Fumio, 79–80
Morse, Edward S.
    on antiquarians, 45–47; friendships among, 47; positive view of, 195; publications for, 46, 62; types of objects collected by, 46, 47–48, 62
    on Archaeological Society of Japan, 160–61
    and archaeology as term, 45, 46
    broad interests of, 199–200, 203
    career of, 198–99, 200–202
    departure from Japan, 204, 205
    and discovery of shell mounds in Ōmori, 45
    epitaph for Matsura, 195
    as example of "the new" for antiquarians, 203
    First Book of Zoölogy, 199
    generation of, and scientific paradigm, 202–7
    Iijima and Sasaki as students of, 192–96, 204
    on illustrated works by antiquarians, 168
    Itō and, 121
    Japanese Homes and Their Surroundings, 130, *130*, 134
    Kashiwagi and, 130
    Mars and its Mystery, 199–200
    Matsurra and, 129
    and Ninagawa, 42n57, 46, 53, 63, 133, 134, 135, 136, 166, 170, 179, 198, 203
    and Ōmori shell mounds, discovery of, 198
    as part professional and part amateur, 200–205
    pottery collection, catalog of, 199, *199*
    Siebold and, 180
    as student of Agassiz, 195, 201, 202–3
    students left behind in Japan, 204
    "study nature" principle of, 195
    at University of Tokyo, 68, 198
    use of "antiquarian" as term, 143
    zoological research, as reason for move to Japan, 198
    See also Japan day by Day (Morse); *Shell Mounds of Omori* (Morse)
Muragaki Norimasa, 74, 75, 76
Murata Fumio, 2, 103

museum at Ueno Park
    construction of, 27–28
    destruction in Great Kanto Earthquake of 1923, 50n15
    exhibition (1873), 27, 90
    exhibition (1874), 27, 90, 101–6, *102*
    as industrial museum, 103
    Machida as director of, 132
    move to Ueno Park, 27–28, 50n14
    original location in Uchiyamashitachō, 27
    role in charting cultural landscape, 29
    transfers of jurisdiction over, 28, 29, 132
Museum Bureau (*Hakubutsukyoku*)
    establishment of, 26, 132
    and exhibition at Yushima Seidō, 26, 44, 140
    Museum and, 27
    staff at, 132, 135, 136, 138–39
    transfers of jurisdiction over, 27, 28, 136, 137
museums (*shūkokan*)
    and age of museology, 73
    Daigaku proposal to build, 26, 58
    early, experience of overseas delegations and, 74
    early proposals for construction of, 26
    and expositions, shared purpose of, 72–73, 106
    gifts to, from South Kensington Museum, 103
    imperial museums, establishment of, 29
    Shōkonsha Shrine exhibition (1871) as first museum-like event, 60
    See also Daigaku proposal to build *shūkokan*
museums, Western, Japanese impressions of
    British Museum, 80, 103
    Paris museums, 79
    Smithsonian Institution, 77–78, 111n20

Nakayama Gen, 17, 149–50
Nakayama Shigeru, 126–28
names and things, study of (*mingwuxue, meibutsugaku*)
    and academic world, lack of intersection between, 198
    antiquarians and, 151–52
    Aoki on value of illustrations in, 152, 168
    archaeology as continuation of, 67, 159–60
    broad vs. narrow conception of, 148–49
    and correspondence of names and things: classical age assumptions about, 149–50, 152; modern linguistic views on, 149–51
    as discipline before Bakumatsu period: Aoki on, 146–49; branches of, 146–47, 149; history of development, 145–47, 148–49; objects of study, 143–44; Sharai on, 143–44; Shirai on, 148; sources used in, 147–48; value of, 144
    exhibitions and, 152–53
    and illustrations of objects, value of, 178
    impact of "the new and the old" paradigm on, 160
    Kanda and, 190
    and mandala-like structure of knowledge, 150–51, 205
    Matsudaira and, 171
    use of illustrations in, 171, 174
"Narrative of My Career" (Tanaka), 127, 196–97
Narushima Ryūhoku, 141, 203–4

national treasures (*kokuhō*), designation of, 31
Natural Objects Categorized (*Butsurui hinshitsu*) (Hiraga), 162–63
necessary *vs.* unnecessary things in exhibitions, 5, 106, 108–10
new and novel things, trend toward pursuit of
    as change in episteme, 57
    as crisis for antiquarians, 57–58
    Daigaku on, 58–59
    Ninagawa on, 54, 55, 56–57, 59–60
    origin in contact with Europe, 59
the new and the old paradigm
    and border between professional and amateur spheres, 68, 200–205
    catalog illustrations and, 63
    as crisis for antiquarians, 57–58, 67–68
    Daigaku proposal to build *shūkokan* and, 58–60
    and "great public benefit" of new, 192–93
    impact on study of names and things, 160
    and *kaichō* shows *vs.* exhibitions, 80–81, 116, 118
    and "new and novel" *vs.* "old and ordinary," 56
    Ninagawa's *Illustrated Book of Past Things* and, 179
    replacement of past and present, 56
    and study of local products, 196–97
    and study of names and things, 160
    See also new and novel things; old and ordinary things
New Chronicles of Yanagibashi (*Ryūkyō shin shi*) (Narushima), 141
Newly Revised Illustrated Explanations of Plants and Trees of Japan (*Shintei sōmoku zusetsu*) (Tanaka), 119–20
New Tales of Tokyo Prosperity (*Tokyo shin hanjō ki*) (Hattori), 101
Nihon sonohi sonohi (Morse), 46–47, 68n1
Ninagawa Noritane
    as antiquarian, 53, 133–34, 143
    background and career of, 59, 129, 134–36, 139, 142
    chromolothographic print album owned by, 177
    circle of antiquarian friends, 47
    clothing and hairstyle of, 134
    death of, 133, 208n23
    and early exhibitions and museums, support for, 136
    and exhibition at Yushima Seidō, Tokyo (1872), 140
    exhibition commemorating (1932), 133–34
    exhibition on, at Archaeological Society, 206
    gatherings of pottery connoisseurs at home of, 166–67
    and government policies on *kokikyūbutsu*, 59
    on illustrations of objects, value of, 178
    interest in determining age of objects, 179
    items shown in Exhibition at Shōkonsha Shrine (1871), 133
    on Japanese antiquarians, 47
    and *Jinshin* survey, 136
    and Kanda's *Notes,* 188
    Kashiwagi and, 131
    Kwan ko dzu setsu: Notice historique et descriptive sur les arts et industries japonais, 14, 15
    and last generation of amateur study, 203–4
    Matsuura and, 128
    and Meiji industrializing policies, 198
    and Ministry of Education survey of treasures, 61
    and Morse, 42n57, 46, 136, 166, 179, 198, 203
    "Photographic Album of the Former Edo Castle" ("Kyū Edojō shashin chō"), 191, 211nn66–67
    portrait photograph of, 134, *135*
    printing business of, 136, 166–67, 175–76
    response to Japanese push for modernization, 4
    See also Illustrated Book of Past Things: Ceramics Section (*Kankozusetsu tōkinobu*) (Ninagawa)
Nishi Amane, 65, 125, 127
Notes on Ancient Stone Implements, etc., of Japan (*Nihon taiko sekkikō*) (Kanda), 139, 187, 188, 190, *191,* 192
Notes on Japanese Archaeology (Siebold), 180–81, *181*
"Notes on Stone Implements from Otaru and Hakodate" (Milne), 182–83, *184,* 186

Okadaira Shell Mound at Hitachi (Iijima and Sasaki), 187–88
    analytic grouping of objects in, 188–89, *189, 192*
Okakura Kakuzō (Tenshin), 28, 205
old and ancient objects (*kokikyūbutsu*)
    Imperial Household Ministry jurisdiction over, 30
    Meiji-era focus on, as government-driven, 30
    preservation of, antiquarians on, 70n31
    revised conceptualization, in exhibition culture, 110
    as term: coining of, 9, 33; and danger of reducing objects to representations, 160
    world of, beyond government policies: importance of studying, 30–31, 33; study of, as antithesis of teleological approach, 32–33
    See also sales of *kokikyūbutsu*
old and ancient objects, catalogs of, 43–44
    edict for creation of, in edict on preservation of *kokikyūbutsu,* 43, 49
    process of creating, 43
    proposal for, in Daigaku proposal to build *shūkokan,* 43
    use for developing exhibitions, 44, 49
    See also Ministry of Education, survey of treasures in shrines and temples
old and ancient objects, edict on preservation of, 21–25
    anti-Buddhist movement and, 33–37, 48–49
    as beginning of significant changes, 25
    categories (sections) of objects in, 21–25; architecture not included in, 44; carriages and palanquin section, 44–45; correspondence to types of objects collected by antiquarians, 47–48; focus on collectible objects, 45; and mandala-like arrangement of knowledge in Tokugawa period, 151
    and confusion about private sales, 42–43, 48, 49
    confusion in, 24

conservation focus of, as retrospective interpretation, 48
Edict on the Separation of Shintoism and Buddhism and, 33–37
effect on exhibitions, 140
and encouragement of industry, 58
inclusion of objects from outside Japan, 22
issuing of, 26
novel conception of *kokikyūbutsu* in, 25
as part of new European-influenced episteme, 59
preparation of exhibitions as one purpose of, 44
unstated connections between categories, 24–25
on value of preserving *kokikyūbutsu*, 25
old and ancient objects, Meiji government focus on, 25–29
and changes in policy, 25, 30
encouraging industry as goal of, 26, 28–29, 30
influence of European models on, 30
postwar focus on "cultural properties" (*bunkazai*), 30
and re-evaluation of objects with new goals, 28–29, 31
and reorganizations of government bureaucracies, 26–28
and research initiatives, 27
turn to political use to support emperor system, 30
old and ordinary things, loss of interest in
as change in episteme, 57
as crisis for antiquarians, 57–58
Daigaku on, 58–59
European values and, 59
Ninagawa on, 54, 55, 56–57
origin in contact with Europe, 59
Ōmori kaikyo kobutsu hen (Morse, trans. by Yatabe), 45, 47, 68n1, 180, 181, *182*, 186
One Hundred Years' History of the Tokyo National Museum: Material Part (*Tokyo Kokuritsu Hakubutsukan hyakunenshi: Shiryōhen*) (1973), 42–44, 79
On the Study of Names and Things in China (*Chūka meibutsukō*) (Aoki), 144–45, 147, 152
The Origin and History of the Great Buddha of Raincoats (*Kappa daibutsu ryaku engi*) (Shiba), 86
Origins of Things Meiji (*Meiji jibutsu kigen*) (Ishii), 73, 90, 94, 97–98, 116–17
Ortega y Gasset, José, 1, 6
Osatake Takeki, 76, 100
The Outline of Archaeology (*Kōko setsuryaku*) (Siebold), 182–83, *183*, 186
overseas delegations
delegation of 1860, 74–79; knowledge of West gleaned from, 78–79; members of, 74–75; visit to Patent Office, 76–77, 111n20; visit to Smithsonian Institution, 77–78, 111n20
to Europe (1862), 77, 78
to France (1863), 78
to France (1865), 78
to France (1867), 79
Fukuzawa and, 73, 76
influence on early museums and exhibitions, 74
puzzlement of members, 74
reports of experiences by, 79–80

painting and calligraphy, early exhibitions of, 163
Paris Exposition Universalle (1878), 27
Paris World Exhibition (1867), 27, 79, 99, 100, 131
Photographs of Submissions at the Vienna World Exposition in Austria (1872), 97, 98
photography in illustrated catalogs, 168, 169–70, 180–81, *181*, 186–87
The Pleasures of Scattering Clouds (*Hatsuun yokyō*) (Matsuura)
artists working on, 174
breadth of, 128
and illustrations in studying names and things, 152
images by Kashiwagi in, 131
kokikyūbutsu discussed in, 128
and polychrome printing, 174
presentation of objects as unique, 190
signing of illustrations by printers, 174
size of illustrations in, 186
use of woodblock prints in, 170, *173*, 173–74, 178, 191
The Politics of Expositions (Yoshimi), 101
printing technology
advances in, 205–6
chromolithography and, 205
collotype and, 169–70, 205
See also lithograph printing
Proceedings of Participation in the Vienna Exposition (*Ōkoku hakurankai sandō kiyō*) (Tanaka and Hirayama), 99
Products of Japan (*Nihon sanbutsu shi*) (1873–77), 122
Les produits de la nature japonaise et chinoise (Geerts), 180
professional *vs.* amateur spheres, development of border between, 68, 200–205
protection and preservation policies. *See* Law for the Preservation of Old Shrines and Teimples (1897); old and ancient objects (*kokikyūbutsu*), edict on preservation of
public display. *See* exhibitions; expositions; museums

"Rambling Notes of Immersion in the Strange" (*Tankimanroku*), 162
Ranking List of Notable Yamato-e Picture Scrolls (*Yamatoe meikan kurabe*) (Kashiwagi), 131
Recollecting the Bakumatsu and the Restoration (*Bakumatsu ishin kaikodan*) (Takamura)
on destruction of Buddhist art after Edict on Separation, 34–35, 36
on Domestic Exposition for the Promotion of Industry (1877), 92–93
on Rakanji Temple and architecture protection laws, 44
on rescue of sculptures from Sazaedō (Rajanji Temple), 35–36; and cultural disruption from Edict on Separation, 41; discrepancies with other sources, 37–38, *38*, *39*; and implicit equality of past and present art, 56; interest in sculptures as artist's models, 39–40; later sale of rescued sculptures, 40–41, 42; possible distorted recollection in, 36–37, 38–39, 41; size of rescued sculptures,

44; statue kept by Takamura Kōun, 36, 41, 42, 45
  on Takamura's work for H. Ahrens & Co., 53–54
Record of Gathering (*Bunkairoku*) (1760), 163–64
A Record of Kaichō Shows of Holy Treasures of Ryūkōji Temple (*Ryūkōji reihō kaichō ki*) (Enkōan), 83–84, *84*, 106
Record of Things Seen and Heard in the West (*Seiyō bunken roku*) (Morata), 79–80, 103
Records of Stones (*Unkonshi*) (Kiuchi), 162
Regulations for the Matsumoto Exhibition in Chikuma Prefecture (*Chikumakenka Matsumoto hakurankai kisoku*, 1873), 94–95
relative merits of objects, judging of
  conditions necessary for, 108
  as point of exhibitions, 91, 93, 107–9
  value of, 109
"Report on Museums of Fine Arts and a Hundred Manufacturers" (Wagener), 99
Report on the Austrian Exhibition (Sano), 107
"Report on the Okadaira shell mound at Hitachi" ("Jōshū Okadaira kaikyo hōkoku") (Iijima and Sasaki), 192
Report on the Vienna Great Exposition (*Ifu daihakurankai hōkoku geijutsu*) (Wagener), 99, 105–6
Reports on Anthropology (*Jinruigakkai hōkoku*) (periodical), 205
Rhopalocera Nihonica (Pryer), 206
roofing tiles, antiquarians' collection of, 48, 109

Saitō Gesshin, 31, 37, 82, 85–86, 163
Sakakibara Yoshino, 138, 140
sales of *kokikyūbutsu*
  confusion about legality of, under Meiji edict on preservation of *kokikyūbutsu*, 42–43, 48, 49
  as part of everyday activity, 42
  sale of sculptures rescued from Sazaedō, 40–41, 42
Sano Tsunetami, 104–6, 107, 197
Sasaki Chūjirō, 187–88, 192–96, 204, 205
  See also *Okadaira Shell Mound at Hitachi* (Iijima and Sasaki)
Satō Dōshin, 2, 3, 7n2
Satow, Ernest Mason, 183–85, *185*
scaling of images in illustrated catalogs, 186–87, 188–89, 192, 205–6
scientific inquiry, emergence as new paradigm
  efforts of old paradigm to accommodate, 196–97
  and fading of antiquarians, 204, 206–7
  as "great public benefit." Iijima and Sasaki on, 192–93
  Morse's generation and, 202–7
  and separation of amateurs and professionals, 193–94
scientists as category of professional
  and advances in printing technology, 205–6
  emergence in late nineteenth century, 196, 203–4
  history of, in America, 200–202
  Morse's generation and, 202–5, 206

Shell Mounds of Omori (Morse), 45, 180–81, *182*, 186–87
Shichijō Sakyō, 40, 52n44
Shimizu Usaburō, 100, 124, 137
Shinmi Masaoki, 74, 76–77
Shirai Mitsutarō, 143–44, 147, 148, 205
Shōun Genkei, 35, 40, 45
Siebold, Alexander von, 99–100, 161, 180
  See also *Notes on Japanese Archaeology* (Siebold)
Siebold, Heinrich von, 180, 182
  See also *The Outline of Archaeology* (*Kōko setsuryaku*) (Siebold)
Siebold, Philipp Franz von, 99, 120, 180
Six Society (*Shōko zuroku*), 139
Smithsonian, Japanese delegation in, 77–78, 111n20
Sonoda Hidehiro, 200–201, 203, 204
South School of Daigaku (*Daigaku nankō*), 26, 29–30, 44, 60, 68, 89, 94, 117, 119, 123, 126, 128, 132, 142, 196
spectacles (*misemono*)
  association with past by mid-19th century, 89, 107, 116
  at early exhibitions, 94–95, 96
  government prohibition at exhibitions, 90–91, 107
  at *kaichō* shows, 81, 85–88, *87*
  as link from *kaichō* to exhibitions, 101, 116
  origin of exhibitions in, 81

Takahashi Yuichi, 61, 137, 169, 191
Takamizawa Shigeru, 101–3, *102*, 103, 106
Takamura Kōtarō, 34, 36, 38–39
Takamura Kōun, 2, 34–35, 37, 40
  See also *Recollecting the Bakumatsu and the Restoration* (*Bakumatsu ishin kaikodan*) (Takamura)
Takamura Tōun, 34–36, 39–40, 45, 92–93
Takemoto Yōsai
  background and career of, 124, 126, 128
  and Exhibition at Shōkonsha Shrine (1871), 118–19, 123–24, 126, 128
  and exhibition at Yushima Seidō, Tokyo (1872), 141
  and exhibitions of local products at Gansui'en (1871), 124–25
  and last generation of amateurish study, 203–4
  Uchida and, 125
Tales of the prosperity of Edo (*Edo hanjō ki*) (Terakado), 101
"A Talk on Experience by Mr. Yoshio Tanaka" (Takaka), 127
Tamamushi Sadaiyū Yasushige, 75–76, 77–78, 79, 111n15
Tanaka Yoshio
  background and career of, 119–20, 126, 127, 136–37
  death of, 136
  and Domestic Exposition for the Promotion of Industry (1877), 115n103
  and early exhibitions and museums, support for, 136
  and exhibition at Shōkonsha Shrine (1871), 118–20, 122–24, 126

and exhibition at Yushima Seidō, Tokyo (1872), 140
exhibition commemorating career of, 127
Itō and, 120, 136
and last generation of amateurish study, 203–4
on life during fall of shogunate, 127
Matsurra and, 129
and Meiji industrializing policies, 196–98
on Ninagawa, 134
as notable collector, 123
scrapbooks of, 120
and study of names and things, 151–52
Takahashi and, 137
Tsuda and, 141
and Vienna Exposition of 1873, 99, 119, 132, 141–42
Tani Bunchō, 162, 163
taxonomy
and absence of color, 190, 191–92
and abstraction of objects, 188–90, 192, 205
development in illustrated catalogs, 188–89
emergence as new paradigm, 192–93
in exhibition of local products at Shōkonsha Shrine, Tokyo (1871), 118
Foucault on required features of, 17–18
Itō's work on, 120
mandala-like system in Tokugawa period, 150–52, 205
Tanaka's work on, 119
See also disciplines for study of things before Bakumatsu period
Terakado Seiken, 83, 85, 101, 106
The Politics of Expositions (*Hakurankai no seijigaku*) (Yoshimi), 73
Things Japanese (Chamberlain), vi, 214
things past, as term, 16
three rites, study of, as study of names and things, 146
Tōdaiji Temple (Nara)
Machida's excavations at, 133
and Shōsōin Repository, 27, 28, 61, 129
Tokugawa Akitake, 79, 99, 141
Tokugawa Yoshinobu, 79, 127
Tokyo Anthropology Society, 205, 206
Tokyo Kaisei School, 29, 68, 196
Tokyo Medical School, 29, 68, 196
Tokyo Numismatic Society, 206
topography, as discipline before Bakumatsu period, 147
To the Barbarian Countries (*Iteki no kuni e*) (Osatake), 76, 100
"Traces of Ninagawa Noritane" (Inokuma), 133–34
Transactions of the Asiatic Society of Japan, 183–85, 186
Treaty of Amity and Commerce, 74, 110n8
Tsuboi Shōgorō, 205, 206
Tsuda Sen, 141–42
Tsuda Umeko, 141, 157n88

Uchida Masao
Akamatsu and, 142
background and career, 125–26
and Exhibition at Shōkonsha Shrine (1871), 118–19, 123, 125, 126
and exhibition at Yushima Seidō, Tokyo (1872), 140
and *Jinshin* survey, 126, 136
and last generation of amateurish study, 203–4
Takemoto and, 125
universities, establishment of, late 1880s–early 1890s, 29
University of Tokyo, 29–30, 45, 68, 194, 196

Vienna World Exposition (1873)
and *bijutsu* (fine art) as term, 29, 214
and development of scientific paradigm in Japan, 204–5
as first Japanese international exhibition, 90, 97
"Guidelines for Exhibiting Objects at the Vienna World Exposition," 29
items obtained by Japan from, 103–4
Japanese preparations for, 27, 44, 49
Japanese success at, 90–91
objects displayed by Japanese at, 27, 97, 97–100, 98
officials working on, 99, 105, 141–42
positive reception of Japan at, 28
Siebold at, 180
A View of a Collection of Things Past, Present, and Novel (*Kokinchinbutsu shūran*) (Ichiyōsai), 12–13, 140
visual perception, exhibitions' focus on, 104–6, 107
public acceptance of, 116
and shifting meaning of objects in cases, 116
and symbolization of objects, 107–10

Watanabe Kazan, 164, 167
woodblock printing, illustrated catalogs and, 170–74, 182
World Art studies (Zijlmans and van Damme), 3
worlding of art, vs. globalization of art history, 3
"The Worlding of the Asian Modern" (Clark), 3

Yamaguchi Masao, 150, 205
Yatabe Ryōkichi, 45, 47, 68n1, 204
Yokoyama Matsusaburō, 61, 97, 98, 175
Yokoyama Yoshikiyo, 171
background and career of, 138, 142
and Exhibition at Shōkonsha Shrine (1871), 138
and Kanda's *Notes*, 188
and Kimura, 138
work on public exhibitions, 138
See also *Illustrated Catalog of Appreciating the Past* (*Shōko zuroku*) (Yokoyama)
Yoshikawa Kōbunkan, 2
Yoshimi Shun'ya, 73, 100, 101, 107–10

zuihitsu essays, 150